PIRATES

ALSO BY ANGUS KONSTAM

Ghost Ships: Tales of Abandoned, Doomed, and Haunted Vessels

The History of Shipwrecks

World Atlas of Pirates: Treasures and Treachery on the Seven Seas in Maps, Tall Tales, and Pictures

PIRATES

THE COMPLETE HISTORY FROM 1300 BC TO THE PRESENT DAY

ANGUS KONSTAM

LYONS PRESS
Guilford, Connecticut

An imprint of Rowman & Littlefield

First published in the UK in 2008 by Osprey Publishing

First Lyons Press paperback edition 2011

Lyons Press is an imprint of Rowman & Littlefield.

Designed by Ken Vail Graphic Design
Maps by Peter Bull Art Studio
Black-and-white images courtesy of Stratford Archive

Distributed by NATIONAL BOOK NETWORK

Library of Congress Cataloging-in-Publication Data is available on file.

ISBN 978-0-7627-7395-4

Printed in the United States of America

CONTENTS

INTRODUCTION

It is hardly surprising that the main contenders for the title of the world's oldest profession—prostitution, law, and journalism—all share a common bond. They all tend to operate on the margins of acceptable society, making money from, or producing stories about, an underworld of crime, corruption, and sleaze. I am probably being a little harsh on prostitutes and journalists, but the point is that crime, and public fascination with it, is as old as civilization itself. It is therefore not unexpected that in 1724, when a London publisher began selling a new book called *A General History of the Robberies and Murders of the Most Notorious Pyrates*, this lurid exposé of a world of crime proved to be a runaway success. It lifted the lid on activities that most of its readers had never dreamed of. It told of violent criminals operating on the high seas and of men (and a few women) who rebelled against the constraints of early eighteenth-century society and who lived by their own piratical code. Of course it also helped that these tales were set against a backdrop of exotic tropical locations and that most pirates met a colorfully violent end. Almost three centuries later this fascination still exists.

The term "pirate" instantly conjures up a picture of a figure in a battered coat and tricorne hat, festooned with weaponry and seeming as if he could fillet you with his cutlass as soon as look at you. Of course we owe most of this to Hollywood and to the piratical images first evoked by Robert Louis Stevenson in *Treasure Island*. Johnny Depp took this classic pirate image in the *Pirates of the Caribbean* films and made it his own, and, like the other pirates of book, stage, and silver screen, Captain Jack Sparrow became a wonderful blend of pirate fact and pirate fiction. Pirates are used to sell everything from rum to cars, from homes to insurance. Like the pirate himself, the skull and crossbones symbol used on pirate flags has become an instantly recognizable and identifiable image —a symbol of piracy and of rebellion against authority.

In a way all this began with Captain Charles Johnson, the man who wrote that bestseller back in 1724. His descriptions of pirates such as Blackbeard and "Black Bart" Roberts, of "Calico Jack" Rackam and Charles Vane, were augmented by a series of engravings that set the standard for the centuries of pirate imagery that followed it. These days, pirates are portrayed either as figures of fun or as romantic characters, rather than as the seafaring criminals they really were. The very phrase the "golden age of piracy" was coined by the creators of pirate fiction rather than by the people who experienced piracy for themselves. There was nothing golden or romantic about being the prisoner of some of these famous pirates—although the gentle readers of Captain Johnson's pirate biography would have felt safe enough in their own homes to cast the pirates he wrote about in their own romanticized light. This process simply continued, so that nowadays Jack Sparrow, Captain Hook, Long John Silver, and Captain Blood are but pale and harmless imitations of the real thing.

This book tells the story of the real pirates of history—the men for whom shipwreck, starvation, disease, and violent death were a constant threat, and whose piratical careers were usually measured in months rather than in years. While these pirates certainly did operate in exotic locations such as the Caribbean, and their story occasionally involves marooning, buried treasure, desert islands, and parrots, the notion that their lives were in any way romantic would have been highly amusing to them. The aim of this book is to allow people to unravel the popular pirate image of today from the far less appealing reality of these historical figures.

Even the term "pirate" has been changed over the years. Scriptwriters who should know better manage to confuse the name with others, such as privateer, buccaneer, filibuster, corsair, freebooter, and swashbuckler. We'll examine these terms throughout the book, but, briefly, all of them have their own separate meanings. A privateer was a man or a ship under contract to a government, allowing it to attack enemy ships during wartime. This contract, called a letter of marque, meant that the government got a share of the profits. In effect the privateer was a licensed pirate who did not attack his own people. The French called these people corsairs, although the term later became associated with Mediterranean pirates rather than just privateers.

In the seventeenth century the term "buccaneer" referred to the English, Dutch, or French raiders who preyed on the Spanish, attacking cities as well as ships on the high seas. A filibuster (or freebooter) was simply a French word for a buccaneer. As for swashbucklers, the term referred originally to a sixteenth-century armed brigand and later to a seventeenth-century swordsman. In the early twentieth century "swashbuckler" was used by writers of pirate fiction, and from there the term was adopted by Hollywood, where it is now used to refer to a particular type of movie. In the piratical heyday the term was never used the way it is today.

Finally there were the pirates. A proper pirate attacked any ship, regardless of its nationality. The dictionary specifies that a pirate is someone who robs from others at sea and who acts beyond the law. Sometimes the pirates themselves crossed the boundaries from one category into another. Captain Kidd was a privateer who later turned to piracy. Benjamin Hornigold was a pirate who attacked only Spanish and French ships, as he wanted to maintain the illusion that he was a privateer. Francis Drake was a privateer, although the Spanish did not recognize his legal status as one and simply called him a pirate. To muddy the waters even further, Henry Morgan was a buccaneer operating under a privateering letter of marque, although England and Spain were at peace when he attacked Panama, so technically he acted as a pirate.

This book aims to provide a general overview of piracy through the ages, from the Ancient Mediterranean to the present day. However, as well as covering this broad range of history, it also concentrates on the periods we now regard as the heyday of piracy in the Caribbean. These fall into two eras—that of the buccaneers who preyed on the Spanish Main in the mid-seventeenth century, and that of the era known to modern historians as the Golden Age of Piracy. This was the time when men such as Blackbeard and "Black Bart" Roberts sailed in search of prey. While it is important to cover the broad picture of piracy through the ages, this approach also allows us to look a little more deeply into these key periods and to tell a more detailed story about some of the most famous pirates in history.

1

PIRATES OF THE ANCIENT WORLD

THE SEA PEOPLES

Piracy was not invented by men like Blackbeard and "Black Bart" Roberts. It has been around since man first took to the sea, a maritime scourge that appeared in historical records since before the building of the Egyptian pyramids. The Mediterranean, otherwise known as the cradle of civilization, was also a pirate hot spot, which we know because the Ancient Egyptians took the time to describe the attacks and their perpetrators.

As in any period, piracy in the ancient world flourished when there was a lack of central control and in areas beyond the reach of major powers such as the Egyptians, the Assyrians, or the Mycenaean Greeks. The first known pirate group was the Lukkans, a group of sea raiders based on the southeastern coast of Asia Minor (now modern Turkey). They first appeared in the fourteenth century BC, when Egyptian scribes recorded that they raided Cyprus, although there are suggestions that their piratical activities started earlier. By the thirteenth century BC they had become a major thorn in the side of the Egyptians and had allied themselves to the Hittite Empire, which offered protection in exchange for naval power. A century later the Lukkans drop from the historic records, a disappearance that was probably linked to the emergence of a new maritime threat. It is highly likely that the pirates were simply assimilated into a collection of maritime nomads and raiders known as the sea peoples.[1]

Historians have blamed these sea raiders for the collapse of the Bronze Age cultures of the eastern Mediterranean and for ushering in a dark age in the ancient world. They single-handedly brought about the collapse of the Mycenaean Greek civilization and the destruction of the Hittite Empire in Asia Minor. Only the Egyptians managed to weather the maritime storm. The term "sea peoples" is a useful collective term to apply to the maritime groups that invaded the Egyptian Empire in the late thirteenth and early twelfth centuries BC. The name was first coined by Egyptian chroniclers, who claimed that the invaders were migrating tribes originating from the Aegean and Adriatic or from the western Mediterranean. It also appears that when they were not waging war or raiding, they traded, developing sea routes that spanned the eastern Mediterranean during the Dark Ages. In other words, they did not exist by piracy alone.

The same sources also mention six clans or tribes—the Shardana, the Denyen, the Peleset, the Shekelesh, the Weshesh and the Tjeker. Some historians have also added two more groups to the list—the Tursha and Lycian peoples who settled in Asia Minor, who did not come into contact with the Egyptians and therefore were not given the same attention by the chroniclers. One of these groups may have been responsible for assimilating the piratical Lukkans. The Shardana, Shekelesh, and Peleset tribes may have originated in the northeast corner of the Adriatic (now Croatia), although the Shardana have also been linked to Sardinia. An inscription at Karnak in eastern Egypt also claims that around this time the Libyans hired mercenaries from what is now Sardinia, Sicily, Italy, Greece and Turkey—then the northern rim of the known world. Whatever their origins, these sea raiders certainly posed a major threat to the Egyptian Empire. They were also the first organized pirate confederation in history, and their actions bear a passing resemblance to those of the buccaneers who spread a path of destruction across the Caribbean in the seventeenth century.

The best evidence for the sea peoples comes from inscriptions in the great temple at Karnak and from the tomb of Pharaoh Rameses II "the Great" at Medinet Habu. In Medinet Habu the inscriptions also provide us with a record of a great sea battle fought around 1186 BC off the Nile Delta. The Egyptians sailed out to do battle with the invading sea peoples, and the fleet of Rameses III emerged victorious. The bas-relief carving of the battle that accompanied the description provides us with the first real image of pirates in action and is probably the earliest ever illustration of a sea battle. The threat did not just end there. Both sets of inscriptions mention that these raiders allied themselves with Egypt's enemies Libya and Palestine, but the swift military response by Rameses broke up the alliance before it could threaten his empire. Although the sea peoples were not strictly pirates in the true sense, but were more like hostile migratory tribes with ships, their actions can still be considered as piracy on a grand scale.[2]

One of the Medinet Habu bas-reliefs tells us a little about how these pirates fought. The sea peoples are shown in smaller and flimsier ships than those of the Egyptians, and they also appear to lack armour, bows and arrows—which the Egyptians had in abundance. The carving supports the idea that the sea peoples depended on light raiding craft, and their style of fighting relied on speed and stealth rather than on brute force. The overall impression is of a rather one-sided fight, but the sea peoples were probably no pushover. After all, the Egyptians later hired the fierce warriors of the Sherden tribe as mercenaries—and these have been linked to the Shardana clan. They are usually depicted wearing armor and carrying swords and shields. Similarly, Mycenaean accounts describe the sea peoples as being great warriors and seamen, armed with long swords and helmets. They also seem to have defeated everyone they came up against—until they met the Egyptians.

The battle with the Egyptians may well have marked the end of the sea peoples. The evidence suggests that from around 1220 until the battle in 1186 BC—just over three decades—they enjoyed an almost total control of the eastern Mediterranean, capturing everything from individual cities to whole ports and their hinterland. After the battle they quickly disappeared from history, which indicates that the Pharaoh Rameses won a decisive victory that effectively put an end to the pirate threat. After the defeat there is evidence that most of the surviving sea peoples settled in Palestine. It has even been proposed that the Peleset clan were the descendants of the Philistines mentioned in the Bible. The Tjeker clan seemed to maintain their maritime traditions and continued to trade throughout the region during the twelfth to ninth centuries BC—indulging in a little piracy on the side. The remains of Tjeker settlements have been found near Dor in Israel, and these may well be seen as the oldest surviving pirate havens in the world. Trading eventually replaced piracy as the main source of Tjeker income, and within a century the clan had developed, or had been amalgamated, into the Phoenicians, who became the economic superpower of their day.

THE PIRATES OF ANCIENT GREECE

Piracy was still commonplace throughout the eastern Mediterranean after the collapse of the sea peoples, and it would continue until the Romans finally managed to establish full control over the Mare Internum (the Inner Sea). While the Ancient Greeks are best remembered for their contribution to Western civilization, they also produced some of the worst pirates in the ancient world. In fact some Greek city-states actively encouraged piracy as a means of generating wealth. Others, such as the Athenians, formed antipiracy fleets to keep the sea lanes clear for their own trading ships.

One of the first known pirate havens was Crete, which sat astride the sea lanes between Greece and the rest of the eastern Mediterranean. In the tenth century BC the last remnants of the Minoan civilization on the island were destroyed by the Dorian Greeks, who raided the coast of Crete in search of slaves. The invaders then used the island as a base from which they launched piratical raids throughout the Aegean. Cretan cities such as Cydonia and Eleutherna became thriving marketplaces for slaves—mainly women and boys—captured in piratical raids and for the sale or barter of plunder. In his *Odyssey,* Homer described the Cretans as being notorious pirates, while his other poems allude to slaving raids carried out by the same people. It was not until the rise of Athens as a dominant naval power during the fifth century BC that the strength of the Cretan pirates was curbed, and they remained an irritant in the region until the end of the second century BC, when the Rhodeans cleared Crete of pirate bases.

Further north in the Aegean, other islands or remote mainland townships were notorious as pirate havens. Plutarch told of the Samians, who were driven from their island by invaders and so moved to Mycale, where they established themselves as pirates. Under the leadership of Polycrates they concentrated their efforts on the island state of Miletus, and in the sixth century BC they incurred the wrath of Corinth and Sparta by attacking their ships. They also prospered from the political instabilities caused by the later clashes between Greece and Persia, successfully playing both sides against each other to increase their own power and profit.

The Athenians finally managed to curb the Samians, and, following a raid on Athens itself by pirates from Lemnos, the Athenian navy devoted much time and effort to clearing pirates from the Aegean. Severe repercussions were threatened against any local rulers who indulged in piracy within the Athenian sphere, while active pirates were hunted down and their lairs destroyed. Apart from Mycale and Lemnos, other pirate strongholds on Cithnos, Myconos and in the Sporades were also destroyed by Athenian antipiracy expeditions during the fifth century BC. Herodotus provides us with a vivid account of pirate attacks, and of these Athenian antipiracy operations.[3]

In the fourth century BC the Aetolian League was formed, and within a century this confederation became the dominant power in central Greece. The Greeks regarded these northerners as semibarbaric, as did the Persians, a view that was encouraged by the Aetolians' practice of using piracy as a means of waging economic war against their enemies.

By the third century BC, Aetolian pirates dominated the region and extorted protection money from coastal towns and cities on both the Greek and the Asian shores of the Aegean basin. It was not until the League was defeated by the Roman Republic in 192 BC that these piratical attacks came to an end. In fact, by that time many of the Aetolian pirates had already set up new bases elsewhere, the majority of them moving to Cilicia on the south coast of Asia Minor. The Cilician pirates would become the largest and most notorious pirate community in the ancient world.

Piracy also flourished on the other side of Greece, along the eastern coast of the Adriatic. The Illyrians and Dalmatians (from what is now Croatia and Albania)

The keelhauling of captured Greek pirates, depicted on an Athenian vase dating from the fourth century BC. Piracy was rife in the Aegean during much of the classical age, although regional sea powers such as the Athenian navy did what they could to hunt down pirates.

raided the Greek and Italian coasts and even ventured out into the central Mediterranean. Their activities reached a peak in the third century BC, when the growing economic prosperity of the Roman Republic meant that there was no shortage of well-stocked Roman and Italian trading vessels to prey on. The islands of Corfu, Cephalonia, and Santa Maria were all used as pirate bases during this period, which allowed the pirates to extend their activities as far as the Tyrrhenian Sea. The Illyrian pirate menace was curbed but not completely eradicated when the Romans conquered the region, and even after the Roman annexation of Illyria in 168 BC, the pirates continued their attacks from relatively secure bases on the Dalmatian coast and from the islands mentioned above.

A series of Roman punitive expeditions finally cleared most of the Dalmatian mainland of pirates during the second century BC, but the pirates still maintained a presence in the islands off the Dalmatian coast until the mid-first century BC, when Pompey the Great dealt with the problem once and for all. Of course accusations of piracy were frequently leveled at coastal peoples by both the Romans and the Greeks, either as a means of character assassination or as a pretext for military or naval action against them. The very name "Tyrrhenian" effectively meant the same as "pirate," and the Romans employed it to refer to the neighboring Etruscans, who used attacks on Roman maritime commerce as a viable tool of war. The Etruscans even took steps to protect themselves against attacks by "Greek" pirates from the east—presumably the Illyrians and Dalmatians—and they actually maintained fleets as a defense against piratical attacks.

The pirates of the Tyrrhenian Sea were certainly a threat to the Etruscans, the Greeks, and the Romans, probably in equal measure. Thucydides recorded several of these pirate attacks, although he claimed they were the work of the Phoenicians. In fact these people were neither Italians nor Greeks but "barbarians" based on the islands of Elba, Corsica, and Sardinia, who concentrated their attacks on Greek shipping operating between Sicily and the Aegean. Other well-known pirate bases existed in the Lipari Islands off the northeast corner of Sicily and as far away as the Balearic Islands and the Ligurian coast of what is now the Riviera. Greek mythology tells how the god Dionysus was captured by Tyrrhenian pirates, who mistook him for the son of a wealthy merchant. Dionysus thought it all a hilarious escapade, but he still turned the pirates into dolphins as punishment for their temerity. The Romans also accused the Sicilians of piracy, although, like the Etruscans, the Greek rulers of the island sanctioned legitimate privateering rather than piracy. However, the result was pretty much the same for both the Greeks in Sicily and the Etruscans, as by the Second century BC both peoples had been conquered by the Romans. The establishment of a Roman hegemony in the western Mediterranean also virtually ended any form of organized piracy in the region.

THOSE TROUBLESOME CILICIANS

If anywhere deserved the reputation of being the cradle of piracy in the ancient world, it was Cilicia Trachea ("Rugged Cilicia"). A narrow strip of land in Asia Minor, in what is now southeastern Turkey, Cilicia perched uncomfortably between the towering Taurus Mountains and the Mediterranean Sea. This mountainous and inhospitable region remained largely unsettled, apart from a few struggling towns that looked towards the sea for their survival. The coastline itself was broken up by rocky headlands, hidden bays, and well-protected anchorages. It was also ideally placed for attacks on shipping traveling between Syria and Greece and Italy, and an attacker could strike then be back in his secret hideaway within hours. In effect it was the perfect hideout for pirate exiles. This was therefore the region that attracted the Aetolian pirates driven out of the Aegean in the early second century BC. They were probably drawn by the reputation of the region as a pirate haven, which had already attracted small pirate communities based around the coastal villages.

It was all a matter of timing. The Aetolian pirates began arriving in Cilicia at exactly the same time that the Seleucid kings of Syria and Asia Minor stopped their regular naval patrols along the Cilician coast. They needed all their available resources to deal with the Romans, who had already overrun the Seleucid territories on the western side of the Aegean. The decisive Roman victory over the Seleucids at Magnesia (190 BC) led to a peace deal in which the western part of Asia Minor became a Roman protectorate. The Seleucid navy was withdrawn for good, and the Romans did not have the naval power or even the inclination to maintain their own naval presence in the area. Soon afterwards the bulk of the Seleucid fleet was taken over by King Mithridates of Pontus, who would sooner ally himself with the pirates than make any deal with Rome. Consequently the pirates were allowed to develop their power base without any interference. Their communities expanded rapidly as thousands fled from the Romans, and soon they possessed the strength to counter any local naval force that might be sent against them.

At first the Cilician pirates limited their attacks to the eastern Mediterranean, preying on passing shipping, then expanding their influence further along the sea lanes until they reached the shores of Crete to the west, Palestine to the east, and Egypt to the south. Their targets were not limited to trading vessels on the high seas; they also raided villages and towns on the coast, gathering captives who could be sold in the slave markets of Crete, while the richest prisoners were held to ransom. Other stolen goods were sold in the nearby cities of Miletus, Ephesus, and Smyrna, all of which were within the borders of the Roman protectorate in Asia Minor. This continued for decades, until the expansion of Roman trade and influence into the eastern Mediterranean meant that the Romans themselves became the principal victims of piratical attacks. Their most celebrated victim was none other than the young Julius Caesar, who—according to Plutarch—was captured by Cilician pirates in 75 BC. The Greek historian described the encounter:

First, when the pirates demanded a ransom of twenty talents, Caesar burst out laughing. They did not know, he said, who it was that they had captured, and he volunteered to pay fifty. Then, when he had sent his followers to the various cities in order to raise the money and was left with one friend and two servants among these Cilicians, about the most bloodthirsty people in the world, he treated them so highhandedly that, whenever he wanted to sleep, he would send to them and tell them to stop talking.

For thirty-eight days, with the greatest unconcern, he joined in all their games and exercises, just as if he was their leader instead of their prisoner. He also wrote poems and speeches which he read aloud to them, and if they failed to admire his work, he would call them to their faces illiterate savages and would often laughingly threaten to have them all hanged. They were much taken with this and attributed his freedom of speech to a kind of simplicity in his character or boyish playfulness.

However, the ransom arrived from Miletus and, as soon as he had paid it and been set free, he immediately manned some ships and set sail from the harbor of Miletus against the pirates. He found them still there, lying at anchor off the island, and he captured nearly all of them. He took their property as spoils of war and put the men themselves into the prison at Pergamon. He then went in person to (Marcus) Junius, the governor of Asia, thinking it proper that he, as praetor in charge of the province, should see to the punishment of the prisoners. Junius, however, cast longing eyes at the money, which came to a considerable sum, and kept saying that he needed time to look into the case. Caesar paid no further attention to him. He went to Pergamon,

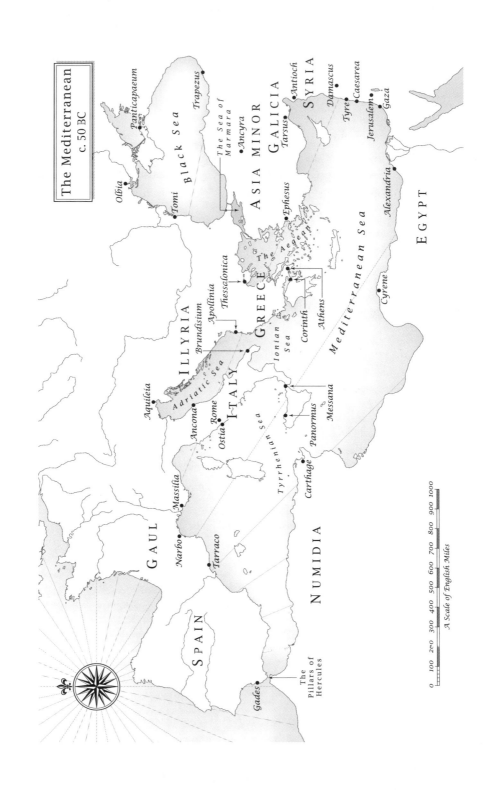

The Mediterranean
c. 50 BC

Panticapaeum
Trapezus
Black Sea
Olbia
Tomi
The Sea of Marmara
Ancyra
ASIA MINOR
GALICIA
Antioch
SYRIA
Damascus
Tarsus
Tyre
Caesarea
Jerusalem
Gaza
Ephesus
The Aegean
Alexandria
GREECE
Thessalonica
Apollonia
Brundisium
ILLYRIA
Corinth
Ionian Sea
Athens
Mediterranean Sea
Cyrene
EGYPT
Aquileia
Adriatic Sea
Ancona
Rome
ITALY
Ostia
Messana
Panormus
Tyrrhenian Sea
Massilia
Carthage
Narbo
Tarraco
GAUL
NUMIDIA
SPAIN
Gades
The Pillars of Hercules

0 100 200 300 400 500 600 700 800 900 1000
A Scale of English Miles

took the pirates out of prison and crucified the lot of them, just as he had often told them he would do when he was on the island and they imagined that he was joking.[4]

It was around this time that the Cilician pirates began to harass shipping and coastal settlements in the Aegean—an area the Romans regarded as their own —and marauding pirate squadrons even conducted raids on the coast of Italy. The Senate decided that the power of the pirates had to be curbed, or else the Roman Republic itself would be threatened through a strangulation of trade. In 101 BC the Senate passed its first antipiracy law. This meant that the pirates could no longer trade with the ports in the Roman protectorate in Asia Minor. Consequently the pirates took their plunder elsewhere, principally to ports within the borders of Pontus. Then in 89 BC King Mithridates invaded the Roman protectorate, and with the help of the Cilicians he besieged the Roman-occupied island of Rhodes. Three years later, in 86 BC, a pirate squadron defeated a Roman naval force off Brundisium in southeast Italy, disrupting communications between Rome and Greece. However, later that year it all began to unravel for Mithridates. He and his pirate allies might have controlled the seas, but on land his troops were no match for Sulla and his veteran Roman army, who drove him out of Greece. By 85 BC Sulla had regained the lost provinces and begun building up naval strength in the region as a means of countering the pirate threat.

For a while this antipirate stance was at best halfhearted as a succession of Roman governors and regional commanders led small but ultimately indecisive punitive campaigns against the pirates. For instance, in 77 BC Publius Servilius Vatia cleared Lycia of the pirates but failed to follow this up with an attack on Cilicia. Then in 74 BC Marcus Antonius Creticus (the father of Mark Antony) attacked the Cretan pirates but was defeated in battle and died shortly afterwards. The Roman attitude hardened after the Cilicians supported the slave revolt led by Spartacus in 73–71 BC. In 67 BC the Romans struck back, and under the leadership of Pompey the Great the Cilician pirates were attacked, defeated, and scattered. After Pompey's campaign, piracy in the Mediterranean was all but eradicated and the Roman Republic could safely enjoy the benefits of the Pax Romana ("Roman Peace"). However, the Roman navy continued its patrols in the centuries that followed. After all, at their height Cilician pirates had threatened the very survival of the Roman Republic.[5]

POMPEY AGAINST THE PIRATES

Today, Gnaeus Pompeius Magnus (Pompey the Great) is best remembered as the bitter enemy of Julius Caesar during the Roman Civil War. However, long before Caesar crossed the Rubicon, Pompey was regarded as the "First Man in Rome," her leading general and the savior of the Roman Republic. Much of this acclaim stemmed from his successful war against the pirates, which effectively ended piracy in the Mediterranean. Following the revolt of Spartacus and the support given to the slaves by the Cilician pirates, the Senate decided to eradicate piracy in the Mediterranean completely. This monumental task would stretch the resources of Rome to its limits. Consequently in 67 BC Pompey was offered an *imperium* (military dictatorship) and ordered to drive the pirates from the Mare Internum, or Mediterranean Sea.

Pompey's *imperium,* granted under the aegis of the *lex Gabinia de piratis persequendis* (antipiracy law) gave him sweeping powers, an immense budget of 6,000 talents, and a military force of some 500 ships and 120,000 Roman troops. He was also given the right to tax and raise militia anywhere in the Roman sphere within 50 miles of the sea. The sheer scale of this enterprise—the equivalent today would be the diversion of over half the U.S. budget and armed forces—showed just how seriously the Roman Senate took the pirate threat. Pompey had fought the pirates before—and he knew exactly how to go about the operation. His ships consisted of both Rhodean biremes (galleys with two banks of oars) and Roman-built Liburnians (purpose-built fast privateering galleys, later called "dromons"), which were fast enough to pursue the pirates on the high seas and trap them. These lighter craft were supported by a fleet of heavier warships, filled with Roman troops—a force the pirates had no means of countering. Following on behind were transports filled with veteran Roman legionaries.

Pompey divided the Mediterranean into thirteen districts, and he placed each of them under the command of a legate (deputy commander). In a coordinated strike, each legate led his forces against the pirate bases and blockaded them, then sent other ships to scout for any unknown pirate lairs. The attacks were launched simultaneously right across the Mediterranean—with one exception The legate covering the Cilician coast was ordered to stay in port. Then Roman troops were sent in to besiege and destroy the pirate bases. Many pirates simply surrendered, and Pompey proved lenient—for a Roman. While ringleaders were executed, others were ransomed and pardoned or released in exchange for information that would help track down other pirate groups.

Once that phase was over, Pompey led his fleets in a sweep through the Mediterranean, working eastwards from Gibraltar, driving any surviving pirates ahead of him as he went. As the pirates retreated, most of them ran into the blockades established by the legates. The lightly armed pirate ships were defeated with ease, and those who were unable to flee were forced either to burn their boats and flee inland or to surrender. Those who escaped capture were inevitably driven towards Cilicia. In less than forty days Pompey had successfully cleared the western and central Mediterranean of pirates and contained the rest in the one remaining safe haven of Cilicia. Then Pompey began the final phase of his master plan.

First he formed a tight blockade around the Cilician coast, using bases in Rhodes, Cyprus, and Syria to supply his ships while they remained at sea. The

The Romans used small, fast biremes to hunt down pirates in the Mediterranean during the final decades of the Roman Republic. This copy of a bas-relief dating from the third century AD depicts similar Roman vessels engaged on an antipiracy patrol.

pirates launched several attempts to break through the naval cordon, but even if they were successful they ran into a second ring of Pompey's warships, patrolling the waters over the horizon from the Cilician coast. Then Pompey tightened the cordon, pushing inwards along the coast to reduce the size of the pirate enclave. Marines were sent ashore to explore every inlet and gully on the coast, to make sure that nobody slipped through the net. In effect this was a tactical repeat of his strategic operation, as the pirates were gradually driven towards the main pirate stronghold of Coracesium, sited on a remote Cilician peninsula. Then Pompey sent in his legionaries to besiege the pirates from the landward side. The Cilicians were no match for the Roman war machine, and within weeks they were forced to surrender.

Once again Pompey was surprisingly lenient, executing the ringleaders and exiling the rest to the hinterland of Cilicia or Greece. By that time the legates had finished their business in the other districts, and Pompey was able to return to Rome in triumph. The whole operation lasted approximately three months, and according to Pompey's report it resulted in the destruction of no fewer than 120 pirate bases, the death through battle or execution of 10,000 pirates, and the destruction of 500 ships. Equally important was the pirate wealth captured by the Romans, which was distributed throughout Pompey's forces. As the holder of the *imperium,* of course, Pompey himself kept the largest share of the plunder.

As a result the Mediterranean was cleared of pirates for the first time in history. Although Pompey did not live long enough to comprehend the lasting fruits of his actions—he was killed in 48 BC—Roman shipping would remain safe from attack anywhere in the Mare Internum for another four centuries. The Pax Romana would break down only following the collapse of the Western Roman Empire, at which point the antipiracy mantle was passed to the Eastern Romans. In the guise of the Byzantine Empire, the war against piracy would continue to be fought well into the Middle Ages—until Byzantium itself finally succumbed to the Turks. However, by that stage piracy was once again big business in the Mediterranean, although the center of piratical activity had moved from Asia Minor to the North African coast.

2

MEDIEVAL PIRATES

THE SEA RAIDERS

Most people don't think of the Vikings as pirates. After all, the dictionary defines pirates as criminals who commit robberies on the high seas, not ones who raid the land. Most Vikings rarely robbed at sea, although certainly there were those who made their living from piracy during the Middle Ages. Rather, they were sea raiders—using their ships as a means of transport, then landing and raiding their coastal targets on foot. Although the Vikings were not the first of Europe's Middle Ages sea raiders, they were arguably the most successful. For over two centuries they terrorized the coastal communities of northern Europe, then returned to conquer, to settle, and to rule. Although not strictly pirates, they did rely on their ships for speed, mobility, and surprise—the hallmarks of the sea raider. Their methods were later copied by both the Elizabethan sea dogs such as Hawkins and Drake and by the seventeenth-century buccaneers—groups of sea raiders whose activities have been closely identified with piracy. Another similarity is the scale of their operations.

Both the Vikings and their buccaneer successors in the seventeenth century began as individual raiders, but by the end of the era they operated in large fleets, capable of landing substantial armies to pillage and conquer. The Anglo-Saxon cleric Alcuin dated the coming of the Vikings to the last decade of the eighth century—the morning of June 8, 793, to be precise. That day a Viking band descended upon the monastic island of Lindisfarne, off the northeast coast of England, and put the monks to the sword. It then pillaged the monastery and set it on fire. Even in an age when murder and mayhem were commonplace, this seemed an unprecedented atrocity. A chronicler described the raid as "an attack on both the body and soul of Christian England," while Alcuin went further, claiming that "never before had such a terror appeared in Britain as we now have suffered from a pagan race, nor was it thought such an inroad from the sea could be made."[1] As Christian clerics, these writers had good reason to be worried.

In 792 King Offa of Mercia had strengthened his shore defenses in Kent, as he considered that his kingdom was threatened by an imminent attack by "pagan seamen." While the Viking appearance off Lindisfarne might therefore not have been a complete surprise to the rulers of Anglo-Saxon England, the ferocity of the attack was something nobody had expected. The attack on Lindisfarne was only the beginning. Just a year later, in 794, an Irish monk recorded "the devastation of all the islands of Britain by the gentiles" as Viking attacks were launched along Britain's eastern seaboard. Over the following years the monastery of Iona off Scotland's western coast was plundered, as were other religious settlements at Jarrow in Northumbria, and Carmarthen, Llancarfan, and St. David's in Wales.

By 798 the Vikings were raiding the northern coast of Ireland, and their winter camps in Orkney and Shetland had turned into permanent settlements as the islands were annexed by the invaders. These secure bases were used to launch raids further afield, until by the start of the ninth century it seemed as if no coastal community was safe from attack. It was clear that the Viking threat was not going to go away. The Celtic and Anglo-Saxon monks who bore the brunt of these attacks were understandably pessimistic, likening the fury of the Norsemen to the apocalypse. The Bible produced a suitably appropriate quote from the Book of Jeremiah: "Out of the north an evil shall break forth upon all the inhabitants of the land." To these monks the arrival of the Vikings presaged the end of the world—the sixth age of the world when "Our Lord Jesus Christ will come to judge the living and the dead and the world through fire." Although this day of judgment never came, the Viking raids would continue.

By the 820s a new breed of Norse overlord was appearing, willing to offer British coastal communities their protection—in return for money. In other words, they ran a Mafia-style protection racket. The era of the Viking raiders was starting to give way to a new phase of colonization and conquest, in which Britain became the battleground of warlords rather than the destination of choice for seaborne plunderers. However, other parts of the British Isles still felt the wrath of these Viking attacks, and the raids would continue in Ireland for another decade. In 820 a cleric wrote in the *Annals of Ulster* that "the sea spewed forth floods of foreigners into Erin, so that no haven, no landing place, no stronghold, no fort and no castle might be found, but it was submerged by waves of Vikings and pirates."[2] Even the monastic communities at Clonfert, Kells, Clonmacnoise, and Armagh were plundered by these Viking raiders— settlements that had been considered far enough from the coast to be safe from attack. In truth, nowhere in Ireland outside the walls of Dublin was safe, and the Emerald Isle lay at the mercy of the sea raiders.

By the late 830s the Viking leader Turgeis followed up these attacks by seizing control of Ulster, and by 840 fortified Viking enclaves were established at Waterford, Cork, and Limerick. Then the Vikings captured Dublin and established a new power base. As the *Annals of St. Bertin* put it, "After they had been under attack from the Vikings for many years, the Irish were made tributaries to them; the Vikings have possessed themselves without opposition of all the islands around about and have settled them."[3]

For the most part the Vikings who raided the shores of Celtic Scotland and Ireland were Norsemen—from Norway. The raiders who devastated much of Anglo-Saxon England during the late eighth and early ninth centuries were Danish. The *Anglo-Saxon Chronicle* entry for 835 declared, "In this year the heathen devastated Sheppey"—an island on the Kentish side of the Thames Estuary. The following year King Ecgberht of Wessex repulsed a large force of Danish raiders that attacked the Somerset coast with thirty-five ships. From that point on the *Chronicle* reported that each year the raids became larger and more numerous. During the 850s the Vikings established their bases in Kent on the islands of Thanet and Sheppey, which provided secure bases for territorial expansion. This heralded a change of emphasis from raiding to conquest—a decade after the same shift took place in Ireland and some three decades after the Vikings first began to colonize the northern and western coasts of Scotland.

The Anglo-Saxons and the Celts were not the only peoples to suffer from Viking attacks. "In the year of our Lord 845, the vast army of the Northmen breached the frontier of the Christians." This was how a friar in the monastery of St. Germain-des-Prés recorded the arrival of a large Viking force at the very gates of Paris. Actually the first Viking raiders had arrived in the Frankish kingdom twenty-five years earlier when they raided the Frisian (Dutch) coastline and probed the defenses of the River Seine. Finding the Franks too organized, they withdrew in search of easier prey—the English.

By the 840s the Frankish rulers were too involved in fighting civil wars to worry about their seaward defenses, and so in 841 the Vikings plundered Rouen, then extorted Danegeld (protection money) from the locals. This was followed by the great attack on Paris in 845, when the sack of the city was prevented only by the payment of some 7,000 pounds of silver. Within six years the Vikings had established a permanent settlement on the lower Seine and Loire Rivers and set about establishing Viking colonies in the territories they now controlled. This meant that at roughly the same time Danes were settling in England, others were carving out their own kingdoms in France—the most famous being Normandy, the land of the Norsemen.

In northwest Europe the period of Viking raids lasted little more than half a century, a period that ended more because there was little left to plunder than because of any change in Viking policy. Whether these raiders can be dubbed pirates is open to question, although contemporaries viewed the term as virtually interchangeable with Viking. The similarity between these Viking raids and the attacks launched by the buccaneers in the seventeenth century is clear. By the end of both eras, these raiders were linked to national powers—Denmark and Norway in one era and England, France, and Holland in the other. What differs is the way the eras ended. While the buccaneers attacked Spanish cities for plunder, the Vikings eventually developed a taste for land and conquest. In effect the activities of individual Viking bands had become subsumed into a larger movement. Although the Viking age would continue into the mid-eleventh century, the days of the sea raider were effectively over by the middle of the ninth century.

PREYING ON THE HANSE

While the ascendancy of the Viking sea raider might have come to an end, the era of the Scandinavian sea trader would continue, forming part of a greater mercantile empire that would transform the economy of Europe. By the twelfth century a new series of major ports had developed along the Baltic and North Sea coasts—Hamburg, Lübeck, Bremen, Stettin, Danzig, and Rostock being the most prominent.

In 1241 Lübeck and Hamburg joined forces to form the Hanseatic League, a merchant guild that supervised maritime trade in the region and provided some protection against pirates. Other ports soon joined the League, until by 1300 the Hanse had become a major power in the Baltic and North Seas and nineteen major ports were united under its banner. Other smaller trading organizations tried to emulate the success of the Hanse, but nobody else was able to match it in terms of ships and resources. The League came to dominate north European trade, and in the process it reduced the power of individual states in the region. The Danes in particular were staunch opponents of the Hanseatic League, and they waged a low-key war against this mercantile monopoly that lasted well into the fourteenth century. Of course this conflict attracted those who sought to claim their own share of this Hanseatic wealth, and so the League's ships often had to arm themselves against attack both by their enemies and by pirates, and pirate-hunting remained a major preoccupation of the League.

One notable small rival was the confederation known as the Cinque Ports, which united Hastings, Dover, New Romney, Hythe, and Sandwich, on England's southeast coast. The towns of Rye and Winchelsea were also associated with this confederation, as were nine later small additions to the alliance. The Cinque Ports was formed in the early fourteenth century to protect local English shipping from pirates and to encourage trade. However, while the Hanseatic League remained a legitimate trading organization, its English equivalent also operated as an extortion racket, a semilegal piratical organization that safeguarded its own shipping but attacked shipping that had not paid for "protection."

In the Baltic, a group of German mercenaries and pirates formed their own brotherhood. Known as the *Vitalienbrüder,* or Victual Brothers, a name coined after running supplies into a beleaguered Stockholm in 1392, they then spent a decade fighting an undeclared war against both the Danes and the Hanseatic port of Lübeck. At first the other Hanse towns supported the brotherhood, as they saw the pirates as a tool to limit Danish expansion in the region. Rostock allowed the brotherhood to use its harbor, while Stralsund and Wismar also provided bases for the pirates.

However, the Victual Brothers soon demonstrated they were pirates first and political allies second when in 1393 they sacked the Hanse port of Bergen in Norway, then followed this up with the seizure of Malmö in southern Sweden. At the same time they harassed shipping and all but halted trade within the Baltic Sea. The Hanseatic League withdrew its support of the brotherhood, allowing the

Danes to concentrate their efforts on countering this pirate threat. In 1394 the
Victual Brothers responded by seizing Visby, on the Baltic island of Gotland, a
move that was probably a response to the Hanse closing their ports. This
coincided with the consolidation of the Danish position through a political
union that united Sweden, Denmark, and Norway under the Danish crown.

Meanwhile the Victual Brothers continued their attacks on Danish (and now
Hanseatic) shipping, which forced Queen Margaret of Denmark to hire English
ships from the Cinque Ports to protect her convoys. As Gotland was technically
part of Denmark's Swedish territories, the Danish queen dealt with the pirate
threat by ceding the island to the Teutonic Knights, who were based in Poland.
Consequently, in 1398 the Grand Master of the Teutonic Order invaded Gotland
and drove the Victual Brothers from the island. The Danes were then able to
clear the survivors out of their remaining hideouts along the Finnish coast. The

*During the Middle Ages the cog was one of the most common ship types to be found in northern
European waters. Although primarily designed as a trading vessel, it could also be used as a warship
and as a pirate vessel. This example of a cog is redrawn from a late twelfth-century German seal.*

last of the brotherhood escaped to establish new bases on the River Schlei on the eastern end of what is now the Danish-German border, around the estuary of the River Ems on the modern German-Dutch border, and on the North Sea island of Helgoland. This new group called themselves the Likedeelers, which meant sharing things in equal measure.

Their most famous pirate leader was Klaus "Störtebeker," which roughly means "emptying the mug with one gulp." It seems that even during the Middle Ages pirates were prone to heavy drinking. It has been suggested his given name was Nikolaus Storzenbecher, and he was born in Wismar around 1360. Störtebeker was one of the brotherhood who escaped from Gotland, and he rose to command the Likedeelers based on Helgoland. The island was ideally placed for attacks on Danish and Hanseatic shipping sailing in and out of Hamburg, and his prizes were not limited to his two enemies, as Muscovite, English, Scottish, and Burgundian Dutch ships were also captured by his men.

Legend has it that his flagship was the *Seetiger* ("Sea Tiger"), and his captains included Gödeke Michels, Hennig Wichmann and the scholar Magister ("Master,", an academic title) Wigbold. Störtebeker finally met his match in the summer of 1401, when the Hanse sent a fleet commanded by the veteran sea captain Simon of Utrecht to destroy the pirate base. Apparently the Hanse flagship enjoyed the marvelous name of *Die Bunte Kuh* ("The Colorful Cow"). The two forces met off the island, and after a running battle lasting three days, the *Seetiger* was captured. German legend includes the story of a Helgoland fisherman who was pressed into pirate service, and had his revenge by disabling the rudder of the pirate flagship.

Störtebeker and seventy-one of his men were captured and taken to Hamburg to face trial. The result was a foregone conclusion, and despite offering a bribe to the Hanse authorities (promising them a gold chain long enough to encircle the city), he was condemned to death in October 1401. As he stood beside the executioner's block he reputedly struck a deal—pardons would be granted to all of the crewmen whom he could walk past after his head was cut off. As the legend goes, he managed to stagger past eleven of his shipmates before he fell—tripped up by the executioner. The heads of the pirates were stuck on spikes along the banks of the River Elbe. The following year Gödeke Michels was captured, along with eighty more pirates, and they met the same grisly fate. Today Klaus Störtebeker is something of a German hero, a cross between Robin Hood and Sir Francis Drake, and has even been immortalized in a poem that dubbed him "The Hell of Helgoland."[4]

THE PIRATE KNIGHTS
OF THE MEDITERRANEAN

During the last century of its existence, the Roman Empire was divided into two spheres—east and west. When the Western Empire collapsed in the face of barbarian invasion during the fifth century AD, the Eastern Empire managed to weather the storm. In fact, under the guise of the Byzantine Empire it survived as a political entity for another millennium. The Byzantine Empire was effectively founded in AD 330 when the emperor Constantine established a new capital in Byzantium, which he renamed Constantinople. The city soon became a major commercial center, connected to the rest of the Mediterranean by prosperous maritime trade routes. Byzantine warships patrolled these sea lanes, keeping pirates at bay and protecting the empire from seaborne attack. Despite the onset of the Middle Ages in Western Europe and the spread of Islam through North Africa and the Middle East, the Byzantines maintained control of the waters of the eastern Mediterranean, and as a consequence maritime trade continued to flourish.

This all started to unravel towards the end of the eleventh century. First came a catastrophic military defeat at the hands of the Turks at the battle of Manzikert (1071). This led to the loss of much of Asia Minor. Then came the Crusaders, who regarded the Greek Orthodox Byzantines as almost as much of a religious enemy as the Muslims they had crossed Europe to fight. By this time the most serious threat to Byzantine naval supremacy was seen as the Normans who occupied Sicily and southern Italy. In the aftermath of Manzikert, the Byzantine navy had been somewhat neglected, and at one stage the emperor Alexios I Komnenos (1081–1118) had to seek naval help from the Venetians to counter Norman attacks on Byzantine sea lanes. This reliance on outsiders proved a mistake, because when the emperor refused to extend a trade agreement with them, the Venetians plundered Byzantine island settlements in the Adriatic Sea.

This and other naval embarrassments prompted a Byzantine naval revival during the mid-twelfth century, and under the emperor Manuel I Komnenos (1143–80) the Byzantine navy was once again regarded as a formidable naval force. As such it was as much a political tool in the power politics of the eastern Mediterranean as a force of naval might and a deterrent to piracy. However, following the emperor's death the fleet was neglected once more, and what remained of it suffered a string of defeats at the hands of both the Normans of Sicily and the Crusader states of the Holy Land. In 1189 the emperor Isaac II was forced to sign a naval treaty with the Venetians and the Genoese. Once again this policy backfired, and in 1204 these Italians and their Crusader allies attacked and sacked Constantinople. What remained of the Byzantine navy was destroyed, and while the tattered remnants of the empire survived, its ability to control the sea lanes did not. From 1204 onwards the waters of the eastern Mediterranean were once again a safe hunting ground for pirates.

This new infestation took root amid the patchwork of petty states, townships, and feudal demesnes of Greece and the coast of Asia Minor, where a new breed of Latin overlord saw piracy as a useful source of revenue rather than as a hindrance to trade. Another encouragement was the distrust between Byzantines and Italians. At one time the Byzantines had recruited Italian seamen into imperial service. With the collapse of Byzantine naval power and a decline in long-range trading, these migrant seamen now had no outlet for gainful employ. They therefore turned their hands to piracy. These pirates used remote bases, well away from Venetian naval patrols or even the last bastions of Byzantine authority. Crete and some of the smaller Aegean islands were favorite haunts, as were remote mainland harbors such as Anaia (now Kusadasi in southwest Turkey) or Monemvasia in southern Greece. This last harbor—known as the Rock—was a medieval fortress built on a rocky outcrop, joined to the mainland by a small causeway. This near-impregnable base became a haven for pirates during the thirteenth century, as did much of the rest of the Peloponnesian coastline.

The Rock lay on the easternmost "finger" of the Peloponnese, but the middle finger, the Mani Peninsula, had been linked to piracy since before the coming of the Romans. Lacking any other source of income apart from fishing, the Maniots were persistent small-time pirates, whose activities enjoyed a boost following the collapse of Byzantine authority in the region. Another pirate haven was the Dalmatian Islands of the central Adriatic—now part of Croatia's picturesque Dalmatian coast. The region was then known as Maria, although the Byzantines knew it as Pagania, a reference to the non-Christian beliefs of the locals, who—confusingly—were known as the Narentines. The region enjoyed a piratical golden age during the eighth and ninth centuries AD, before the establishment of Byzantine control over the islands. When the Byzantine shackles were broken in the late twelfth century, these islands, like the Peloponnese, provided pirates with a secure base astride the Venetian sea lanes.

Probably the most successful medieval pirate leader in the region was Margaritone of Brindisi (1149–97), an Italian knight who came to be nicknamed the New Neptune. He began his maritime career as a Paganian pirate, then became a privateer working under contract to the Norman rulers of Sicily. He eventually rose to become the Grand Admiral of Sicily. In 1185 he seized control of the islands from the Byzantines, proclaiming himself the Count of Cephalonia and Zante. He established the islands as a privateering base, declaring himself a supporter of Tancred of Sicily. His exploits in Sicilian service took him as far away as the Holy Land, but following the death of Tancred's father in 1189 he returned to the Adriatic.

The new Sicilian ruler was at war with the Holy Roman Emperor, and Tancred called on Margaritone to help defend Naples from the Imperialists. He was captured when the city fell in 1194 and ended his days in a German prison. The Dalmatian Islands remained a pirate base for another decade, until the archipelago was attacked and captured by the Venetian fleet in 1204 as it passed by on its way to Constantinople. During the century that followed, Italian and Greek renegades established a new pirate haven amid the Ionian islands of Corfu, Zante, Ithaca, and Cephalonia, and these islands remained the lair of small-time pirates until their formal annexation by Venice in the late fourteenth century.

The real pirate heyday in the waters surrounding Greece came in the later thirteenth century. The emperor Michael III recaptured Constantinople from the Italians, but he lacked the resources to rebuild the navy. Instead he resorted to the hiring of mercenary naval captains—the majority being the pirate leaders who infested the waters of the Aegean and Adriatic Seas. Under the Byzantine banner they preyed on Venetian and Genoese ships throughout the eastern Mediterranean, and these privateers were even reported off Venice itself. The irony of this policy was that the majority of these Grecian pirates were Italians themselves—the same group of predominantly Venetian and Genoese seamen who had once joined the colors of the official Byzantine navy. According to the Italian historian Torsello, the majority of pirates in the Aegean Sea during the early fourteenth century were originally from one of these two Italian ports.

His claim is supported by a document drawn up in 1278, in which Venetian merchants sought compensation for losses at the hands of these Byzantine privateers. The names Michael Balbo, Manuel de Marino, and Bartolomeo Foscolo all suggest northern Italian rather than Greek or Balkan roots. However, a few names, including Bulgarino d'Anaia, George de Malvasia, and George

Makrycheris, suggest that although the Italians may have been in the majority, their ranks included local pirates as well. One of these Byzantine privateers—the Genoese pirate Giovanni de lo Cavo—seized Rhodes from the Genoese in 1278 and became the overlord of the island, ruling in the name of the emperor Michael VIII Palaiologos (1223–82). Under de lo Cavo's rule the island attracted both pirates and slave traders, and despite Turkish raids it remained a thriving pirate haven until 1306, when another Italian renegade, Vignolo de Vignoli, encouraged the Knights Hospitaller to conquer the island.

By that time the rest of the region had been subjugated by the Turks, by the Byzantines, or by the Italians. The growing naval power of the Ottoman Empire and the regional dominance of the Venetians and the Knights Hospitaller meant that lawlessness was curbed and maritime trade encouraged. Rhodes was the penultimate pirate bastion in the Aegean during this period. The one remaining pirate refuge was Athens, where from 1311 they briefly flourished under the protection of Duke Manfred of Athens. He was a mercenary commander, part of the Catalan Company, which hired its services to Latin and Byzantine rulers alike. These Catalan pirates remained a scourge in the region until the Turkish conquest of the city in 1458, at which point the survivors of the pirate band entered the service of the Turks.

By the late fourteenth century the center of piratical activity in the Mediterranean had moved west, from the Aegean and Adriatic to the Mediterranean coast of North Africa. While Turkish privateers still operated against the Italian enclaves such as Crete and the Morean coast of Greece, for the most part Turkish naval dominance in the eastern Mediterranean meant that such activities became secondary to the Turkish naval effort—the campaign for maritime dominance in the central Mediterranean. At a time when the merchants of northern Europe were reestablishing long-abandoned maritime trading routes, the Mediterranean was being divided into a religious battleground, where naval power rather than trade or piracy would be the new driving force.

PIRACY AROUND THE BRITISH ISLES

Pirate attacks were not just limited to the Baltic Sea. One of the characteristics of the feudal system was that the central power of the crown was fairly limited. This made it difficult to maintain a state navy powerful enough to root out pirate dens, while the feudal barons often lacked the power to do much about the sea robbers on their doorstep. Therefore piracy thrived wherever it could, particularly in the English Channel and the Irish Sea, where national and regional rivalries meant that pirates could play neighboring powers off against each other. In the Channel Islands pirates even became semifeudal lords themselves, thriving amidst the dynastic struggle between England and France.

By the early thirteenth century, piracy had become such a serious problem in the English Channel that only the best-protected ships were guaranteed a safe cross-channel passage. One of the most notable pirates of this period was Eustace the Monk, also known as the Black Monk, who was simultaneously hired as a privateer by both King John of England and King Philip II of France. From his base in Jersey he dominated the waters of the English Channel, demanding protection money from shipping and attacking those who refused to cooperate. His exploits were celebrated by a French poem written in 1284, and, while much of this work was little more than romantic fiction, contemporary records provide us with some idea of his activities.

From 1205 until 1212 he served King John, leading raids on the French coast from Calais to Brest. He fell from favor when his men attacked English settlements, and King John retaliated by invading the Channel Islands, driving Eustace from his base. The pirate monk then allied himself with King Philip and led a revenge attack on Folkestone. Eustace finally met his end during the struggle following King John's death. He supported a rebellion against the new English monarch, Henry III, and in 1217 used his fleet to transport a rebel army across the Channel. This pirate fleet was lying at anchor off Sandwich on the southeast coast of England when it was surprised and destroyed by a larger English fleet. Eustace was captured, and together with his fellow pirates he was put to the sword.[5]

Another pirate chief of the period was Savary de Mauleon, who used the English-controlled port of La Rochelle as a base. In fact King John even made the French pirate the town's governor, although de Mauleon also allied himself with the French king, effectively playing both sides in order to maintain his pirate fiefdom. However, his was an isolated case, as by the middle of the thirteenth century both the English and French governments had managed to contain the pirate problem through the issuing of privateering licences, or letters of marque. This was part of a carrot and stick approach to piracy that would be repeated in the eighteenth century. As long as the pirates did the bidding of their chosen monarch, then they enjoyed the protection of the crown. If they attacked the shipping of the ruler's country, or failed to provide the monarch with a share of the profits, then all legal protection would be removed and the pirates would find themselves outlaws with a price on their heads and denied access to the ports they needed to sell their plunder.

On the Celtic fringes of Britain—in the west of Scotland and in Ireland—this small-time piracy continued to thrive well into the sixteenth century. The Lords of the Isles were descendants of the Vikings who once controlled the west coast of Scotland, and they operated in much the same way as Eustace the Black Monk, extorting protection money from shipping and attacking passing ships that refused to pay them their "feudal" dues. The fight to repulse English invaders, feuding nobles and a lack of hard cash prevented the Scottish crown from dealing with this problem for some three centuries. Finally James VI of Scotland managed to break up this power base in the early seventeenth century—first by countering the authority of the notorious Ruari Macneil of Barra and then by the capture of Neil Macleod of Bereasaidh.

In Ireland the lack of central authority meant that pirates enjoyed the same immunity from the law. The Viking invaders were soon replaced by English ones, ushering in centuries of rebellion, warfare, and instability. Probably the most notorious Irish pirate—and certainly the most unusual—was Gráinne Ní Mháille (or Granuaile), known to the English as Grace O'Malley (c. 1530–1603).[6] In Irish legend she enjoys the marvelous title of the Sea Queen of Connemara. Her father, the clan chief of the Ní Mháille (O'Malley), controlled much of the coastline of what is now County Mayo, charging taxes on fishermen using his coastal waters. Her name—which derives from the Irish word for being bald, or having cropped hair—was explained by her father's refusal to take her on a trading voyage to Spain. The story goes that she cropped her hair and hid amongst the crew until the ship had sailed.

In 1546 she married Donal O'Flaherty, heir to the O'Flaherty clan title and part-time pirate, and bore three children to him before he was killed in battle. Much of his time was spent waging a trade war with Galway and putting down rebellions against his authority, and his wife seems to have taken control of his pirate operation. In 1564 he was killed during a battle with a rival to the clan chiefdom, and Granuaile withdrew to her father's fortified stronghold on Clare Island, off the west coast of County Mayo. Although she remarried two years later, from that point on she seems to have carved out her own piratical career. Eventually the authorities decided to deal with the threat she posed, and in 1577 they sent a force to besiege her stronghold. She was duly captured and imprisoned, although for some unknown reason she was soon released.

Following a second incarceration by Sir Richard Bingham, the English governor of Connaught, her children were kept in prison as surety against her good behavior. She immediately sailed to London, where she was granted an audience with Queen Elizabeth I. The result was that her children were freed, and the now elderly pirate queen continued her small-scale raiding until her death. While much of this story is shrouded in Irish legend, her visit to the court generated sufficient interest for her life to be chronicled by English-speaking contemporaries. Similarly, the records of her English jailer also provide us with a list of her piratical "crimes," which consisted mainly of the harassment of local coastal shipping. Still, despite the relatively small scale of her activities, her sex guaranteed that she would be remembered long after the raids carried out by other minor Irish pirates and clan leaders were long forgotten. However, set against the activities of the English sea raiders of the same era, she was little more than a local tearaway.

3

SEA DOGS
OF THE RENAISSANCE

PRIVATEERS OR PIRATES?

There really is some truth in the idea that one country's privateer is another country's pirate. This famously swashbuckling age of Elizabethan sea dogs, Spanish treasure galleons and daredevil raids on the Spanish Main was a time when national and individual interests could be pursued in tandem, and a fortune could be won while ostensibly serving the state. For much of this period Catholic Spain and Protestant England, while not exactly at war with each other, were rivals. While this undeclared war continued, rulers, diplomats, and sea captains had to tread a fine line between taking advantage of the hostility and overstepping political and diplomatic boundaries.

In 1585, after three decades of these diplomatic niceties, the rivalry turned into full-blown war, a conflict brought on largely through the actions of sea captains such as Francis Drake, whose raids on the Spanish Main effectively constituted a declaration of war. Freed from her diplomatic restraints, Queen Elizabeth I was able to let slip her sea dogs, and for the next two decades they terrorized Spanish coastal settlements in Europe and the New World, attacked Spanish shipping on the high seas, and thwarted Spanish attempts to invade England.

However, the English were not the only national group to attack Spain's newfound overseas empire. They certainly were not the first to see the potential offered by the poorly defended Spanish settlements in the New World, and by the stream of specie—silver ingots, gold bars, and coins of both metals—piling up in Central American ports ready for shipment to Spain. The French began attacking Spanish treasure ships in the 1520s, some four decades before the English began their attacks on the Spanish Main. Then, almost as soon as James I of England (and VI of Scotland) made peace with Spain, Dutch fleets began preying on Spanish convoys in American waters.

Throughout this period the Spanish regarded those who preyed on their New World possessions as interlopers. The phrase "no peace beyond the line" referred to the division of the newly discovered New World into Spanish and Portuguese sectors. According to the Treaty of Tordesillas (1494), the longitudinal line of 36° 47' West, which ran through Brazil, set the boundaries of the Spanish New World. Everything to the west of this line belonged to Spain, even lands that were still to be discovered. Clearly other emerging maritime powers in Europe felt they were being excluded, and so the scene was set for centuries of conflict.

For the Spanish the situation was very simple. With the exception of Brazil, they considered the Americas to be Spanish territory and so would resist any attempt by outsiders to establish their own colonies beyond the line, regardless of the diplomatic situation back in Europe. Therefore they regarded interlopers as pirates, even though they arrived to trade rather than to fight, as did Sir John Hawkins in 1568. This heavy-handed reaction only served to antagonize other European powers and led to a cycle of escalation that would inevitably result in open war. For example, Queen Elizabeth issued Hawkins with a letter of reprisal, which allowed him to attack Spanish shipping and property as a means of redress for the losses he suffered at the hands of the Spanish. In English (and for that matter French and Dutch) law, reprisal was considered a perfectly legal act, which effectively bestowed privateering status upon these raiders.

A privateer was essentially an individual or crew who was given a licence or letter of marque by their national government, which allowed them to attack the shipping of another belligerent state. Privateering was governed by an internationally recognized set of rules, which at least in theory meant that if caught by the enemy, then the privateer was considered an enemy combatant rather than a pirate. In return for this legal protection, the state that had issued the letter of marque usually received a percentage of the profits. As long as they abided by the rules and attacked only the enemies of the state listed on their letter of marque, privateers could not be hanged as pirates, condemned to a lifetime of servitude in the galleys, or simply killed outright.

However, the Spanish refused to observe these international niceties, particularly if the privateers operated beyond the line. While the English regarded Sir Francis Drake as a national hero, the Spanish likened him to the Devil and labeled him as a pirate. The Treaty of Tordesillas gave the Spanish the legal right to take such a stance, and they rightly regarded the stalwart defense of their New World possessions as vital to the prosperity and security of the Spanish Empire. Therefore, as long as the sea dogs continued to prey on the Spanish Main, the Spanish denied them any legal protection, treating them as pirates to be hunted down without mercy and executed without leniency.[1]

THE SPANISH MAIN

A privateer leaving from one of the ports in England's West Country for the New World would begin by sailing south rather than west and running down to the Canary Islands, or even the Cape Verde archipelago, to take on water. The ship would then pick up the northeast trade winds, which allowed it to cross the Atlantic Ocean in a matter of weeks rather than months. It would make landfall somewhere in the Lesser Antilles, that great necklace of islands that marked the edge of the Caribbean. The privateer would then take on water and supplies, and if necessary the crew would careen their ship, cleaning the hull of weeds and marine growth to make sure it sailed as fast as possible. The islands were not settled by the Spanish, so for the moment the Englishmen were safe. However, these precautions were necessary, because from that point on the ship would be operating in the enemy waters of the Spanish Main.

In theory, this term referred to the northern coastline of the South American mainland—the region Spanish settlers called the Tierra Firme, or "dry land." However, the term "main," or sea, was soon extended far beyond these coastal waters, and by the mid-sixteenth century it had become synonymous with anywhere in the Caribbean basin. After all, the Spanish regarded the whole area as theirs, so calling the waters and coastline of the Caribbean basin the Spanish Sea was no exaggeration. To avoid confusion, the Caribbean Sea itself soon became labeled the Mar del Norte (North Sea). All this meant that once past the line of the Lesser Antilles, any privateer would be facing hundreds of miles of open sea, bounded in the south by the Tierra Firme, in the west by the newly

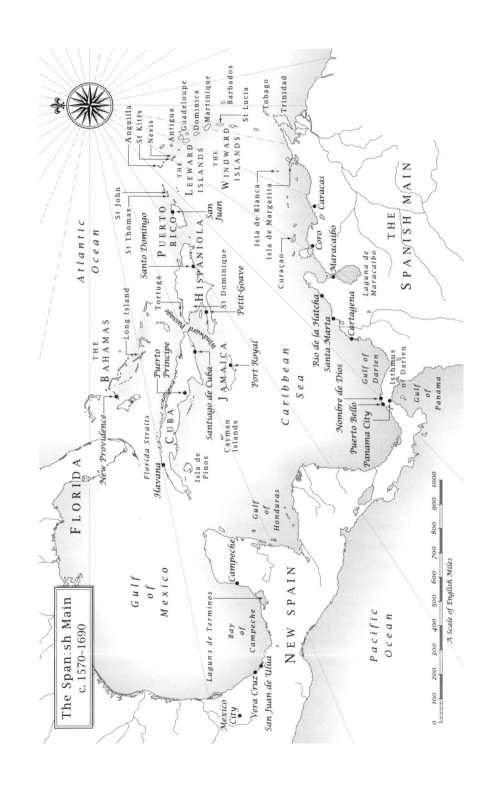

The Spanish Main
c. 1570–1690

FLORIDA

Gulf of Mexico

Atlantic Ocean

THE BAHAMAS

New Providence

Florida Straits

Havana

Isla de Pinos

CUBA

Santiago de Cuba

Cayman Islands

Long Island

Puerto Principe

Tortuga

Santo Domingo

St Thomas

St John

PUERTO RICO

San Juan

HISPANIOLA

St Dominique

Petit-Goave

Windward Passage

JAMAICA

Port Royal

Caribbean Sea

Anguilla
St Kitts
Nevis
Antigua

THE LEEWARD ISLANDS

Guadeloupe
Dominica
Martinique

THE WINDWARD ISLANDS

Barbados
St Lucia
Tobago
Trinidad

Caracas
Coro

Isla de Blanca
Isla de Margarita

Curaçao

Maracaibo

Laguna de Maracaibo

THE SPANISH MAIN

Rio de la Hatcha
Santa Marta
Cartagena

Gulf of Darien

Isthmus of Darien

Nombre de Dios
Puerto Bello
Panama City

Gulf of Panama

NEW SPAIN

Gulf of Honduras

Campeche

Laguna de Terminos

Bay of Campeche

Campeche

Vera Cruz
San Juan de Ulúa

Mexico City

Pacific Ocean

A Scale of English Miles

0   100 200 300 400 500 600 700 800 900 1000

conquered lands of Mexico—now called New Spain—and in the north by the La Florida Peninsula and the North American mainland. The privateer had crossed the line and would now be regarded as an interloper.

The Caribbean basin itself was divided by numerous islands, the largest being Cuba, which separated the Gulf of Mexico from the Mar del Norte. To the east of Cuba lay the large island of Hispaniola, the place where the Spanish established their first colony. Further to the east lay Puerto Rico, and beyond it lay Las Virgines (the Virgin Islands), where the chain of islands began curving southwards towards the Tierra Firme, marking the eastern rim of the basin. To the north of Cuba lay the Lucayos, the jumble of islands, reefs, and deserted cays now known as the Bahamas. Around the fringes of the basin lay numerous smaller places where an interloper could hide, or where an ambush could be laid.

In the midst of this tract of warm seas and tropical islands lay the Spanish settlements, ranging from substantial and well-defended cities such as Havana and Cartagena to the smaller ports, little more than coastal villages, found on the shores of Cuba, Mexico, and Hispaniola. Some of the larger settlements also served as regional administrative centers, and during the sixteenth century some, but not all, were protected by fortifications. Ports such as Havana, Cartagena, Santiago de Cuba, Vera Cruz, Nombre de Dios, and San Juan were all protected by substantial stone-built defensive works, garrisoned by a combination of regular Spanish troops and locally raised militia. Following the Huguenot attacks of the mid-sixteenth century, the Spanish crown poured substantial sums into the building of fortresses, the placing of shore batteries, and the training of troops to deal with any threat. However, many smaller ports lay open to attack, and a well-armed visiting ship would find itself the temporary master of the settlement if its commander wished.

This ramshackle overseas empire was administered by the Council of the Indies, which was established in 1524, and attached to the royal court. It was also responsible for the Casa de Contratación (House of Trade) in Seville, which controlled shipping to and from the New World and the transport of specie. In 1535 the Council established the viceroyalty of New Spain, which had its headquarters in Mexico City. In theory, as a royal official, the viceroy governed the region in the name of the king, but there was also considerable scope for individual profit. In 1544 a second viceroyalty was created in Peru.

Eventually smaller regional *audencias* were created, administered by one of the two viceroys. *Audencias* were Spanish administrative districts in the New

World, each ruled by a local governor. The *audencia* at Santo Domingo (Hispaniola) was already established to govern the larger Caribbean islands, and it duly fell under control of New Spain, along with the new *audencias* of Mexico (founded in 1527), Guatemala (1543), and New Galicia (Guadalajara—1548). The viceroyalty of Peru was responsible for the *audencias* of Panama (1538), Santa Fé de Bogotá (New Granada, now Colombia—1548), and Lima (Peru—1543). While on paper all this sounded impressive, the system itself was open to misuse, to corruption, and to neglect. While some Spanish administrators were noted for their zeal, others did little to protect their territory, and so all but invited the attention of foreign interlopers.

THE TREASURE FLEETS

The impetus behind most of the Spanish conquests in the New World was the search for gold, and while the conquistadors and the regional administrators who followed them were entitled to the largest share, the Spanish crown was also entitled to its *quinto,* or fifth. By the 1520s Spanish ships were transporting this specie back to Spain, but in 1526, after Spain had lost several treasure ships to French pirates, these shipments were transported as part of a *flota,* or fleet. What therefore amounted to an annual convoy transported the wealth of the New World back to Spain, presenting the Spanish crown with a windfall and daring interlopers with an opportunity for plunder.

For almost two centuries this convoy followed a set routine. There were two treasure fleets. The first of these, the New Spain fleet, sailed from Seville in April, and after a transatlantic crossing from the Canary Islands, it made landfall in the southern part of the Lesser Antilles. In September the Tierra Firme fleet followed the same route but once in the Spanish Main took a different direction. After collecting the royal quota of the silver produced in Mexican mines, the New Spain fleet wintered in Vera Cruz, then sailed on to Havana in the early summer. The Tierra Firme fleet wintered in Cartagena, where it collected Colombian emeralds and Venezuelan gold. In the spring it continued on to Nombre de Dios, where it collected the king's share of Peru's vast silver production, which had been shipped up the coast from Lima to Panama then transported by pack mule across the isthmus to the Caribbean port. Following Drake's attack on the town in 1572, the treasure terminus was moved just up the coast to Porto Bello, which was considered more defensible. It then sailed on to join the New Spain fleet in Havana.

Usually the two *flotas* returned home separately. The aim was to sail from Havana by July at the latest, in which case the New Spain fleet was due back in Seville in September, and the Tierra Firme fleet in October. However, in time of war the two convoys would often band together for protection, even if this meant putting off the sailing for a month or so—a decision that involved a substantial risk, as it could delay departure until well within the hurricane season, which lasted from June until November. The *flotas* of 1544, 1622, and 1715 were all overtaken by major hurricanes, and in the case of the last, the storm and its aftermath played a major part in the story of piratical activity in American waters, as the wreckage proved a magnet for treasure hunters, many of whom turned into pirates (see p.155). The safe arrival of a treasure fleet was a cause for rejoicing in Seville, and on the few occasions when the fleet never arrived, due to the intervention of either man or nature, the Spanish economy suffered.[2]

Naturally enough, these Spanish treasure fleets were attractive targets for interlopers, particularly for large piratical or privateering expeditions, such as those led by Sir Francis Drake in the 1570s and 1580s. Even Drake found the well-guarded treasure fleets too difficult a target, as did his buccaneering successors such as Sir Henry Morgan. The only occasion in which a *flota* was captured in its entirety was in 1628, when a Dutch squadron drove it ashore on the coast of Cuba. However, Drake and Morgan found the weak point in the Spanish system. Although work had begun to defend the treasure ports of Nombre de Dios, Vera Cruz, Panama, and Porto Bello, by the time Drake arrived in the Caribbean these improvements were still not fully complete. Worse still for the Spanish, there was no easy way to protect the transport of silver across the isthmus of Panama, and a well-planned attack could seize a fortune in plunder before the mule trains ever reached the coast.

Then there was always the chance that a treasure ship could be caught on its own, as shipments from Spanish possessions in the Philippines to Mexico were still made by single ships, called Manila galleons. For much of the sixteenth and seventeenth centuries, the Spanish would make every effort to protect their coastal colonies from attack and, above all, preserve the flow of specie from the New World to the Old. For their part, men like Sir Francis Drake regarded the Spanish Main as their hunting ground and the treasure fleets as their elusive prey.

THE FRENCH CORSAIRS

The first serious attack on Spain's overseas empire came just two years after the conquistador Hernando Cortez captured Tenochtitlan, the capital city of the Aztecs. A portion of the Aztec gold seized by Cortez and his men was earmarked for the emperor Charles V and was shipped back to Spain. In May 1523, the three caravels (small two-masted vessels with lateen-rigged sails) carrying this treasure made their landfall at Cape Sagres, the very southwest corner of the Portuguese coast. Their voyage from Havana had been uneventful, and the crews looked forward to their arrival in Seville, less than three days of easy sailing away. Within hours they would pick up their escort, a pair of well-armed carracks (larger and more robust ships with three masts, two of which carried square-rigged sails) waiting for them off Cabo de Santa Maria (Cape St. Vincent). It was then that the lookouts spotted five strange sails to the north, so the Spanish commander veered away to the southeast, towards his waiting escorts.

The Spanish were out of luck. Within hours the five ships overhauled two of the Spaniards and threatened to board. Outmatched, the Spanish were forced to surrender. The trio of mystery ships turned out to be a squadron of French privateers under the command of the corsair Jean Fleury (or Florin) of Honfleur. To the French, corsair was synonymous with privateer; the word was derived from the French term *la course*, which in nautical terms meant a cruise. France and Spain had been intermittently at war with each other since 1495, and by 1523 the French army was on the defensive in northern Italy, fighting a campaign that would culminate in the great French disaster at Pavia (1525). The French crown had issued a privateering licence to the Dieppe ship owner Jean Ango, who in turn had ordered Fleury to sea in search of Spanish plunder. Off Cape Sagres he hit the jackpot.

The plunder reputedly included chests filled with Aztec statues and religious artefacts cast in gold, exquisite jewelry including an emerald the size of a fist, discs and ingots of gold and silver, bejeweled cloaks and headdresses … even a live jaguar. The total value was later placed at 800,000 ducats. Another version of the encounter involved a sea battle between the French corsairs and the Spanish escorts waiting off Cabo de Santa Maria, while a third set the encounter off the Azores. However, the report sent by Jean Ango to King Francis I made no mention of a full-scale battle and firmly placed the encounter off the southwestern tip of Portugal. When Fleury returned to Dieppe the news of the French success caused a sensation. For the first time, the rest of Europe became

SPANISH COINAGE

In the sixteenth century the basic unit of Spanish currency was the *maravedi*—the equivalent of a penny. Across Europe the standard unit of international currency was an 8oz (227g) gold coin called the *ducat,* whose stability was assured by its adoption by German and Italian banking houses. The Spanish crown introduced its own golden equivalent—the *mark*—but in 1537 this gave way to the *escudo,* which was valued at 374 maravedis. In 1566 the Spanish also minted a half-escudo coin and also a two-escudo coin called the *doblon*—more famously known as the *doubloon.* Later, other larger coins were minted, worth four and eight escudos apiece. In sixteenth- and seventeenth-century England the *pound* (coin) was the equivalent of a pound (weight) of silver and was therefore the equivalent of an escudo.

The silver coin used by the Spanish was the *real,* which contained an ounce of silver. Before the depreciation of silver prices caused by the huge influx of specie from Peru, 11 silver reales were the equivalent of one gold escudo. However, from the 1560s on the rate was set at 16 reales to the escudo. These coins were minted in half-, one-, two-, four- and eight-real denominations, although the most common was the eight-real coin—also known as the silver *dollar* or *peso.* This coin became popularly known as a *piece-of-eight.* This meant that a golden doubloon was the equivalent of four silver pieces-of-eight.

Using the retail price index as a guide, a silver "piece-of-eight" of 1585 was the equivalent of $180 in 2007, while the same coin in 1675 is the equivalent of $120 today. This meant that when Francis Drake captured the Spanish treasure galleon *Nuestra Señora del la Concepción* in 1578, the plunder was worth approximately $72 million in modern money—making it one of the most lucrative pirate attacks in history.

aware of the full scale of Spain's plunders and conquests in the New World and of the wealth being transported in Spanish ships from the New World to the Old.[3]

After Jean Fleury's encounter, the floodgates were opened and a veritable wave of French corsairs put to sea, patrolling off the Spanish and Portuguese coasts, cruising off the Azores, and even probing beyond the line into the waters of the Spanish Main. By 1525 the Spanish reported that French pirates were operating beyond the line, and in 1527 Spanish and Portuguese ships were being attacked off the coast of Brazil. Jean Fleury never lived long enough to reap the benefits of his discovery, however. After leading a series of highly successful raids on Spanish shipping in the western Mediterranean, he was finally cornered in 1527, on his return voyage to France. He surrendered after a six-hour fight, and on being landed in a Basque port he was turned over to the Spanish authorities. Under torture he confessed to the capture of more than 150 Spanish ships, which may have been an exaggeration, but which at least highlights the scale of the privateering problem facing the Spanish at the time. Jean Fleury was duly tried and executed as a pirate.

By the 1530s the French threat became even more serious. In 1533 another Spanish treasure ship was captured off the Azores, while between 1535 and 1547 no fewer than 23 Spanish ships operated by the Casa de Contratación were lost to French corsairs in the Spanish Main, with further losses reported in home waters. Corsairs captured nine ships in 1537 alone, reducing Spanish royal income from the New World by half—to just over one million pesos. In his *Historia del Mondo Nuovo* (1565) the Italian scholar Girolamo Benzoni claimed that as a result of these losses, "of the captains, pilots and clerks who traded in the Indies, few escaped without having been captured by the French once or twice." These attacks led directly to the creation of the *flota* system in several stages from 1526, in which the treasure ships were formed into convoys. However, it took time to perfect this system, and these heavy Spanish losses continued until 1559, when the Treaty of Cateau-Cambrésis brought the war to an end.

Spanish treasure ships were not the only victims. In 1536 a group of French interlopers attacked Havana, while the following year smaller Spanish settlements in Honduras and the isthmus of Panama were also sacked. Five years later Havana was plundered again, after which the raids spread to the Tierra Firme—the South American coast—with attacks on Cubagua and the pearl farming settlement on the island of Margarita. In 1540 the corsairs sacked San Juan in Puerto Rico, and in 1544 another group of corsairs fell upon Santa Marta on the Venezuelan coast and even managed to capture and sack Cartagena, one of the most important settlements on the Spanish Main. A brief few years of peace gave the Spanish something of a respite, but when war resumed in 1551 the corsairs returned with a vengeance.

The most successful of these French privateers was François le Clerc, a corsair known as "Pegleg" (*Jambe de Bois*). After making landfall in the Leeward Islands his force of ten ships cruised westwards, attacking several small coastal settlements on Puerto Rico and Hispaniola as he went. In early 1554 he fell on Santiago de Cuba, capturing the town, then holding it for a month. Although le Clerc returned home with his plunder—sacking Las Palmas in the Canary Islands on the way—one of his captains, Jacques de Sores, remained in the Caribbean, where he commanded a small force of three privateers. After cruising and raiding off the coast of Venezuela he headed back north, and in July 1555 de Sores descended on Havana. The settlement was still poorly protected, and after a siege lasting two days the Cuban governor was forced to yield the city to the corsairs. A botched attempt at a surprise attack led de Sores to slaughter his Spanish prisoners, and after plundering what he could from the town, he burned it to the ground.[4]

It was de Sores who introduced a new sectarian element to these attacks. Although it took some two decades for the Protestant Reformation to make its mark in France, when it did arrive it was in a stronger, more virulent form than the brand of Protestantism that had swept Germany. This second wave of reformation was symbolized by the beliefs of John Calvin (1509–64), the French-born reformer who refused to compromise on his beliefs. The result was a new breed of Calvinists who viewed the Spanish as their sworn religious enemies, and therefore privateering expeditions to the Spanish Main inevitably took on a religious element. As a Calvinist, de Sores made sure he desecrated the Catholic churches in Havana before putting them to the flame. The devastation of Havana was so efficient that another corsair band that arrived off the city the following winter could find nothing left to plunder.

Although peace was declared in 1559, a clause in the treaty stated: "West of the prime meridian ... violence by either party to the other side shall not be regarded as a contravention of the treaties." There would be no peace beyond the line. In France, the end of the Spanish war was followed by a series of internecine sectarian conflicts known as the French Wars of Religion (1562–98). On the one hand the withdrawal of privateering letters of marque ended state-sponsored attacks on the Spanish. Further, the growing religious war in France meant that former privateers such as le Clerc and de Sores became enmeshed in their own homegrown religious struggle and let the Spanish alone. On the other, it also meant that when the French Protestants (Huguenots) suffered a string of reverses and were driven from their homes, groups of exiles elected to establish settlements of their own in the New World.

In 1564, French Huguenots established a settlement on the banks of the St. Johns River, near the modern city of Jacksonville, Florida. This settlement, named La Caroline (or Fort Caroline), was established near the spot where two years earlier the French privateer-turned-explorer Jean Ribault had raised a stone marker, proclaiming that the surrounding land belonged to Charles IX of France. The Spanish had other ideas. Their great fear was that a rival European power would manage to establish a base within striking range of their Caribbean settlements, which would then serve as a haven for pirates and interlopers. A Spanish force under the command of Pedro Menendez de Avilés was sent north from Havana to remind the Huguenots that Florida belonged to Spain.

The Spanish expedition established a forward base at St. Augustine, some 30 miles south of La Caroline. Ribault and the bulk of his force put to sea in an attempt to destroy the Spanish ships as they lay at anchor. Unfortunately for the French, their squadron was hit by a hurricane, which dashed the ships onto the Florida coast. Meanwhile Menendez had marched north, and on September 20, 1565, he attacked the fortifications of La Caroline. Heavily outnumbered, the company-size force left behind to defend the settlement was overwhelmed and butchered. After putting all male prisoners to the sword, the Spanish marched south again to round up the shipwrecked survivors of Ribault's squadron. These 350 Frenchmen were then given the option to convert to Catholicism, an offer which they rejected outright. Menendez ordered his men to massacre the prisoners. The Spanish must have congratulated themselves on dealing with a serious threat to their overseas empire. However, an even more serious threat was just over the horizon—another group of interlopers that would threaten the very survival of the Spanish colonies in the New World.

HAWKINS AND THE ARRIVAL
OF THE ENGLISH

When word of the riches of the Spanish New World reached the rest of Europe, few other European powers were in a position to take advantage of the opportunities presented by a poorly defended Spanish overseas empire. Henry VIII of England was an ally of the Spanish, and it was not until 1527 that he switched allegiance and formed an alliance with his old French rival, Francis I. A few letters of marque were duly issued to English sea captains, and later that year the Spanish recorded the arrival of the first English interloper beyond the line. An unnamed English captain landed a force of around 40 men and a ship's cannon near Santo Domingo in the southwest corner of Hispaniola. These interlopers tried unsuccessfully to force the port's inhabitants to trade with them—at gunpoint if necessary. Faced with rejection, the English plundered what they could, then withdrew to their ship. This might have been an isolated incident, but it proved that the Spanish settlers were more scared of their own administrators than they were of interlopers.

The sack of Havana by French Huguenot corsairs led by Jacques de Sores in 1555.

49

While this process was repeated several times over the next four decades, the political status quo in Europe dictated against English interference in the Spanish Main. After all, France remained the great rival to Henry VIII's England, and so an alliance with France's greatest rival, Spain, made sound political sense. Trading expeditions to the Spanish Main were forbidden, and while the French made the most of these opportunities for plunder, the English had to content themselves with privateering operations closer to home. This cosy arrangement even survived Henry's break with the Catholic Church in the mid-1530s. However, following the accession of his daughter Elizabeth I in 1558, relations between England and Spain became considerably cooler. As an active Protestant, Elizabeth saw Spain as both a religious and a political rival. Although open war was avoided for over a quarter of a century, the rivalry between the two countries provided ample opportunities for English sea captains to take up where the French had left off.

John Hawkins (1532–92) was the first of these Elizabethan interlopers. Ironically, the man responsible for preparing the Elizabethan navy to take on the Spanish Armada entered the Spanish Main with peaceful intentions. His first voyage in 1562 was more of a slave trading expedition than an attempt to break the Spanish monopoly in the New World. After collecting a cargo of slaves on the Guinea coast in West Africa, Hawkins crossed the Atlantic, making landfall in the Leeward Islands somewhere near Antigua during the spring of 1563. His three ships—the *Solomon* (120 tons), the *Swallow* (100 tons), and a Portuguese slaver captured off the Guinea coast—were crammed with 300 Africans, whom Hawkins hoped to sell to Spanish plantation owners in Hispaniola. Avoiding the principal port of Santo Domingo, Hawkins landed his human cargo some miles from the settlement and opened negotiations with local landowners. Lorenzo Bernárdez, the captain of a cavalry squadron sent to intercept the interlopers, even offered to protect the English during their visit in return for a cut of the profits. Hawkins returned to England a wealthy man, the richest in Plymouth.

It was inevitable that Hawkins would try his luck again. This time he was offered royal backing, and as part of her share the queen agreed to lease him a royal warship—the 700-ton *Jesus of Lubeck*. Although it was an impressive warship, this was not a particularly good deal for Hawkins, as he had virtually to rebuild it at his own expense, modernizing the 20-year-old ship by reducing her superstructure in an attempt to make her less of a cumbersome vessel. Once again Hawkins picked up a cargo of slaves in West Africa, but this time the

Spanish were less willing to cooperate. Turned away from the island of Margarita, off the Venezuelan coast, he tried elsewhere, selling part of his human cargo at Bourbarata on the mainland and the rest in Rio de la Hatcha, further up the coast in what is now Colombia.

Even this last transaction was far from straightforward, as Hawkins had threatened to turn the guns of his flagship on the port unless the locals agreed to the sale. In fact, this might have been a means of providing the locals with an excuse for trading with an interloper—a prearranged gesture that "forced" the Spanish to complete the transaction. Still, in late 1565 Hawkins managed to return home with an even greater profit than before, although this time his actions had earned an official complaint from the Spanish ambassador at Elizabeth's court. However, the system seemed to be working, and Hawkins had proved that, if its commander wanted to, a well-armed expedition could break the Spanish monopoly of trade on the Spanish Main.

Hawkins then embarked on a third attempt.[5] This time the *Jesus of Lubeck* was accompanied by a second royal warship, the 120-ton *Minion*, as well as Hawkins's own ships *Swallow, Solomon,* and the *Judith,* commanded by Hawkins's young kinsman Francis Drake. The expedition sailed from Plymouth in October 1567 and made for the West African coast. This time things went wrong from the start. A slaving raid near Cape Verde ended with the death of eight sailors, killed by poisoned arrows as Hawkins was forced to retreat back to his ships. In what is now Sierra Leone Hawkins found that two local chiefs were at war with each other. He sided with one against the other and helped his ally capture Conga, the enemy capital. The Englishman's reward for his alliance was a cargo of 500 Conganese slaves. Hawkins then sailed for the Spanish Main.

In June 1568 he visited Rio de la Hatcha again but found that a newly installed Spanish garrison prevented him from selling his cargo. After a brisk exchange of fire, the interlopers withdrew but managed to sell about half of their slaves at Santa Marta further up the coast. Once again, the sale involved a pretense. As had probably happened three years before at Rio de la Hatcha, the locals put up a token resistance, and Hawkins threatened to bombard the town— almost certainly a prearranged display of force. Hawkins hoped to sell the rest of his slaves at Cartagena, but after the two sides began firing at each other, it became clear that the English were not welcome there.

He then sailed north, but in September 1568 his fleet was overcome by a hurricane off the western tip of Cuba, and Hawkins was forced to put in to Vera

Cruz in Mexico for repairs. This was the port built by Cortez when he invaded the Aztec Empire, and it also served as a treasure port for Mexican silver. Clearly the Spaniards would be none too pleased to see such a powerful force of interlopers, so Hawkins decided to use subterfuge. His squadron flew the Spanish flag as they entered port, and his men seized the port's defenses before the garrison realized they had been tricked. Hawkins thought he could repair his fleet in relative security, but then his luck ran out. Two days later the annual Spanish treasure *flota* arrived, a powerful force commanded by Admiral Francisco Luján. The English were now outnumbered two to one.

A truce was arranged, but the Spanish fleet carried a passenger who had decided to teach the interlopers a lesson. Martín Enríquez, the new governor of New Spain, had traveled from Seville with the fleet and had no intention of being dictated to by Hawkins. Under cover of darkness a powerful force of Spanish troops lay hidden on board a hulk moored between the two fleets. As dawn rose on September 23, Hawkins spotted the hidden soldiers and ordered his ships to open fire. The Spanish immediately leaped ashore and overran the English garrison on San Juan de Ulúa—the island in Vera Cruz's harbor where the ships were moored. Having captured the shore batteries the Spaniards turned their guns on the English. The battle that followed lasted all day, but it was clear that the situation facing Hawkins was a hopeless one. He gave orders to make a break for the open sea.

The *Jesus of Lubeck* was trapped, as was most of the rest of Hawkins's fleet, but eventually the *Minion* managed to cut her way through the enemy and escape, carrying Hawkins and 200 men to safety. The only other English vessel to escape from San Juan de Ulúa that evening was Drake's *Judith*.[6] The two English ships had no provisions and were far from home. Over 100 crewmen requested to be put ashore and take their chances with the Spanish, while disease and starvation took its toll of many of the rest. By the time the *Minion* limped back into Plymouth, fewer than 20 men were left alive, one of them being Hawkins. The expedition had ended in complete disaster, but it awoke in both Hawkins and Drake a burning hatred of the Spanish, whom they viewed as breaking their word. While Hawkins concentrated on shipbuilding and transforming Elizabeth's Navy Royal, Drake vowed to return to the Spanish Main, and to take the fight to the enemy. What would begin as a private war would end up as a clash between nations—an attempt by England to attack the Spanish where they were most vulnerable.

OF SHIPS AND GUNS

The popular myth of the period is that the Spanish sailed in large, cumbersome ships, while the English preferred smaller, faster vessels. Like all such myths, the story contains an element of truth—and a lot of misleading generalizations.

The galleon was a Spanish invention—a faster and more maneuverable version of the cumbersome carrack (or nao). Until the 1520s most large warships were carracks—three-masted square-rigged ships with high forecastles and sterncastles. These ships made excellent warships, as they were large and stable enough to carry artillery. When it first appeared in the 1530s, the galleon was a streamlined version of the carrack, with a lower superstructure and better sailing qualities. Originally designed as a treasure carrier for the *flotas*, the galleon was soon used as a warship.

By the 1550s the English fleet included three galleons—copies of the Spanish ships. In Queen Elizabeth I's reign English shipbuilders developed the design, which reached its peak with the fast, "race-built" galleons designed by Sir John Hawkins. These same features were also found in smaller privateers. A prime example of these is the 100-ton swift-sailing *Golden Hind*, built to carry a powerful armament of 18 heavy guns.

This armament was important, as the English regarded accurate gunnery as the key to victory. While the Spanish considered that guns should be fired once, just before boarding, the English liked to keep their distance. Most Spanish carriages were two-wheeled, while the English preferred more sophisticated four-wheeled carriages, which could be reloaded faster. The Spanish advantage was the quality of their sea soldiers. The two protagonists of the era followed different tactical doctrines—one emphasizing firepower and the other close combat.

Conditions on board were primitive. The *Golden Hind* was less than 70 ft (21.4 m) long, with a 20 ft (6.1 m) beam. Belowdecks space was taken up by the stores, by guns and ammunition, and by the crew of 80 men and boys. While Drake had his own tiny cabin, his senior officers only had alcoves on the deck below. The crew only had space to swing a hammock amidst the guns of the lower deck. Drake enjoyed some comforts—he reputedly had oak furniture in his cabin—and it was just big enough to entertain. He circumnavigated the globe in this little floating world, which was typical of the Elizabethan privateers sailing on the Spanish Main.

DRAKE'S FIRST RAIDS

Francis Drake (c. 1540–96) was already an experienced sea captain in 1570, having been at sea since his teens. Having participated in his cousin John Hawkins's expeditions, he had more knowledge of the Spanish Main than most other Englishmen. In 1570 the queen granted him a letter of reprisal—a peacetime version of a privateering letter of marque. It allowed him to attack the Spanish in an effort to seek redress and reimbursement for the losses he suffered at San Juan de Ulúa. Hawkins was granted the same licence, but his newfound duties at the royal shipyard at Deptford meant that he was unable or unwilling to return to the Caribbean. For his part, Drake had no hesitation, and in 1570 he led the first of three small annual expeditions beyond the line. His force comprised just two small ships—the *Swan* of 25 tons and the *Dragon*, which was probably the same size. Little is known about what exactly he got up to that year, although he probably treated the raid more as a reconnaissance than as a serious cruise in search of prey. Certainly there is no record of plunder being brought back to Plymouth.

We know a little more about what happened the following year, when Drake returned to the Spanish Main in the *Swan*. He cruised off the isthmus of Panama, no doubt gathering information on the treasure port of Nombre de Dios and its tenuous overland supply link to Panama itself. He also captured several Spanish vessels, having teamed up with a group of French Huguenot pirates operating off the mouth of the Chagres River. As the Spanish put it in an official letter of complaint, he "upon the coast of Nombre de Dios did rob diverse barques in the river of Chagres, and in the same river did rob diverse barques that were transporting of merchandise." It may be that the French leader was Jean Bontemps, who was killed during a failed attack on Curaçao later that same year. By the time Drake returned to Plymouth, the *Swan*'s hold contained "forty thousand ducats, velvets and taffeta, besides other merchandise with gold and silver." Drake's reputation was secured.

His backers would have been delighted, and were quick to finance a new expedition. So in 1572 Drake set out again from Plymouth in two ships—the 70 ton *Pasco* (or *Pasha*) belonging to Hawkins, and Drake's own *Swan*. They carried just 73 men between them. By July Drake was back in his old hunting ground off Nombre de Dios, having established a secret base which he called Port Pheasant. Most probably this was the half-hidden bay south of Nombre de Dios now called Puerto Escoces—so named because it became the site of the Scottish settlement of New Edinburgh during the doomed Darien Expedition of 1698–1700. It was there that a third ship joined Drake's force—an English barque (a small three-masted sailing vessel using a combination of square- and fore-and-aft-rigged sails) crewed by 50 men, commanded by Captain James Raunce (or Ranse).

Deciding to attack the port, Drake left Captain Raunce in charge of the ships, and on the evening of July 28 he landed the rest of his force—some 70 men—on the beach, a few miles from the town. What should have been a straightforward night attack against an unsuspecting town went horribly wrong. A passing Spanish ship saw Drake's boats and warned the town, just as the Englishmen stormed the town's outer defenses. By the time the English sea dogs reached the port's marketplace they found the local militia drawn up waiting for them. A brisk exchange of fire followed, during which Drake was wounded in the leg. A mêlée ensued, and the Spanish were eventually broken. For the moment, Drake was in control of the town, but the Spanish were regrouping. A sudden rainstorm had kept the two sides apart as dawn broke, but the English realized they were now heavily outnumbered and all but surrounded. When Drake fainted through loss of blood, the attackers melted away, retreating back to their ships. Drake's first real attack on the Spanish Main had ended in ignominious failure.

Back in Port Pheasant Captain Raunce decided to quit the expedition, leaving Drake with just two ships and some 60 men, some of whom were wounded. He had too few men to sail his ships properly, let alone continue raiding. Drake then sailed east, towards the coast of Colombia, but found that news of the small English force had preceded them. Having captured a handful of prizes, Drake scuttled the *Swan* and moved his crew onto the *Pasco* and his two pinnaces (small vessels that could use either sails or oars). He then returned to the Panama isthmus, hoping to capture a few more lucrative prizes before he returned home. After all, so far the expedition had little to show for its efforts. Forewarned, the Spanish kept in port. Drake headed east again, and by January 1573 he had reached Curaçao. There was little to plunder. It was there that Drake made the bold decision to return to Nombre de Dios in an attempt to intercept the annual convoy of Peruvian silver which was due to be transported across the isthmus.

The timing was crucial. Drake had to intercept the mule train carrying the silver before it reached Nombre de Dios, and he had to avoid the powerful Tierra Firme fleet which arrived off the port in January. After all, he did not want another repeat of the San Juan de Ulúa debacle. Returning to the Panama coast, Drake made contact with the local Cimaroons—runaway slaves who now lived in the jungle. They offered to act as guides. Hiding his ships, Drake led his men inland, their advance screened by his newfound Cimaroon allies. On reaching the Royal Road, Drake ordered his men to take cover in a wood just outside Vente Cruces, some 18 miles from Panama. His Cimaroon scouts reported that a shipment was on its way, accompanied by the Treasurer of Lima and his family. The military escort was minimal. All Drake and his 18 English sailors had to do was stay in hiding and trip the ambush at the right moment.

Unfortunately, Drake reckoned without Robert Pike. The sailor had been drinking heavily to pass the time, and when he heard the pack train approaching he leaped up and cheered. His companions dragged him back into cover, but it was too late. A Spaniard on horseback spotted Pike and sounded the alarm. The treasure convoy was immediately turned around, and Drake had no option but to order his men back into the jungle. In order to return to his ships he needed to cross the Royal Road again, but when he tried it his party ran into a Spanish patrol. The Spanish retreated back through the village of Vente Cruces, and Drake slipped across the road and into the jungle. Within a week his men were back on their ships, while Drake thought up a new way of turning what had become a disastrous expedition into a profitable one.

In April he joined forces with the Huguenot pirate Guillaume le Testu (or Têtu), and together they decided to have another go at the Spanish treasure train, as the next shipment of silver was due to be moved from Panama to Nombre de Dios the following month. This time Drake landed some 20 miles east of the Spanish treasure port, and once again he relied on local Cimaroons to act as his scouts. He selected an ambush spot, and his 40 men—half French and half English—lay in wait. This time there was no mistake. The escort was taken completely by surprise and driven off after a sharp fight, leaving Drake's men to capture the mule train. They found it packed with specie—about 15 tons of silver, plus a small amount of gold. It was too much to carry, so the raiders buried the silver, then returned to their ships. Captain le Testu had been the only casualty of the fighting, and the badly wounded French commander had to be left to the mercy of the Spanish. The Spanish were not in the mood to be merciful, and le Testu was executed on the spot.

Drake's plan was to wait for the furore to die down, then to hire more Cimaroons to help him move the treasure. Unfortunately a Spanish patrol captured one of the Frenchmen, and under torture he revealed where the plunder had been buried. All Drake had left was the gold, which he had to share with the Frenchmen before sailing for home. In August 1573, Drake returned to Plymouth, with little to show for the 15 months he had spent on the Spanish Main. Still, it has been estimated that the haul of plunder he brought back was 50,000 pesos, or pieces-of-eight—which after division between crew and investors was a healthy enough profit. It also seemed sufficient to establish Drake as his own man, free of any lingering debt to the Hawkins family.

The sea dog would return to the Spanish Main four years later, but in the meantime he found himself something of a celebrity, cheered in the streets and feted at court. He quickly became a favorite at Hampton Court, and in 1575 he was used as an auxiliary naval commander during an attack on Rathin Island, off the northeast tip of Ireland. Encouraged by discussions of court-sponsored scientific expeditions, or voyages of discovery, Drake proposed a voyage into the Pacific—one that combined these noble motives with that of profit. By finding a way into what the Spanish considered a private sea, Drake would be able to intercept the fabulously wealthy Manila galleons, which sailed between the Philippines and Mexico. Queen Elizabeth I shared his enthusiasm, but for diplomatic reasons she was unable to give such an aggressive expedition her official sanction. Instead she became a secret shareholder in the expedition. After all, his plans included a piratical cruise off the coast of Spanish-held Peru—the "treasure house" of the Spanish overseas empire.

DRAKE'S SECRET VOYAGE

In December 1577 Drake sailed from Plymouth with five ships—the *Pelican*, *Elizabeth, Swan, Marigold,* and *Christopher*. The latter was a supply vessel, while the *Swan* and *Marigold* displaced less than 30 tons apiece.[7] They headed south to the Cape Verde Islands, where Drake plundered local Portuguese shipping, then veered west-southwest across the Atlantic Ocean. He made landfall off Brazil in early April, then the expedition continued southwards, down the South American coast. This stage of the voyage was marked by three incidents—the abandonment of the *Swan* and *Christopher* due to their poor condition, the renaming of the *Pelican*, which became the *Golden Hind*, and the execution of Captain Thomas Doughty, whom Drake accused of plotting against him. It was a strange way to prepare for a trip around Cape Horn.

Drake's ships threaded their way through the Straits of Magellan, between Tierra del Fuego and the South American mainland, an extremely dangerous transit that took two weeks. However, as soon as they entered the Pacific they were struck by a major storm, a tempest stronger than anything the veteran seamen had experienced. The *Marigold* went down with all hands, while the *Elizabeth* and the *Golden Hind* were scattered. Captain John Wynter of the *Elizabeth* waited for Drake off the Peruvian coast, but when he did not appear Wynter considered sailing west into the Pacific, heading for the Moluccas, an archipelago that Drake had talked about exploring. In the end he decided to return to England through the Straits of Magellan, and he eventually arrived home in June 1579. He would later be arraigned on charges of piracy, the result of Drake's attack on Portuguese shipping off the Cape Verde Islands. However, on Drake's return the charges were quietly dropped; after all, the queen was hardly going to accuse the man whose expedition she had secretly invested in.

For his part Drake had been driven south, past Cape Horn, and was almost dashed against the ice of Antarctica. When the storm abated he sailed north, following the Chilean coast as far as Valparaiso, where he captured a Spanish ship and plundered the town, netting some 25,000 pieces-of-eight. Finding no sign of Wynter and his ship, Drake continued north, attacking Arica, the loading port for the Potosi silver mines, and then Callao, the port that served the regional capital of Lima. In both ports Drake took the Spanish completely by surprise, and the interlopers were able to loot whatever they could—which wasn't much. The Spaniards had enough warning to land a cargo of silver, and it now lay behind the well-defended walls of the local governor's residency. However, just as important as plunder, Drake captured vital Spanish charts of the Pacific coast, which he used to plan his next move, and, even more importantly, he learned that a treasure ship had left Callao a few days before and was on its way to Panama. This 120-ton galleon was called the *Nuestra Señora del la Concepción*, although the Spanish nicknamed her the *Cacafuego* (which translates as "shit-fire"). Drake set off in pursuit.

As the *Golden Hind* sailed north it picked up the trail. Passing coastal craft reported that the galleon was three days ahead, and then the lead dropped to just two days. It was Drake's younger brother John who first saw their prey, 4 leagues (12 nautical miles) in front of them. To avoid suspicion Drake increased sail but also streamed objects astern, which slowed his ship down—giving it the appearance of a lumbering merchantman. It took some nine hours before the *Golden Hind* overhauled the *Concepción*—it was the evening of March 1, 1579, when the two ships closed within hailing distance. The Englishmen would have been pleasantly surprised to discover that their prey carried no ordnance, while for his part the Spanish captain San Juan de Anton was taken completely by surprise.

Caca Fogo.   Caca Plata.

The capture of the Nuestra Señora de la Concepción *by Francis Drake in the* Golden Hind.
*The Spanish treasure ship was attacked off the Pacific coast of South America in early 1579
and yielded the English pirate a fortune in plunder.*

When the Spaniard refused to surrender, Drake ordered his men to run out the
guns, and a broadside brought down the treasure ship's mizzenmast. Musketeers
sent the Spanish crew diving for cover. Then a boarding party was sent over, and
within minutes the *Concepción* was in Drake's hands—her crew securely locked up
below decks and her Spanish captain taken aboard the *Golden Hind*.

To the victors go the spoils, and so the Englishmen threw open the prize's
hold. The haul would have dumbfounded even the most avaricious sea dog. The
hold contained 14 small chests filled with silver pieces-of-eight, others filled with
small finger-size gold bars and discs—some 80 lbs in all—and no fewer than 26

tons of silver ingots, cast in 80 lb ingots. That was only the official cargo, and more unregistered specie was found on board—probably in the captain's cabin. The total amount was later valued at 400,000 pesos, or £200,000 in Elizabethan England—a little more than half the annual income of the English crown. It was an astounding haul, even though it represented only about 3 percent of Spain's annual haul of specie and around 15 percent of Philip II's share of this New World bonanza. However, for Drake and his men their fortunes were made. All they had to do now was to make it home with their plunder.

Drake continued up the coast, where he made one last raid, this time on the little Mexican port of Guatulco. While the attack achieved little, it did reveal something about Drake's attitude during a conversation with one of his prisoners—one Francisco Gomez Rangifo. While explaining his motives, Drake said, "I would not wish to take anything except what belongs to King Philip and Don Martín Enríquez [the viceroy of Mexico] ... I am not going to stop until I collect two millions, which my cousin John Hawkins lost at San Juan de Ulúa." In other words he saw himself not as a pirate or even a privateer—just a man seeking retribution, in accordance with the licence granted by Queen Elizabeth. However, quite how he estimated Hawkins's losses to be the equivalent of five treasure galleons like the *Concepción* is difficult to see.

The English avoided the well-protected port of Acapulco and continued north up the Pacific coast of North America, possibly in an attempt to find the mythical Northwest Passage—a sea route around the top of the American continent. Beaten by the weather, Drake dropped back down again and put in to the coast of what is now California. He already realized that the only safe way now was across the Pacific to the Indian Ocean, a plan he had already discussed with Captain Wynter. However, before such a mammoth voyage was attempted, Drake needed to careen his ship, replenish her provisions, and rest his crew. The location of this anchorage has long been debated, but the most likely candidate is Drake's Bay—in what is now San Francisco Bay. He named the area Nova Albion (New England)—a name that might well have been inspired by the white cliffs in the area. Drake stayed there for five weeks, until finally on July 23 the *Golden Hind* raised her anchor, then headed west towards the setting sun.

In terms of piracy and plunder, the rest of Drake's voyage was unexceptional. However, as a piece of maritime history it was a monumental achievement—the first circumnavigation of the globe by an English captain, the exploration of the Spice Islands, the details of which had hitherto been kept secret by the Portuguese, and a safe return, the globe-trotting little ship laden with Spanish plunder. In late September 1580 Drake returned to Plymouth a hero—and a rich man. For her part the queen was delighted, and after a dinner invitation to the *Golden Hind* as she lay at Deptford, Elizabeth even knighted Drake on the quarterdeck of his own ship. A merchant turned privateer turned national celebrity and royal favorite, Sir Francis Drake was at the height of his fame and fortune. After all, if the queen secretly called you "my pirate," you could do little wrong.

THE GREAT RAID OF 1585

By 1585 the rivalry between England and Spain was heating up. When the Dutch revolted against their Spanish overlords in 1566, a religious war had begun that threatened to drag the English into the fighting. It went through phases—the Spanish nearly crushed the rebellion in the late 1560s, but in 1572 it flared up again. By the mid-1580s the Dutch rebels held the north (now Holland itself), while the Spanish controlled the south (now Belgium). In 1585 the Duke of Parma's army was on the offensive again, and Dutch resistance was crumbling. Fearing a Spanish base in Holland, Elizabeth openly supplied the Dutch with money and troops—support which brought England and Spain to the brink of open war. Barring a diplomatic miracle, war between the two powers was now inevitable.

In 1584 the Spanish had impounded English ships trading in Spanish ports. Elizabeth immediately offered the ship owners the right of retribution—the old excuse used by Drake since the San Juan de Ulúa incident in 1568. However, this time the legal niceties were abandoned, and instead Elizabeth's advisor and spymaster Sir Francis Walsingham planned a full-scale raid on the Spanish Main, with secondary attacks launched against the Spanish whaling and fishing fleets off Newfoundland. Inevitably, Drake was given the job of commanding this state-sponsored expedition, and during the spring and early summer of 1585 he busied himself in Plymouth gathering ships and men. Once again this was organized as a business venture, with the queen being just one of many investors. Her stake was the lease of two royal warships—the *Elizabeth Bonaventure* (600 tons), which became Drake's flagship, and the smaller *Aid* (250 tons). Drake's deputy was Martin Frobisher, who flew his flag in the *Primrose*, an armed merchantman from London that had recently escaped internment in the Spanish port of Bilbao.

This was no halfhearted raiding party. Including the two royal warships Drake's fleet comprised 21 well-armed ships, not counting the eight small pinnaces that would be towed behind the larger vessels. Equally significantly, as well as the 1,000 crewmen in the fleet, Drake's force also included 12 companies of soldiers—around 800 men—commanded by Walsingham's son-in-law, Captain Christopher Carleille. This was a force capable of dominating the Spanish Main, and of striking virtually anywhere it wanted. However, the queen was having second thoughts. After all, sending Drake off with a force like this was tantamount to a declaration of war—and Spain was the superpower of her day. Fearing a recall, Drake hurriedly put to sea on September 14. The die was now cast.

Drake's first stop was the port of Vigo, in the northwest corner of Spain. He seized the town, then used the port as a shelter to ride out the equinoxial storms of late September which roared out of the Atlantic. After a week he continued southwards to the Canary Islands, where he hoped to intercept the returning Spanish treasure fleet. The combined treasure *flota* had a narrow escape, having passed through the Canaries just a week before the English arrived. Drake continued on to the Cape Verde Islands, where he planned to launch the first of his attacks. On the evening of November 16, Drake's fleet anchored in the roadstead of Santiago (now called Praia)—the leading Portuguese settlement in the islands. Carleille's troops were sent ashore under cover of darkness, and by dawn the men were in position. As Drake's fleet bombarded the town, the English soldiers stormed Santiago from behind, only to find that the defenders had already fled. There was little to plunder, nor was any real treasure found on the island's inland settlement of São Domingos (Santo Domingo). In fact, all Drake had to show for his efforts was the capture of a few artillery pieces. The disappointed Englishmen razed the settlement then returned to their ships.

While the principal settlement of the Cape Verde Islands might have been captured without a fight, the action still took its toll on the fleet, as during the transatlantic voyage that followed the fleet was struck by disease brought on board during the raid. By the time Drake made his Caribbean landfall and put in to St. Kitts for water and to celebrate Christmas, he had lost some 300 of his crew. From there, Drake continued on to Hispaniola, where he planned to attack the island's capital of Santo Domingo. As a colony it had long been surpassed in importance by Havana and was no longer considered a major port, although it was still well defended. However, Drake thought it would make an excellent place to test out the potential of his powerful fleet.[8]

The English arrived off Santo Domingo during the last days of December, and Carleille and his men were landed some 20 miles west of the town. Drake also made contact with the local Cimaroons, who promised to support the attack.

The town's defenders had plenty of warning of the attack, but they expected the assault to come from the sea. Instead, at 8:00 a.m. on January 1, 1586, the English soldiers appeared to the west of the town and soon managed to drive back the three companies of Spanish troops and horse sent to bar their way. The Spaniards even tried to drive cattle into the path of Carleille's men—a trick repeated during Henry Morgan's attack on Panama almost a century later. It was no use, and after splitting his force in two, Carleille led his main body through the town's main gate, following hard on the heels of the retreating Spanish soldiers, who simply kept running through the town and into the jungle beyond.

Closer to the beach, the other English column led by Captain Powell stormed a second gate, and the two columns met in the town's main square. Meanwhile Drake's ships bombarded the town, receiving almost no return fire from the formidable coastal defenses of the port. He ceased fire only when he saw the English flag flying above the city. Drake was now the master of the town. While his men combed the houses for plunder, the English commander opened negotiations with representatives of the Spanish governor, Ovalle, proposing that Drake would spare the town if the Spaniards paid him a ransom. When the negotiations stalled, Drake had his men begin to systematically level the principal buildings of the town, and by the end of the month the offer of 25,000 ducats was placed on the negotiating table. Drake duly took the money, reembarked his men, and sailed away, leaving the Spanish to reclaim the shattered remains of what was once the premier city on the Spanish Main.

For his next attack, Drake selected Cartagena, second only to Havana in its importance as a port—a major destination for the Tierra Firme *flota*, and a city regarded as the richest prize in the Americas. The port was extremely well defended, and this time the Englishman realized there would be no easy solution, no undefended approach he could use to assault the place. Instead he would have to rely on the professionalism of Captain Carleille and his men and on the skill of Drake's sailors. Worse, the governor, Don Piero Fernandez de Busto, already knew the English were coming, having been tipped off by a messenger sent from Hispaniola. Drake's only real advantage was that the Spanish reports placed his force at around 10,000 men—ten times the troops available to him. In fact the two sides were fairly evenly matched. On February 19 the fleet arrived off the port, and once again Drake made contact with local Cimaroons, who gave him details of the Spanish dispositions. This gave the English something of an edge.

To test this intelligence Drake began by launching a probe against the fort of El Boquerón, which guarded the landward side of the town. Heavy fire from the defenders convinced Drake that the Cimaroon reports were quite correct—and that a repeat of his standard landward assault gambit would lead to disaster. Instead, Drake landed his soldiers on the tip of La Caletta—the coastal spur that ran westwards from the city, dividing the outer roads from the sea. The Spaniards had built strong defenses on the seaward and landward sides of the town, but the earthworks covering the narrow spit to the west were only half finished. To compensate, the Spanish governor ordered two galleys to cover the exposed western approach to the town with their guns. Drake then led the fleet into the roads and blockaded the inner harbor. This time his ships would be able to do little to influence the course of the battle. For once, Drake was a spectator, watching the drama as it unfolded.

Warned of poisoned stakes blocking his path, Carleille ordered his men to wade through the surf, and the advance continued unimpeded. Then a Spanish cavalry patrol appeared on the beach, and although it was driven off, the element of surprise was now lost. Carleille decided to keep going. As dawn arrived the English appeared in front of the western edge of the town, which was protected by a makeshift barricade built up using wine casks. Staying put was impossible, as the two galleys had pulled close inshore and were firing into the English flank. The soldiers charged with Carleille at their head, and despite significant casualties they took the position, overturning the wine casks and breaking into the town that lay beyond them. Four hundred native bowmen ordered up to plug the gap also turned and followed their Spanish overlords as they pulled back through the town.

In a similar way to Carleille, Don Pedro Vinque, the commander of the galleys, pulled in to the beach and landed at the head of a group of 20 Spanish horsemen. However, these few men could do nothing to prevent the rout, and, while the riders joined the retreat, Don Pedro returned to his galleys, only to find that one of them had caught fire and the second had run aground. Disgusted, the Spanish officer gave orders to torch the beached galley, and then followed the rest of his men in their flight. Meanwhile Carleille had fought his way through the streets to Cartagena's marketplace, defeating all attempts by Governor Fernandez to organize a new line of defense. His troops gathered around the town's half-built main church, but the combined firepower of English small arms supported by a few rounds from a supporting field piece was enough to break the Spanish will. With his men now in headlong retreat, the governor bowed to the inevitable and joined the rout. Against the odds, Drake had won the day—at the cost of just thirty casualties.

Once again, as his men plundered the town, Drake contacted Governor Fernandez and demanded a ransom—this time of a million pieces-of-eight. The Englishman held the city for almost two months, and the negotiations dragged on. Eventually the attackers settled for a ransom of just 107,000 pieces-of-eight. However, another 250,000 pesos were looted in the town itself, while Drake also seized artillery, church bells, and even slaves from the Spanish port—a haul valued at a further 150,000 pesos. By the time the fleet sailed again on April 12 Drake's force had been whittled away by disease, and he probably now had less than half his original strength. Still, he decided on one last dramatic assault before heading home with his plunder.

Drake considered an assault on Havana, where the New Spain *flota* was sheltering, but after probing the port's defenses he decided the Cuban city was too well defended. Instead he headed north through the Bahama Straits towards the Carolinas, where he planned to put in for supplies at Sir Walter Raleigh's new settlement at Roanoke and unload his cargo of freed galley prisoners and African slaves. However, the route took him past the Spanish settlement of St. Augustine, on the eastern coast of Florida. This was the base established by the Spanish when they destroyed Jean Ribault's Huguenot settlement. Drake decided to raid the port—settling an old score on behalf of his fellow Protestants.

On May 27 English lookouts spotted a Spanish coastal watchtower which marked the mouth of the Matanzas River. The Spanish settlement lay a few miles inland. Once again Carleille's troops were landed on the beach and marched across the sandhills until they came to the town—the river separating the English troops from their objective. Artillery was landed, which duly bombarded the town's fort into submission, while Drake's men made camp, ready for an assault at first light. A nighttime attack by local natives loyal to the Spaniards was repulsed, and at dawn pinnaces ferried the English soldiers across the river and into the town. They found St. Augustine deserted, the Spaniards having fled inland as Carleille's men approached. The townspeople also seemed to have taken their possessions with them, as all that Drake's men found of value was a strongbox in the fort containing wages for the garrison. Drake ordered the settlement razed, after which his fleet continued its voyage northwards. Few would have guessed it at the time, but this was Drake's last fully successful raid on the Spanish Main.[9]

The expedition put in to Roanoke, only to find that the settlement was on its last legs. The English settlers accepted Drake's offer of a passage back home, and on June 18 the fleet raised anchor, slipped out past the Outer Banks, and set course for England. He arrived back in Plymouth five weeks later to find that the long-awaited war had finally broken out, and the country was preparing for what was seen as an inevitable Spanish assault. As a plundering expedition Drake's raid of 1585 was largely unsuccessful; his force was simply too large to ensure everyone made a substantial profit, and most investors—including the queen—had to make do with a return of just 75 percent of their original investment. However, as a means of discomfiting the Spanish the raid had worked perfectly, proving that an area once regarded by the Spanish as theirs by default was now open to attack by anyone with the ships, the men, and the determination.

PLUNDERING FOR THE GREATER GOOD

War brought a temporary halt to these expeditions, as privateers along with merchant ship owners found their vessels called up for service with the Navy Royal. In theory this should have reduced the opportunities for piratical acts, but in effect it made little difference. When not actually serving as part of a naval

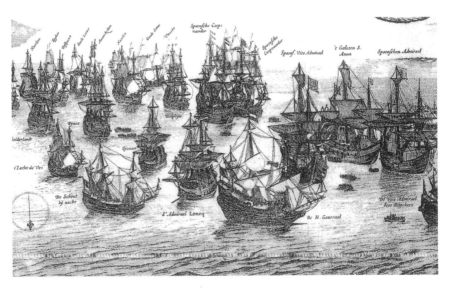

In 1628 the Dutch admiral Piet Heyn cornered an entire Spanish treasure fleet in Cuba's Matanzas Bay. The Spanish ships were driven ashore, where they were captured, plundered, and burned. In the process, the Spaniards lost a fortune in New World silver.

force, many privateers simply fought their own private war, or even continued to trade with the enemy. The balance between patriotism and profit was a fine one in Elizabethan England, and men like Drake did their utmost to gain political kudos with one hand while lining their pockets with the other.

The most notorious example of this was the capture of the *Nuestra Señora del Rosario*. During the Spanish Armada campaign of 1588 this 1,150-ton warship was the *Capitana* (flagship) of the Squadron of Andalusia—commanded by Don Pedro de Valdés. During the first battle of the campaign—fought off Plymouth on July 31—the Armada was formed up in a giant crescent, while two squadrons of the English fleet under Drake and Lord Howard harried the enemy's rear guard and left wing. However, the English were unable to disrupt the Spanish formation or stop its stately progress up the English Channel. Then, around 4:00 p.m., the *Rosario* collided with another ship in her squadron, and her bowsprit was damaged in the collision. Other Spanish ships came to her aid, and one of them collided with her again, bringing down the foremast of Valdés's flagship. Attempts to tow her to safety were thwarted by rough seas, and as night fell the *Rosario* fell behind the rest of the fleet—a vulnerable and tempting prize.

Drake had explicit orders to shadow the Spanish fleet, allowing time for Howard's main force to regroup, then follow on behind. The stern lanterns on Drake's flagship, the *Revenge*, were meant to serve as Howard's beacon, allowing him to move into position to attack the Spanish again as soon as dawn broke. However, Drake had other ideas. He later claimed he forgot to light his stern lanterns, and under cover of darkness he veered off to starboard in pursuit of the stricken *Rosario*. Without a guiding light, Howard's force straggled for miles, and the English commander was in no position to launch a coordinated attack the following morning. As for Drake, as the sun rose Don Pedro de Valdés found him lying 500 yards (457m) off their stern quarter, his guns trained and his men ready for action.[10]

Drake later expressed surprise at finding the *Rosario* so close to him at dawn. He wasn't fooling anyone. His former deputy, Martin Frobisher, responded to Drake's protestations of innocence by saying, "Aye marry, you were within two or three cables length [at dawn, as] you were no further off all night!" After some prevarication Valdés agreed to surrender his ship, and later that day the *Rosario* was towed into Dartmouth by the privateer *Roebuck*—a vessel of Drake's command. On board was a chest containing 50,000 gold escudos—the equivalent of 100,000 pieces-of-eight. As an admiral in the English fleet, Drake's duty lay in following the Armada, not pursuing a lone Spanish ship in search of plunder. The sea dog came in for some sharp criticism after the campaign, particularly when the queen discovered that half of the plunder had disappeared before it reached London. Rather foolishly Drake bought a magnificent new mansion the following year. After that the cloud of distrust and suspicion never quite went away.

The Armada campaign itself is not really part of this story, nor are the attacks launched by Elizabeth's fleet on the Spanish coast both before and after 1588. However, by using privateers such as Drake, Frobisher, Raleigh, Grenville, and Hawkins as her naval commanders, the English monarch blurred the line between private enterprise and public service. This was further exacerbated by her tendency to run these expeditions as financial ventures, even though they were ostensibly conducted as official naval operations. It is therefore hardly surprising that the majority of English seamen saw such ventures as little more than an opportunity to plunder on a grand scale.

Never was this spirit of opportunism more evident than when the English fleet attempted to intercept the annual treasure *flotas*. For example, in 1592 an English fleet that included royal warships and privateers set sail from Falmouth, under the joint command of Walter Raleigh and John Norris. When Raleigh was recalled to England to answer legal charges his place was taken by Martin Frobisher. However, as Raleigh's deputy refused to work with his new commander, the fleet was divided into two forces, leaving Frobisher with just six ships. This squadron was then dispersed by an unseasonable storm, and a Spanish force chased Frobisher back to the safety of Falmouth. Norris continued on alone but returned home empty-handed after failing to intercept the treasure *flota*. However, Raleigh's old deputy, Robert Crosse, remained at sea, and somewhere off the Azores he was joined by a second ship—the *Dainty*—belonging to Sir John Hawkins. The pair came across a Spanish straggler, the treasure galleon *Madre de Dios*, commanded by Fernando de Mendoza. The Spaniard was forced to surrender after an epic fight, and the prize was duly escorted into Dartmouth.[11]

At that point the arguments started. According to Mendoza, his galleon was carrying specie worth around one million pieces-of-eight, or half a million pounds. However, only the equivalent of 300,000 pesos was ever handed over to the queen's assessors, and soon accusations began flying. Inevitably Crosse and his deputy were accused of stealing the rest of the plunder, while lawyers working on behalf of Hawkins and Norris claimed a share of the missing treasure. After all, as fleet commanders, they should have been entitled to something. Eventually Elizabeth appointed Drake to sort out the mess. After all, he was probably an expert in the business of hidden treasure. However, apart from a paltry £9,000 of undisclosed specie, even he failed to find the missing plunder. Still, the queen and other investors made a fortune on the business, while Crosse—and probably his partners in crime Raleigh and Hawkins—managed to keep the loot.

As well as these "official" expeditions, numerous smaller privateering raids were launched against the Spanish during the years following the defeat of the Armada. While some of these were small affairs involving just one or two ships, a few were more substantial. It has been estimated that during the three years between 1589 and 1591, some 236 privateering ships were at sea, and while the majority of these displaced less than 100 tons, at least 16 were much larger—with a displacement of 200 tons or more. Of these, most came from either London or the Devon ports. The picture is repeated in 1589, when some 86 licensed privateers were operating. This time over a quarter of the ships displaced more than 200 tons, which suggests a general move towards larger and better armed private men-of-war.

Not all of these privateers were successful. For example, in 1596 Sir Anthony Shirley led an expedition to raid the Portuguese settlement of São Tomé, off the West African coast. He had five ships under his command, but disease took its toll, and by the time he reached the Cape Verde Islands he barely had enough hands left to man the ships. He decided to storm Santiago—the same port raided by Drake a decade earlier. He took it, but the attackers suffered heavy losses. Shirley found little worth looting, so when his men recovered he crossed the Atlantic to cruise off the coast of Venezuela. There he fell upon the largely undefended small settlement of Santa Marta, and again he found nothing to plunder. His only success came in Jamaica, where the expedition captured La Ville de la Vega (near modern Kingston) and gained enough supplies to fill the holds of the ships. Next came a cruise off the Yucatan Peninsula, followed by a fruitless march across the Central American isthmus. At this point Shirley's captains refused to continue, so the expedition commander was forced to return home "alive but poor."[12]

Others were equally unsuccessful. In 1592 Captain John Myddelton, commanding the 50-ton *Moonshine,* was driven off when he tried to attack the *rancheria* (pearl fishing station) at Margarita, off the Venezuelan coast. He then joined up with a force of four privateers commanded by Captain Benjamin Wood, but their cruise proved fruitless. The following year another privateering captain, Sir John Burgh, was also driven off by the defenders of Margarita, even though he outnumbered the Spaniards. However, in early 1597 a Captain Parker successfully looted the *ranchería* at Margarita, but his lucky streak came to an abrupt end a few months later when he joined forces with the unfortunate Sir Anthony Shirley.

Parker's fortunes improved when he abandoned Shirley off the Yucatan Peninsula, as he plundered the port of Campeche before being driven off by Spanish reinforcements. He eventually managed to return to England with enough plunder to delight his backers, who funded another equally successful raid on the Spanish Main in 1600. These successes were unusual. The Earl of Cumberland financed over a dozen such raids, only one of which showed a profit. Still, the overall climate was one of fiscal greed and opportunism, despite the failure of many of these expeditions. After all, the war meant that English merchants could no longer trade with the ports of Spain or her allies; consequently privateering seemed to offer the best return for their investment. However, none of these small raids was powerful enough to take on the treasure *flotas* or to capture the Spanish treasure ports. It was left to the old sea dogs Drake and Hawkins to show these lesser captains how it was done.

THE LAST OF THE SEA DOGS

In 1595, Elizabeth's advisor William Cecil, Baron Burghley, devised a new plan to renew the offensive against the Spanish. It involved a two-pronged attack.[13] Lord Thomas Howard and Sir Walter Raleigh would attack Cadiz, where they would unleash the Earl of Essex and his army on the port. Meanwhile an expedition jointly commanded by Sir Francis Drake and Sir John Hawkins would descend on the Spanish Main, where it would cause as much damage and rake in as much plunder as it could. Another secondary objective was the establishment of a permanent English settlement within the Caribbean basin. They had a fleet of 27 ships and 25 pinnaces at their disposal, including six royal warships, crewed by 2,500 men. Unfortunately the animosity between the two commanders did much to limit the effectiveness of the force. They had fallen out when Hawkins publicly censured Drake for his capture of the *Nuestra Señora del Rosario*, and consequently the two ageing sea dogs found it hard to agree on strategy—or anything else.

The expedition sailed from Plymouth in late August 1595, and its first port of call was Las Palmas in the Canary Islands, where a major attack was thwarted by heavy seas and a powerful Spanish garrison. The troops were unable to secure a beachhead, and Drake withdrew, leaving a handful of prisoners in Spanish hands. Unfortunately one of them knew the fleet's next destination, so within days a fast ship raced across the Atlantic to warn the governor of San Juan that the English were coming. The fleet reached Puerto Rico on November 12, having made its Caribbean landfall at Dominica two weeks earlier. By that time Hawkins was dying from fever, as were many of his men. He finally succumbed some days later—leaving Drake in sole command of the expedition.

Drake found San Juan bristling with troops and saw that fresh batteries had been installed to cover both the harbor and the landward approaches to the town. A scuttled galleon even blocked the harbor entrance, while the defenders covered all possible landing places on the north side of the island. This was clearly going to be a tough nut to crack. On November 22—two days after Hawkins's death—Drake led his squadron in for a closer look but was driven back by the accurate fire of the Spanish guns. One roundshot even hit Drake's own cabin, where he was entertaining his senior officers. The following day an attempt to disembark was foiled by defenders on the beach, who shot fire arrows into the English launches. The Spanish later claimed that as many as 400 English soldiers were killed in the attempt, although Drake asserted that the total was nearer 50. A second halfhearted landing attempt two days later was also repulsed, by which time even Drake realized that he had no chance of achieving anything.[14]

On November 28 the fleet upped anchor and sailed away, rounding Puerto Rico before heading south towards the coast of South America—the scene of Drake's great triumph at Cartagena a decade earlier. This time he considered Cartagena too well defended to assault. After a brief sojourn in Curaçao he went on to raid the coastal town of Rio de la Hatcha, the place where Drake had had his first taste of the Spanish Main 30 years before. There the *ranchería* provided enough plunder to make up for the failure of San Juan, although a second raid on nearby Santa Marta produced next to nothing. Next the fleet headed west towards the isthmus of Panama, and Drake arrived off his old stomping ground of Nombre de Dios on January 6. The port was no longer the all-important Caribbean terminus of the silver mines in Peru; this had moved to Porto Bello, just down the coast, since Drake was last there. The town had already been abandoned, so Drake established a base there and prepared his men for an assault on Panama, 30 miles away on the Pacific side of the isthmus.

While Drake probed the defenses of the Chagres River, Sir Thomas Baskerville led the soldiers across country, and three days and 30 miles later he reached the mountain barrier that marked the center of the isthmus. There his path was blocked by Spanish troops, dug in across the only pass, their flanks protected by the heights on either side. Baskerville launched three assaults, but each time his men were forced back with heavy losses. Worse, more Spanish arrived to reinforce the defenders. Baskerville had little option but to retreat back to Nombre de Dios, the Spanish native allies hounding his rear guard as it withdrew. On January 12 they reached the safety of the fleet, and after burning the port Drake withdrew up the coast.

His plan was to raid the coast of Honduras, but many of his men were sick, most probably with yellow fever. As the fleet rode gently off the coast the death toll mounted, and within days Drake himself caught a fever and took to his cabin. His condition worsened, and on the evening of January 27 he signed his will. Within hours the venerable sea dog was dead. Drake was placed in a lead-lined coffin and then buried at sea within sight of Porto Bello.

It was time to leave. Not only was Drake dead and the fleet due back in England, but a powerful Spanish fleet had been gathered to intercept and destroy the English expedition. This force caught up with Baskerville off the Cuban Isle of Pines, but the English fleet managed to repulse the Spanish attack, and Baskerville was left in peace to continue his voyage home. He arrived back in Plymouth in late April 1596, where reports of the death of both Hawkins and Drake were finally confirmed.[15]

This homecoming and the deaths of these two men marked the end of an era. Within a few years Elizabeth herself would be dead, and her passing marked both the end of the Tudor dynasty and the end of what many regarded as a golden age of English history. Her successor, James I of England and VI of Scotland, united the monarchy of those two kingdoms, made peace with Spain, and ushered in a time when merchants rather than pirates or privateers dominated the waters of Europe and the Americas. The days of the sea dogs had passed into history. Colonies would flourish in North America during the years that followed, and the Spanish overseas empire would be left in relative peace— at least for a while. However, the establishment of European colonies in the Americas marked another historical turning point, and within a few short years a new breed of seaman would turn the Spanish Main into its hunting ground. At least the Elizabethan sea dogs followed the established gentlemanly rules of war. The buccaneers who followed them would have no such inhibitions.

4

MEDITERRANEAN CORSAIRS

GREEK PIRATES AND MUSLIM CORSAIRS

Following the collapse of the Western Roman Empire, the western Mediterranean became something of an economic and political backwater. The barbarian states that occupied Italy, France, and Spain did little to develop their economies, and consequently there was no return to the commercial heyday of the Pax Romana. Instead they preferred to eke out a living from fishing, raiding, and piracy. It was a different story in the East, where the Roman Empire turned into that of the Byzantines, who not only developed an extensive trading network but also protected their merchantmen from pirates.

After the fall of the Western Roman Empire, Byzantium remained a bastion of order in the Mediterranean for several centuries, despite the rise of Islam and the advent of the Middle Ages in Europe. However, by the late twelfth century the boundaries of the Byzantine Empire had been pushed back both by the Turks and by Frankish Crusaders until its power was limited to Greece, the Aegean, and western Asia Minor. Following the sacking of the Byzantine capital of Constantinople by the Crusaders in 1204, the Byzantine navy could barely patrol its own home waters. Consequently piracy thrived in the Aegean and in the ancient pirate haunts of Crete and Asia Minor. On the other side of Greece the Ionian islands of the southern Adriatic became notorious pirate dens, ruled by

Margaritone of Brindisi, discussed earlier. Later, both Italian and Greek pirates established additional lairs on the nearby islands of Corfu, Zante, Ithaca, and Cephalonia. These Adriatic pirates continued to pose a threat to Italian merchant shipping until the Venetian navy cleared the area of pirates in the late fourteenth century.

The thirteenth century was a time when piracy thrived in Greek waters, as the feudal Italian overlords who reclaimed the country from the Byzantines did little to halt its spread in both the Aegean and the Adriatic. Many of these pirates were Italians, and according to the Italian historian Torsello, mentioned in chapter 2, most Aegean pirates were natives of either Genoa or Venice. Some of these pirates were even hired by the Byzantines, who used them as naval auxiliaries. In fact, in 1278 the pirate mercenary Giovanni de lo Cavo even became the Byzantine governor of Rhodes. Other Greek, Balkan, and Turkish pirates also operated in Grecian waters, many of them being little more than local fishermen who made a living by moonlighting as pirates on the side.

Then from the late thirteenth century onwards the naval vacuum created by the rapid contraction of the Byzantine Empire was partly filled by the rise of three independent navies. Rhodes was technically a Byzantine province until 1308, when it became a stronghold of the Knights of St. John. A succession of island Grand Masters built up the power of the Rhodean navy, which soon became a bulwark against the rising power of the Ottoman Turks. At the same time the Venetians were expanding their control of the Adriatic and establishing useful naval bases along the Greek coast and in Crete. The powerful Venetian galley fleets operated against pirates within their new sphere of influence, then sent patrols into the Aegean, where they supported the Rhodeans and Byzantines in antipiracy operations. However, by that time there was a new naval power in the region.

By the 1360s the Ottomans had reached the Aegean coast of Asia Minor, and galley fleets were built to extend Turkish influence into the Aegean itself. The Turks had already cleared the rest of the eastern Mediterranean of pirates, and they gradually extended their power base to include the entire coastline of Asia Minor. Unlike the more rigidly controlled Christian fleets in the area, the Turks relied heavily on mercenary forces—effectively fleets of privateers who augmented their pay by indulging in a little coastal raiding and the plunder of Christian shipping. The Ottoman method of administration lent itself to this kind of practice, as regional governors often used privateering as a means of generating income. In effect, apart from a core of dedicated warships, the bulk of the Ottoman navy was made up of privateers—although their Christian victims made no distinction between Turkish privateers and pirates.

On the African shore of the Mediterranean, a similar transformation was taking place. Following the Arab conquests of the seventh and eighth centuries, the entire coast of North Africa fell under Muslim control, as too did Sicily and most of Spain. Although these vast territories were united by religion, there was little or no political unity, and the fragmentation of the Almohad dynasties resulted in a string of petty chiefdoms dotted along the African coast from Morocco to Libya. The reconquest of Sicily by the Normans in the late eleventh century and the beginning of the Reconquista in Spain meant that by the late fourteenth century the battle lines had been drawn across the Mediterranean, with intermittent religious wars being fought in Spain at one end and Greece at the other, while in between, both Christians and Muslims eyed each other with suspicion.

Although pirates had operated along the North African coast since the collapse of the Western Roman Empire, it was not until the expansion of European maritime commence in the late fifteenth century that these pirates became a serious threat. By that stage the African coast was firmly in Muslim hands, and the ports of Algiers, Tunis, and Tripoli, plus a score of smaller coastal towns, were ideally located to serve as privateering bases from which to harass passing shipping. As these Barbary ports lay on the edge of the Sahara Desert, and the sparsely populated hinterland produced little in the way of wealth, any riches had to come from the sea. Consequently during the late fifteenth and early sixteenth centuries these local rulers encouraged corsairs to use their ports as havens. In return, these rulers (known as beys, governors, or beyerliks, chief governors) expected a percentage of the profits. Privateering was a hugely profitable business, and their ports soon became bustling markets for the sale of slaves and plunder.

THE BARBARY CORSAIRS

In theory these local potentates who ruled the Barbary States owed feudal allegiance to the Ottoman sultan. Following the Turkish conquest of Constantinople (now Istanbul) in 1453, the last surviving part of the Byzantine realm, the Ottoman sultan established his court in the former Byzantine capital. Of course this was far enough away from the North African coast for the beys of the Barbary Coast to be left pretty much on their own—unless the sultan needed their help to fight a war. While the privateering fleets of the Barbary Coast took part in several major naval campaigns during the sixteenth century, for the most part they operated independently of both the Turks and each other and limited their activities to the western and central Mediterranean.

While the Barbary galleys would most accurately be described as privateers—operating under a licence issued by the bey—the terms corsair and pirate were both used freely. Technically the French term corsair also means privateer, although by the sixteenth century it was also used to describe pirates who operated in the Mediterranean, including those from the Barbary Coast. These days the term pirate is widely used, although this was rarely a term applied at the time. The difference came later, during the seventeenth and eighteenth centuries, when the maritime powers of Europe refused to recognize the authority of the Barbary rulers. Consequently they viewed all the privateers or "corsairs" who operated out of ports on the Barbary Coast as pirates. The American assault on the Barbary ports in the early nineteenth century was carried out as an antipiracy operation, and therefore it was expedient to call the Barbary sailors pirates rather than privateers. For clarity, we will stick to the term corsair during the period up to the mid-seventeenth century, when the Barbary raiders were strictly controlled by the Ottoman sultan. After that we will use the term pirate to reflect their lack of international recognition.

By the early sixteenth century many of the Barbary beys were elected from the ranks of the corsairs themselves, which meant that privateering became an integral part of the political and economic framework of the Barbary coast. They were certainly well organized. A ruling captains' council called the Taife Raisi supervised the running of the Barbary ports and the corsair fleet but remained answerable to both the local rulers and, in time of war, to the Ottoman sultan. The Taife Raisi ruled over any disputes, supervised the sale of plunder and slaves, and made sure that the bey was given his share of the spoils. While he nominally served the Ottoman Empire and both the local potentate and the Taife Raisi, each captain (or *rais*) owned his own ship and had almost complete freedom of action. He was assisted by the *agha*, who commanded the boarding party, and a scribe appointed by the Taife Raisi ensured that any booty would be shared between the *rais* and the local potentate at the end of the cruise. Typically, the local bey would claim 10 percent, plus a fee for use of his port. As the Barbary ports provided excellent markets for the sale of contraband and captured slaves, the system suited both the corsairs and the local authorities.

However, as privateers rather than pirates, the Barbary corsairs had to abide by the terms of their privateering letters of marque. This meant that they had to limit their attacks to non-Muslim shipping, collect only non-Muslim slaves on raids, and abide by any treaty arranged between their local Barbary rulers and the Christian states on the far side of the Mediterranean. The result was that sometimes their attacks were restricted—for instance, Genoese targets were sometimes deemed off-limits because of a trade agreement, or attacks on French shipping were avoided due to a temporary peace treaty. To further complicate things, as the sultan was their feudal overlord, the Barbary corsairs also had to abide by the terms of treaties arranged between the Ottoman sultan and the rulers of Christian states. For instance, Venice was at peace with the Ottoman Turks for much of the sixteenth century, and therefore attacks on Venetian ships were forbidden—which was not to say that they did not happen; only that the Barbary beys had to make sure that reports of such attacks did not reach the ears of the sultan in Constantinople. Effectively this followed the old piratical adage that "dead men tell no tales," or that slaves had no legal rights.

Of course the feudal obligations between the Barbary States and the Ottoman sultan worked both ways. The city-states of the Barbary Coast were technically considered part of the Ottoman Empire, and so Turkish regular garrisons were assigned to help the local bey defend his territory. On occasion they were called upon to defend the port from Christian (frequently Spanish) attackers. Conversely the corsairs often combined piratical attacks with service in the Ottoman navy, and corsair commanders and their galley fleets fought in all of the major naval battles of the sixteenth century. The Spanish followed their Reconquista of Spain by launching a series of assaults against the ports of the Barbary Coast, initiating a long-running struggle for control of the North African coast.[1]

This rivalry began with the expulsion of the Moors from Spain in 1492. The exiles settled in the North African ports and sought revenge by launching attacks and slave raids against the Spanish coast and on Spanish shipping. They were assisted by the other Barbary States and by Muslim adventurers from the eastern Mediterranean, the most notable of these being Aruj and Hızır—the Turkish sea captains known as the Barbarossa brothers. The Spanish retaliated by assaulting and capturing a series of major Barbary ports—Oran, Algiers, and Tunis—forcing the local beys to appeal for help to the sultan. In 1529 the Turkish counterattack began, which eventually drove the Spanish from most of their coastal enclaves.

From then until the death of the leading Barbary potentate, Uluch Ali of Algiers, in 1587, a string of sultans took a personal interest in the defense of the Barbary Coast, lending full support to the local potentates who ruled over the coasts of Tripoli, Tunisia, and Algeria. In fact many of these beys were the sultan's appointees—pashas sent from Constantinople to rule the Barbary Coast. Ultimately this intermittent conflict with Spain ended in a stalemate as the sixteenth century drew to a close largely because, through a series of peace treaties, the Spanish were forced to recognize that the region was officially part of the Ottoman Turkish Empire. Peace with the Turks therefore meant peace with the corsairs—as long as they did not attack Spanish ships. This changed in 1659, when Turkish rule collapsed following a revolt against the pashas. As a result, although the beys were nominally under the control of the Turks, in effect they ruled over their own city-state, answerable to nobody save the corsairs who kept them in power.

By that stage the Barbary corsairs had plenty of other victims to attack. The mercantile growth of north European maritime nations such as England and Holland meant that their merchant ships would increasingly become subject to piratical attacks—and technically these were pirate actions, as no state of war existed between Turkey, England, or Holland. However, these countries also possessed powerful fleets of sailing man-of-war ships, which were potentially far more powerful than the galley fleets found in the Mediterranean. Consequently the English and Dutch navies inflicted a string of defeats upon the Barbary corsairs during the seventeenth century, and by its end the offensive power of the Barbary States had been broken. Although Barbary corsairs (and pirates) still attacked passing ships and even small convoys, they did so in small groups and not as large galley fleets. They would never again be able to rival the Christian powers for control of the Mediterranean.

This does not mean they were no longer considered a threat. In Europe the Barbary corsairs were often depicted as cruel and fanatical Muslims, who waged an undeclared war against their religious enemies. Their reputation for slave trading was well known, and both the Church and humanitarian organizations frequently raised money to purchase the release of Christian slaves from the beys and landowners of the Barbary Coast. The surprising element in this view of religious antagonism was that many of the corsairs were actually born as Christians and were either slaves who converted to Islam or else were European adventurers who did so in order to pursue a potentially lucrative career as a corsair. Renegade Christians made up a substantial portion of corsair numbers. This did not alter the fact that for much of the early modern period, the Barbary corsairs were the boogeymen of the Mediterranean—the people you threaten your children with if they don't behave. The rapacity and ferocity of the corsairs was widely recognized, and therefore their appearance instilled fear—a useful

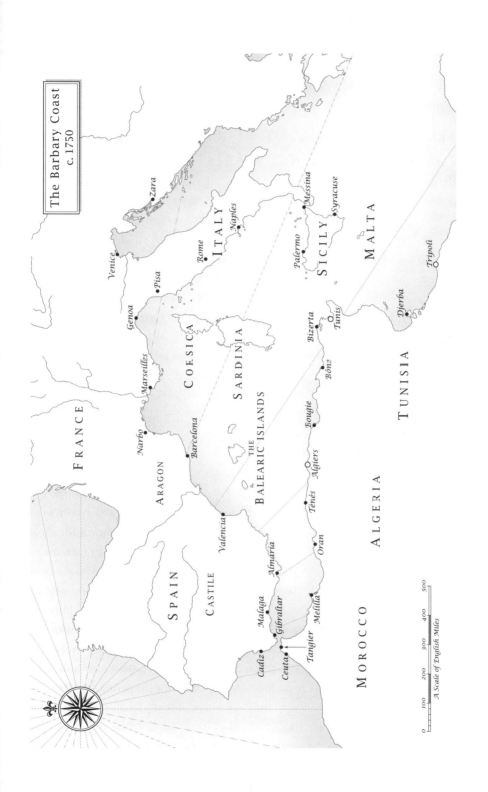

The Barbary Coast
c. 1750

FRANCE

SPAIN
ARAGON
CASTILE

Narbo
Marseilles
Barcelona
Valencia
Almaria
Malaga
Gibraltar
Cadiz
Ceuta
Tangier
Melilla

Genoa
Pisa
Rome
Venice
Zara

ITALY
Naples

CORSICA
SARDINIA
THE BALEARIC ISLANDS

Messina
Syracuse
Palermo
SICILY

MALTA

Tripoli

Djerba
Tunis
Bizerta
Bône
Bougie
Algiers
Ténès
Oran

TUNISIA
ALGERIA
MOROCCO

A Scale of English Miles

0   100   200   300   400   500

device for any pirate or privateer, who would always prefer a victim to surrender than to put up a fight. While much of this unsavory reputation was simply Christian propaganda, some of it was well deserved.

ARUJ "BARBAROSSA": THE FIRST CORSAIR

The first real corsair heroes of the Barbary Coast were Aruj and Hızır—the Barbarossa Brothers. Aruj (also written as Oruç) and his younger brother Hızır (also written as Khızır) were both born on the Aegean island of Lesbos at some time in the 1470s, although some accounts place their home on the nearby island of Mytelene. The story goes that they were the oldest and youngest of four sons, born to a Christian mother and a Muslim father. The father, Yakup Aga, was a former Turkish cavalryman who had been granted land on the island following his help in its capture by the Turks in 1462. He then worked as a potter and used a boat to sell his products to neighboring islands. One version of their lives claims that Aruj and his brother Ilyas were returning from a trading voyage to Tripoli when their boat was stopped and plundered by a galley from Rhodes, operated by the Knights of St. John. The Christians killed Ilyas and took Aruj prisoner. He spent the next year as a galley slave, until his family could arrange the payment of a ransom for his release.

Another less colorful version of the tale claims that by the end of the fifteenth century, Aruj was serving on board a local pirate galley, which operated in the northern Aegean. This is certainly possible, as at that time Lesbos was officially part of the Ottoman Empire, but in reality it was a semiautonomous island. It was also a notorious haven for pirates, both Greek and Muslim. It boasted a busy port where the cultures and religions of the Mediterranean mixed freely—and where the pirates could readily sell their plunder. The pirate galley was captured by the Knights of St. John, and the pirates became galley slaves until their release was negotiated as part of a peace treaty between the knights and the emir of Egypt.

The different versions of the tale also provide us with different versions of what happened after Aruj was released. One has him return to Lesbos, where he enlisted the help of his brother Hızır and joined a pirate crew. The brothers soon rose to command their own small galley (or galliot). The other version has him brought to Alexandria following his release, and tells that it was there that he asked his brother to join him. He persuaded the local Mameluke emir, Qansuh al-Ghawri, to fund the fitting out of a corsair galliot, allowing him to have his revenge on the Christians who had made him their slave. A third version—supported by the

Turkish archives—places Aruj in Antalya on the Turkish coast, where he was granted a privateering licence by the port's bey, the Ottoman prince Shehzade Korkud. It was there that he began his piratical career, moving to Alexandria only when Shehzade fled to Egypt following a dispute over succession. In any event the next phase of the lives of the two brothers is reasonably well documented, and the strands of the story merge into known historic fact.

The brothers proved to be gifted corsairs, and they learned their piratical trade in the waters of the eastern Mediterranean. They expanded their force by capturing Christian trading galleys, augmenting their numbers by recruiting freed Muslim galley slaves. Peace between the Ottoman Empire and the Knights of St. John forced the brothers to move their corsair operation further west, and in 1505 they arrived in Djerba, a small island port off the coast of Tunisia, and some 200 miles south of the regional Barbary city-state of Tunis. The brothers obtained a privateering licence, and they then led their two well-armed galliots across the Mediterranean to the Tyrrhenian Sea, where they cruised northwards along the Italian coast in search of prey. They ranged as far north as the Ligurian Sea, harassing the Italian coastal trade off the busy port of Genoa before heading home. Then off the island of Elba they ran into two galleys flying the colors of Pope Julius II. The papal ships turned out to be a rich trading galley and an escorting warship, both of which were captured by the corsairs after a stiff fight. The advantage the corsairs enjoyed over the papal galleys was that every one of their crewmen was free, and therefore available to fight. The papal vessels relied on galley slaves, who were hardly going to fight to protect their captors. The brothers returned to the Tunisian port of La Goulette in triumph, and their reputation was assured.

The Spanish historian Diego Haedo wrote:

> The wonder and astonishment that this notable exploit caused in Tunis, and even in Christendom, is not to be expressed, nor how celebrated the name of Aruj Rais was to become from that very moment; he being held and accounted, by all the world, as a most valiant and enterprising commander. And by reason his beard was extremely red, or carroty, from thenceforward he was generally called Barbarossa, which in Italian signifies Red Beard.

In a Mediterranean world filled with black hair, the two redheaded brothers would certainly have stood out from the crowd, and so their nickname was born.[2]

The next victim was the *Cavalleria*, a Sardinian warship bound for Naples, which the corsairs found becalmed near the Lipari Islands, off the northeast corner of Sicily. The big advantage of a galley over a sailing ship was its ability to operate regardless of the wind. However powerful it might be, a becalmed sailing ship—with its guns pointing out on either broadside—was completely defenseless against a galley firing into her from her bow or stern. Another tactical trick used by the brothers was to operate in light and speedy galliots, but to keep a larger and better armed galley in reserve, just in case. The result of this lucrative capture and a string of others was that the Barbarossa Brothers became the most successful corsairs of the Barbary Coast. Hundreds flocked to join their band, and their new base of La Goulette filled with both prizes and plunder. The Barbarossa Brothers were now some of the richest men on the Barbary Coast. In 1509 they were joined by their remaining brother, Ishak, who helped them lead further raids against the coast of Calabria and Sicily.

In 1511 a disagreement between the corsair brothers and the bey of Tunis, Abu Abdullah Mohammed Hamis, led to another change of base—this time further west along the coast to Djidjelli (now Jijel), between Tunis and Algiers, where the emir of Algiers had asked for their help fighting the Spanish who were threatening to attack him. The Spanish had captured Oran in 1509 and Bougie (now Beijaia) the following year, so the Algerians expected that with the Spanish on either side of them they would be next. At first the corsairs enjoyed some degree of success. Then they overreached themselves. The brothers attacked Bougie, and this time they were repulsed. Aruj lost an arm in the engagement, and almost lost his life. They returned two years later, but once again they were driven off by the Spanish defenders.

From that point on the brothers became embroiled in a war against the Spanish—defending their Barbary lair by harassing Spanish outposts on the North African coast, attacking Spanish shipping operating between Oran and Spain, and even leading raids against settlements on the Spanish coast. While the brothers were waging their own private war, the emir of Algiers seemed happy enough to let them fight his battles for him, doing nothing to help them or to improve his own defenses. The Spanish already had a trading settlement at Peñón on the far side of the Bay of Algiers, and they took advantage of this lack of enterprise and turned the trading colony into a fortified base. Finally in 1516 the Algerians had had enough of their ineffective leader and rose up in revolt. Aruj immediately realized the potential in the situation, took his men west to Algiers, and led a coup, killing the bey and establishing himself as the new ruler of the city.

Aruj realized that he could not fight off the Spanish on his own, so he appealed to the Ottoman sultan for help. In return for his fealty to the Turkish Empire he was made bey of Algiers, and beylerbey (effectively governor-general of the lesser beys) of the western Mediterranean—making him the de facto ruler of the Barbary Coast. Better still, the sultan promised men, galleys, and guns. The struggle between the Barbarossa Brothers and the Spanish reached a climax in 1518. First the Spanish launched an attack from Peñón, but the assault was thwarted by the Algerian defenders, who were aided by a sudden storm. Then in May the emperor Charles V arrived in Oran at the head of a large army. He planned to attack Algiers, but it was Aruj who struck first, landing behind Oran and striking inland to destroy a large force of Arab auxiliaries who were marching to join the Spanish expedition.

When the emperor learned of the attack he immediately sent his lieutenant Garcia de Teneo with a force of Spanish and Bedouin troops to intercept the raiders. The veteran Spanish general caught the corsairs before they could escape, and Aruj and his brother Ishak were besieged in the inland town of Tlemcen. Aruj had 5,000 corsairs under his command, supported by 1,500 Turkish troops, but he was still heavily outnumbered by the Spaniards, who had upwards of 10,000 men, supported by artillery. After a siege of 20 days the Spanish assaulted the town, and Aruj and Ishak were killed as they defended the breach. It was the end of an era, but not the end of the fight. Hızır would continue the struggle and would eventually prove an even greater threat to the Spanish than his elder brother.

KHAIR-ED-DIN

Hızır "Barbarossa" was now the head of the Barbary corsairs, and he was determined to avenge the death of his two brothers.[3] The Turkish sultan Selim I made him the new beylerbey, and he sent reinforcements. In December 1518 he led an army west which threatened Oran, and recaptured Tlemcen—a dramatic gesture that came a little too late to help his brother. More useful was his assault and capture of Bône (now Annaba), a Spanish-held port to the east of his corsair base at Djidjelli and midway between Bougie and Tunis. Then in 1519 he defeated an expedition sent from Oran to capture Algiers. As a reward he was named as the emir (pasha) of Algiers. With his base reasonably secure, he was then able to resume his attacks on Christian targets.

Over the next few years Hızır Rais raided the southern coast of France and the Balearic Islands and even attacked Spanish shipping off Cadiz. He managed to

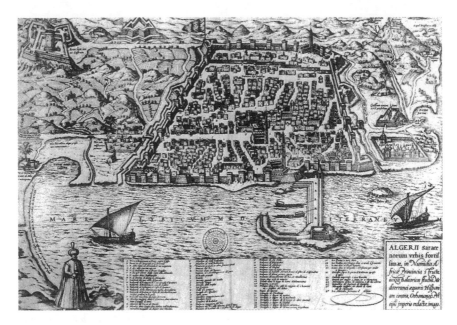

In the early sixteenth century, Algiers was the chief stronghold of the Barbary pirates, having been captured from the Spanish by the Barbarossa brothers in 1519. The port became a pirate haven, where slaves and plunder were sold in the city's marketplace.

avenge another long-standing wrong in 1522, when the sultan ordered him to join an expedition against Rhodes, the eastern Mediterranean bastion of the Knights of St. John. The Christians were driven from the island in January the following year, and as a result the Barbary corsair was named "Khair-ed-Din" (or Hayreddin) by the sultan, meaning "goodness of the faith" or "gift of god." He had come a long way since his youth on Lesbos. Also, as the last of the four redheaded brothers, he became known simply as Barbarossa.

After returning to the Barbary Coast he led raids on Corsica, Sardinia, and the Italian coast, before being driven away by the combined fleets of Genoa and the Maltese Knights of St. John. He returned the following year, and in the meantime he continued his raids in Spain. This pattern would continue for six years, from 1525 until 1531, by which time he had achieved an even more important victory at home. In May 1529 he captured the Spanish stronghold of Peñón in the Bay of Algiers, thereby ensuring the safety of his home base. In 1531 he also launched a major assault on Tripoli, which had been captured by the Spanish in 1510 and handed over to the Knights of St. John as compensation for their loss of Rhodes. This time Khair-ed-Din was repulsed, and the city remained in Christian hands until 1551.

The following year he was called back to serve the sultan, who needed his help to counter a Venetian offensive in the Adriatic that threatened the newly won string of Ottoman outposts in the Ionian Islands. Not only did he recapture many of the islands from the Christians, but he also managed to raid the Italian coast while he did so, and he even caused the church bells of Rome to ring an alarm as he cruised off the mouth of the River Tiber. Meanwhile the Christians were gathering their strength, and it was clear that a major clash was about to take place.

It began when Barbarossa seized Tunis, where the local bey, Mulei Hassan, had decided to support the emperor Charles V. The exiled ruler asked the emperor for help in recapturing his city, and consequently the Spanish sent an overwhelming force to Tunis, which succeeded in recapturing the city the following year. Unable to tackle the Spanish head on, Barbarossa headed west in time to thwart the second phase of the Spanish offensive—an expedition sent from Oran to recapture Tlemcen. He then led an Ottoman force against Naples, which captured this major Spanish-held Italian port in 1537. This prompted Pope Paul III to form a Holy League, and so in 1538 the Imperial Admiral Andrea Doria led a large League fleet into the Aegean to corner and destroy Barbarossa once and for all.

The Christian Holy League consisted of galleys from Spain, Genoa, the papacy, and Venice—and the contingent commanders could barely be restrained from attacking each other, let alone the Turks. The two fleets met at Prevesa on September 28, 1538, and the result was a victory for Barbarossa, who sank or destroyed 13 enemy vessels and captured 38 more. This stunning victory meant that Turkish naval supremacy in the Mediterranean would remain unchallenged for another three decades, until the results of Prevesa were overturned at the battle of Lepanto (1571). Clearly Charles V decided that Barbarossa could not be beaten, as two years later he tried to bribe him to change sides. The Barbary leader was having none of it, and the long war between Spain and the Barbary corsairs continued.

In 1540 Charles V tried and failed to capture Algiers, which might have ended the Barbary threat in the western Mediterranean in a single battle. Meanwhile Barbarossa cruised the Mediterranean at will, capturing Reggio in the toe of Italy and Nice on the French Riviera (1543), and operated in support of his newfound allies, the French, who hated the Spanish almost as much as the corsairs did. The following year he arrived off Genoa to negotiate the release of the Barbary corsair Turgut Rais, then wreaked havoc in the coastal communities of Italy as far south as Naples. It was the old corsair's last cruise. In 1545 he was called to Istanbul, and he left Algiers in the hands of his son Hasan Pasha. In the sultan's court the aged Barbarossa dictated his memoirs, and he died peacefully there the following year. During their lives the two Barbarossa Brothers had saved the Barbary Coast from the Spanish invaders and helped ensure that these fragile semi-independent city-states would survive long after their passing. In the process they established a fearsome reputation for the Barbary corsairs they commanded, which would last for more than a century.

THE SULTAN'S CORSAIRS

The Barbarossa Brothers were only the first of many Barbary corsairs who divided their time between privateering and service in the Ottoman navy.[4] A lieutenant of Khair-ed-Din, Turgut Rais was born in Bodrum, on the coast of Turkey. He joined the army and served in Egypt until he joined a band of corsairs as a master gunner. He soon rose to command his own galliot and operated in the Aegean, where he specialized in attacking Venetian shipping. In 1520 he joined Khair-ed-Din in Algiers, and he was soon promoted to command a squadron of Barbary corsairs. Operating in concert with his emir and as an independent commander, he soon developed a reputation both for skill as a corsair on the high seas and as an amphibious commander, raiding his way around the coasts of Sicily and southern Italy.

Turgut Rais took part in the battle of Prevesa (1538), where he commanded 30 vessels—one wing of the Turkish fleet. The following year he fought his way up the Adriatic, defeating Venetian squadrons sent to fight him and conquering a string of islands and fortresses in the name of the sultan. His next challenge was as the bey of Djerba, taking command of one of the most notorious corsair havens on the Barbary Coast. He seemed born to the job, leading raids on Malta, Sicily, and Corsica. However, it soon went badly wrong. In 1541 he was surprised and cornered by a Genoese squadron while repairing his ships in a secluded Corsican bay. The Barbary corsair and his men were captured, and he spent the next three years working as a galley slave on the ship of Giannettino Doria, the nephew of the Imperial Admiral. It was only when Khair-ed-Din arrived off Genoa in 1544 and threatened to besiege the city that Turgut Rais was finally released in exchange for a ransom of 3,500 ducats—the equivalent of $1.25 million today. It turned out to be money well spent.

Back at the helm, Turgut Rais spent the next three years raiding the Genoese coast and preying on Genoese shipping, becoming such a threat that Andrea Doria was forced to mobilize a major fleet and tried to destroy him. The wily corsair simply hid in the friendly French port of Toulon until the Genoese returned to port. Following Khair-ed-Din's death in 1546 he became the new commander of the Ottoman fleet, and two years later he replaced his former commander's son as the bey of Algiers and the beylerbey of the western Mediterranean. Effectively he had become the new leader of the Barbary corsairs. He continued to lead his own attacks, and that August he succeeded in capturing a Maltese galley carrying a fortune of 70,000 ducats ($25 million) on board, which more than covered the cost of his ransom four years before.

Then came a determined Christian assault on the Barbary bases in Tunisia. In 1550 Andrea Doria captured Mahdia and blockaded Turgut Rais in Djerba. Although the corsairs managed to escape capture, the port fell to the enemy, who held on to it for a decade. After summoning up Turkish reinforcements he returned to the Barbary coast in August 1551 and succeeded in capturing Tripoli from the Knights of St. John. In recognition of his achievement, a grateful sultan named Turgut Rais the bey of Tripoli. Five years later he became the region's pasha. This gave the corsairs another useful base, which they used to good effect. His galleys defeated Andrea Doria at the battle of Ponza (1552), which opened up the coasts of Sicily, Sardinia, and Italy to a fresh wave of corsair raids—attacks which continued intermittently for another three years. Andrea Doria made another attempt to defeat Turgut Rais, a campaign that ended in another humiliation for the Christians at the battle of Djerba (1560). From then until his death five years later during the Siege of Malta, he was able to continue his policy of raiding the coasts of the Christian powers and whittling away at their footholds on the Barbary Coast.

The south Italian fisherman Giovanni Dionigi was captured by Barbary corsairs in 1536 and became a slave, an experience that left him with the marks that earned him the nickname "Farta," meaning scarred by disease. When he was eventually given the opportunity, he converted to Islam and joined the corsairs based in Tripoli. By 1560 he was known as Uluj Ali, a corsair serving under Turgut Rais as the commander of a galliot, and he rose to prominence during the fighting off Djerba. He also distinguished himself during the Siege of Malta, and as a result he was named as the new bey of Tripoli after Turgut Rais's death. His corsairs attacked shipping and coastal settlements in Sicily and southern Italy, and within three years he was given the even more prestigious title of beylerbey of Algiers. For the next decade he led his galleys against the Spanish and the Knights of Malta, and in 1570 he captured a powerful Maltese squadron in a battle that earned him a post as an Ottoman naval commander.

CORSAIR GALLEYS

While in the rest of Europe the sailing ship replaced the oared longship as the principal warship, in the Mediterranean the oared galley remained supreme. Renaissance galleys were similar to those used by the Romans and Byzantines, but by the sixteenth century, most galleys carried guns, used to fire into an enemy seconds before the two met, and then the crew would board the enemy through the smoke.

Galleys were vulnerable to being rammed, and so the only offensive part of the vessel was the bow. This was used as the gun platform and boarding point, and most galleys were also fitted with a ram.

Most galleys relied on galley slaves for propulsion, although the Barbary corsairs were all freemen. Galleys also carried masts fitted with lateen sails, allowing them to take advantage of the wind. A typical war galley of the sixteenth century would carry 20–30 oars or sweeps, each manned by three, four, or even six rowers.

The Barbary corsairs avoided using their ram or artillery except in a crisis, as damage to a potential prize lowered its value. The Barbary corsairs' galleys also carried swordsmen and musketeers. A preferred tactic was to maneuver behind an enemy ship, then swarm aboard it, overpowering its crew in a melee.

Most Barbary corsair galleys were not galleys at all but were of the smaller, faster vessel type known as the galliot. A typical galliot was flush-decked with a single mast. Between six and 12 oars per side were manned by an average of two oarsmen per sweep, and on true corsair galleys or galliots these oarsmen were free pirates not slaves. Larger galleys went on raids, or were used as command vessels, and often were used as backup for the galliots. The advantage of a galley or galliot was that it was not reliant on the wind for propulsion. In light winds this meant that Barbary corsairs could outmaneuver their opponents, but if a sailing warship fired a broadside at close range, the effect was devastating. Consequently a good Barbary corsair knew when to attack, and when to keep away.

He took part in the disastrous battle of Lepanto in 1571, and in the aftermath of the defeat he took command of the battered Turkish fleet and remoulded it into a fighting force that helped prevent the collapse of Ottoman power in the eastern Mediterranean.[5] However, he was a corsair at heart, and he was soon allowed to return to Algiers. His next triumph came in June 1574, when he masterminded the recapture of Tunis from the Spanish. Uluj Ali made the most of his victory, consolidating his control of the Barbary Coast from Tripoli to Oran and strengthening the defenses of the Barbary ports under his command. Eventually the Spanish signed a truce with the Ottomans, ending the best part of six decades of near-constant threat to the Barbary Coast. That left Uluj Ali free to pursue his responsibilities to the sultan, and from then until his death in 1586 he helped maintain Turkish control over its coastal territories along the Adriatic and North African coast.

Probably the last and perhaps the greatest Barbary corsair was Murat Rais, who rose to prominence during the second half of the sixteenth century. He was probably born in Albania around 1534, and in 1546 he was captured by a roving band of corsairs and elected to convert to Islam and to join their crew. By 1565 he had command of his own galliot, and he slowly gained a reputation as a daring corsair and as something of a maverick. Rather tactlessly he annoyed his superior, Uluj Ali, during an attack on a Maltese galley by boarding it ahead of his admiral. It is therefore not exactly surprising that it took two decades for him to be called upon to command an Ottoman fleet.

However, he was gaining influence on the Barbary coast. In 1574 he was appointed the "Captain of the Sea" by the bey of Algiers, an appointment that reflected his growing prowess as a corsair commander. Four years later he captured the Spanish viceroy of Sicily, who was returning home to Spain in two powerful galleys. This sent shockwaves throughout the Mediterranean and enraged King Philip II, almost prompting a full-scale expedition to raze Algiers to the ground. For the next decade he fought an undeclared war against the Spanish, raiding their coastline, preying on their ships, and filling the slave market of Algiers with Spanish captives. In 1586 he even sailed as far as the Canary Islands, where he attacked Lanzarote and held the inhabitants to ransom. By this time he was widely regarded as the most notorious corsair in the Mediterranean.

In 1594 he was given official recognition by the Ottoman court and became the sultan's admiral. In that capacity he led a large-scale Ottoman attack on southern Italy, and in 1595 he fought off a superior force of galleys and sailing warships off the coast of Sicily. For the next four decades until his death in 1638 he was the sultan's commander in the eastern Mediterranean, his galleys defending the waters against Christian interlopers, raiding Christian ports, and keeping the seas safe for Muslim traders. He finally met his end during the Ottoman siege of Vlorë in Albania, ending the best part of a century of corsairing and naval service within miles of his original home.

THE DECLINE OF THE BARBARY PIRATES

Although he would never have admitted it, by the time Murat Rais died in 1638, the heyday of the Barbary corsairs was over. It probably didn't seem so at the time, and some historians have even referred to the early seventeenth century as a golden age for the Barbary States. After all, the slave markets had never been busier—Algiers alone was said to have 20,000 Christian slaves within its walls at any one time. A few might try to escape from captivity by converting to Islam—a process described by other Europeans as "turning Turk." Under Islamic law a Muslim could not be fettered or be made to row a galley. Although this was not always a way to escape servitude, it usually meant a great improvement in conditions. However, the majority of slaves on the Barbary coast were not given this opportunity. Similarly the richest captives were held prisoner until they were ransomed, while the poor were condemned to a life of servitude. The most sought-after captives were young women and good-looking boys, although men with useful trades—skilled gunners, sailors or tradesmen—were all highly prized.

Miguel de Cervantes, the Spanish author of *Don Quixote,* was captured by the corsairs in 1575. He remained their slave for five years and described the constant fear of execution or punishment for unknowingly offending the Islamic religion. While Christian propaganda may have made the most of such stories, there is little doubt that the life of the average slave was a hellish one. By the start of the seventeenth century, slavery rather than corsair attacks on the high seas was the main source of income for the Barbary States. An uneasy peace with the Europeans meant that these slave raiders were no longer considered privateers or "corsairs," and so the term pirates or slave traders would probably be more appropriate.

To keep these slave markets stocked, the corsairs became slavers more than privateers. For the most part these captives were gathered during raids of the Sicilian, Italian, Spanish, or Balkan coasts, but sometimes the corsairs traveled further afield in search of slaves. For instance, in 1627 a Flemish convert to Islam called Murat Rais the Younger (no relation to the elderly admiral) led a force of

15 Barbary galliots into the Atlantic. He raided his way up the Atlantic coasts of Portugal, Spain, and France, and he eventually landed upon the small island of Lundy, in the Bristol Channel. For the next five years he used the island as a base to prey on coastal communities and shipping as far away as Iceland.

Murat Rais the Younger was not unusual in being a Christian renegade. Around the same time many Christian pirates were accepted into the ranks of the corsairs without renouncing their religion, particularly if they brought with them a knowledge of maritime technology or warfare or could demonstrate skills in navigation or a knowledge of a particular coast. In the early seventeenth century European ports were filled with unemployed seamen, many of whom had been trained as privateers during the long war between England, Holland, and Spain. It was inevitable that some of these men would seek employment on the Barbary Coast. A prime example was John Ward, an Elizabethan seaman who entered the service of the bey of Tunis and rose to command a Barbary flotilla of ten galliots. These renegades seemed to have no reservations when it came to enslaving their fellow Christians.

A typical slave raid of this period was the assault of Murat Rais the Younger and his pirates on the Irish village of Baltimore in County Cork, in which the entire population was rounded up, then carried off to a lifetime of slavery. A priest who witnessed their arrival in the slave market in 1631 wrote: "It was a piteous sight to see them exposed for sale at Algiers, for when they parted the wife from the husband, and the father from the child; then, say I, they sell the husband here, and the wife there, tearing from her arms the daughter whom she cannot hope to see ever again." Only two of the captives ever managed to return to Ireland. One of Rais' Icelandic captives was Oluf Eigilsson, who was ransomed in 1628 and wrote a detailed account of his experiences, as did the Frenchman Jean Marteille de Bernac, who spoke of his experiences as a galley slave:

> Think of six men chained to a bench, naked as when they were born, one foot on the stretcher, the other on the bench in front, holding an immensely heavy oar, bending forwards to the stern with arms at full reach to clear the backs of the rowers in front, who bend likewise; and then having got forward, shoving up the oar's end to let the blade catch the water, then throwing their bodies back on the groaning bench. A galley oar sometimes pulls thus for ten, twelve, or even twenty hours without a moment's rest. The boatswain ... puts a piece of bread steeped in wine in the wretched rower's mouth to stop fainting, and then the captain shouts the order to redouble the lash.

If a slave falls exhausted upon his oar (which often chances) he is flogged till he is taken for dead, and then pitched unceremoniously into the sea.[6]

The only hope for many of the poorer captives was that some Christian religious order would buy their freedom. One of these groups—the Redemptionists—organized the purchase and freedom of some 15,500 Christian slaves of all nationalities between 1575 and 1769. Another Catholic organization called the Lazarists was equally successful. Sometimes governments took a hand in the business of raising money. For example, in 1643, seven women petitioned the English Parliament to allow churches to take up collections because "Their husbands and others were taken by Turkish pirates, carried to Algiers, and there now remain in miserable captivity, having great fines imposed on them for their ransoms."[7]

A Christian religious order known as the Redemptionist Fathers raised funds to buy back Christian slaves from the Barbary pirates during the sixteenth century. These pirates regularly raided the coast of Christian Europe in search of slaves during this period.

Another source of income was extortion, or protection money. Merchants whose ships passed through the Mediterranean frequently arranged to pay a fee, which secured immunity from attack. In northern Europe, these payments were often passed off as presents to local dignitaries or as the payment of a ransom in order to protect the merchants and their backers from charges of collusion with pirates. In fact, just as the French had allied themselves with the Barbary corsairs in the sixteenth century during their war with Spain, Dutch and English merchants actually seemed to encourage the payment of these bribes as a means of limiting the effectiveness of less wealthy competitors. As late as 1816, as the British admiral Lord Exmouth bombarded Algiers in another punitive gesture, he expressed the private opinion that the complete suppression of piracy in the region would probably not be acceptable to the British trading community.

It has been argued that when the English and the Dutch began a long-running series of punitive actions against the Barbary pirates from the mid-seventeenth century on, these actions were undertaken more to ensure a good deal for their merchants than as a serious attempt to end slavery and piracy in Mediterranean waters. For instance, in April 1655 the English admiral Robert Blake arrived off the Barbary Coast with orders to extract compensation from the beys for attacks on English shipping.[8] From his letters it seems that this was merely part of the deal, and that a negotiation over protection money was also an important part of his mission. When the bey of Tunis refused to negotiate, Blake set his fleet of 15 men-of-war into the harbor of Porto Farina (now Ghar al Milh), destroying the port's defenses and nine pirate galleys. The bey immediately entered into negotiations.

A further series of punitive actions was undertaken by Charles II's navy, following his acquisition of Tangier in 1662 as part of his wedding dowry. His forces held the port for two decades, despite fierce opposition from the Muslim rulers of Morocco. As a trading post it was considered vital that English merchants have free access to other Mediterranean ports—which meant coming to an arrangement with the Barbary States. However, the English monarch had learned a lesson from Blake, and negotiations were conducted from a position of naval strength. The French also pulled the same trick, and in 1682 and 1683 they bombarded the port of Algiers when trade negotiations with the beylerbey failed to achieve the results they wanted. Of course the corsairs could match force with force. When the French reappeared in 1683, the beylerbey seized the French consul, loaded the struggling diplomat into an oversize mortar, then fired him at the French fleet.

By the eighteenth century the extortion of protection money had replaced slavery as the region's main source of income. However, as a newcomer to the business of maritime trade, the United States of America were less willing to negotiate the payment of protection money, which they rightly saw as a tool that benefited their British, French, and Dutch competitors rather than their own merchants. In 1784 the Americans negotiated a trade agreement with the sultanate of Morocco, but they proved less willing to make any deal with the beys of the Barbary Coast. Consequently American ships became prime targets for the pirates, and American captives began to appear in the slave markets.

The American response was to ask their merchants to operate in convoys and to send their fledgling navy to the area to protect American interests. Certainly the main European powers were not going to help the Americans, as they were embroiled in their own conflict—the fight with France, which lasted almost without a break from 1789 to 1815. The administrations of Thomas Jefferson and James Madison still refused to pay protection money, or to negotiate for the release of captives, and the slogan "millions for defense, but not one cent for tribute" was coined. What followed was a series of punitive actions that became known as the Barbary Wars.

In 1801 Jefferson sent the U.S. Navy to Tripoli, and the port was blockaded. During the conflict that followed the USS *Philadelphia* was lost when she ran aground in Tripoli harbor, and the US Marines achieved success by taking the fight "to the shores of Tripoli." By 1805 the bey was willing to sign a peace deal. In return for $60,000 he returned all his American slaves, offered free passage to American ships, and promised to behave himself in the future.

A second conflict (also known as the Algerine War) erupted in 1815, and this time the British and French allied themselves with the Americans.[9] The conflict ended with the allied bombardment of Algiers (1816) and the promise by the beylerbey that he would no longer enslave Christians. This was really the end of the Barbary States. Within two decades Algiers became a French colony, while Tunis followed suit later, in 1881. In 1835 Tripoli returned to the Turkish fold and remained part of the Ottoman Empire until 1911, when it became an Italian colony. The long history of privateering, slave trading, and piracy ended more with a whimper than with a bang, the result of a changing world and the growing importance of military technology and global trade—of which the Barbary rulers had little or no understanding.

5

BUCCANEERS

DUTCH COURAGE

By the end of the sixteenth century, the long-running war between England and Spain seemed to be running out of steam. When the French king Henry IV made peace with the Spanish in 1598, he left the English and the Dutch to continue the war on their own. By the time Queen Elizabeth I died in 1603, it was clear that the war was bankrupting the country. However, it was her successor, James I of England and VI of Scotland, who finally ended the conflict—and in 1604 the Treaty of London brought the long war to an end. All privateering letters of marque were immediately canceled, and English ship owners were quick to take advantage of the new trading opportunities that peace presented to them. This just left the Dutch.

By 1604 the Dutch were already considered a threat to the Spanish New World, as, after three decades of warfare in the English Channel, their privateers had recently begun organizing themselves into large fleets, operating under the command of the Dutch state. This spirit of cooperation between privateers and the government went back to the very start of the Dutch revolt against the Spanish in 1572, when a loose confederation of Dutch pirates, smugglers, and privateers who styled themselves the sea beggars had captured the port of Brielle (Brill), then used it as a base to attack Spanish coastal shipping.

They managed to combine their old piratical skills with their newfound patriotism and spent the next decade raiding coastal towns held by the Spanish, harassing their supply convoys, and even—in 1574—helping to enforce the blockade of Bergen-op-Zoom, which was being besieged by Dutch rebels. Another high point came in 1585, when the Spanish were besieging Antwerp. The Duke of Parma built a giant pontoon bridge above the city, which the sea beggars duly attacked using fireships. Although the result was a spectacular conflagration that destroyed the bridge and sapped Spanish morale, the city still fell four months later. However, the attack reinforced the already apparent fact that while the Spanish army might be triumphant on land, the sea beggars controlled the rivers, estuaries, and coastal waterways of Holland.

The Spanish solution to this was to create a rival pirate threat. In 1583 the Duke of Parma captured the port of Dunkirk, which had already established itself as a haven for pirates and privateers. Parma issued his own letters of marque, and within five years these Dunkirkers had irritated the Dutch so much that they were declared pirates rather than legitimate privateers. During the Twelve Year Truce (1609–21) the lack of official privateering letters of marque seemed to offer few problems to the Dunkirkers, most of whom continued to operate as pirates until the fighting resumed. After the truce ended in 1621 the gloves were off again, and between then and 1648 when the war finally came to an end, the Dunkirkers were responsible for the capture of over 200 Dutch ships each year, ranging from small fishing boats to large East Indiamen. By way of retaliation, in 1587 the Dutch States General ordered that any captured Dunkirkers should be "beaten into the sea" (i.e. thrown overboard). In other words, they treated them as pirates—men to whom the normal privateering rules of justice did not apply.

While the Dunkirkers may have hindered the Dutch, the privateers were unable to stop the steady expansion of Dutch maritime power during the last decades of the sixteenth century.[1] By the late 1580s Dutch squadrons were operating with the English fleet, and by the 1590s fleets of up to 70 Dutch privateers were capable of operating as far afield as the Azores. In 1599 a fleet of 72 Dutch privateers under the command of Pieter van der Does attacked the island of Gran Canaria. However alarming these attacks were for the Spanish, it was the Dutch penetration of the Pacific that caused them the greatest concern. In 1599 a five-ship expedition worked its way through the Straits of Magellan and attacked Spanish shipping on the Chilean coast. Although the interlopers were dispersed and destroyed, a second Dutch force repeated the attacks the following year, then returned home across the Pacific, attacking Spanish shipping in the Philippines as they did so. While these expeditions yielded little in the way of plunder, they did show just how far the Dutch had come since they first revolted against Spanish rule.

In 1602 the Dutch founded their own East India Company in a bid to secure a trade monopoly with the East Indies. While the principal route involved sailing round Africa, the Dutch also tried to establish a sea route via the Straits of Magellan, which inevitably brought them into conflict with the Spanish. In 1615, and despite the truce, a Dutch squadron plundered its way up the Pacific coast of Peru, almost causing the two countries to resume their long war. With the Dutch actively seeking to expand their overseas commercial interests into the Caribbean and the Far East, it was inevitable that when the truce ended in 1621, the war that followed would be fought for control of international sea routes as much as for the survival of the Dutch Republic. As if to emphasize their enthusiasm for a maritime war, the Dutch even founded a West India Company, designed to challenge the Spanish trade monopoly in the Caribbean.

While a few Dutch raids were indeed launched against the Spanish Main, the main assault fell on the Portuguese colony of Brazil. In March 1624 a Dutch fleet of 35 ships arrived off Bahia (San Salvador) and claimed the port in the name of the Dutch Republic. The Iberian response was immediate—a joint Hispano–Portuguese fleet of 63 ships under the command of Don Fadrique de Toledo was sent to recapture the colony. In May 1625 Toledo arrived off the Brazilian coast to find the Dutch fleet had escaped. In fact, while Toledo busied himself with the recapture of Bahia, the Dutch were attacking San Juan in Puerto Rico. Although the attackers managed to sack the town, the garrison held out in the city's fortress, and eventually the attackers withdrew. Rather than return home empty-handed, the Dutch then cruised off the coast of the Spanish Main, snapping up whatever prizes they could and plundering a string of small coastal settlements. Nevertheless, by the spring of 1626 the fleet was back in Holland, having achieved very little for all its efforts.

However, the next Dutch raid was going to be different. The second-in-command of the Brazil venture was Piet Heyn, a former privateer who became a vice admiral in the West India Company in 1623. In 1624 he led a secondary expedition to Luanda in Angola—the major Portuguese trading post on the African coast. He failed to capture the town and arrived back off the Brazilian coast in time to be chased off by Don Fadrique. So far Piet Heyn hadn't covered himself in glory. However, in 1626 he led a small privateering expedition back to Bahia, and this time he managed to capture and plunder the town. Lacking the men to hold the Brazilian port, he returned home, receiving a hero's welcome. The Dutch had found their own Drake.

In 1627 Piet Heyn returned to the Spanish Main at the head of a powerful fleet of 36 Dutch privateers crewed by 3,300 men. By September he was off the northern coast of Cuba, where he hoped to intercept the combined annual treasure *flota*. The Spanish sent dispatch boats from Havana to warn the fleet that the Dutch were there, but Heyn's men intercepted most of these messages. Only the Tierra Firme *flota* in Cartagena was warned in time. Consequently, when the New Spain *flota* finally appeared off the Cuban coast, the Dutch took it by surprise. The first victim was the small Honduras squadron, bound from Trujillo to Havana. Cut off from Havana, the Spaniards were driven towards the coast and forced to surrender. Next came the bulk of the New Spain fleet, where Heyn repeated his successful tactic, this time driving the Spanish into Matanzas Bay—10 miles to the east of Havana. On September 8 the Dutch followed their victims into the bay. Trapped like fish in a barrel, the outgunned Spanish treasure ships had no choice but to surrender.

By the time Piet Heyn and his men returned home in January 1629, news of their exploits had reached Holland before them, and the well-planned celebrations that followed included firework displays, services of thanksgiving, and triumphal parades. However, the real cause for celebration was the plunder—worth some 11.5 million ducats ($6.9 billion in modern money). While the Dutch were celebrating, the Spanish were struggling to cope with their loss. Historians have often explained Spain's subsequent political, military, and economic relegation in Europe by citing the loss of the Matanzas treasure, and they could well be right. By the time the Thirty Years' War ended in 1648, it was the Dutch who were the economic top dog in Europe, while the Spanish had slipped from being a world power and were struggling to maintain their grip on a continent that was increasingly dominated by their French rivals. Meanwhile, over in the Americas, the Spanish were facing a new threat, which made the Dutch seem like a minor irritant.

TROUBLE ON HISPANIOLA

In a way, the Spanish brought all this trouble on themselves. After the end of the war with England, and throughout the long truce with the Dutch, they continued as if nothing would ever change. While the Spanish should have used this respite to fortify their ports, build up defensive fleets, and train local garrisons, they did next to nothing. Worse, a loophole in the Treaty of London signed in 1604 allowed interlopers to trade beyond the line, but only with the express permission of the king of Spain or his council. In fact, this need to seek permission was waived if the rulers of the region or country beyond the line allowed the interlopers to trade with them. In the past, local governors and the inhabitants of isolated settlements had been more than happy to trade with outsiders, and so the English, French, and Dutch assumed this would continue. However, the Spanish had other ideas.

Philip III regarded illegal trade with his overseas colonies as a serious problem—it encouraged smuggling and even piracy and led to a loss of royal revenue. One solution was to allow local governors to benefit from impounding the ships and possessions of interlopers, in the hope that the Spanish colonists would police themselves. When this failed, he resorted to more dramatic measures. First, a belated program of fortification building was begun, concentrating on the main ports in the Spanish Main. A small guard fleet—the Armada de Barlovento (Windward Fleet)—was also created, with squadrons based in Havana and Cartagena. These units were charged with hunting down smugglers, and they were moderately successful. Then someone dreamed up the idea of depopulation.[2]

The Spanish authorities had long known that the northern side of Hispaniola was a lawless place. The island lacked the resources of nearby Cuba, and consequently its hinterland was never fully developed by Spanish colonists. The one successful economic development in the island was the introduction of cattle, and by the early seventeenth century beef and leather production became the mainstay of the island economy. Away from the cattle ranches of the hinterland, small and impoverished settlements clung to the northern coast, and the farther they were from the administrative center of Santo Domingo, the more independent they became. Fraternization between Spanish colonists and interlopers had always gone on in northern Hispaniola, but during Philip III's reign the region became known as a haven for smugglers, who stopped off there for beef, leather, and water.

As early as 1598, the island governor had proposed moving the cattle herds closer to Santo Domingo in an effort to reduce the opportunities for smuggling. At first local landowners successfully opposed any such move. However, the king's envoy López de Castro refused to be thwarted and ordered Governor Osorio forcibly to depopulate the northern coast of the island. One of his principal reasons had nothing to do with economics. It was argued that heretical Protestant Bibles were being introduced to the island by these smugglers, and the drastic action by the authorities was undertaken in part to protect the colonists from spiritual temptation. During 1605 Governor Osorio's men destroyed a string of settlements and moved their inhabitants to new colonies established closer to Santo Domingo.

On paper the operation was a success. However, many colonists fled into the hinterland or founded new settlements hidden from the eyes of the Armada de Barlovento. With no legitimate source of income left to them, they took to cattle rustling and smuggling in order to survive. Whole stretches of coastline were depopulated, becoming a wilderness uncontrolled by the Spanish authorities in Santo Domingo. In effect the northern part of the island became a political vacuum, and while the Spanish might have benefited from this in the short term, by the 1620s they were beginning to reap the ill effects of their policy.

When the population of Hispaniola was forcibly clustered around Santo Domingo, the authorities also tried to move the cattle closer to the capital. This proved a disaster, and only a portion of the herds was successfully moved to the new ranches. The rest simply roamed wild, and after a period of adaptation they survived and even thrived in their new mountainous, forested environment. While the legitimate cattle ranching business never fully recovered from its relocation, these wild cattle provided those Spaniards who stayed behind with a new source of income. In effect they became *boucaniers*—a French term meaning those who smoked meat, or *boucan*. These locals continued to sell their meat to interlopers, and in time this trade not only prospered, it also attracted others to Hispaniola, who saw in the depopulation of the northern part of the island an opportunity to establish their own safe haven in the heart of the Spanish Main.

The Spanish were certainly aware of the problem. Patrols were sent out from Santo Domingo with orders to round up any stray cattle and to hunt down *renegados* (renegades, existing outside the authority of the Spanish crown) hiding in the forest. Invariably both cattle and *boucaniers* simply melted into the trees, and the Spanish punitive expedition would achieve little apart from the destruction of temporary hunting camps and the capture of a stray animal or two. The business of cattle hunting and meat smoking would continue as before. The process of smoking involved laying the carcass out on a green wood frame over an open fire. The technique was supposedly taught to the settlers by the few local Arawaks who survived the Spanish occupation of the island. These natives called the process *barbicoa*, which in Arawak meant "the stick with four legs and many sticks of wood on top to place the cooking meat." Today we call it a barbecue.

A French observer described these early *boucaniers* as looking like "the butcher's vilest servants who have been eight days in the slaughterhouse without washing themselves." It might have been a fairly apt description, as they lived, worked, and slept in rough leather hunting shirts or working clothes, coarse homespun shirts, and boots made out of pigskin. Animal fat was smeared over the skin to repel insects, which probably accounts for the repugnance shown by the Frenchman. These men roamed the hills, rounding up wild cattle, then butchering them, smoking them, and curing the hides. The barbecued meat and the hides were eventually transported to the coast, where they could be sold to interlopers or in one of the secluded coastal trading settlements that sprang up. In exchange the *boucaniers* would buy weapons, powder and shot, rum, and any other goods that they needed back in the hills. They operated in small groups, developing their own complex codes of behavior which would later develop into the buccaneering codes so beloved of pirate fiction.

Meanwhile, the Spanish were continuing their policy of depopulation by force. During the first years of the seventeenth century, other European powers began establishing small unofficial settlements in the West Indies. In 1600 the Dutch colonized the barren island of St. Eustatius, but the settlement failed, and the island was abandoned. However, when the Dutch West India Company was founded in 1621, a fresh wave of Dutch settlement began. A small colony was established on St. Croix in 1625, then on nearby St. Martin. In 1622 the English settled St. Kitts, and the French joined them on the island three years later. Barbados was colonized in 1625—part of a privately funded drive "to cut the King of Spain at the root and seek to impeach or supplant him in the West Indies."[3] Other colonies would follow throughout the West Indies, an area that had never been properly settled by the Spanish. Clearly King Philip III had to deal with the problem or else face the collapse of the Spanish monopoly beyond the line.

The Spanish response was predictable. The king's favorite admiral, Don Fadrique de Toledo, was already gathering an armada to drive the Dutch from Brazil when news of the St. Kitts settlement reached the Spanish court. He was duly ordered to visit St. Kitts at some stage during his Brazil voyage and to crush any French or English settlement he found there. In September 1627 Don Fadrique's fleet arrived off the island, and troops were landed near the main French settlement of Basseterre, driving back the French defenders at swordpoint. The French capitulated after being granted a safe passage home. Unfortunately for the Spanish many of these settlers simply took passage as far as the neighboring islands of Monserrat and St. Barts and founded new settlements there. For their part the English promised to leave, then went back on their word as soon as the Spanish left.

A number of French refugees from St. Kitts headed west, seeking out a new place to settle somewhere along the deserted northern shore of Hispaniola. They selected the island of La Tortuga, off the northwest corner of the island, which seemed to offer everything they needed. Within a few years a thriving tobacco crop was being harvested there, while the island also attracted local *boucaniers*, Dutch and French smugglers, and other refugee interlopers. It was the Dutch who gave this new settlement some degree of legitimacy, as the Dutch West India Company offered to protect the fledgling colony in exchange for leather hides. In other words, the greatest pirate den on the Spanish Main began its life as a backwater trading post.

TORTUGA: THE BUCCANEERS' HAVEN

The island settlement of Tortuga had a rocky history. The first Europeans to settle there were the Spanish—the planters who arrived in 1598 discovered the hard way that the island was unsuitable for sugar production, but it could support a tobacco crop. Then came the forcible resettlement, which meant that any Spaniards who remained in Tortuga did so as *renegados*. By the time the first wave of French settlers arrived in 1627, they found that the island already supported a small but thriving business, where the locals ran a trading post, serving as a link between the *boucaniers* and interlopers.

The French soon discovered that the island was not well suited to farming. First, it was small—just 40 miles in circumference—and shaped like the turtle which gave it its name, Isle de la Tortue ("Turtle Island"). The soil was poor and rocky, while the hinterland was covered in forest. The northern coast of the island was fringed with cliffs, while the only suitable harbor lay on the southern side— where the Spanish *renegados* had established their trading post. The best tobacco-growing area was on the western side of the island. The French simply took over the plantations for themselves—calling the area La Ringot—and they then established their own settlement, called Basseterre in honor of their lost colony on St. Kitts. The trading post of Cayonne by the main harbor remained in business, run by the local *renegados*.

The Dutch offer of protection never materialized, although, from 1630 on, Dutch ships began a lucrative trade with the island, shipping hides back to Europe and supplying the colony with weapons, manufactured goods, and rum. By that stage another trading organization—the Providence Island Company—had also begun trading with the islanders. Founded by Robert, Earl of Warwick, and the parliamentarian John Pym, the company soon sent its own colonists to augment the settlers who already occupied the island. Anthony Hilton, the governor who represented the Providence Island Company, was given titular control of the island.

Just as on St. Kitts, the English and the French coexisted on the same island, although following the death of Governor Hilton in 1634, the English left the island to join another colony on Providence (Santa Catalina)—an island off the coast of what is now Nicaragua. The Providence Island colony, first established in 1630, was after all the main focus of the English company's efforts. This left the French in sole control of Tortuga, although they still enjoyed the protection of the Dutch West India Company. However, the Dutch were nowhere to be seen in 1635 when the Spanish attacked Tortuga. The island may have been raided before—in 1629—but this time the Spanish meant business.

That January a punitive expedition sent from Santo Domingo under the command of Captain Ruy Fernández de Fuenmayor forced its way ashore at Cayonne, reputedly guided by John Murphy, an Irish Catholic settler who sold his information on the island's defenses to his coreligionists. Another source names Captain Francisco Turillo de Yelva as the Spanish naval commander who forced his way into the harbor. Whoever commanded the expedition, the Spanish managed to destroy the colony and capture some 240 colonists and 30 slaves. Of these colonists, all but 30 Spaniards and French Catholics were summarily executed, while the rest were taken back to Santo Domingo in chains. Incidentally the Spanish then continued on to Providence Island, but this time the attackers were repulsed. The English colony survived for another six years but, deprived of supplies due to the civil war at home, was finally overwhelmed by the Spanish.

In Tortuga, the Spanish may well have left behind a small garrison, but the settlers who survived the Spanish attack by fleeing to Hispaniola eventually returned to reclaim their property. In 1636 a group of English privateers from Nevis attacked the fledgling settlement on Tortuga, reportedly killing the 40 Frenchmen they found there. However, more settlers began arriving, and by 1638 the Spanish were forced to launch another expedition. This time the raid was carried out by the Armada de Barlovento, commanded by Carlos de Ibarra. Once again they managed to disperse or capture the colonists, but the islanders simply returned as soon as the Spanish left. This time a Captain Robert Flood, formerly of the Providence Island Company, established himself as the leader of the 300 Anglo-French settlers who survived.

In 1639 the new French governor of the West Indies (or Lieutenant General of the Isles) sent Jean le Vasseur to take control of Tortuga on behalf of the French crown. Le Vasseur established a base at Port Margot, another island off the Hispaniolan coast, and then in August 1640 he led an assault on the island at the head of some 100 well-armed Huguenots. Tortuga fell without much of a struggle, and as the new governor, le Vasseur set about improving the island's defenses. He began by building Fort du Rocher (La Rocca), overlooking Cayonne harbor, and then called on the original settlers to join him in protecting the island as a Protestant enclave in the heart of the Spanish Main. Naturally this did not go down well in Paris, but by this stage Tortuga had become a magnet for pirates and smugglers, and, lacking the power to recover the island, the French decided to leave le Vasseur well alone.

This marked a new phase in the history of Tortuga. Until the arrival of le Vasseur the islanders had busied themselves with growing tobacco, trading with the *boucaniers,* and acting as a trading post for Dutch West India Company ships. However, under his leadership Tortuga became a haven for fugitives of any nation, who all shared a common distrust of the Spanish authorities. From around 1640 on, these settlers began to attack passing Spanish ships. Tortuga lay at the northeastern end of the Windward Passage between Cuba and Hispaniola, and this busy shipping lane became the new hunting ground for le Vasseur's pirates.

The way these attacks were conducted was simple but effective. The pirates used small sailing or rowing boats (flyboats or pinnaces) and attacked at night. Their aim was to creep up astern of larger Spanish ships, then board them before a lookout could sound the alarm. While marksmen shot the helmsmen and officers, others wedged the ship's rudder to prevent their prey escaping. They then swarmed up the side of the enemy vessel, and in most cases the attackers would have outnumbered the Spanish crew. These pirates soon developed a reputation for cruelty and torture, whether deserved or not, and this worked in their favor. It was often enough to encourage the Spanish to surrender without firing a shot, in the hope that their lives would be spared.

In his book *Buccaneers of America*, published in 1678, Alexander Oliver Exquemelin claims that the first of these attacks was carried out by a Frenchman called Pierre le Grand (Peter the Great). According to this account, Pierre le Grand was born in Dieppe and arrived in Tortuga soon after 1640. Gathering a group of followers together, he began cruising the waters off Tortuga in a small canoe, hoping to intercept a small Spanish trading ship. According to Exquemelin he managed to capture a small pinnace, and then used it to hunt for larger prey. After months of fruitless searching he finally stumbled across one of the most lucrative prizes on the Spanish Main—a straggler from a Spanish treasure fleet. He brought his boat up behind the Spanish ship, then boarded her before the Spanish realized they were being attacked. To encourage his 28 followers to attack, he scuttled his own craft, so they had no option but to board their prey. The Spanish ship was duly captured, and rather than take her back to Tortuga, Pierre le Grand sailed her home to Dieppe, where he retired on the proceeds of his venture.

If Exquemelin is to be believed, Pierre le Grand was the first real pirate of the Caribbean, and his exploits served to encourage others to follow in his stead.[4] However, the story lacks any real corroborative evidence, and we are probably expected to see the tale as symbolic of a new breed of pirates rather than to accept it as a straightforward account. More interesting than the actual details of the attack is the way in which the French pirate was said to have carried out his raids. It suggests a trend in the waters off Tortuga—small canoes being used to prey on coastal shipping, after which these captured Spanish vessels were turned into pirate ships in their own right, cruising a little further afield in search of larger victims.

While the accuracy of Exquemelin's account is probably less important than the bigger picture, his evidence is supported by a letter written by the Spanish governor of Santo Domingo in 1646, which stated that Tortuga had become a pirate haven populated by Englishmen and Dutchmen as well as by le Vasseur and his French Huguenots. According to Exquemelin two important events took place around this time. First, the Tortugans began collectively to refer to themselves as buccaneers. Secondly, they also started calling themselves the Brethren of the Coast. In effect the Tortugan incomers had adopted the name and collective identity of the *boucaniers* of Hispaniola, which suggests that by the 1640s the two groups had become so intermingled as to become one body.

THE BRETHREN OF THE COAST

Our understanding of buccaneering society comes from Exquemelin. He claims that the buccaneers of Hispaniola operated in hunting parties of six to eight men, pooling their resources and making decisions by consensus. He also suggests that a pairing of buccaneers was also common—a male union known as *matelotage*—a term which essentially meant "bunk mate," but which has been more commonly linked to the French word *matelot*, meaning a sailor. This union—essentially a single-sex marriage—was recognized in the self-administered buccaneering laws or guidelines known as the way of the coast. A *matelot* stood to inherit the possessions of his partner on his death and may well have had other rights akin to marriage that have gone unrecorded. The Brethren of the Coast was no tightly knit brotherhood but more a loose confederation built up of these smaller partnerships and hunting groups.

While the business of hunting and meat smoking continued, the suggestion is that by the time Tortuga became established as a pirate haven, the *boucaniers* who traded with the island had crossed the 7 miles of sea between Tortuga and the mainland of Hispaniola and formed the core of the island population. In the process they brought their own rules and ways with them. In fact, according to Exquemelin, around 1650 the French governor le Vasseur imported prostitutes to the island in an attempt to break up the *matelotage* system. What these men shared with the incomers from Europe such as le Vasseur's Huguenots and Robert Flood's Englishmen was a strong antipathy to Spanish authority and a will to thrive at the expense of the Spanish crown. The Brethren of the Coast would soon grow from an island brotherhood into a maritime force capable of terrorizing the whole of the Spanish Main.

Calling Tortuga a pirate den is something of a misnomer. It was a gathering place, a trading center, and a place where crews could be recruited. It was not, however, a particularly safe haven. On at least two occasions—in early 1635 and again in early 1654—the Spanish assaulted and captured the island. Each time the inhabitants fled to the safety of the Hispaniola coast (which they called the "Tierra Grande") or else disappeared over the horizon. Even the building of Fort du Rocher did little to prevent the Spanish from capturing the place. After the assassination of Jean le Vasseur by discontented buccaneers in 1653, the French privateer the Chevalier de Fontenay became the new governor. As a devout Catholic, Fontenay was probably the wrong man for the job. However, the Spanish governor of Hispaniola, Juan Francisco Montemayor Cuenca, saw the change of leadership as a divisive step, which presented him with an opportunity to assault Tortuga.

The following January Juan Francisco landed a powerful expeditionary force on the western side of the island, then marched on the Fort du Rocher. By all accounts he carried the stronghold by a direct assault, then held its defenses in the face of a series of counterattacks launched from the island hinterland. Within a week the resistance had been crushed, although it soon became clear that the majority of the buccaneers had fled the island before the Spanish arrived. A total of 330 buccaneers were captured, including the French governor's brother, while another 170 inhabitants—presumably women and slaves—were shipped to Santo Domingo with the rest of the captives. All the prisoners would become slaves on Spanish plantations. In addition the Spanish captured some 70 artillery pieces and goods valued at approximately 160,000 silver pesos, or pieces-of-eight.

Although the Spanish left behind a small company-size garrison, it was evacuated in April 1654 after the troops slighted the island's defenses. This was shortsighted, as within a year the buccaneers started to return to Tortuga, and by 1660 the island was fully operational again as a buccaneering haven. However, by that stage a new buccaneering den had become established on Jamaica, and, unlike the shantytown of Cayonne, this would soon develop into one of the most bustling and best-defended ports in the Spanish Main. The days of Tortuga were numbered, although the French government's encouragement of privateering meant that the island would enjoy one last hurrah—a golden age when Tortuga became the busiest buccaneering haven in the New World.

In 1664 the French West India Company took over the administration of Tortuga, and the English governor in Jamaica removed the restrictions he had imposed that prevented English buccaneers from using the French island as a base. The new French governor, Bertrand d'Ogeron, tried to convert the freewheeling buccaneering society he found there into something more akin to an established colony, but the locals had little sympathy for his reforms. His solution was to introduce new French colonists, but his country's policy of encouraging privateering meant that he needed the buccaneers, so his plans came to nothing. Instead he concentrated his efforts on gaining some control over the buccaneering fleets by imposing restrictions on the letters of marque he issued.

The 1660s were a period when Tortuga was the center of a large-scale privateering operation, directed by Louis XIV's government through Bertrand d'Ogeron. In theory, when Spain and France signed the Treaty of the Pyrenees in 1659 the two countries were officially at peace—the first time that Spain had not been at war with somebody since 1621. However, in 1661 Philip IV of Spain ordered his armies to invade Portugal, so beginning a seven-year conflict that drained the Spanish treasury for little practical gain. The English sided with the Portuguese, which meant that the Spanish colonies were fair game for English privateers. Then in 1667 Louis XIV invaded the Spanish Netherlands, uniting the Dutch, the English, and the Imperialists (Spain and Germany) against him. Although the war only lasted a year (by which time the Dutch and the English were at war with each other), the fighting was resumed in 1673. This time it lasted for six years. Meanwhile the Third Dutch War (1672–74) had broken out.[5]

While this all seemed a little confusing, it meant that the issuing of letters of marque by governors such as Bertrand d'Ogeron was fraught with difficulty. Given the delay in communications between colony and home country, and governor and privateering captain, it was inevitable that privateering would often continue for some time after a war officially ended in Europe. Therefore the English governors of Jamaica and Barbados, the French governors of Tortuga and Martinique, and the Dutch governors of St. Eustatius and Curaçao all adopted the expedient policy that, while wars might come and go between their three powers, the Spanish would always remain the enemy. Therefore, unless direct orders came from Europe, the Spanish were regarded as fair game. This meant that Dutch, English, and French buccaneers tended to work together, regardless of the political situation at home.

The notorious buccaneer L'Ollonnais (see p.121) used the island as a base for raids against the cities of the Spanish Main, aided by his deputy Michel le Basque. Together with Port Royal, Tortuga provided a base for substantial buccaneering fleets, and this heyday of buccaneering continued well into the 1670s. What brought it to an end was not the activities of the buccaneers themselves but the interference of national governments, who had been trying to control the buccaneers since the 1640s. The final death knell was the Treaty of Ratisborn (Regensburg) of 1684, a Franco-Spanish peace treaty that ended the days of freely issued letters of marque. The French buccaneers drifted away, and although privateering work would resume by the end of the decade, it was too late for Tortuga. By the mid-1680s at the latest, the island had become little more than it had been when the buccaneering phenomenon first began—a trading post built on the declining trade in wild Hispaniolan beef.

A TALE OF TWO BIOGRAPHIES

In 1678, the Amsterdam publisher Jan ten Horn began selling copies of a new book, *De Americaensche Zee-Rovers*, written by one Alexander Oliver Exquemelin. It proved an instant success in Holland, and it was soon reprinted in several other languages, including Spanish, French, and English (as *Buccaneers of America*).

Exquemelin was a French doctor who was employed by the French West India Company and participated in the filibuster raids of the 1660s and early 1670s. He had firsthand experience of these men and would have talked to others who sailed with Myngs and Morgan. He returned to the Spanish Main in 1697 and participated in the French attack on Cartagena, but he was back in Amsterdam the following year and died there nine years later.

The next pirate biography was even more successful. In 1724 the London publisher Charles Rivington began selling a small book by an unknown author, Captain Charles Johnson. *A General History of the Robberies and Murders of the Most Notorious Pyrates* proved so popular that Rivington was forced to reprint a new and expanded edition of the book within months. The book contained a series of pirate biographies, all of British or British-born swashbucklers, and is still in print today.

We know next to nothing about Captain Charles Johnson, except that his writing demonstrates an intimate knowledge of seamanship and maritime life and that much of what he wrote about the pirates of the golden age of piracy was substantially accurate. Captain Johnson was probably a pseudonym, concealing a piratical past, or simply a nom de plume. Several candidates have been proposed, including Rivington himself and Charles Johnson the playwright— neither of whom had the necesssary maritime experience.[6]

A stronger candidate is Daniel Defoe, the author of *Robinson Crusoe* (1719) and *Captain Singleton* (1720). Defoe was widely traveled, and could have gathered enough nautical knowledge to write such a salty tale. While the identity of the author remains a mystery, there is no escaping the contribution Johnson's book made to pirate history. Like Exquemelin before him, his writing forms the cornerstone of all subsequent pirate histories and remains one of the most useful tools for the pirate historian.

As for the Brethren of the Coast, it was never a united confederation—a force to be reckoned with. Throughout the 1660s and 1670s it remained what it had always been—a loose alliance of individuals, pairs, groups, and crews of buccaneers, unified by a common temporary goal rather than by any larger political union. As such they were willing to join forces under the leadership of a dynamic buccaneering captain such as L'Ollonnais or Henry Morgan, but as soon as the expedition returned to Port Royal or Tortuga, any allegiance became null and void. By the 1670s the term was mainly used to refer to the English buccaneers based in Port Royal, and Morgan even styled himself the "Admiral of the Coast"—suggesting that at least for a while he was the top dog in what was otherwise a society of equals.

THE WESTERN DESIGN

While the English managed to secure a few of the Windward Islands during the early seventeenth century, these small islands—Barbados, Antigua, St. Kitts and Nevis—all lay far from the heart of the Spanish Main. During the 1650s England's Lord Protector, Oliver Cromwell, decided that now that he had won the civil war, England was free to embark on a war with Spain. The reason was largely economic; English merchants wanted free access to the ports of the East Indies and the Spanish Main, and by striking at the heart of the Spanish overseas empire, Cromwell hoped to secure his own national stake in the New World.[7]

During the Anglo-Spanish War of 1654–59, General-at-Sea (Admiral) Robert Blake blockaded Cadiz, while in 1656 one of his commanders—Vice Admiral Richard Stayner—intercepted a homebound treasure fleet as it tried to run the blockade, capturing two galleons filled with an estimated one million gold escudos, or eight million pieces-of-eight. However, most of the plunder was divided amongst the English sailors long before it reached the safety of London. However lucrative it might be, this blockade was only a diversion. The centerpiece of Cromwell's "Western Design" was an assault on the very heart of the Spanish Main.

Cromwell hoped to attack the Spanish in the Caribbean but also to avoid being drawn into a full-scale war at home in Europe. Cromwell's planners decided to raise a special force and use it to assault Hispaniola, which an intelligence source claimed was only lightly defended. This force consisted of raw troops—adventurers in search of a new life in the Caribbean, augmented by the sweepings of the regular army. The experienced commander Richard Venables was placed in command of the expedition, supported by General-at-Sea William Penn and Daniel Searle, the governor of Barbados. The 3,000 newly raised troops and some 18 warships were placed at his disposal, while a further 6,000 men were promised—to be raised in the English colonies in the West Indies.

The fleet arrived off Barbados in early 1655, and, augmented by these fresh recruits, the expedition headed towards Hispaniola, arriving off Santo Domingo on April 13. By that time Venables and Penn were at loggerheads, and sickness amongst the troops meant that morale was low. Nevertheless Venables went ahead with the invasion, landing his raw army 25 miles west of the port. It took his men four days to reach Santo Domingo, by which time the shortage of supplies and water, and pinprick attacks by the Spanish, had further sapped morale. After repulsing a Spanish attack Venables decided to fall back to the beachhead. After resupplying his army he tried again, but on April 24 another Spanish attack all but broke the English force. Venables called off the assault and returned to the safety of Penn's ships.

Hoping to salvage something from the disaster, Venables and Penn decided to attack Jamaica, which was reportedly held by a negligible Spanish force. On May 11 the fleet arrived off the island and this time the main settlement of Santiago de la Vega was captured without any major setback. Within a week the Spanish were forced to abandon the island and fled to the safety of nearby Cuba. Although thwarted on Hispaniola, the English now had a useful consolation prize—Jamaica was sited in the very center of the Caribbean basin and was therefore well placed as a base for further raids against the Spanish Main. While the two English commanders returned home, their unfortunate troops left behind built their own strongpoint, Fort Cromwell, on the tip of the sand spit known as the Palisadoes, which closed off the entrance to the island's main anchorage—now Kingston Harbor. The fort was later renamed Passage Fort, and a small settlement known as Cagway (or sometimes the Point) was built up on the spit beside the fort.

Santiago de la Vega (renamed Spanish Town) became the main agricultural center of the island, while Cagway became the maritime hub—attracting buccaneers, traders, shipwrights, and prostitutes. However, the island's economy was slow to develop, despite the influx of 1,600 English settlers drafted in from Nevis in late 1656. Many of the soldiers who stayed behind took to farming, while others looked for an easier way to make a living. Inevitably it was the war with Spain that provided them with the chance to make some easy money.

Although Jamaica never caught on as a privateering and buccaneering center until after 1660, it was clear that if the colony was to survive, it could only do so with the help of the Brethren of the Coast.

Captain Christopher Myngs was one of the first to realize that the buccaneers were the island's initial line of defense. The Norfolk-born sailor served in the English Navy Royal before the English Civil War, and along with most of the fleet he sided with Parliament in the war against King Charles. By 1656 he commanded the modern 44-gun warship *Marston Moor*—one of the most powerful vessels in Cromwell's Commonwealth navy. In January that year the *Marston Moor* arrived off Cagway, and Myngs became the deputy to Vice Admiral William Goodson, the commander of the Commonwealth squadron based in Jamaica. Goodson was a firm advocate of the policy of proactive defense, and he encouraged Myngs to enlist the aid of English buccaneers based in Tortuga, offering them the use of Cagway in exchange for their help in defending the island. The Jamaican governor, Edward d'Oyley, fully supported Myngs's scheme, issuing letters of marque to Goodson's and Myngs's new allies.

In early 1656, Goodson and Myngs led a raid on the South American coast, attacking the small town of Santa Marta in what is now Colombia. A second raid was launched that spring, this time against Rio de la Hatcha, further up the same coast. When Goodson was recalled to England in January 1657, Myngs assumed command of the Jamaican squadron of three Commonwealth frigates—and he also became the de facto leader of a buccaneering fleet. The success of these first raids attracted more buccaneers from Tortuga to Cagway, which meant he could stage even larger raids. The Spanish tried their best to respond; in May 1658 an expedition sent from Vera Cruz landed some 550 troops on the island, but Myngs countered the Spanish move by destroying their transports, thus buying time for d'Oyley to contain and then defeat the Spanish force.

By way of retaliation Myngs led another expedition to the Tierra Firme coast, attacking Santa Marta again, then the smaller settlement of Tolú, below Cartagena. He then split the fleet, leading part of it towards Cumana on the Venezuelan coast, while the rest operated off Cartagena. Off Coro he managed to intercept a Dutch ship transporting specie on behalf of the Spanish—a haul valued at £50,000, or 400,000 pieces-of-eight. Unfortunately on his return to Cagway he discovered that the crew had stolen the bulk of this plunder, although Governor d'Oyley was not convinced and sent Myngs back to England to face charges of theft. However, luck was with him, as in the interim Cromwell had died, and the exiled Charles II had been invited to reclaim his father's throne. In a remarkable reversal of fortune, Charles II not only accepted Myngs's protestations of loyalty, but he also removed d'Oyley from office. Myngs returned to Jamaica in August 1662 as a captain in the new Royal Navy—a free man and a powerful one. He must have taken particular delight in giving passage to Lord Windsor, d'Oyley's replacement as the governor of Jamaica.[8]

PORT ROYAL: THE WICKEDEST CITY ON EARTH

In the spirit of the Restoration, Fort Cromwell was renamed Fort Charles, while Cagway became Port Royal. Charles even enticed a new wave of settlers to Jamaica, who helped transform the island's fragile economy. In fact the only thing that seemed to remain the same was the policy of encouraging privateering, despite the official end of the war with Spain in 1659. In the process Cagway—now Port Royal—developed into a boisterous haven for buccaneers. As the reappointed commander of the Jamaica squadron, Myngs flew his flag in the 46-gun man-of-war HMS *Centurion*, although he realized that his real strength lay in the buccaneer vessels clustered beneath the guns of Fort Charles. Spain and England might now be at peace, but both Myngs and Lord Windsor refused to let that little technicality get in the way of the policy of a proactive defense. After all, the Spanish still refused to recognize the English claim to Jamaica and barred her merchants from trading with Spanish ports. Clearly it was time to teach the Spanish a lesson.

In September 1662 Windsor offered to grant letters of marque "in order to subdue our enemies on land and at sea, along the entire coast of America." Although it was never stated, it was obvious who the enemy was meant to be. By the end of the month Myngs had gathered a small fleet and raised a force of some 1,300 men—400 of whom were former Western Design soldiers, the rest buccaneers. On October 1 he headed out to sea, sailing westwards around Jamaica to avoid Spanish naval patrols. Off Cape Negril he held a council of war and told his followers their target was Santiago—the second-largest city in Cuba, some 200 miles away to the northeast. Just over two weeks later he anchored off the mouth of the San Juan River—the same place the Americans would land during the Santiago campaign of 1898. By dawn the following morning Myngs and 1,000 men were just 3 miles east of the city.

Governor Pedro Morales knew the English were coming, but he never expected them to attack so quickly. He had just 250 men under his direct command, while his deputy Cristobal de Isasi Arnaldo commanded a 500-man reserve. Unfortunately for Morales, Myngs had already come to an agreement with de Isasi, and when the buccaneers attacked, the Spanish reserve turned on their heels and fled. Morales was overwhelmed, and the city fell to the attackers, along with seven trading ships riding at anchor in the harbor. The plunder turned out to be disappointing, particularly when it had to be shared with the turncoat de Isasi and his men. However, Myngs turned his men loose on the city, then set about systematically destroying all its defenses and major buildings, including the cathedral. It was later said that it took the inhabitants a whole decade to recover from the damage caused by Myngs and his men.

The following year Myngs led his buccaneers out for another large-scale raid, this time against the coast of New Spain (Mexico). On this occasion his force of 1,500 men included a handful of Dutch and French buccaneers, making it a truly international privateering force—albeit one operating under the protection of the king of England. He headed to Campeche, on the western side of the Yucatan Peninsula, but part of his fleet was dispersed by bad weather, and so by the time the *Centurion* made landfall just south of Campeche, only two-thirds of the buccaneer force remained. Myngs decided to attack anyway. Despite the alarm being raised by Spanish patrols, the defenders were unable to halt the dawn onslaught, and within an hour most of Campeche was in English hands.

However, a spirited group of 150 militiamen still held out in the fort, and Myngs was forced to lay siege to the defenses, his troops supported by the guns of the *Centurion*. Although the defenders were eventually forced to surrender, Myngs was wounded in the fighting and taken back to his flagship to be treated. His deputy, Captain Edward Mansfield, took over the command, and it was he who negotiated the official surrender of the province by Governor Antonio Maldonado de Aldana. The buccaneers remained in Campeche for two weeks, then returned to Port Royal with their spoils. This time Myngs wasn't taking any chances and kept the plunder well guarded during the voyage home. In all some 150,000 pieces-of-eight were turned over to Acting Governor Thomas Lynch in Jamaica when the *Centurion* returned to port in April 1663, and Myngs and his men were the toast of the town.

Unfortunately Charles II then yielded to Spanish diplomatic pressure and forbade further raids. In 1665 a fresh war with the Dutch led to Myngs and the *Centurion* being ordered back to England. On his return home he was promoted to the rank of vice admiral, and in June 1666 led a squadron into action during the engagement known as the Four Days' Battle. Myngs proved himself a gifted commander and was knighted for his services in the engagement. However, just seven weeks later he was dead—killed by a Dutch sharpshooter during the battle of North Foreland on August 5, 1666. England had lost a valuable naval commander and a highly successful buccaneer. In Jamaica Myngs had almost single-handedly turned Port Royal into the largest buccaneering haven in the Caribbean, and his example would be followed by others—men like Henry Morgan—who would lead Myngs's buccaneers on larger and more daring raids and in the process wreak havoc in the very heart of the Spanish Main.

As for Port Royal, the town prospered in the decade following Myngs's departure. He might have encouraged the buccaneers to use the place as their own, but he would have been surprised and not a little alarmed by his success. After all, Port Royal was ideally placed for raids on the Spanish Main, from the Tierra Firme coast of South America to the Mexican coast of New Spain. Jamaica also lay south of Cuba, allowing buccaneers to lie off both ends of the islands, yet still remain within easy sail of their base. Its harbor could hold hundreds of ships, while the authorities actively encouraged the buccaneers to plunder from the Spanish, regardless of whether England and Spain were at war. In effect, Myngs and others created the perfect pirate haven.[9]

The conversion of Port Royal into a buccaneering haven did not stop there. It was inevitable that merchants would follow in the wake of the buccaneers, making sure that Port Royal provided a ready market for plunder—cloth, rum, slaves, tobacco—whatever the buccaneers could lay their hands on. Warehouses were built to hold this merchandise, which was then sold on to more legitimate merchants for a substantial profit. By the late 1660s Port Royal was a thriving but lawless boomtown of some 6,000 people, and the authorities were keen to turn a blind eye to any excesses. After all, many of Jamaica's leading landowners and merchants had a stake in buccaneering—they owned the businesses and warehouses that supported all these privateering activities—and consequently they grew rich from their share of Spanish plunder. During its heyday Port Royal was larger and more prosperous than any other city in the Americas, apart from Boston.

These landowners did not restrict themselves to merchant ventures. Taverns, brothels, and gambling dens sprang up by the score, all vying with each other to deprive the buccaneers of their money. In fact it was said that a fifth of the town's buildings were "brothels, gaming houses, taverns and grog shops." It was the perfect party town—a sailor's dream. However, others were less impressed. A visiting English clergyman said of Port Royal: "This town is the Sodom of the New World … its population consists of pirates, cutthroats, whores and some of the vilest persons in the whole of the world."

More accurately, he probably took exception to the population's laissez-faire attitude towards religion. Unlike the straitlaced towns of colonial America, Port Royal provided a welcome haven for people of all religious persuasions, including Jewish and Catholic practitioners. However, it was still a rough and often violent place. For example, one particularly unsavory buccaneer, a Dutchman known as Roche Braziliano, was known to roam the streets of Port Royal in a drunken frenzy, attacking anyone unlucky enough to cross his path. No wonder another visitor called Port Royal "the wickedest city on earth."

What finally killed Port Royal as a pirate den was the same thing that ended Tortuga's glory days—good government. Henry Morgan's great raid on Panama took place between 1670 and 1671, three years after a peace treaty had been signed with the Spanish. The same treaty allowed English merchants to trade with Spanish colonies, thereby removing the long-term economic threat to the survival of Jamaica. Peace also meant that the island was no longer threatened by a Spanish invasion. In 1671 the governor, Sir Thomas Lynch, threatened to take legal action against buccaneers who continued to attack the Spanish. After all, with no war going on, these privateers had effectively become pirates. As a pragmatist, Lynch also saw the need to pardon some of the worst (and most powerful) offenders, as part of a carrot-and-stick approach to illegal buccaneering.

In 1675 Sir Henry Morgan became deputy governor and served as acting governor twice—in 1678, then again from 1680 to 1682. Ironically, under his leadership an antipiracy law was passed by the Jamaican legislature (1681), and the following year Sir Thomas Lynch resumed control of the island and continued his policy of discouraging buccaneering. The result of all this was that by the early 1680s at the latest, buccaneering was no longer considered a viable business in Port Royal. Slaves, sugar, and rum became the new staples of the Jamaican economy. As the merchants turned to more legitimate pursuits, and the selling of plundered goods became harder, sailors were forced to operate elsewhere; for instance, many ventured into the Pacific.[10]

The final blow came in 1692, at exactly 11:40 a.m. on June 7, when the first tremors of an earthquake hit Port Royal. The first shock was followed by other stronger ones, and within minutes buildings throughout the town had collapsed, while the northern section of Port Royal slid into the sea, taking most of the docks with it. Clearly building a town on the end of a sandy spit had its drawbacks.

Thousands were trapped in the rubble or drowned in the tsunami that followed. Some 2,000 townspeople died that day, and a similar number perished in the next weeks from disease or injury. The town never recovered, and a fire in 1702 destroyed much of what had been rebuilt amidst its ruins. Following another earthquake in 1722 the town was abandoned, and the sands slowly covered over what ruins were left. There were those who saw this as a final divine judgement on what was once described as "that wicked and rebellious place, Port Royal."

LOWLIFES OF THE CARIBBEAN

It is inevitable that any account of the buccaneers who preyed on the Spanish Main in the seventeenth century will be dominated by the most spectacular of them—men such as Henry Morgan, whose story is covered later in the chapter, L'Ollonnais, and Christopher Myngs. However, the buccaneers were made up of small groups of individual vessels and their crews, who joined forces under these great captains for a particular venture. This meant that for every Henry Morgan, there were dozens of less successful buccaneers—men who barely scraped a living from their activities. A quick survey of a couple whose careers were recorded by Exquemelin also reveals a little about the type of men who turned to buccaneering during this period.

Roche (or Rock) Braziliano was one of the Dutchmen who settled in Brazil, as part of the Dutch West India Company's venture there. In 1630 the Dutch company captured Recife (Pernambuco) from the Portuguese—the most westerly part of the Brazilian coast. This colony, known as New Holland, was short-lived. The Portuguese besieged Recife intermittently from 1645, and despite several relief attempts the colony finally capitulated in January 1654. When the garrison was evicted "Rock the Brazilian" somehow drifted elsewhere in the Americas—probably to Curaçao—and at some time after 1655 he turned up in Cagway, where as a sailor and probably an experienced Dutch privateersman, he found himself in demand. However, at some point he quarrelled with the captain of his ship, and together with a small group of followers he deserted in the ship's boat.

According to Exquemelin, Braziliano succeeded in capturing a small Spanish vessel, probably by using the techniques adopted by Pierre le Grand. He therefore returned to Cagway as a buccaneering captain and continued to operate out of Jamaica during the late 1650s, either on his own or as part of a larger expedition. His big break came when he captured a Spanish galleon outward bound from Vera Cruz in Mexico—a prize that catapulted him further up the buccaneering league table. However, his successes were tempered by spells of wild behaviour. On his return to Cagway he and his followers "wasted in a few days in taverns all they had gained, by giving themselves to all manner of debauchery." After a bout of heavy drinking he "would oftimes shew himself either brutish or foolish … he would run up and down the street, beating and wounding whom he met, no person daring to oppose him or make any resistance."[11] Even compared with the worst excesses of the buccaneers, Braziliano sets himself apart as a particularly unlikable psychopath.

During one expedition to Campeche, he was captured by the Spanish and thrown into the port's jail. Exquemelin is a little vague on the timing here, but Braziliano may well have been tortured while in prison and revealed the location of a hidden cache of plunder the buccaneers had established on Cuba's Isla de la Juventud (Isle of Youth). While in prison Braziliano forged a letter, supposedly written by accomplices outside the city, who threatened to sack Campeche and slaughter its inhabitants if the captives were executed. The governor felt intimidated enough to cancel the planned execution, and instead he shipped Braziliano and his crew onto the next ship bound for Spain. Once there, Braziliano managed to escape and make his way back to Jamaica.

Like many of Exquemelin's tales, his account of Roche Braziliano lacks dates or much in the way of corroborative evidence. However, he places him back in Cagway (now Port Royal) at the time the buccaneering captain L'Ollonnais was active there, probably around 1668, and he suggests that Braziliano joined the Frenchman's party. Like his leader, the Dutchman gained an unsavory reputation for the brutal execution and torture of Spanish prisoners. Exquemelin said of Braziliano: "He perpetrated the greatest atrocities possible against the Spaniards. Some of them he tied or spitted on wooden stakes and roasted them alive between two fires, like killing a pig." He certainly was not a man to be crossed, although to be fair many other buccaneers also tortured prisoners in an attempt to discover the location of hidden plunder. However, Braziliano's excuse was that the Spaniards he roasted had withheld the whereabouts of their pigs.

Roche Braziliano wasn't one to learn from his mistakes, as by 1669 he was back in the Gulf of Campeche, and just as before, the expedition ended in disaster. This time Braziliano ran his ship aground and was forced to abandon it. He knew that buccaneers frequently used the far side of the Yucatan Peninsula near the island of Cozumel as a watering place, and so he decided to lead his men across country in an attempt to find a passing friendly ship. Pursuing

Spanish patrols were kept at bay by musket fire, and eventually Braziliano and his men cut their way through to the coast, where he stumbled upon a logwood camp. The harvesting of logwood—valuable for the dye it produced—was a lucrative industry in Central America during this period. The buccaneers drove off the loggers, then stole their supplies and a boat—probably a small pinnace—and made their way home to Port Royal. After that Roche Braziliano fades from the history books, which means he probably died in Port Royal soon after his return in or around 1670. Given his reputation, it is far from unlikely that he ended his days in a Port Royal alleyway with a knife in his back.

A buccaneer who was even less successful than the psychotic Dutchman was Bartolomeo el Portugues. Exquemelin places the Portuguese buccaneer in Jamaica soon after the island's capture by the English. At first he served as a buccaneering crewman, participating in raids on the Spanish Main. These might well have been the expeditions led by Christopher Myngs against the Tierra Firme in 1657 and 1658. However, within a few years Bartolomeo had secured his own modest command—a small pinnace armed with four guns and crewed by 30 men. He cruised off the southern coast of Cuba, evidently hoping to prey

The Dutch buccaneer Rock, or Roche, Braziliano was regarded as something of a psychopath.

The buccaneer Bartolomeo el Portugues (Bartholomew the Portuguese) was dogged by consistent bad luck during his brief career.

on Spanish coastal shipping. However, in his first attack he was repulsed, losing half his crew in the struggle. Undeterred he attacked again, and this time he captured the prize, which contained a coin chest and a cargo of cocoa beans. Bartolomeo was forced to abandon his pinnace, as he lacked the crew to sail both vessels. However, strong contrary southwesterly winds prevented him from sailing directly back to Cagway, so instead he headed east, parallel to the southern coast of Cuba, hoping for a more fortuitous wind. Instead he bumped into a patrol from the Armada de Barlovento.

The encounter took place off Cape San Antonio—the western tip of Cuba— and the buccaneers found they had nowhere to run. Bartolomeo el Portugues was captured and found himself shackled in the hold of one of the warships. The same winds that had hampered the buccaneers now developed into a full-blown tropical storm, and, unable to bear round towards Havana, the Spanish naval squadron was driven into the Gulf of Campeche. It was decided to try to execute the prisoners in Campeche itself, before the squadron sailed on to Havana. Somehow the buccaneers escaped and swam for the shore. Like Roche Braziliano in 1669, Bartolomeo and his fellow survivors elected to hack their way through the jungles of the Yucatan Peninsula, hoping to rendezvous with a friendly ship somewhere near modern-day Cancun. Amazingly they made it, and even managed to find a passing ship that took them back to Jamaica.

Bartolomeo el Portugues was hell-bent on revenge, so, as soon as he could, he returned to Campeche, this time with 20 men in a piragua—a form of large seagoing canoe. He approached Campeche to find a ship at anchor in the roads. Exquemelin suggests it was the warship that had captured him, but this is highly unlikely. If anything, it might have been his original prize—the cocoa transport. The buccaneers stealthily entered the harbor, overwhelmed the men on watch, and cut out the prize from under the noses of the Spanish garrison. The ship was even fully laden with cargo, and at last it seemed as if Bartolomeo's luck had changed. However, disaster struck again when he ran the prize aground near the Isle of Pines. He had no option but to abandon ship and take to the boats, which is how he made his ignominious return to Cagway.

During the years that followed—the Restoration period and beyond— Bartolomeo continued to serve as a buccaneer working out of Jamaica. Unfortunately his story did not have a particularly happy ending. As Exquemelin put it, Bartolomeo made "many violent attacks on the Spaniards without gaining much profit from marauding, for I saw him dying in the greatest wretchedness in the world."[12] Presumably he was another buccaneer who ended his days begging, starving, and dying on the rum-sodden streets of Port Royal. What is particularly interesting about both of these characters is that they highlight two things. First, buccaneering was a risky business, and while the profits could be huge, so too were the inherent dangers. Second, both buccaneers shared the same trait—an intense drive that let them continue on in the face of often severe setbacks. Buccaneers might have been united by their hatred of the Spanish, but they also showed a remarkable collective determination that allowed them to achieve much.

L'OLLONNAIS: THE FLAIL OF THE SPANIARDS

According to Exquemelin, "the flail of the Spaniards" hailed from the fishing town of Les Sables d'Olonne, just up the coast from La Rochelle, on the French Atlantic coast. It was his birthplace that provided him with his buccaneering nickname— "L'Ollonnais," the man from Olonne. That whole region of France was considered a Huguenot enclave, so the chances were that the buccaneer the Spanish called El Olonés was a Protestant. Exquemelin also provided a name for the buccaneer— François Nau—although his real name might well have been Jean David Nau (or Naud). It seems typical of the buccaneers, many of whom adopted a new identity when they arrived in the Caribbean, or rather when they turned to buccaneering.

As a teenager, probably around 1660, he was sent to the French colony of Martinique as an indentured servant—someone who had to spend several years as an unpaid laborer in exchange for working off their passage. After three years he was freed from his obligations and drifted to Tortuga, which by then would have been recovering from its latest assault by the Spanish. Apparently he spent time hunting with the *boucaniers* on the mainland of Hispaniola before turning to piracy. On Tortuga he was given, or more likely bought, a small vessel—a ten-gun sloop, probably a prize captured by other buccaneers. As the donor was Governor Bertrand d'Ogeron, it seems likely he purchased it during a privateering auction and division of plunder. By 1667 France and Spain were officially at war again, although the conflict only lasted a year. Still, it gave d'Ogeron the excuse he needed to issue privateering licences—and to encourage up-and-coming buccaneers. L'Ollonnais therefore gathered a crew of some 20 men, prepared his vessel for sea, and set off in search of Spanish prey.

He proved highly successful. In the Mona Passage off the eastern coast of Hispaniola he intercepted a Spanish merchantman, which he captured after a hard fight. Another Spanish ship carrying a military payroll fell to the buccaneers, and each time L'Ollonnais sent the prize back to Tortuga, where he sold the cargo, refitted the vessel, and crewed her with more pirates. However, according to Exquemelin, it was around this time he suffered a temporary setback. One of his earliest raids was against the unfortunate town of Campeche. Exquemelin suggested that L'Ollonnais lost part of his force through shipwreck during the voyage from Tortuga and so he lacked the men to capture the city. L'Ollonnais threw himself into the assault anyway. The attack was a disaster, and the buccaneering leader only escaped by playing dead, lying amongst the corpses until dark. He finally managed to steal a couple of piraguas and escaped together with a handful of his men.

Unfortunately, there is no evidence that Campeche was attacked between Myngs's raid in 1663 and another raid by the filibusters de Graaf and Grammont in 1685. What is more likely was that some time around 1666 or 1667—before he built up a substantial following—he was shipwrecked near Campeche, then hounded by Spanish patrols until he and his men were able to escape. The next anecdote supplied by the biographer fits neatly with this story. Shortly afterwards—probably on his way back to Tortuga—he was passing Cayo Largo, a cay lying off the southern coast of Cuba. Local fishermen had reported the presence of buccaneers, so the governor of Havana sent a patrol boat to deal with them; its crew included a hangman.

Instead the hunters became the hunted, as L'Ollonnais and his men boarded the Spanish vessel as she lay at anchor, her crew asleep. The buccaneers massacred their prisoners, leaving one man to take a message back to the Cuban governor. As Exquemelin phrased it, L'Ollonnais' note declared:

> I shall never henceforward give quarter to any Spaniard whatsoever; and I have great hopes I shall execute on your own person the very same punishment I have done upon them you sent against me. Thus I have retaliated the kindness you designed to me and my companions.

In other words, L'Ollonnais was fighting his own personal war against the Spanish, and from that point on he would take no prisoners and give no quarter. The Frenchman then sailed his prize back to Tortuga. By keeping his prizes and crewing them with buccaneer volunteers, L'Ollonnais rapidly built up his force from a single small ship to a powerful buccaneering squadron—by late 1667 he commanded eight ships crewed by at least 400 men.

He was now a force to be reckoned with and was able to contemplate launching raids against substantial Spanish coastal settlements. His deputies at this time were Michael the Basque (Miguel el Basco to the Spanish), Pierre le Picard, and the Dutch buccaneer van Klijn. L'Ollonnais selected the Tierra Firme as his first real target, and in September 1667 his squadron arrived in the Gulf of Venezuela—the entrance to the great lagoon known as the Lago de Maracaibo. He began his assault by storming the battery that guarded the entrance to the Lago, at Maracaibo Bar. This allowed him to enter the lagoon. By the time the buccaneers descended on the region's main port of Maracaibo, they found the town had been abandoned—the inhabitants having fled into the hinterland. L'Ollonnais spent two weeks there, his men rooting through the town in search of hidden caches of money and patrolling the region looking for townspeople to interrogate. The haul was still pitifully small.

Undeterred, L'Ollonnais crossed the lagoon to the smaller town of Gibraltar (now called Bobures), which was not only still occupied but was also defended by a Spanish garrison. Landing just outside the town, the buccaneers stormed the defenses and captured Gibraltar after a particularly bloody fight that probably ended with the massacre of L'Ollonnais's Spanish prisoners. This time the buccaneers stayed in the town for a month, demanding a ransom from the

The French buccaneer L'Ollonnais developed a reputation for excessive cruelty.

123

governor of 10,000 pieces-of-eight. When this was paid L'Ollonnais led another surprise raid on Maracaibo, where another ransom of 20,000 pieces-of-eight was paid to prevent him from destroying the settlement. After a brief visit to the Isle à Vache (Cow Island) off the southern coast of Hispaniola to divide the booty, then a call to Port Royal to sell off some of his prizes, L'Ollonnais returned to Tortuga, where he would have been feted as a buccaneering hero. The total haul of plunder was estimated at around 260,000 pieces-of-eight.

Another account of his activities suggests that in 1668 L'Ollonnais led a major raid against the Central American coast, but, instead of Campeche, his objective was the Mosquito Coast—now Nicaragua. The area had only just been raided by a group of English buccaneers, who had launched their attack from Port Royal three years before. On that occasion the buccaneers sailed up the San Juan River to the inland town of Granada, sacked it, then withdrew before the Spanish could react. L'Ollonnais was less fortunate, as bad weather and contrary winds prevented him from making a landfall on the Mosquito Coast and instead he landed up off the northern coast of Honduras, off the small Spanish port of Puerto Cabellos (the "port of horses," now called Puerto Cortés). He landed and captured the town together with a well-armed Spanish merchant ship at anchor in the harbor. He then led 300 of his men towards San Pedro Sula, the regional capital, which lay some 30 miles (48 km) from the coast.

The Spanish made several attempts to ambush the buccaneers as they marched on the town, but it was no use. L'Ollonnais and his men pressed on and eventually stormed San Pedro, driving the Spanish defenders into the jungle. After plundering the town the buccaneers razed it to the ground, then returned to their ships, carrying their loot with them. L'Ollonnais then learned that the annual Honduras treasure galleon was due to arrive in the area, so he decided to intercept it. The Spanish ship finally showed up three months late, and after it was captured in a particularly bloody action, L'Ollonnais discovered it had already unloaded its cargo in Trujillo, just up the coast. The buccaneers had wasted their time.

Long before he arrived in Honduras L'Ollonnais had developed a reputation for barbarity. In a way this played against him, as Spanish captains such as the commander of the Honduras galleon would prefer to fight to the end rather than surrender to L'Ollonnais and face being tortured to death. After all, as Exquemelin put it, "It was the custom of L'Ollonnais that, having tormented any persons and they not confessing, he would instantly cut them to pieces with his hanger (sword) and pull on their tongues." That was when he was feeling magnanimous. On other occasions he would resort to "burning with matches and suchlike torments, to cut a man to pieces, first some flesh, then a hand, then an arm, a leg, sometimes tying a cord about his head and with a stick twisting it till his eyes shoot out, which is called woolding." He continued, "When L'Ollonnais had a victim on the rack, if the wretch did not instantly answer his questions he would hack the man to pieces with his cutlass and lick the blood from the blade with his tongue, wishing it might have been the last Spaniard in the world he had thus killed."[13] An example of this barbarity is provided during his march on San Pedro. He used two Spanish prisoners as guides, and after being ambushed by Spanish troops he suspected that the men had deliberately led him into a trap. Consequently he "ripped open one of the prisoners with his cutlass, tore the living heart out of his body, gnawed at it, and then hurled it in the face of one of the others." The remaining prisoner immediately decided to cooperate and suggested an approach route that would not be covered by the Spanish defenders. The buccaneers then captured and burned San Pedro.

It was just after the attack on the Honduras galleon that L'Ollonnaiss's expedition fell apart. Van Klijn and Pierre le Picard refused to continue, and they returned to Tortuga accompanied by most of the ships in the squadron. L'Ollonnais was left with just his own flagship and a crew of around 400 men. He worked his way south but ran aground near Punta Mono ("Monkey Point"), just south of Bluefields, on the Mosquito Coast. The survivors made camp on the shore, and while one group made a small boat from the wreckage, L'Ollonnais led the rest on a raid up the San Juan River towards the settlement of Solentiname. This time the Spanish managed to ambush the buccaneers, who were driven back to their camp. L'Ollonnais used the newly built boat to head south towards the comparative safety of the Gulf of Darien.

However, while the area might have been empty of Spanish patrols, it was full of hostile natives. Half-starved, the buccaneers attacked what they thought was a small native village, hoping to find stocks of food. Instead they were surrounded and captured. According to Exquemelin there was only one survivor, who recounted that, along with his men, L'Ollonnais was hacked to pieces, then eaten by the cannibalistic natives. Another version claims that the victors burned the severed pieces of his body, then scattered the ashes to the winds. Whatever the real story, it seems that one of the most brutal and psychopathic of all the buccaneers met a fate that in all probability he richly deserved.

THE RISE OF HENRY MORGAN

These days, Henry Morgan is generally seen as a Falstaff character, a bluff, plump and somewhat comic figure known for swashbuckling his way across the Spanish Main. Such is the legacy of pirate fiction. Certainly he would have appeared larger than life to his contemporaries—that impression was first supplied by Exquemelin in 1678, while Morgan was still very much alive. However, Morgan was so much more—a born leader, a skilled tactician, and a consummate politician. In other words he was a far more complex character than history gives him credit for. For that matter, if he was ever seen as a comic figure during his lifetime, the Spanish failed to get the joke.

Henry Morgan was probably born into a Welsh farming family around 1635, although he never spoke of his early life. It is rumored he went to Barbados as an indentured servant and then moved to Jamaica soon after the island was seized by the English in 1655. In between he might well have visited Tortuga, where his first contact with the buccaneers probably took place. Morgan's reticence to discuss his past meant that even Exquemelin was reduced to speculation rather than relying on hard fact. For the next few years little or nothing is known of him, although he may have participated in a buccaneering raid as early as 1659. In 1662 he was appointed as a captain in the Jamaican militia, which suggests some military experience. Later that same year he was granted a letter of marque, which of course legally empowered him to participate in buccaneering raids against the Spanish.

It is highly probably that Morgan took part in Christopher Myngs's attacks on Santiago de Cuba in 1662 and in his subsequent assault on Campeche the following year. Exquemelin suggests that Morgan owned a small sloop and consequently was a bit player in these early buccaneering dramas. However, by February 1665 his stock had risen sufficiently for him to serve as one of three co-commanders in another raid. Together with the English buccaneer John Morris and the Dutchman David Martien, Morgan landed on the Mexican coast near Santa Maria de la Frontera, at the swampy mouth of the River Grijalva, which ran through Tabasco province. The buccaneers made their way upriver by boat and fell upon the regional capital of Villahermosa, taking the town by complete surprise. Two coastal vessels were commandeered to carry the plunder and captured supplies back to the coast.

The raiders retraced their steps, only to find that a Spanish naval squadron of three powerful frigates sent from Campeche had appeared in their absence. The three buccaneer ships left behind off Santa Maria had been captured or driven off, leaving the raiders with nothing but their little coasters. Undaunted, the three buccaneer captains elected to work their way westwards up the coast in search of a larger ship that could take them to safety. However, the Spanish tracked them down, landing a force of 300 militiamen to capture the interlopers. The buccaneers were ready, having thrown up a defensive palisade, and the Spanish attack was repulsed without much difficulty. The following day—March 19— the buccaneers stumbled across the two Spanish ships, still waiting for their troops to return. Instead they were captured by the English raiders, who discovered they were two of their own ships, which had been captured by the Spanish three weeks earlier. The buccaneers were therefore able to sail off with their plunder.

Rather than head back to Port Royal, the three captains worked their way around the Yucatan Peninsula into the Gulf of Honduras. They raided Trujillo, cutting out a Spanish ship lying at anchor in the port, then continued on to Nicaragua's Mosquito Coast. In early June 1665 they anchored off Punta Mono at the mouth of the San Juan River, then repeated the tactic they had used at Villahermosa—using boats to race up the river before word of their approach reached the inhabitants of Granada, the regional capital. Crossing the Lago de Nicaragua, they fell on the unsuspecting town at dawn on June 29 then spent the next day plundering the place. This time their three ships were waiting for them on their return, and by the end of August the buccaneers were safely back in Port Royal.

Morgan used his share of the plunder wisely, buying the first of several Jamaican plantations, then courting and eventually marrying his cousin Mary, the daughter of his soldier uncle Sir Edward Morgan, the deputy governor of the island. Henry Morgan also cultivated a friendship with the new governor, Thomas Modyford. As a governor Modyford seemed reluctant to turn his buccaneers on the Dutch (with whom the English were currently at war), but instead he favored the continuation of raids against the Spanish—a country with which England was at peace. In fact, one Jamaican merchant complained that "although there has been peace with the Spaniards not long since proclaimed, yet the privateers went out and in, as if there had been an actual war without commission."[14]

This was not strictly fair. Bowing to pressure from London, Modyford authorized at least two expeditions against the Dutch. The first, led by Sir Edward Morgan in 1665, was directed against the island of St. Eustatius, one of the Leeward Islands. Although the raid was a success, Henry Morgan's uncle died of a stroke during the attack. Another larger expedition was launched later that year against the Dutch island of Curaçao, off the Venezuelan coast. Its leader was Captain Edward Mansfield, the former deputy of Christopher Myngs. However, Mansfield was unable to make his buccaneers attack their fellow Protestants, and so he bowed to the inevitable and led them against the Spanish instead.

This expedition almost ended in disaster off the coast of what is now Costa Rica. Having taken on water in the well-known buccaneering rendezvous of the Bocas del Toro (Mouths of the Bull) archipelago, now in northern Panama, Mansfield raided Portete, on the Costa Rican coast. However, when he marched inland towards the regional capital of Cartago he found himself outnumbered by the Spanish, who drove the buccaneers back to his ships. Mansfield was forced to return home empty-handed, but as a consolation he attacked the Spanish island of Santa Catalina as he passed. This island—once the home of the Providence Island Company's colony—was captured and garrisoned by Mansfield and his men, who thought it would make a useful base for future raids.

Back in Jamaica, Henry Morgan missed out on these two raids, but he spent the time consolidating his social and political standing in Jamaica, and may have been influential in securing Governor Thomas Modyford's official support for privateering raids against the Spanish. Consequently, despite a nonaggression pact that was signed between England and Spain in 1667, Modyford claimed that this encouragement of buccaneer raids was necessary because the Spanish still harbored plans to invade Jamaica. In January 1668 he ordered Henry Morgan "to draw together the English privateers and take prisoners of the Spanish nation, whereby you may gain information of that enemy." Although this was essentially a reconnaissance mission, Morgan's letter of marque permitted the capture of Spanish ships on the high seas. However, it said nothing about conducting raids on the coast, which meant that such attacks were technically illegal acts. Morgan's subsequent actions pushed the boundaries of what he and Modyford could get away with.[15]

His first raid showed that Morgan could operate on a scale similar to Christopher Myngs. He assembled a force of ten ships and 500 men and then rendezvoused off the southern coast of Cuba with a force of French buccaneers, who joined him from Tortuga. Together the two groups entered the shoal waters of the Costa de Ana Maria, on the southern side of Cuba's narrow waist. On March 28, 1668, the buccaneers disembarked, then advanced inland for some 40 miles until they reached the provincial capital of Puerto Principe (now called

Camaguey). The buccaneers drove off a Spanish attack, and three days later they stormed and captured the city. Morgan and his men found there was little there to plunder. According to Exquemelin, the raiders locked the inhabitants in a church. Morgan agreed not to burn the building down in return for a ransom of 50,000 pieces-of-eight—a meager reward for such a substantial raid. The buccaneers remained in Puerto Principe for two weeks, unsuccessfully trying to extort an even larger ransom from the Spanish authorities.

Once the buccaneers returned to their ships, the French decided to head home to Tortuga, while the English elected to try attacking an altogether more lucrative target—Porto Bello, the great treasure port on the isthmus of Panama. It was a bold decision—the port was guarded by three forts, although Morgan's sources told him they were undermanned and poorly equipped. In addition the governor of Panama could call on a sizable force of militia and regular troops, meaning the raiders could easily be outnumbered—just as Mansfield's men were three years earlier. Like Mansfield he used the Bocas del Toro as a gathering point, transferring his men into smaller boats before the final approach to the treasure port, some 150 miles to the east across the Golfo de los Mosquitos. It took four days to make the approach, but by the afternoon of July 10 Morgan and his men were just a few miles from their objective.

His force disembarked that evening, and, using the darkness as cover, Morgan marched his men along the coast. The port lay on one side of a bay, with a fort on either side of the harbor, and a third partly built fort covering the beach. Capturing the city would require a combination of speed, surprise and luck. The buccaneers reached Porto Bello's western outskirts just before dawn, and Morgan launched an immediate attack on the city. Within minutes his men were in the town, firing their guns "at everything alive—whites, blacks, even dogs, in order to spread terror." There was still no reaction from the garrisons of the three forts, so later that morning Morgan decided to assault Fort Santiago, which covered the western side of the harbor and was therefore the fort closest to the town.

Morgan had his men gather a human shield of nuns, friars, local gentlewomen, and even the mayor. Understandably the Spanish defenders were reluctant to fire on their own people, and so the buccaneers were able to reach the walls having suffered only one casualty. Within minutes the fort was taken, the Spanish garrison killed or wounded to a man. The unfinished fort had already been abandoned, which just left the substantial Castillo San Filipe, covering the eastern entrance to the harbor. The following morning—July 12—Morgan led

200 men across the bay in an amphibious assault, landing beneath the walls of the fort. After a brief resistance the outnumbered defenders surrendered. The last thing they wanted was a repeat of the massacre they had witnessed on the other side of the bay.

With Porto Bello in Morgan's hands, the buccaneer recalled his fleet, which entered the harbor a week later. Meanwhile Morgan and his men set about ransacking the government warehouses and torturing the inhabitants, forcing them to reveal where they had hidden their personal possessions. He also wrote to the governor of Panama, telling him that "tomorrow we plan to burn this city to the ground, and then set sail with all the guns and munitions from the castle."[16] To avoid this, all the governor had to do was pay a ransom of 350,000 pieces-of-eight. Instead of sending money, Agustin de Bracamonte sent troops— some 800 men—along with the dismissive note that "vassals of the King of Spain do not make treaties with inferior persons." Morgan replied: "We are waiting for you with great pleasure, and we have powder and ball with which to receive you. If you do not come very soon, we will, with the favor of God and our arms, come and visit you in Panama." It was all stirring stuff, but the real test would come when the two forces met in battle.

That took place on July 24, after a weeklong delay while the Spanish waited for more reinforcements. The assault was repulsed, and as Bracamonte's army fled back towards Panama, his emissaries brokered a deal with the buccaneers, paying a ransom of 100,000 pieces-of-eight in exchange for the safe return of their town. It took a week to arrange the payment, but once it was made, Morgan honored his agreement and sailed off, back to Port Royal. The ransom money brought the Porto Bello plunder up to a respectable total of 250,000 pieces-of-eight—the equivalent of $300 million in today's money. That summer Henry Morgan was the toast of the Caribbean, and as hundreds of fresh volunteers flocked to him, it seemed as if he could do no wrong.

"HARRY MORGAN'S WAY"

Within a few months Morgan put to sea again, this time at the head of a powerful buccaneering force, escorted by the English 34-gun frigate HMS *Oxford*—a parting loan from Governor Modyford. Morgan headed east to the Isle à Vache (Cow Island), off the southwestern coast of Hispaniola—a well-known buccaneer rendezvous. He had arranged to meet a French contingent there, and when the two groups met in early January 1669, the union was considered a cause for celebration. While Morgan and his captains sat down to dinner in the quarterdeck of the *Oxford*, the rest of the crew celebrated in their own way, which meant that the rum flowed freely. Then disaster struck. Some drunken buccaneer fired off his musket, and the spark ignited a powder barrel. The resulting explosion set off the gunpowder in the forward powder magazine, and Morgan's flagship was ripped apart. The mainmast fell across the dining table, killing several of Morgan's captains, but amazingly their leader and his other guests survived the disaster, along with a handful of the *Oxford*'s crew. While this was a singularly unlucky event, it also seemed to demonstrate that Morgan led a charmed life.

Morgan made his 14-gun privateer *Lilly* his new flagship and held a council of war with his surviving captains. Before the *Oxford* disaster, the plan was to attack Cartagena, the richest and most powerful city on the Spanish Main. Without the English frigate that would now be impossible, so Morgan suggested Trinidad as an alternative target. Even this proved too much when four of his captains deserted him, leaving Morgan with just eight ships and 500 men—most of them English. It was then that someone suggested a repeat of L'Ollonnais's raid on the Lago de Maracaibo of just two years before. Morgan and his captains immediately set sail for the Maracaibo Bar, arriving there on March 9. The battery there had been rebuilt since L'Ollonnais's visit, and its defenses had been strengthened, turning it into a small 11-gun fortress. The trouble was that fewer than ten men garrisoned the place, and they ran away as the buccaneers landed.

The fort was taken without loss, but not before Morgan's men discovered that the departing Spaniards had set a fuse in the magazine, which—according to Exquemelin—was just an inch away from the gunpowder when it was discovered and stamped out. With the fort in buccaneering hands, Morgan was able to pass his squadron over the bar and so enter the Lago de Maracaibo, which appeared to be at his mercy. On reaching Maracaibo, Morgan found the town had been abandoned, so the buccaneers spent the next three weeks sending out patrols to round up townspeople hiding in the hinterland, then torturing them to reveal the whereabouts of their hidden valuables. They then sailed across the lagoon to fall upon Gibraltar, where once again the buccaneers found the town abandoned.

So far the raid had proved a move-by-move repeat of L'Ollonnais's attack, although less plunder was found by Morgan's men, mainly because the French buccaneers had already stripped both towns of much of their wealth. Still, plunder valued at some 100,000 pieces-of-eight was gathered from the two towns, so Morgan's men were still delighted. By April 17 Morgan was back at Maracaibo, having captured a large merchantman off Gibraltar. The buccaneers divided what booty they had and prepared to sail home. It was then that Morgan discovered that the lagoon had become a trap. While the buccaneers were sacking Gibraltar, Admiral Alonso de Campo y Espinosa had arrived from Cartagena at the head of a powerful squadron of the Armada de Barlovento. Having learned of the pirate attack, he sailed for the lagoon with four warships—his 400-ton, 38-gun flagship *Magdalena*, accompanied by two frigates (*San Luis* and *Nuestra Señora de la Soledad*), plus the smaller brig *Marquesa*. Although this force was outnumbered by the buccaneers, the Spanish ships were heavily armed, and crammed with soldiers.

Admiral Campo's first move was to bottle up the only exit from the lagoon, working his squadron over the Maracaibo Bar, and sending troops ashore to refortify the Maracaibo battery, on the tip of the San Carlos Peninsula. He then sent Morgan a challenge, which stressed he was there to "revenge the unrighteous acts you have committed against the Spanish nation in America."[17] Morgan's reply to this was to sail up the lagoon and anchor his fleet just outside gun range of the enemy. Admiral Campo made no move, so for the next two days the two squadrons faced each other, the Spaniards trapped by the bar behind them but covered by the six guns that Campo had managed to reinstall in the battery. Then, on the morning of April 27, Morgan made his move.

Led by the captured merchantman, which flew Morgan's flag, the buccaneers bore down on the waiting Spanish ships, which hurriedly prepared for action. The merchantman headed straight for the *Magdalena*, and hardly believing their luck, Campo's men grappled the buccaneer flagship then sent their soldiers swarming on board. They were just in time to see the last of the merchantman's skeleton crew heading over the side into a boat, leaving their vessel to the Spanish. Then the flames appeared, licking out of the English ship's hold. Morgan had converted his prize into a fireship, filling her with tar, old sails, and gunpowder. The *Magdalena* was inextricably locked to the fireship, and the fire soon spread to the Spanish flagship. Unable to extinguish the inferno, Admiral Campo and his men abandoned ship just before the flames reached the magazine. Minutes later the *Magdalena* and Morgan's prize blew up in a shattering explosion.

Eager to avoid the other buccaneer ships which followed behind the fireship, two of the Spanish vessels—the *San Luis* and the *Marquesa*—ran themselves aground under the guns of the fort, where their crew set fire to their ships and fled for the safety of the shore. The buccaneers managed to salvage the smaller

Marquesa and towed her to safety, but the *San Luis* burned to the waterline. Of Admiral Campo's squadron, only the *Nuestra Señora de la Soledad* survived, having fled over the bar when the flagship blew up. Still, the Spanish still controlled the battery, and Morgan could not risk working his ships over the bar right in front of those guns. Despite all their efforts, the buccaneers were still trapped. Morgan ordered his ships back to Maracaibo, while he worked out what to do next.

Admiral Campo survived the loss of his flagship, and he set up his command post in the battery. He and Morgan continued to exchange messages, but the Spanish commander remained adamant. He was not prepared to strike a deal with Morgan, regardless of what the buccaneers threatened to do to their Spanish prisoners. The impasse lasted a week, and then Morgan made his next move. Prisoners reported that only six of the fort's guns were mounted—not enough both to cover its landward approach and to sweep the waters of Maracaibo Bar.

Morgan moved his ships up towards the bar, then began ferrying troops ashore, his beachhead screened from the fort by a wood. To the Spaniards it looked as if the buccaneers were planning to launch an assault from the land. Consequently Admiral Campo ordered his six guns transferred to the west face of the battery, where they could cover the open ground of the San Carlos Peninsula. In fact Morgan's landing was a ruse—each group of longboats contained the same men, who simply hid from view each time the boats returned to the fleet. To the Spanish it looked like a steady stream of men being landed on the shore, while in fact the buccaneers remained on their ships, ready and able for action. That night the Spanish stood by their guns, expecting Morgan to launch an assault under cover of darkness. Instead his ships spent the night working their way over the bar, and by dawn they were safely riding at anchor on its seaward side. Morgan had successfully outfoxed Admiral Campo, who was unable to redeploy his guns before Morgan deposited his prisoners on the beach, then set sail for Port Royal.

The buccaneers returned home on May 27 with their plunder from the two towns, plus a further 20,000 pieces-of-eight found on board the *San Luis*. The equivalent of $14 million shared out among 500 men was certainly a substantial haul and ensured that the taverns and brothels of Port Royal were kept busy for months. However, the political climate had changed while Morgan had been away. Governor Modyford had come under pressure from London to abandon his aggressive policy towards the Spaniards, and consequently he revoked all outstanding privateering licences. Then, on June 24 he was forced to issue a proclamation, which stated that "the subjects of His Catholic Majesty be from now until further order treated and used as good friends and neighbors."[18] It seemed as if Henry Morgan had led his last raid, and so he used his share of the plunder to expand his Jamaican estates, exchanging his career as a buccaneer for one as a plantation owner. However, events soon overtook him, and Morgan would be given one last great opportunity to lead his buccaneers against the Spanish.

THE SACK OF PANAMA

Henry Morgan's return to buccaneering came about as a result of poor communications. As a response to Morgan's raid on Porto Bello in July 1668, the Spanish crown decided to allow colonial governors on the Spanish Main to commission their own privateers. However, the delays inherent in Spanish bureaucracy and the distance between Madrid and Cartagena meant that it was not until early 1670 that these privateering letters of marque were actually issued—six months after Governor Modyford's declaration of peace beyond the line. The Spanish saw the raids that followed as an opportunity for revenge; the Jamaicans saw them as a betrayal.

The most successful of these Spanish privateers was a Portuguese captain called Manoel Rivero Pardal, who operated out of Cartagena in his ship the *San Pedro y la Fama*. In late January 1670 he raided an English fishing settlement in the Cayman Islands, then attacked and captured an English privateer off Manzanillo, in southeastern Cuba. This prize turned out to be the *Mary and Jane*, commanded by the Dutch privateer Bernard Claesen Speirdyke—known as Captain Bart, who was killed in the battle. At the time Speirdyke was sailing under a flag of truce, delivering a notification of Modyford's peaceful intentions to the local Cuban governor. The Jamaicans were outraged, while Rivero returned to Cartagena, where his return was celebrated with a fiesta. In May the Portuguese privateer returned to Jamaica, driving an English sloop ashore, then burning coastal villages in Montego Bay. He even issued a challenge to Morgan, offering to meet the buccaneer in an equal fight, with both sides having two ships of 20 guns apiece. That way Morgan "might see the valor of the Spaniards."

To Morgan and Modyford this was fighting talk, and it provided the governor with the excuse he needed to resume hostilities. Although Morgan never accepted Rivero's challenge, he began planning an even more dramatic response to this new Spanish initiative. On July 9, 1670, Modyford proclaimed Morgan "Admiral and Commander-in-Chief of all the ships of war belonging to this harbor … to attack, seize and destroy all the enemy's vessels that shall come within his reach."

He was also rather ambiguously permitted "to do and perform all matter of exploits which may tend to the preservation and quiet of Jamaica."[19] The buccaneers flocked to sign up, and within a month Morgan had a fleet of 11 privateers and 600 men at his disposal. He raised his flag in his 22-gun privateering frigate *Satisfaction*, and on August 11 he led his newfound fleet out to sea. Henry Morgan was back.

His target was none other than Panama, a city regarded as the richest prize in the Americas. Morgan had already arranged to rendezvous with the French buccaneers of Tortuga at the Isle à Vache, where more English and French ships eventually joined him. On September 16 he sent his deputy Edward Collier ahead with three ships and 600 men, with orders to get prisoners for intelligence from the Spanish Main. For his part Morgan remained at the Hispaniolan rendezvous until all his ships were ready, giving him a buccaneer force of some 33 (or possibly 38) ships and 2,000 men. He also appointed the Dutch privateer Captain Laurens Prins as his deputy. While the *Satisfaction* and 12 others of these ships were substantial enough, carrying ten or more guns apiece, the rest of the fleet comprised much smaller vessels, many without any guns at all. Still, between

After his capture of Panama in 1671, Henry Morgan returned to Jamaica to discover that a peace treaty had been signed with the Spanish while he was away. Morgan was shipped to London, where he was a prisoner for two years until circumstances changed again.

them they carried just about every buccaneer on the Spanish Main. One of his most welcome recruits was Captain John Morris and his privateer *Dolphin*, who arrived at the rendezvous in late October, followed by the *San Pedro y la Fama*. He had run into the Spanish privateer off the eastern tip of Cuba. Morris ,attacked, and in the brief fight that followed, Manoel Rivero Pardal was killed and his ship captured.

In the meantime Collier had made landfall at Rio de la Hatcha, where he promptly captured the fort, the town, and one of Rivero Pardal's privateers that was at anchor in the harbor. After the usual round of interrogation and torture he sailed back to the Isle à Vache with 38 prisoners, all encouraged by Collier to tell Morgan whatever they knew. He rejoined Morgan on December 8, and ten days later the great buccaneering fleet got underway, setting course towards the coast of Panama. Morgan visited Santa Catalina on the way (now renamed Providence Island) and discovered that the Spanish had recovered the place in 1668, three years after Mansfield's capture of the island. Morgan promptly reclaimed Providence on behalf of the Jamaican government, although a small Spanish garrison still held out on the well-fortified Isla Chica. The next morning—on Christmas Day—the Spaniards agreed to capitulate after staging a face-saving mock battle. Morgan now had a secure base to fall back to if things went wrong in Panama.

His next move was to send a detachment of three ships and 470 men on ahead under Captain Joseph Bradley, with orders to capture the Castello San Lorenzo, which guarded the mouth of the Chagres River. Morgan followed on a few days later with the rest of the fleet. On January 6, 1671, Bradley landed his men a few miles from the fort, then advanced "with flags and trumpets."[20] The buccaneers were confident of an easy victory and advanced straight at the walls—where they were met by a storm of musketry. The commander Pedro de Elizalde had recently had his garrison reinforced and was in no mood to capitulate. His men repulsed two attacks, holding the buccaneers at bay until nightfall.

Bradley decided to change his tactics. He sent a small group forward in the dark, who reached the walls, then hurled incendiaries and grenades over the wooden palisade. The defenses caught fire, and by morning the palisade had been destroyed and half of the garrison had fled into the night. The remaining defenders managed to repulse Bradley's dawn attack, but the fort was carried in the next assault. Having suffered such heavy casualties—30 killed, including Bradley himself, and over 70 wounded—the buccaneers were in no mood to give quarter, and so Elizalde and his fellow defenders were cut down to a man. When Morgan arrived on January 12 he found the buccaneers still licking their wounds and lamenting the death of Captain Bradley. Still, the way now lay open for an advance up the river to Panama, the city that had eluded Sir Francis Drake some seven decades before.

On January 19 the raiders made their way up the river. After leaving behind a garrison, Morgan had some 1,500 men at his disposal, crammed into seven small pinnaces and 36 piraguas. It was a bold move, as Panama lay 70 miles away across the isthmus, and the governor Juan Perez de Guzman would have time to call out his militia and to organize his defenses. If Morgan failed, then his men would be hard-pressed to make it back to their ships. Actually, as seventeenth-century jungle expeditions went, the whole operation went fairly smoothly. After abandoning the boats halfway to their destination, Morgan's men entered the small town of Venta de Cruces, where in 1573 Drake had ambushed the Panama treasure convoy. For the last 18 miles the buccaneers advanced down the Royal Road, and on the morning of January 27 they stood on a hill overlooking Panama.

In the meantime Governor Juan Perez de Guzman had been busy, and as the buccaneers approached he marshaled his Spanish defenders out onto the plain, deploying into line a mile in front of the city. He had some 1,200 foot under his command supported by 400 cavalrymen, split into two units—one deployed on either flank. Unfortunately they lacked artillery—and experience. Morgan's buccaneers attacked in three groups, the vanguard led by Laurens Prins advancing on the left flank, the other two groups echeloned behind and to the right of him. Each contained around 500 men, almost all of whom were armed with muskets—and knew how to use them.

As Prins's men contacted the enemy, Guzman unleashed a herd of cattle hidden behind his center, which stampeded towards the buccaneer ranks. Rather optimistically he ordered his men to follow on behind, hoping the cattle would disrupt the buccaneers sufficiently to make them an easy target. However, one good volley was enough to make the cattle stampede the other way, and it was the Spaniards who ended up in disarray. Meanwhile Prins defeated the Spanish right wing, after which his men stood on the high ground there and fired into the flank of the wavering Spanish line. A Spanish counterattack against Prins was stopped dead by musket fire, at which point Morgan's other divisions burst into the Spanish, who were still reeling from the cattle stampede. Within minutes the whole affair was over, and the defenders were running back into the city, leaving some 600 of their companions dead or dying on the battlefield.

Guzman paused long enough to give orders to fire the town's main buildings before he fled towards the safety of the harbor. Behind him small groups of Spaniards still tried to put up some kind of a defense, but it was a hopeless task. The buccaneers flooded into Panama and made their way down to the harbor—arriving in time to see the governor sail out into the Pacific, one of hundreds of refugees who were spirited away to safety by the ships in the harbor, escorted by the warships of the Armada del Sur (the Southern Fleet). Unfortunately for Morgan and his men, the warships also carried away the bulk of the city's treasury. That night the majority of Panama burned to the ground, and the following morning the buccaneers began sifting through the ruins, looking for hidden caches of plunder.

Morgan and his men remained in the smoking ruins for the best part of a month, sending out patrols to find Spaniards to interrogate and gathering whatever treasures they could find. During their stay they missed one of the greatest—the golden altarpiece in the cathedral, which the clerics had whitewashed to camouflage it just before the buccaneers arrived. However, the torture and ransoming of prisoners proved reasonably lucrative, and by February 24 when Morgan began the return march, his men had gathered approximately 750,000 pieces-of-eight as plunder (worth $90 million today). Of this haul, Morgan's personal share was a healthy 400,000 pieces. It took some 175 mules to transport the haul back to the ships. Unfortunately that was where the arguments began. The English and French contingents had already fallen out, the latter suspecting that Morgan planned to cheat them of part of their share.

The bickering would continue long after the buccaneers returned to Port Royal, mainly because, after Morgan deducted his share, the rest had to be divided between 1,500 men. This meant that most buccaneers received little more than 200 pieces-of-eight for their troubles—or $24,000. Given all they had gone through, this seemed a poor recompense. Faced with dissention, on March 16 Morgan simply upped anchor and sailed home to Jamaica, leaving the rest of his fleet to follow on as best they could. Some of the French buccaneers stayed on to raid the coast of New Spain, but the majority of the buccaneers just went home. Back in Port Royal Morgan discovered that Thomas Modyford had fallen out of favor in London and that any further attacks against the Spanish would be seen as open acts of piracy.

The climate cooled even further in June when Modyford was relieved by a new governor, Sir Thomas Lynch, who promptly arrested his predecessor and shipped him home to answer charges. In April 1672 Lynch arrested Morgan, who was duly sent to London aboard the frigate HMS *Welcome*. On his arrival he discovered that the government was fully occupied by a new war with the Dutch, and privateers were suddenly back in demand. When Spain sided with Holland, the charges against Morgan were as good as dropped. In January 1674 Governor Lynch was recalled and Morgan found himself appointed as the new deputy governor, with orders to advise Lynch's replacement—John, Lord Vaughan—on Jamaican matters. In effect it was a complete exoneration, and Morgan's reversal of fortunes was completed the following November when he was knighted by Charles II.

Morgan returned to Jamaica the following spring and spent his last years drinking with old comrades, tending his plantations, assisting Lord Vaughan and his successor the Duke of Carlisle, and, rather bizarrely, prosecuting pirates— former buccaneers who had stepped over the line from privateering into piracy. He was to live another 13 years, growing fatter all the while, until he finally died of dropsy (now called edema) in 1688—the goutlike swelling of the legs and ankles brought on, according to Morgan's physician, by "drinking and sitting up late." His passing marked the end of an era. Already the days of the buccaneers had passed, replaced by smaller and highly regulated groups of privateers, whose actions were controlled as much by London as by the Jamaican governor. However, other English buccaneers simply ventured further afield, and in the process they created a whole new chapter in the history of piracy.

DAMPIER AND THE BUCCANEERS OF THE PACIFIC

In early 1679, William Dampier arrived in Port Royal, having just sailed from London on a merchantman. Born in Somerset in 1651, he served as a shipwright's apprentice in Weymouth before going to sea as a seaman in 1669. For the next ten years he served on an East Indiaman and on a Royal Navy warship fighting the Dutch and then worked as a logwood cutter in Central America. As an experienced seaman Dampier was recruited by a group of die-hard buccaneers, who continued to wage their own unofficial war against the Spanish. This group included the experienced buccaneering captains Bartholomew Sharp, Basil Ringose, Peter Harris the Elder, John Coxon, John Cook, Edmond Cook, and Richard Sawkins. In December 1679 they formed a raiding party which sacked Porto Bello, yielding some 36,000 pieces-of-eight. They then worked their way across the isthmus of Panama, pillaging the gold mining camp of Santa María el

Real as they went. On reaching the Pacific coast they captured a number of local coastal vessels and then defeated a force sent out from Panama to capture them. However, the buccaneers were unsure what to do next, as they did not have enough men to attack Panama, the only really lucrative city in the region.

At that point the expedition moved up the coast to Coiba Island, some 160 miles (258 km) west of Panama on the Pacific coast. There the expedition split up. Coxon elected to head home, taking some 70 men with him. Sawkins raided the nearby settlement of Pueblo Nuevo (now Remedios), where he was killed. The rest elected Sharp as their leader and Ringose his deputy. Dampier decided to join them as they headed south down the Pacific coast with the remaining 150 men. Sharp proved a highly unpopular captain, and despite his leading them on a few small and marginally successful raids, his crew mutinied twice in as many months. Finally in April 1681 a group of 50 men had had enough, and under the leadership of John Cook they left Sharp's band to return home. Dampier went with them, and eventually they retraced their steps to the Caribbean, where they were picked up by fellow buccaneers and went their own way. Cook quarreled with his new Dutch captain and was marooned for his troubles on the Isle à Vache. He was rescued by a French buccaneer, Captain Tristian, and Cook rewarded his benefactor by stealing his ship, using it to capture two French prizes, then fleeing to Virginia, which he reached in April 1683.

Meanwhile Sharp struck it rich, plundering 37,000 pieces-of-eight from two prizes, the *San Pedro* and the *Santa Anna*. In this last ship the buccaneers also captured a detailed set of charts of the Pacific coast—yielding information that would benefit those who followed them. He then headed for home, and Sharp's captured Spanish vessel, the *Trinity*, finally arrived in Barbados in February 1682. On his return to England Sharp was arrested and tried for piracy, the prosecution basing their case on evidence supplied by a Spanish teenager Sharp captured off Peru then kept on as a cabin boy. However, the charts saved him, and the trial was conveniently abandoned after he presented them to the Admiralty.

As for John Cook, several of his former shipmates had joined him in Williamsburg, and so in August 1683 he decided to return to the Pacific. William Dampier was one of the 70 former buccaneers who joined his expedition. After replacing his French prize with a Danish ship captured off the west coast of Africa—he renamed the vessel the *Bachelor's Delight*—Cook headed for Cape Horn and entered the Pacific in March 1684. He then encountered Captain John Eaton in his privateer the *Nicholas*. Eaton had sailed from London six months before, and by the time he encountered Cook off the coast of Chile he had only managed to capture one small prize.

Cook and Eaton then headed northwards to the Juan Fernandez Islands, then on to the Galapagos. They captured a few Spanish ships, but none of their prizes yielded much in the way of plunder. The two captains then decided to strike eastwards to cruise the South American coast. Cook died before the buccaneers made landfall off Cabo Blanco, the most northerly part of the Peruvian coastline, and his shipmates buried him on the headland. Edward Davis assumed command of the *Bachelor's Delight* and led the buccaneers on a largely unprofitable raid on the nearby town of Paita. Eaton decided to make his own way home. However, their luck changed in October when they ran into another buccaneer, Charles Swan.

Swan had sailed with Henry Morgan during the earlier expedition and had since teamed up with Bartholomew Sharp's old deputy, Basil Ringose, who sponsored Swan's voyage into the Pacific. Swan left London in October 1683, and the following spring he reached the Pacific coast of Panama, where he spent several months trying to intercept a treasure galleon. In July he teamed up with Peter Harris, a Jamaican buccaneer who had crossed the isthmus six months before, following in the footsteps of Sharp's expedition of 1680. On the Pacific coast Harris stole a ship, then used it to capture several other Spanish prizes. The two groups met off the coast of Chile, where Swan, Harris, and Davis decided to make an attempt on the treasure fleet which was due to sail from Lima to Panama the following summer. Eaton elected to return home and sailed off into the Pacific.

The rest headed north to lie in wait, where they were joined by three other privateering crews, commanded by a Captain Townley and the French captains François Grogniet and Pierre le Picard. All of these newcomers had crossed the isthmus and captured ships on the Pacific coast. In all some 1,000 buccaneers joined forces that winter, when they made the Isla del Rey in the Gulf of Panama into their temporary haven. However, when the fleet finally arrived off Panama in June 1685, the buccaneers discovered that it outnumbered them. They attacked anyway but were driven off.

At that point Dampier jumped ship, signing on with Captain Swan and joining the crew of his privateer *Cygnet*. Swan planned to sail home via the Orient, and Dampier had a taste for adventure. The *Cygnet* crossed the Pacific to Mindanao in the Philippines, where Swan spent the best part of six months enjoying the delights of the local women. By that time his crew had had enough, and sailed on without him. They crossed the South China Sea to Indochina, then headed south past the East Indies to make landfall on the western coast of New Holland (now Australia) in January 1688.[21]

Meanwhile Dampier's old skippers Edward Davis and Peter Harris moved on to Nicaragua, where they launched a few more unsuccessful raids. Harris eventually went his own way and was never heard of again, while Davis decided to return home. The *Bachelor's Delight* was now operating in consort with another buccaneer, William Knight, who had joined the force on the Isla del Rey the previous winter. During 1686 the two buccaneers operated off the coast of Peru, and this time the raids proved moderately successful, the Englishmen garnering a haul of over 60,000 pieces-of-eight. They split up in the Juan Fernandez Islands that November, and by the summer of 1688 Davis and the few remaining survivors of John Cook's original crew finally returned to Virginia, where they were unsuccessfully charged with piracy.

On his voyage home Dampier jumped ship again, this time in the Nicobar Islands, halfway between Sumatra and India. He spent the next two years serving aboard a local trading vessel before returning home in 1691—12 years after he first sailed from London.

Dampier wrote about his voyage, and his *A New Voyage Around the World* proved a runaway success. He made two other voyages, one of them as the unsuccessful commander of a privateer; then in 1708 he was asked to join a new buccaneering expedition into the Pacific, this time commanded by an experienced Bristol seaman, Captain Woodes Rogers. What followed would make pirate history and would inspire a semifictional best seller.

The expedition set sail from Bristol in August 1708 and reached the coast of Brazil in mid-November. By January they had safely rounded Cape Horn, and on February 2, 1709, Rogers's two ships *Duke* and *Duchess* reached the Juan Fernandez Islands. Rogers sent a boat ashore to investigate a light they had seen during the night, and when the landing party returned it was accompanied by a strange-looking man, clothed in goatskins. He turned out to be Alexander Selkirk, the former master of the privateer *Cinque Ports*, who had stayed behind on the island when his ship sailed away five years before. He lived off goats, and when Rogers arrived he soon ingratiated himself with his rescuers by demonstrating his hunting skills. Selkirk soon became the mate of the *Duke* and was later given command of one of Rogers's prizes. The story later inspired Daniel Defoe to write *Robinson Crusoe* (1719).[22]

After quitting the islands Rogers headed for the Peruvian coast, where he captured a small coasting vessel, then a large, well-armed merchantman. This was followed by a raid on the Ecuadorian port of Guayaquil, which yielded a substantial haul of plunder. To avoid any Spanish pursuit Rogers headed back into the vastness of the Pacific, and by May he had reached the Galapagos Islands. By that time half his crew were stricken by fever and scurvy, so he spent two months there while his men recovered. During this sojourn, Dampier told Rogers what he knew about the Manila galleons, the treasure ships that made an annual trip from the Philippines to Acapulco, on the Pacific coast of New Spain. From there their cargoes of gold and porcelain were transported overland to Vera Cruz, where they were shipped to Spain on board the galleons of the New Spain treasure *flota*. The buccaneer decided to intercept them.

Rogers was in luck. Following Dampier's advice he headed northeast towards the coast of what is now Mexico's Baja California. It was there that the galleons made landfall after their voyage from Manila and Guam. He lingered there for a month, long after the scheduled time of the galleons' Mexican landfall. Then, in mid-December 1709, when he had almost given up the search, a lookout spotted a galleon—the *Nuestra Señora del la Encarnacion Disengaño*. The *Duke* and *Duchess* gave chase and captured the treasure galleon after a hard-fought engagement, during which Rogers was wounded in the jaw. His prisoners told him that a second galleon was not far behind them, so, leaving a prize crew on board, Rogers went off in search of her. On Christmas Day they found her, but the *Nuestra Señora de Begona* was a tougher prospect, and this time the buccaneers were driven off. However, Woodes Rogers and his men still had their earlier prize.

The captured Manila galleon yielded a fortune in specie, porcelain, spices, and Chinese silks—enough to delight Rogers, his crew, and their English backers. Renamed the *Bachelor*, the galleon was added to Rogers's squadron. On January 10, 1709, the three ships set course for Guam, following the course already sailed by Dampier 13 years before. From there they continued on to Batavia in the East Indies, then across the Indian Ocean to the Cape of Good Hope. By October 1711 they were back in the port of London, with plunder valued by some contemporaries at 1,600,000 pieces-of-eight, or $192 million. Dampier's own share was £1,500—worth £180,000 ($291,000) today. It wasn't a bad haul for a writer, even a best-selling one.

Woodes Rogers was acclaimed as one of the most successful privateers of all time—and as the last of the buccaneers. Actually, the days of the buccaneers were long gone, and Dampier alone remained the last link with that swashbuckling past, completing a cycle of events which began when he stepped off the ship in Port Royal, back when Sir Henry Morgan was still holding court in the local taverns and Jamaica was still a haven for a dwindling band of buccaneers. For his part, Dampier went on to write a fresh account of his voyages, while Woodes Rogers is now best remembered as the poacher-turned-gamekeeper who cleared pirates such as Blackbeard out of the Bahamas.

THE FRENCH FILIBUSTERS

At the time it must have seemed as if English buccaneering was passing into history just as the French were getting into their swashbuckling stride. Part of this impetus came from colonization, as during the 1660s a string of French settlements were established on the western part of Hispaniola.[23] Although a handful of Frenchmen had lived on the coast for decades, this new impetus was driven by a new wave of colonists, and by French political ambition. In 1664 the French government officially claimed the area as their own, naming the region Saint Dominique (now Haiti), although the Spanish still claimed control of the whole of Hispaniola. This Spanish claim was only dropped in 1697, when the Treaty of Ryswick finally established French political ownership of western Hispaniola. Tortuga continued as a buccaneer haven until the early 1670s, by which time Petit Goâve in southwestern Saint Dominique overtook it in importance. This new settlement provided better supplied markets for the sale of contraband, as unlike Tortuga it had its own hinterland of French plantations and towns. As the seventeenth century drew to a close, Tortuga became a backwater, a lingering reminder of a violent past.

This change of base also led to the creation of a new breed of French buccaneer. One of the most prominent to emerge during the 1670s was Michael de Grammont. His origins are obscure, but Exquemelin claims he was born in Paris and then served in the French navy. By 1672, France was at war with both Holland and Spain, and Grammont commanded a French privateer operating in the Caribbean. However, he crossed the line from privateering into piracy when he captured a Dutch vessel in the Leeward Islands before the official declaration of war that March, and was therefore unable to return to the more established French colonies. Instead he based himself in Saint Dominique, where fewer questions were asked. He soon became one of the colony's most successful privateers, although the men themselves preferred the term "filibusters" (or *flibustiers* in French), which itself was derived from the Dutch term for freebooter. In effect they were prepared to operate against the perceived enemies of France, regardless of whether these countries were at war with the French or not. By 1678 Grammont was accepted as the de facto leader of the Saint Dominique filibusters, and he adopted the title of Chevalier as a form of unofficial acknowledgement of his status.

In May 1678 Grammont and his filibusters sailed out on a raid against the prosperous Dutch island of Curaçao. His flotilla of six large and 13 smaller ships filled with 1,200 men sailed from Petit Goâve and then rendezvoused with an official French expedition sent from Martinique, commanded by Jean, the Comte d'Estrees. However, the expedition was caught by a hurricane, and many of the ships were dashed against the Isla de Aves (Island of the Birds), some 100 miles east of their objective. Once the tempest passed, d'Estrees limped back to Martinique, leaving the filibusters to salvage what they could from the wreckage. According to Exquemelin, in the weeks that followed the filibusters "were never without two or three hogsheads of wine and brandy in their tents, and barrels of beef and pork."[24]

Left to his own devices, Grammont decided that his force was too weak to assault Curaçao on its own, so he decided to pick on the Spanish instead. In June 1678 he arrived off the Maracaibo Bar with six ships and 700 men. Confronted by a newly built fort on the tip of the San Carlos peninsula, Grammont landed a battery of ship's guns and bombarded the Spanish into submission. He left some of his ships behind to guard the lagoon entrance, and then pressed on. Once inside the Lago de Maracaibo he discovered that Maracaibo and Gibraltar had not really recovered from Morgan's and L'Ollonnais's raids a decade before. However, Grammont used captured horses to move his raiders inland, falling on the poorly defended Venezuelan town of Trujillo, which he stormed on September 1. He razed Trujillo and Gibraltar to the ground, then moved back to Maracaibo, which he continued to hold until early December, when he led his fleet back to Saint Dominique, his ships laden with plunder.

In May 1680, Grammont led another raid against the Venezuelan coast, this time attacking La Guaira, the harbor that served Caracas, the provincial capital. A small assault force was sent ahead of the main body to capture the two forts that guarded the port, and the rest of the buccaneers then followed on behind to capture the town itself. The following day a counterattack was launched by the Caracas militia, and the filibusters soon found themselves besieged. The Spanish launched several assaults against the port, but the Frenchmen held on, despite mounting losses. Grammont himself was badly wounded in one of these attacks. The situation was hopeless, so he gave the order to retreat back to the ships. The filibusters managed to escape, taking several Spanish hostages with them, whose ransom proved the only source of plunder of the whole expedition.

In May 1683, Grammont joined forces with those of the Dutch buccaneer Laurens de Graaf for a joint assault on Vera Cruz, the principal harbor of New Spain (Mexico) and one of the most important treasure ports on the Spanish Main. In all the raiding force consisted of five large privateers, eight smaller vessels, and around 1,300 men. Grammont sent two ships disguised as Spanish merchantmen ahead of the fleet, who reported that the annual treasure *flota* was not moored beneath the guns of San Juan de Ulúa—the fortress island off Vera Cruz where Sir John Hawkins was defeated over a century before. This was good news, as it meant the buccaneers would probably have a numerical advantage over the Spanish. That night Grammont landed 200 filibusters a mile north of the city, while de Graaf's larger force began landing at Punta Gorda, a few miles further up the coast. The Frenchmen sneaked into the city, and on May 18, just as dawn broke, the Dutch assaulted the town's defenses from the north, while Grammont's men fell on the Spanish from behind.

It was all over in minutes, and the raiders set about securing captives and plundering the city. Although a Spanish garrison still held out on San Juan de Ulúa, they could do nothing but impotently watch the sacking of the port. To cap it all, Grammont then led thousands of the city's inhabitants to a nearby island, where they were held until they were ransomed. What was particularly striking about this affair was that the three nations were at peace at the time, so Grammont's actions amounted to nothing more than piracy. However, the French governor of Saint Dominique preferred to turn a blind eye to the activities of his filibusters.

In the summer of 1685 Grammont and de Graaf joined forces again for another attack on New Spain, this time assaulting Campeche, the scene of so many attacks a decade earlier. On July 6 some 30 privateers anchored off Beque, a fishing village south of Campeche, but Spanish troops deployed in the tree line above the beach managed to prevent the raiders from landing. The following morning the buccaneers tried again, and this time they lured the Spaniards into the open by feigning a retreat to their boats. The milita were routed, and de Graaf led a column of 700 men northwards towards the city, leaving Grammont circled behind Campeche, preventing any escape. The town fell within a few hours.

A Spanish counterattacking force was sent south from Mérida in the Yucatan Peninsula, but Grammont's filibusters defeated the Spanish militia with ease. He then organized flying columns mounted on captured horses to raid the hinterland, and this tactic proved highly lucrative until the main column was ambushed by the Spanish at Hempolol, some 25 miles to the north. The buccaneers remained in Campeche until early September, when Grammont returned home. Although the haul of plunder had been relatively poor, the reputation of the Chevalier was at its height. The governor of Saint Dominique, Jean du Casse, even offered him the post of his lieutenant general, defending the French colony from attack. Instead Grammont elected to continue raiding, and in May 1686 his flagship was lost at sea somewhere off the west coast of Florida during a reconnaissance of the Spanish settlement of St. Augustine.

THE LAST GREAT RAID

In 1688, the French became embroiled in the War of the League of Augsburg, a conflict that pitted them against the English, the Spanish, and the Dutch—all at the same time. As Governor Jean du Casse in Petit Goâve was now able to issue privateering letters of marque to almost any filibuster who wanted one, this conflict, and the War of the Spanish Succession (1701–14) that followed on its heels, made the filibusters legal again. Suddenly the French government began viewing them as a strategic asset rather than as an embarrassment.

In Paris, as the war began to draw to a close, French strategists looked for the opportunity to launch a devastating attack on the Spanish overseas empire—one that they could use as a major bargaining counter during the forthcoming peace talks. After some debate Cartagena was nominated as the ideal target. After all, it was reputed to be the richest city on the Spanish Main, and since it had last been sacked by Francis Drake over a century before, its defenses had been greatly strengthened. So far they had succeeded in deterring the buccaneers. However, this time the French strategists planned to combine the enterprise of the buccaneers with the steady professionalism of the French army and navy. As the plan developed it took on some of the aspects of the Elizabethan ventures of a century before, a sort of government-sponsored business opportunity, complete with investors, "gifted" royal troops and semi-independent privateers. In March 1695 a French admiral, Bernard Jean-Louis de Saint Jean, the Baron de Pointis, arrived in Petit Goâve to take command of the expedition. He brought with him a squadron of ten French warships and a fleet of transports carrying

3,000 veteran troops. The Saint Dominique filibusters supplied another seven ships, while Governor du Casse commanded his own squadron of four vessels.

Unfortunately the French admiral soon fell out with the filibusters, who were only persuaded to stay thanks to the diplomatic intervention of Governor du Casse, who was more successful in hiding his dislike of his superior. Fearing that the admiral planned to trick them, the filibusters demanded written contracts, which specified exactly how any plunder would be divided up. Placated, they finally agreed to sail under the admiral's orders. The fleet set sail from Saint Dominique at the end of March, and on April 13 it arrived off Cartagena. Baron de Pointis was all for an immediate attack, but du Casse counseled for a thorough reconnaissance first. It was just as well, as the seaward side of the city was protected by a reef, which would have prevented the assault boats from reaching the shore.

In the end Baron de Pointis and du Casse followed the route taken by Drake back in 1586. The fleet would force the entrance to Cartagena Bay, then assault the city by way of La Caletta—the coastal spur which ran westwards from the city. The only problem was that the entrance to the bay was now guarded by the Fort San Luis, an imposing structure, at Bocachica, the tip of La Caletta. On April 15, some 1,200 men landed on La Caletta, beside the fishing hamlet of Los Hornos, just out of range of the San Luis guns. The following day the fort was stormed, and it surrendered after a token resistance (not such a token for du Casse though, as he was wounded in the assault).

The French could now enter Cartagena Bay, but the inner harbor with the city behind it was still protected by two more forts—Fort Santa Cruz on a spur of La Caletta and Fort Manzanillo on the opposite side of the harbor entrance. Baron de Pointis ordered an advance up La Caletta, and the French were delighted to discover that Fort Santa Cruz had been abandoned just minutes before the French troops arrived in front of its walls. The admiral then ordered the filibusters to play their part, ordering them to land on the northeastern side of Cartagena Bay, then skirt round Fort Manzanillo to occupy La Popa, a hill overlooking the landward approach to Cartagena. With du Casse indisposed, the Saint Dominique contingent were led by Joseph d'Honon de Gallifet.

It was with some misgivings that the filibusters did what they were asked, but by April 20 they had seized the high ground, thereby sealing Cartagena off from its hinterland. Next, heavy guns were landed from the fleet, and a formal siege got under way. By April 28 the batteries were in place on La Popa, and they began bombarding the town, supported by the warships lying off the seaward side of the city. After two days a breach had been made on the landward defenses of Cartagena, although this side of the town was still protected by the Fort San Lazaro. Baron de Pointis ordered an assault, which was launched at dawn the following morning—May 1. The first attack was repulsed with heavy losses, mainly caused by the enfilading fire from the fort, but the French attacked again, and finally, on the evening of May 2, the garrison surrendered. Cartagena had been captured.

That was when the deceit began. After learning that a relief column was approaching the city, de Pointis ordered the filibusters to block their approach, supported by a sizable contingent of French regulars. The attack never materialized, and by the time the filibusters returned to Cartagena, the city gates were shut in their faces. Worse, they soon discovered that the admiral had spirited the bulk of the plunder onto his flagship, leaving his filibuster allies just 40,000 pieces-of-eight between them. This time neither du Casse nor de Gallifet could control his men's anger. On May 30, when the French garrison withdrew, the filibusters stormed the city and occupied it for themselves. They soon fell back on their traditional methods of extorting money from the Spanish, and within three days they raised another million pieces-of-eight from the poor inhabitants. The result was that when du Casse and the filibusters sailed home to Petit Goâve on June 3, each man had around 1,000 pieces-of-eight in his pocket—the equivalent of $120,000.

Still, the Baron de Pointis had his revenge. On June 4 his squadron was intercepted by an Anglo-Dutch squadron commanded by Vice Admiral Neville. The allies chased de Pointis for a week before he managed to give them the slip, somewhere to the west of Cartagena. However, as they turned back, Neville's ships ran into the filibusters on their way home. Four of the 11 French privateers were captured or driven ashore on the Tierra Firme coast, and those who struggled back into Petit Goâve were in no mood for any further forays against the Spanish Main, or partnerships with the French authorities. The majority of the filibusters returned to privateering on their own, while a few quit the Caribbean in search of prey elsewhere, for example in the Indian Ocean.

Cartagena marked the last great hurrah of the buccaneers, the end of an era. By the turn of the century, the era of the buccaneers was over and a new age, in which privateers hunted on their own, would take its place. It was also inevitable that some of these men would reject the tight controls imposed on privateers and would take the law into their own hands.

6

THE GOLDEN AGE

A GOLDEN AGE?

In recent years the period of piratical history from roughly the start of the eighteenth century until about 1730 has been dubbed the golden age of piracy. Some historians have narrowed it down even further. For instance, maritime historian David Cordingly established it as starting in 1698, when the privateer-turned-pirate Captain Kidd captured the *Quedah Merchant*. He dated its end as 1722, when the surviving members of "Black Bart" Roberts's pirate crew were executed in a mass hanging at Cape Coast Castle in West Africa. In *Blackbeard: America's Most Notorious Pirate*, I argued for an even tighter historical span—from 1714 until 1725. In the end it is all subjective, as the parameters we use to define the period are a matter of personal opinion. What everyone agrees on is that during the first decades of the eighteenth century there was a marked increase of piratical activity in the waters of the Americas, off the African coast, and in the Indian Ocean. The phrase the "golden age" is therefore a useful historical shorthand to describe this phenomenon.

Tracking down the origin of the phrase is a little difficult. The obvious source is Captain Charles Johnson's *A General History of the Robberies and Murders of the Most Notorious Pyrates*, first published in 1724, but the phrase never appears in the book. Neither does it appear in any of the newspapers, court records, official letters, or any other correspondence of the time. That means that it was not in contemporary use during this period and was invented some time after the golden age came to an end. Modern pirate historians such as David Cordingly, Marcus Rediker, Richard Zacks, Peter Earle, Jan Rogozinski, and I have all used the phrase, but none of us invented it. Neither did Robert Louis Stevenson, whose adventure novel *Treasure Island* (1883) first put piracy on the literary map. At the moment the likely candidate is Rafael Sabatini (1875–1950), the British author who penned pirate novels such as *Captain Blood* (1922) and *The Black Swan* (1932), both of which were transformed into Hollywood swashbucklers. However, the origin of the phrase is largely immaterial, as its importance today is to define an era in which some of the most notorious pirates in history plied their trade.

Whoever first dubbed the period the golden age of piracy clearly did so with their tongue firmly in their cheek. The irony was certainly lost on those who had fallen victim to men like Blackbeard, "Black Bart" Roberts, or Charles Vane. In a way, both the pirates and the victims they preyed on were created by official policy back in Europe. We have already seen how the buccaneers who operated in the Caribbean during the later seventeenth century were gradually brought under government control. By the 1670s it was no longer considered acceptable for these men to prey on the Spanish unless there was a war on. The Dutch never developed a powerful buccaneering fleet, and the actions of their privateers were regulated fairly effectively from the 1620s onwards. The English managed to establish a firm grip on their buccaneers in the aftermath of Henry Morgan's raid on Panama in 1670–71, and Morgan himself was involved in the introduction of legislation designed to prevent illegal forays.

The French took longer to establish control over their buccaneers, mainly because—as did the Jamaican authorities in the late 1650s—the French governor of Saint Dominique in what is now Haiti saw his filibusters as his main form of defense. Elsewhere the French were successful in turning filibusters into law-abiding privateers, and in Saint Dominique the same tight controls were successfully introduced in the aftermath of the War of the League of Augsburg (1688–97). This meant that when a new and long-lasting war broke out, namely the War of the Spanish Succession (1701–14), all of the leading maritime powers—England, France, Spain, and Holland—had managed to control the way in which privateers operated, making sure they kept within the bounds of the law.[1]

The conflict—also known as Queen Anne's War—pitted the French against the other three powers. Although neither the Dutch nor the Spanish made extensive use of privateers in Caribbean waters, the French and the English (or rather the British after the Anglo-Scottish Union of 1707) both made great use of this form of naval warfare. In Europe, ports such as Dunkirk for the French and Bristol for the British turned into major privateering havens, while in the Caribbean, Fort-de-France in Martinique, Bridgetown in Barbados, Petit Goâve in Saint Dominique, and Port Royal in Jamaica were all filled with seamen and captains bearing letters of marque. Given the long history of conflict "beyond the line," things weren't quite as simple as all that. When the Spanish joined the allied cause, many British and Dutch privateers surreptitiously applied for letters of marque from French colonial governors. After all, many of the older hands had known little else except waging war against Spain's overseas empire. Then a series of allied victories in Spain led to the division of the country into two camps, each supporting their own rival for the Spanish throne.

During these years privateering was a highly lucrative business, and places like Port Royal attracted merchant seamen in their hundreds, all eager for the opportunity of better working conditions and the chance of earning big money. Port Royal became a boomtown again, and everyone benefited from the war—apart from those ship owners and merchants whose vessels were captured by the French, of course. However, not everyone was so enamored of the conflict, and in 1711 the British government opened secret peace talks with the French. The result was the Treaty of Utrecht, signed in April 1713, which put an end to the hostilities. However, the French and the Imperialists continued to fight in Europe until the following year.

Peace revealed the full extent of the problem Britain had created for herself. When the war ended, all outstanding letters of marque were immediately canceled. As many as 6,000 former privateersmen—all trained to prey on merchant shipping—found themselves unemployed, and the major British and colonial ports were soon filled with former privateersmen, all looking for work. Many were lucky, as when the war ended the British merchant fleet expanded dramatically. With more merchantmen at sea, the demand for sailors gradually increased, and many former privateers were more than happy to accept the poor conditions and pay they were offered by merchant captains. Others decided to use their privateering skills by continuing their private naval war, almost as if the peace had never happened. In other words they turned to piracy but tried to cover their actions by maintaining a fiction of legitimacy. While these former privateers-turned-pirates limited their attacks to their old French or Spanish enemies, other men, such as Blackbeard (see p.188) and Bartholomew Roberts (p.233), had no such scruples. They simply attacked whomsoever they wanted.

Consequently the end of the war meant an increase in both pirates and potential victims, particularly British pirates and British (or colonial American) merchantmen. Although the worst affected areas were the Caribbean and the Atlantic seaboard of America, this new breed of pirate ranged further afield, and both the West African coast and the Indian Ocean became pirate hot spots. In other words, although these pirates did not operate in large fleets like the seventeenth-century buccaneers, their attacks were not confined to the Caribbean or to one enemy, and therefore they proved a greater disruption to the maritime economy. Another contributory factor was the lack of authority. Piracy tends to develop in areas where the authorities lack the power or the will to deal with the problem. The lack of strong government in many of the American colonies during the early eighteenth century made the Atlantic seaboard an attractive area for pirates to operate in, and these waters remained a pirate hunting ground until the governments took firm action to deal with the threat. Often this action came about when the benefits of illicit trade between pirates and colonists were outweighed by the disruption of shipping and rising insurance prices, although in some places, such as the Bahamas, there was a far more aggressive drive to deal with piracy.[2]

The golden age of piracy came to an end when one by one these pirates were hunted down and killed in a series of high-profile pirate executions—those of Stede Bonnet, Charles Vane, Jack Rackam, and the crews of Blackbeard and "Black Bart" Roberts are prime examples. These all tended to discourage other seamen from choosing a piratical career, as did the hardening of attitudes towards piracy amongst seafaring communities who were becoming increasingly reliant on maritime trade. By 1725–30 at the latest, the "age" had passed, and all that remained was the romanticized view of a past era. During their careers, pirates attracted the full attention of the press, and pirate trials and executions all helped to sell newspapers and broadsheets. This contributed to the creation of a somewhat glamorous image of piracy that was largely undeserved and that completely failed to account for the brutal realities of pirate life, save the almost certain prospect of an early death.

This golden age produced some of the most famous pirates in history, men who now seem almost improbably colorful and larger than life after centuries of romanticized accounts of their lives. Writers such as Robert Louis Stevenson and J. M. Barrie, painters such as Howard Pyle, or film stars such as Errol Flynn and Johnny Depp have all added to this, so that today the reality of piracy in the golden age has largely been hidden by the myth. Even the phrase the golden age of piracy is a misleading one, as it suggests a romantic movement rather than a decade of brutal attacks and economic disruption. So scraping away the romance is vital if we want to reveal the true nature of piracy during this period, and if we want to understand anything about the real lives of these desperate men. The result is far removed from the image created by Hollywood.

NEW PROVIDENCE

One of the many drawbacks of being a pirate was that unlike the buccaneers of old, who spent their time raiding the rich treasure ports of the Spanish Main, the plunder captured usually did not come in the form of coins, which could easily be divided up amongst the crew. The merchant ships that were the victims of pirate attacks were not the towering Spanish treasure galleons of the late sixteenth century but everyday trading vessels and transatlantic merchantmen, which sailed through pirate-infested waters to deliver their cargo. These could be slavers bound for Jamaica from the West African coast, ships carrying rum or sugar from the Caribbean to Europe or colonial America, or else the vessels that brought manufactured goods to the colonies of the Americas and returned home laden with tobacco, cotton, furs, timber, or tar. Even the fishing fleets that operated off Newfoundland and the Grand Banks were targeted.

For the most part the pirates simply drank the rum, although other cargoes were sometimes destroyed in an orgy of wanton destruction, just for the simple pleasure of it. Like any criminals, in order to turn anything that remained into money, the pirates needed to find someone willing to buy stolen property without asking too many awkward questions. Clearly places such as Port Royal or Martinique were no longer an option due to an increasingly tough line on piracy and illegal trade. The larger ports of colonial America were also out of the question for the same reason. This left the smaller settlements and island colonies, or else prearranged rendezvous where merchants, smugglers, and pirates could gather to exchange or sell the merchandise. Of course it was much better if the pirates could have their own town filled with shady merchants, brothels, taverns, and gambling dens. In 1715 they got it.

The pirate haven on the island of New Providence in the Bahamas came about because of a Spanish maritime disaster. On June 30, 1715, the annual Spanish treasure *flota* was homeward bound, heading north up the Bahamas Channel between Florida and Grand Bahama. The winds had risen steadily all day, and that evening the fleet ran into a hurricane. One by one the ships were dashed against the Florida coast, and by morning only one of the dozen ships in the *flota* remained afloat. It sped back to Havana with the news, and the Spanish governor wasted no time in sending a salvage expedition to rescue the survivors and to recover the shipwrecked silver.[3]

Unfortunately others had the same idea. In late November a force of some 300 raiders attacked the salvage camp, driving off its small garrison of 60 soldiers and capturing the salvaged treasure. These men—mainly former privateers from Port Royal—made off with an estimated 60,000 pieces-of-eight. For many it must have been just like the old days. Earlier that month the governor of Jamaica sent the former privateer Captain Henry Jennings to the area with orders to see if anything could be salvaged. Jennings took that as an excuse to loot, and it was he who led the raid on the salvage camp. Then, on the return voyage, he ran into a Spanish merchantman, a ship that had just left St. Augustine for Havana, carrying the first batch of recovered treasure. Jennings promptly captured it, and so doubled his haul of plunder.

As the Jamaican governor turned a blind eye to the raid, Jennings returned to the Florida coast in January 1716 and attacked the camp again, this time capturing some 120,000 pieces-of-eight. However, that was the last of the raids, as the Spanish turned their salvage camp into a heavily armed fortress. That summer two galleons carried the salvaged treasure home to Spain, and the camp was abandoned. However, the work was not completed, and by Spanish estimates a total of some 250,000 pieces-of-eight still lay scattered amongst the wreckage. That was when treasure fever swept the Caribbean. Within weeks Henry Jennings had returned, accompanied by a horde of treasure hunters, who established their own salvage camp. Florida was Spanish territory, so, bowing to pressure from London, the Jamaican authorities disowned the salvors.

This left the salvors without legal protection and denied them the opportunity to spend their gains in the fleshpots of Port Royal. However, they now had an alternative. In November 1715 the privateer-turned-pirate Benjamin Hornigold arrived off the struggling British settlement on New Providence in the Bahamas and traded with the locals. By the time he returned a few months later, the island population had grown, as a handful of Jamaican merchants had established small trading posts there. By the following summer, when the treasure hunting was in full swing, New Providence had grown into a small pirate haven, capable of providing a marketplace for stolen goods and of supplying the more basic needs of Hornigold's men. It was inevitable that Henry Jennings and his salvors would gravitate towards this friendly port, and so New Providence grew into a bustling den of pirates, treasure hunters, smugglers, and illicit traders. In June 1716 the governor of Virginia wrote to London complaining that pirates had taken over the Bahamas, which means that the new pirate den was already well established.

New Providence was ideal. It was close to major trade routes and to the Florida wreck sites, and favorable winds allowed an easy passage to these pirate hunting grounds. Its natural harbor of Nassau was large enough to hold a hundred ships or more. The island had a good supply of food, water and timber, vantage points for lookouts, and even a small fort, built by the island's original (and now heavily outnumbered) settlers. Above all New Providence contained a thriving shantytown that provided for the pirates' every need.

What few indigenous people lived there were probably wiped out by disease soon after the arrival of the first European settlers in the mid-seventeenth century. The land was about 60 square miles in size, barely large enough to support a small settlement. By the time Hornigold arrived, most of the population had already moved to nearby Eleuthera, and the settlement at Nassau was all but abandoned, as was the fort. Even better, although it was nominally a British colony and the capital of the British Bahamas, there was no governor to impose the authority of the crown. In other words there was nothing that could prevent the takeover of the island by the pirates.

By the summer of 1717 over 500 pirates were reportedly using the island as a base, serving in at least a dozen small vessels—mainly sloops and brigantines. Men such as Benjamin Hornigold, Charles Vane, Henry Jennings, "Calico Jack" Rackam, Edward Teach ("Blackbeard") and Sam Bellamy all passed through New Providence and called the island home during these few heady years. This meant that the makeshift shanty taverns of Nassau would have read like a veritable pirates' *Who's Who* in late 1717 and early 1718. Merchants and traders bought or traded with these men and then smuggled the goods—including slaves—into the established markets of colonial America and the Caribbean. Captured ships were bought, then sold on elsewhere. Meanwhile shipwrights earned a living repairing pirate ships or mending prizes, while blacksmiths repaired guns and weapons or remounted artillery on new carriages. New Providence must have been a robust and bustling place, where the only form of government stemmed from the collective wishes of the leading pirate captains.

Then the party came to an end. As complaints about all this piratical activity reached London it was decided that something needed to be done. Consequently, on September 5, 1717, King George I signed *A Proclamation for Suppressing Pyrates*. In brief it complained about the "divers Pyracies and Robberies on the High-Seas" of the Bahama pirates, and then went on to offer a solution.[4] If these pirates surrendered to a representative of the crown by September 5, 1718, they would be granted a full pardon—but only for crimes committed before January 5, 1718. Those who refused to accept the pardon would be hunted down, and a sizable reward was offered to anyone willing to help bring them to justice. It was a classic carrot-and-stick policy and was based on the sensible notion that many of these pirates would turn their back on piracy if they were given a second chance.

A copy of the proclamation reached New Providence in December 1717, prompting a winter of debate and argument. The effect was to create two political groups: the one, headed by Hornigold and Jennings, who favored accepting the offer, and the others—the die-hards—led by Charles Vane, who refused to surrender. In March 1718 HMS *Phoenix* sailed into New Providence harbor, its captain eager to discover how the pirates had taken the offer. Captain Pearce was somewhat surprised to receive a cordial welcome, and on April 6 he sailed back to New York with the names of 209 pirates who had accepted his provisional offer of a pardon—the list including both Hornigold and Jennings. Vane's name was nowhere to be found. Pearce also warned the pirates that the British authorities were sending a governor to the island, who would not only establish British rule but would also formally approve the provisional pardons.

The man the British government chose for this delicate job was none other than Woodes Rogers, the buccaneer who had cruised in the waters of the Pacific less than a decade before, and whose privateers *Duke* and *Duchess* had captured a Manila galleon. Rogers would be a poacher-turned-gamekeeper. Since his return to Bristol in early 1711 he had published an account of his voyages, and used his profits to set up a successful slave trading business, shipping his human cargoes from West Africa to the Dutch East Indies. His acceptance of the Bahamian governorship was part duty, part commercial venture, as he hoped to turn the islands into a profitable colony using funds supplied by financial backers in Britain. Just before nightfall on July 26, 1718, Rogers appeared off

New Providence harbor with a squadron of seven ships: his own 30-gun flagship the *Delicia*, the brigantine *Willing Mind*, two hired sloops (the *Buck* and the *Samuel*) transporting a company of British soldiers between them, and an escort of three Royal Navy warships—HMS *Milford* of 32 guns, and the sloops HMS *Rose* and HMS *Shark*. He decided to anchor just outside the harbor for the night and land with full pomp and ceremony the following morning. However, Charles Vane had other plans.

That evening Vane bundled his 90 fellow hard-liners onto two sloops—his own vessel the *Ranger* and a recently captured French prize. He was well prepared, having stocked the prize with enough combustible materials to turn her into a fireship. He raised anchor and set course towards the entrance and Rogers's squadron. He tucked the *Ranger* in behind the now fiercely blazing fireship, and watched as the British crews were forced to cut their anchor cables and make sail to avoid it. To add to the confusion Vane had double-shotted the fireship's guns, and these fired off in the heat. Her crew slipped overboard and rowed over to the *Ranger*, which managed to slip out of the harbor and escape into the darkness.

It was a spectacular gesture on Vane's part, but it left Jennings and Hornigold in firm control of the island. When Rogers finally stepped ashore the following morning, the pirates presented their new governor with a guard of honor, and the two captains escorted the newcomer to the fort, where Rogers raised the Union Jack. New Providence was now under British control. The majority of the pirates were true to their word, and while Jennings retired to Bermuda with his salvage money and plunder, Hornigold accepted the post of Rogers's pirate-hunter, charged with tracking down any of his former shipmates who returned to their old ways. The first test of Rogers's government came in December, when he staged a mass hanging of former New Providence pirates who had been caught within Bahamian waters. There was no uprising, and the hanging served to demonstrate that both Rogers and the law and order he represented were there to stay. His authority was further enhanced when, with the help of the former pirates, he repulsed a Spanish attack the following year. It was clear that the days of New Providence as a pirate haven were over.

Unfortunately, without the economic impetus of piracy, both New Providence and the Bahamas quickly turned into an economic backwater. Rogers never managed to make the islands into a profitable colony, as all his schemes for agriculture and industry came to nothing. By 1721 the money had run out and Rogers returned to Britain, where he was promptly arrested for debt by his

London backers. Although imprisoned, he was later released on appeal and was even paid the salary that the government had withheld from him for the past five years. He returned to New Providence with his family, where he died in 1732. By that time the golden age of piracy was well and truly over, and Woodes Rogers was appropriately remembered as the man who dealt the first blow to this pirate scourge.

CHARLES VANE AND HIS DIE-HARDS

By the time Charles Vane made his dramatic exit from New Providence in August 1718, he was already seen as one of the toughest pirates on the high seas. He began his career with Henry Jennings, attacking the Spanish treasure camps on the Florida coast. Before that he was probably a privateer, working out of Port Royal. By early 1718 he had command of his own sloop, the *Ranger*, and that April he took her on his first independent cruise. He captured two Bermudan sloops, and in depositions written by the sloops' owners Vane was accused of beating and torturing the two crews. One captain claimed that Vane had beaten him and his men and then tortured one of the crew by tying him up, then jabbing burning matches into his eyes. On the other sloop Vane hanged one of the crew until he was almost dead, then slashed at him with his cutlass until his fellow pirates calmed him down. Clearly Charles Vane was something of a murderous psychopath, who was quickly gaining a reputation for cruelty.[5]

We have already heard how the men who declined to accept the King's Pardon—the hard-liners or die-hards—looked towards Vane for leadership. By the time Woodes Rogers was expected, the island had split into two camps, and Vane had already made preparations to sail off on a fresh piratical spree. However, it says a lot about the man that he deliberately waited until Woodes Rogers arrived before making his escape, choosing such a flamboyantly provocative way of doing so. It was almost as if Vane was challenging Rogers to a duel. After quitting New Providence Vane headed towards Charles Town (now Charleston, South Carolina) and was reported loitering off the Charles Town Bar that August. Rogers sent Benjamin Hornigold after the *Ranger*, and although he never caught Vane, he did run into a sloop captured by Vane's former quartermaster—a pirate called Yeats.

According to Captain Johnson, Yeats had been given command of a prize by Vane, but, instead of operating in concert with the *Ranger*, Yeats sailed off on his own cruise. Hornigold encountered one of Yeats's victims in the Bahamas and captured its newly installed pirate crew. Former New Providence pirates to a man, they were taken back to Nassau, where they were tried and hanged. This was the first real test of Woodes Rogers's leadership, and fortunately for the authorities the mass hanging took place without incident. However, Charles Vane was still at large, and he was reportedly still operating in the waters of the Carolinas. By that time the South Carolina colony had sent a two-ship antipiracy squadron out on patrol, with orders to track Vane down. Although Vane managed to avoid them, another pirate, Stede Bonnet, was less lucky and was cornered and captured in the Cape Fear River. Bonnet and his men were taken back to Charles Town, where they too were tried and executed—the second mass hanging of pirates in as many months.

By September the *Ranger* was lying off Ocracoke Island in North Carolina's Outer Banks, a haven then being used by Blackbeard. The two pirate crews spent a week together, and by all accounts they had a marvelous beach party, complete with rum and women shipped across from nearby Bath Town. When the authorities heard of this union they feared that it might herald the creation of a pirate confederation and the start of a marauding pirate squadron. They need not have worried, as Blackbeard and Vane soon parted company, and Vane sailed off northwards, bound for the busy waters off New York and Long Island. Captain Johnson places Vane off Long Island on October 23, 1718, when he captured a small brig on her way from Jamaica to Massachusetts.

Then, with the onset of winter weather, the pirates decided to return to the warmer waters of the Caribbean. This was a common enough practice for pirates and privateers—like migrating birds they tended to head south for the winter. By late November Charles Vane and his men had reached the Windward Passage between Saint Dominique and Cuba after a monthlong voyage which brought no prizes, no plunder, and no rum. The crew were already a little disaffected when, on November 23, they sighted a French merchantman. It seemed as if the pirates' luck had turned. Captain Johnson described what happened next:

Then they fell upon a ship, which 'twas expected would have struck as soon as their black colors were hoisted; but instead of that, she discharged a broadside on the pirate, and hoisted colors, which showed her to be a French man-of-war. Vane desired to have nothing further to say, but trimmed his sails, and stood away from the Frenchman; but Monsieur having a mind to be better informed who he was, set all his sails, and crowded after him. During this chase, the pirates were divided in their resolutions what to do; Vane, the captain, was for making off as fast as he could, alleging the man-of-war was too strong to cope with; but one John Rackam, who was an officer that had a kind of check upon the captain, rose up in defense of a contrary position, saying that though she had more guns, and a greater weight of metal, they might board her, and then the best boys would carry the day.[6]

There was no such thing as a mutiny on a pirate ship—after all, the captain and quartermaster were both elected, and decisions were usually reached by consensus. However, when it came to decisions made in action, the captain should have had the last word. What Vane was facing amounted to a mutiny. Although he managed to have his way and the *Ranger* veered away from the French warship, the taint of cowardice was left behind in its wake. The quartermaster Jack Rackam called a vote, and a resolution was passed, branding Vane a coward and removing him from his captaincy. Rackam would be the next pirate captain. At the time the *Ranger* was accompanied by a small sloop, a prize captured off Long Island. Vane and 16 supporters were moved into her, and the *Ranger*, with its new captain, "Calico Jack" Rackam, sailed off into the sunset, heading towards Jamaica.

Vane seemed undeterred by being left with a small sloop and a skeleton crew. He decided to head off towards the Gulf of Honduras, and so he sailed round the north side of Jamaica, capturing a sloop on the way, then made landfall off what is now Belize in mid-December 1718. He established a base on an island that Captain Johnson called "Barnacko," and then used this haven while he raided southwards into the Gulf—the home of the logwood cutters. Then disaster struck. Sometime in February 1719 a violent storm hit the two sloops and, after being pummeled by the seas for two days, Vane and his men were shipwrecked on a small island—probably around what is now Lighthouse Reef off Belize. As Captain Johnson claimed, "Vane himself was saved, but reduced to great straits, for want of necessaries, having no opportunity to get anything from the wreck."

The pirate castaways survived for several weeks before a ship put in to the island for water. Unfortunately the skipper—a Captain Holford—recognized Vane and refused to rescue him or his men. However, the next ship was more obliging, and the marooned men were rescued. Then, in an unlikely twist of fate, the rescue ship encountered the one whose captain had refused to pick up Vane and his men, as he knew them to be pirates. As the two passing ships heaved in the middle of the ocean, the captains yelled greetings to each other, and one invited the other for dinner. After the feast, as he was returning to his own ship,

Captain Holford spotted Vane amongst the crew. The game was up. He told the rescuers who the castaways were, and Vane and his men were captured. The pirates were transferred to Holford's ship, which returned to Jamaica.

By November 1719 Charles Vane was back in Jamaica, this time safely locked away in a Spanish Town jail. His trial began on March 22, 1720, and the result was a foregone conclusion. After all, Vane had refused the King's Pardon some 20 months earlier and fired on Governor Rogers. The condemned pirate was taken to Gallows Point overlooking Port Royal harbor, where he was hanged, after which his body was displayed in a cage as a warning to others.

The second of Vane's two sloops—the one that had parted from him in the storm off Belize—was commanded by Robert Deal, Vane's right-hand man. He was captured by a British warship just a few weeks after he parted company with Vane, and he and his small crew were swinging from Gallows Point while Vane was still a castaway. Of course Vane was not the last of the die-hards who defied Woodes Rogers and the king. His nemesis "Calico Jack" Rackam remained at large—the last of the Bahamian pirates to remain in business.

"CALICO JACK" RACKAM

The capture and execution of Charles Vane was something of a triumph for the British authorities, and a stern warning to others. As Captain Vernon, the commander of the Royal Naval squadron based in Port Royal, put it, "He has been tried, condemned and executed, and is now hanging in chains … These punishments have made a wonderful reformation here."[7] However, the unfortunate Vane was merely a figurehead, and most of the 90 men who sailed from Nassau with him in the summer of 1718 were still at large. After the crew rebellion on board the *Ranger*, "Calico Jack" Rackam became the new leader of the 50 or so die-hards who had rejected Vane as their captain. That made Rackam rather than Vane the real focal point of the Bahamian hard-liners.

We know nothing of Rackam's life before he sailed with Vane, apart from his nickname—"Calico Jack." Calico is a textile made from unbleached cotton, less coarse than canvas, and far cheaper than processed cotton. Its name came from the Indian port of Calicut (now Kozhikode), where it was mass-produced. In 1700 its import into England or the American colonies was banned in an attempt to protect the English cotton industry, and so Rackam may well have earned his nickname as a smuggler of cloth into American or Caribbean ports. However, this is mere speculation, and the real reason for his unusual nickname may never be known.

After sending Charles Vane on his way, Rackam cruised the waters of the Leeward Islands, where he captured a few small prizes. He then headed west to the Jamaica Channel, between Jamaica and Saint Dominique. He captured a merchantman bound from Madeira to Jamaica, and his men spent two days drinking their way through her cargo of wine. By late December Rackam was somewhere north of Hispaniola, where he careened the *Ranger*—scraping the

The pirate "Calico Jack" Rackam (often written as Rackham) was elected the captain of the New Providence "die-hards" when they deposed Charles Vane.

marine growth from her hull so she could sail faster. Apparently Christmas was one big drunken beach party for Rackam and his men. They had little to celebrate over the next few months, as they cruised the Windward Passage without capturing anything more than a convict ship, bound for the Jamaican plantations. The pirates freed the convicts, and sent them on their way in their ship. Their freedom was short-lived, as a few days later the ship was recaptured by a British warship.

Rackam then decided to head north towards the Bahamas, which is where the accounts become a little confused. According to Captain Johnson he captured two large merchantmen, and when news of this reached New Providence, Woodes Rogers sent out a well-armed sloop to hunt down the pirates. He then claims that as Rackam and his men were busy securing two more prizes, the Bahamian sloop-of-war arrived and drove them off. The pirates then spent the next few months hiding out on the southern coast of Cuba. However, the truth was a lot less spectacular. In December 1718 Britain declared war on Spain—a conflict that lasted just 14 months. The British government decided it needed privateers again, and so to boost numbers Woodes Rogers reissued his offer of a pardon. Rackam and his die-hards must have decided they had enough of being on the wrong side of the law, for in May 1719 Rackam applied for and was awarded a pardon.

It seemed as if the last of the die-hards had hauled down their black flag for good. It appears that the *Ranger* was sold off, which meant that the profits would have been divided amongst her crew of former pirates. Rackam and his shipmates would have made some effort to look for honest work, probably signing on as the crew of privateers. However, the end of the war in February 1720 would have ended that lucrative opportunity. It was during this time that Rackam met the first of two women who would scandalize polite society. We shall hear more of Anne Bonny and Mary Read later, but suffice it to say that Anne met "Calico Jack" in New Providence that year, and when he decided he wanted to return to piracy, she left her husband and sailed with him.

On August 22, 1720, Rackam and 13 of his followers—including Anne Bonny—rowed out to the 12-gun Bahamian sloop *William*, which was riding at anchor in Nassau harbor. They seized the ship and escaped before the authorities could stop them or give chase. Amazingly, one of the dozen men in his crew turned out to be another woman—Mary Read, who had disguised herself as a man. Woodes Rogers responded by issuing a proclamation, which declared: "John

Rackum and his said Company are hereby proclaimed Pirates and Enemies of the Crown of Great Britain, and are to be so treated and Deem'd by all His Majesty's subjects."[8] The document also listed two of Rackam's crew—Anne Fulford, alias Bonny, and Mary Read.

It seems that Rackam took the *William* south through the Windward Passage, pausing only to raid a small fleet of Bahamian fishing boats. On October 1 he captured two sloops off the northwest corner of Saint Dominique, somewhere near Tortuga, and by the middle of the month he captured a third vessel off the northern coast of Jamaica. The Jamaican authorities immediately sent the pirate-hunter Captain Jonathan Barnet out to find Rackam in the 12-gun sloop the *Eagle*, but the pirate seemed oblivious to the reaction his actions provoked and continued westwards along the Jamaican coast, past Montego Bay and on to Negril Point—the most westerly tip of the island. There, on November 15, he overtook a small piragua crewed by nine turtle-hunters, and they offered their catch in exchange for drink. The pirates dropped anchor and a drinking session began, which continued into the evening.

A few hours later Barnet was approaching the Point from the south when he heard the sound of musketry coming from closer inshore. He altered course to investigate and came upon the *William* and the piragua. (The musket shot was probably fired off by a drunken pirate.) Rackam slashed his anchor cable and tried to escape, but within an hour the *Eagle* had overhauled them. Evidently an excess of rum was not conducive to good seamanship. Barnet hailed the *William*, asking her captain to identify himself. The reply—"John Rackam from Cuba" was enough for Barnet, who ordered the pirates to surrender.

They replied by firing a swivel gun at the *Eagle*, and Barnet replied with a full broadside. A roundshot cut through the *William's* boom, and the pirate sloop swung up into the wind. Barnet seized the opportunity to come alongside and boarded the *William*. Only Bonny and Read seemed to have been in a fit enough state to offer any resistance, cursing their drunken shipmates as they fought. As Captain Johnson put it, they "called to those under deck to come up and fight like men, and finding that they did not stir, fired arms down the hold amongst them, killing one and wounding others."[9] These two firebrand women were soon overpowered, and the pirates were taken back to Spanish Town in chains.

On November 16, 1720, the Vice Admiralty Court tried and convicted Rackam and his nine remaining male shipmates, and the following morning "Calico Jack" and four others were hanged on Gallows Point—the same place where Charles Vane had met his end eight months before. The remaining six were hanged the next day, this time at a gallows erected on the outskirts of Kingston. Rather unjustly the court also condemned the poor turtle-hunters, whose only crime was being in the wrong place when Barnet appeared out of the darkness. As for the two women pirates, their arrest caused a storm of interest. After all, this was a time when women simply didn't do that kind of thing. So began a public fascination with the lives of Anne Bonny and Mary Read that has never really gone away.

ANNE BONNY AND MARY READ

On November 28, 1720, the two women pirates were tried in the Vice Admiralty Court in Spanish Town, and like their male shipmates they were sentenced to be hanged. However, no sooner had the sentence been passed than they both claimed they were pregnant. It was not normal British policy to hang women, let alone ones with child, so the execution was delayed while a doctor was found to examine the pair. It turned out that both were telling the truth, although exactly who the fathers were has never been explained. Rackam may well have been responsible—at least for the pregnancy of his partner Anne Bonny, although it was also claimed that both women repeatedly offered themselves to their jailers, knowing that only pregnancy could guarantee their escape from the gallows.

Mary Read died in prison five months later, still carrying her unborn child. As for Anne Bonny, "She was continued in prison, to the time of her laying in, and afterwards reprieved from time to time; but what became of her since, we cannot tell; only this we know, that she was not executed."[10] Like many others, she probably ended her days in the brothels or gutters of Port Royal or Kingston, although like anything involving these somewhat larger than life characters, rumors continued to circulate that she lived to become a respectable mother and model citizen in the American colonies.

Whatever the truth behind the lives of Anne Bonny and Mary Read, the two women seemed to fascinate, scandalize, and titillate contemporary society in equal measure, the most shocking revelation being that both had dressed as men and had passed themselves off as seamen. In other words, Bonny and Read had broken all the rules, and had escaped from the restrictions imposed on the lives of women of the time. If this was not shocking enough, they had also turned to a life of crime and had used their bodies to avoid sharing the fate of Rackam and his men. It was little wonder that the newspapers of the day were full of the

The Atlantic Seaboard
c. 1718

A Scale of English Miles
0   100   200   300   400   500

The
Grand
Banks

Halifax

Salem
Massachusetts Bay
Cape Cod
Boston
Newport
Block Island

NH
NY
MA
RI
CT

Long Island
New York
Delaware Bay

NJ
Philadelphia
Baltimore
MD   DE
PA

Chesapeake Bay
Williamsburg
James River
VA

Cape Hatteras
Bath
Okracoke Island

NC

Cape Fear

SC

Charles Town

GA

Atlantic
Ocean

CT	Connecticut
DE	Delaware
GA	Georgia
MA	Massachusetts
MD	Maryland
NC	North Carolina
NH	New Hampshire
NJ	New Jersey
NY	New York
PA	Pennsylvania
RI	Rhode Island
SC	South Carolina
VA	Virginia

THE
BAHAMAS
New
Providence

Florida Straits

CUBA

story, and what was not actually known about the two women was happily made up for the readers. The public was gripped by the scandalous notion that two women could turn to piracy. However, this was probably not the first time that women had followed the black flag.

There was the medieval French noblewoman Jane de Belleville, who reputedly sided with the English following the invasion of Brittany in 1345. She was supposed to have fitted out three privateers and led them on raids of the Normandy coast. Then there was Charlotte de Berry, a seventeenth-century English-woman, who according to tradition dressed as a man to follow her husband to sea. She was captured by a privateer, and after being raped by its captain, she engineered a mutiny, which ended with the murder of her assailant. The trouble with these tales is they cannot be substantiated, unlike the account of the Irish pirate Grace O'Malley, whose exploits have already been mentioned (see p.35). Another verifiable woman privateer was Lady Killigrew, who commanded a ship that operated in the English Channel during the mid-sixteenth century. However, these were very isolated cases, and so female pirates were very much a novelty when Bonny and Read made the headlines.

Consequently both of them warranted their own chapter in a revised edition of Captain Johnson's pirate biography. Unfortunately, despite all the contemporary newspaper coverage, we know very little about the two women. The biographer probably embroidered what was known about their backgrounds from the stories that had circulated in the press. However, although much of his information may have been made up, Captain Johnson still remains our best source of information on Bonny and Read.

According to him, Anne Bonny (or Bonn) was Irish, the illegitimate daughter of a lawyer from County Cork and his maid. Johnson gives a long-winded account of Anne's early family life, explaining how Anne was passed off as a boy during most of her formative years, the deception allowing the father to collect a maternal allowance set aside for a son. Eventually the ruse was discovered, the allowance was stopped, and to avoid any further shame, Anne's father emigrated to the Carolinas, where he passed off his maid as his wife. He began by practising law again, but after Anne's mother died he took to commerce, building up a respectable fortune. It was hoped that Anne would marry well, but instead she ran off with a sailor who "was not worth a groat." When her father threw her out of his house, she ran off with her husband to New Providence in the Bahamas, arriving there sometime around the end of 1719.

Before the mid-1st century BC piracy was considered an endemic problem in the Mediterranean. This Roman mosaic depicts the Greek god Dionysus fighting pirates. (Charles & Josette Lenars/Corbis)

In 67 BC the successful Roman general Pompey was ordered to clear the Mediterranean of pirates. By the time the operation ended Pompey had brilliantly achieved his goal. (The Art Archive/Corbis)

This Swedish stela (or boundary stone) depicts Scandinavian longships of the type used by Viking raiders to prey on the coastlines of northern Europe during the 8th and 9th centuries AD. (Charles & Josette Lenars/Corbis)

The Osberg *ship formed part of a burial mound, dating from the 9th century AD. It remains one of the few extant examples of a Norse longship—the kind of craft used by Viking sea raiders during their heyday. (Christophe Boisvieux/Corbis)*

This portrayal of Sir Francis Drake by Marcus Gheeraerts the Younger captures the charisma of the Elizabethan sea dog who terrorized the Spanish for the best part of three decades. (National Maritime Museum, Greenwich, London)

John Hawkins was one of the first Englishmen to risk crossing the line. His first two ventures as an interloper were successful, but his luck finally ran out at San Juan de Ulúa. (National Maritime Museum, Greenwich, London)

This painting by Aert Anthonisz entitled An English & a Dutch Ship Attacking a Spaniard *illustrates how Spanish treasure ships presented lucrative targets for interlopers. (National Maritime Museum, Greenwich, London)*

This colored engraving by Baptista Boazio depicts Sir Francis Drake's privateering fleet off Santo Domingo during his assault on the Spanish-held port in 1586. (National Maritime Museum, Greenwich, London)

Drake followed up his assault on Santo Domingo with an attack on the well-defended city of Cartagena on the Spanish Main, which was then the largest city in the Americas. Engraving by Baptista Boazio. (National Maritime Museum, Greenwich, London)

For much of the 16th century the Spanish were locked in a bitter fight with the Barbary pirates. Spanish Engagement with Barbary Pirates, *by Andries van Eertvelt. (National Maritime Museum, Greenwich, London)*

ABOVE *By the late 16th century the Spanish supported their galley fleet with sailing galleons, armed with large batteries of heavy guns.* Spanish Men of War Engaging Barbary Corsairs, *by Hendriksz Cornelis Vroom. (National Maritime Museum, Greenwich, London)*

LEFT *Hizir Barbarossa, known as* Khair-ed-din *("The Gift of God").* Portrait of Barbarossa, *Florentine School, c. 1550. (Christie's Images/Corbis)*

This painting depicts the Dutch assault on Bahia, now the Brazilian port of San Salvador. Attack on San Salvador, 1624, *by Andries van Eertvelt. (National Maritime Museum, Greenwich, London)*

By the 1620s the Dutch were sending whole fleets of warships to the Caribbean to disrupt Spanish treasure shipments. Dutch Squadron Attacking a Spanish Fortress, *by Adam Willaerts. (National Maritime Museum, Greenwich, London)*

In the mid-17th century, Port Royal developed into Jamaica's main harbor and the leading buccaneering port in the Caribbean. View of Port Royal, Jamaica, *by Richard Paton. (National Maritime Museum, Greenwich, London)*

The Bristol-born privateer turned colonial administrator Woodes Rogers was the man responsible for driving the pirates from the Bahamas. Woodes Rogers and his Family, *by William Hogarth. (National Maritime Museum, Greenwich, London)*

Blackbeard finally met his match in November 1718, when he was attacked by two sloops commanded by Lieutenant Maynard of the Royal Navy. The Capture of the Pirate Blackbeard, 1718, *by Jean Leon Gerome. (Bettmann/Corbis)*

The Portuguese, the Dutch, and later the English grew rich on the spice trade, making their East Indiamen prime targets for pirates by the end of the 17th century. Ships Trading in the East, *by Hendrik Cornelisz Vroom the Elder. (National Maritime Museum, Greenwich, London)*

By the late 17th century the English East India Company had grown into one of the biggest commercial organizations in the world, and its ships transported a fortune in spices and other goods from India to London. An English East Indiaman, c.1720, *by Peter Monamy.* (National Maritime Museum, Greenwich, London)

After the pirate Bartholomew Roberts was killed in a sea battle fought against HMS Swallow, the surviving members of his crew were taken to Cape Coast Castle, where they stood trial for piracy. (Werner Forman/Corbis)

During the 18th and early 19th centuries the maritime powers of Europe and America made extensive use of privateers to prey on enemy merchant shipping in time of war. An English Privateer off La Rochelle, *by Cornelis Claesz van Wieringen. (National Maritime Museum, Greenwich, London)*

Ruses of all kinds were employed by pirates in an attempt to lure their victims within range. Early 19th-century engraving by Auguste-François Biard. (National Maritime Museum, Greenwich, London)

ABOVE *The brief resurgence of piracy in the years following the end of the Napoleonic Wars presented the navies of the world with a fresh challenge.* A Man-of-war Chasing a Pirate Lugger, *painting by an unknown artist of the English School. (National Maritime Museum, Greenwich, London)*

LEFT *The White Rajah of Sarawak, the British officer James Brooke, waged his own private war against the Dyak pirates of Indonesia.* Portrait of James Brooke of Sarawak (1803–68). *(National Portrait Gallery, London)*

The climax of James Brooke's campaign against the Indonesian pirates came in 1845, when he assaulted the main pirate enclave on the coast of Borneo. Cutting the Boom at Malludu/Pirate Headquarters Destroyed, Borneo 1845. *(National Maritime Museum, Greenwich, London)*

During the 18th and early 19th centuries the British safeguarded trade in the Indian Ocean and the Persian Gulf by attacking pirate dens along the coast of India and Persia. The Storming of Schinaass, Persian Gulf, 1810. *(National Maritime Museum, Greenwich, London)*

The Destruction of Chuiapoo's Pirate Fleet, 1849, *by Nam-Sing. The wooden junks of the Chinese pirates were no match for Western firepower. (National Maritime Museum, Greenwich, London)*

The destruction of the Chinese pirate Shap-'ng-Tsai's fleet in Vietnam's Tong King (Honga) River at the hands of the East India Company. Drawing by Edward Cree, 1849. (National Maritime Museum, Greenwich, London)

By the mid-19th century the navies of the world were able to employ steam-powered warships to hunt down pirates in the South China Sea. British Paddleship Nemesis in Action against Pirate Junks at Kut-O, 1850. *(National Maritime Museum, Greenwich, London)*

This silken flag once belonged to the Chinese pirate leader Shap-'ng-Tsai and depicts T'ien Hou, the Calmer of Storms and the Empress of Heaven. (National Maritime Museum, Greenwich, London)

Today, one of the most pirate-infested stretches of water in the world is the Malacca Straits, between the Malaysian Peninsula and the Indonesian island of Sumatra. (Reuters/Corbis)

Most modern pirates operate from fast speedboats and tend to be equipped with a fearsome array of automatic weapons. (Michael S. Yamashita/Corbis)

Many fictional pirates are based loosely on real historical characters. In Roman Polanski's film Pirates *(1986), Captain Red, the character played by Walter Matthau, incorporated elements of both Blackbeard and Captain Kidd. (J. P Laffont/Sygma/Corbis)*

Captain Jack Sparrow, as portrayed by Johnny Depp in Pirates of the Caribbean: Dead Man's Chest *(2006). Depp's character bears little resemblance to the real pirates of the "Golden Age," although he brilliantly captures their reckless spirit. (Bureau L.A. Collection/Corbis)*

Johnson's description of her relationship with "Calico Jack" Rackam is particularly revealing. "Here [New Providence] she became acquainted with Rackam the pirate, who making courtship of her, soon found means of withdrawing her affections from her husband, so that she consented to elope with him, and go to sea with Rackam in men's clothes."[11] However, Johnson went on to claim that Anne became pregnant, and so Rackam lodged her with friends in Cuba until after the child's birth. He also places this before Rackam accepted the King's Pardon, which is virtually impossible given the timing of known events in Rackam's life. It is much more likely they met after he returned to New Providence and signed the pardon.

After Rackam returned to piracy, Johnson claims that "Anne Bonny kept him company, and when any business was to be done in their way, nobody was more forward or courageous than she." He continued by recounting that she visited Rackam in his cell the morning of his execution, when she told him that "she was sorry to see him there, but if he had fought like a man, he need not have been hanged like a dog." Johnson makes little mention of the pregnancy which saved her from the gallows, but hinted that her father might have had a hand in her reprieve. "Her father was known to a great many gentlemen, planters from Jamaica, who had dealt with him ... Wherefore they were inclined to show her favor, but the action of leaving her husband was an ugly act against her."[12] According to the strict laws of early eighteenth-century society, being a female pirate was bad enough, but abandoning your husband was nigh-on unforgivable. The implication of Johnson's mention of her father's influence is that she may well have returned to her parental home after her release from the Jamaican prison.

Johnson provides even less information about Mary Read. She was English, born in London, and her mother's second child. The first, a son, was legitimate, the father being a sailor who for some unexplained reason never returned home after his birth. Mary's pregnant mother moved to the country to give birth to her, and while she was there her infant son died. After three or four years the mother returned to London, and in order to claim support from her husband's family she passed Mary off as the legitimate child—the son. That means that, like Anne Bonny, Mary spent her childhood being raised as a son rather than as a daughter. When she became a teenager she left home, and served for a time in the Royal Navy, then as an ensign in an English infantry regiment. This is all pretty far fetched, and probably Johnson drew his biography from the sensationalist newspaper reports that circulated around the time of the trial in Jamaica.

The story becomes even more unbelievable. Mary then became a cavalryman, fighting in several engagements before she fell for a Flemish soldier. The two soldiers courted in secret, and at the end of a season's campaigning she revealed herself to be a woman and married her lover. They both quit the service and opened a restaurant in Breda, and for a while everything went well. Then around 1697 her husband died, and business fell away to nothing. She then ran away to sea, on a vessel bound for the West Indies. When her ship was captured by English pirates they took her with them, and she remained part of their crew until they accepted the King's Pardon. The crew ended up in New Providence, enticed by the prospect of a privateering letter of marque. Woodes Rogers granted them the licence, but then a group—including Mary—returned to their old ways.

Once again, this version does not hold up under scrutiny. From the death of her husband to her return to piracy in 1720 she is supposed to have spent most of her time at sea. Even the most hardened seaman of the period would have been hard pushed to spend a decade before the mast in those days, where danger, poor conditions and a near-constant risk of death through disease, war, or injury were the lot of the common sailor. According to Johnson, she would have been around 13 or 14 when she first ran away to sea, and in her early 20s by the time her husband died—an event Johnson sets around the end of the War of the League of Augsburg in 1697. That means she spent the best part of 23 years at sea and was in her mid-40s when she met Anne Bonny. This was extremely unlikely in those days, and also makes her pregnancy in Jamaica another near-impossibility.

If we accept a grain of truth in the account, it makes far more sense to suggest that her husband died around 1713—around the time of the War of the Spanish Succession—and she took passage to the West Indies a year or so later. That fits in with a short piratical career, the granting of a pardon, and her meeting with Rackam and Bonny. However, there is also nothing to say that Johnson's account is any more than a complete fabrication, based on garbled and melodramatic newspaper stories of the time.

Johnson goes on to describe how Read dressed as a sailor, and only revealed her real identity to Anne Bonny, possibly Rackam, and a young sailor she took a fancy to. As Johnson put it: "When she found he had a friendship for her, as a man, she suffered the discovery to be made, by carelessly showing her breasts, which were very white." If such a romance took place it was short-lived, as within three months of joining Rackam's crew, the young man was hanged as a pirate along with his captain, while the pregnant Mary Read remained in jail, where "she was seized of a violent fever soon after the trial, of which she died in prison." She was buried on April 21, 1721, still carrying her unborn child.

The proceedings of the trial provide us with a superb description of the two women pirates. One witness—a woman whose canoe was stopped and pilfered by Rackam—said: "The two women, prisoners at the bar, were then on board the

The female pirate Anne Bonny was one of two women in "Calico Jack" Rackam's crew.

said sloop, and wore men's jackets and long trousers, and handkerchiefs tied about their heads, and that each of them had a machete and pistol in their hands."[13] Another claimed of the women that "they were both very profligate, cursing and swearing much." It was a sensational image at the time, and one which guaranteed the inclusion of Anne Bonny and Mary Read in any fictional or historical account of piracy during the golden age. However, apart from the circumstances surrounding their last few weeks at sea, their capture, their trial, and their escape from the gallows, everything else we know about them is little more than supposition, the word of a contemporary biographer whose account of their lives smacks of a rush job—making the most of their notoriety to sell a revised copy of his book. Of course, one can hardly blame Captain Johnson for that.

THE RISE OF BLACKBEARD

These days, if anyone shuts their eyes and conjures up an image of a historical pirate, the chances are they'll think of Blackbeard. He owes his fame to Captain Johnson, whose vivid description of the man certainly captures the imagination:

> So our hero, Captain Teach, assumed the cognomen of Blackbeard from that large quantity of hair which, like a frightful meteor, covered his whole face and frightened America more than any comet that has appeared there a long time. The beard was black, which he suffered to grow of an extravagant length; as to breadth it came up to his eyes. He was accustomed to twist it with ribbons, in small tails, after the manner of our ramilies wigs, and turn them about his ears.
>
> In time of Action, he wore a Sling over his Shoulders, with three brace of Pistols, hanging from Holsters like Bandaliers; he wore a Fur-Cap, and stuck a lighted Match on each Side, under it, which appearing on each side of his Face, his Eyes naturally looking Fierce and Wild, made him altogether such a Figure, that Imagination cannot form an idea of a Fury, from hell, to look more frightful … If he had the look of a fury, his humours and passions were suitable to it.[14]

Clearly Blackbeard—or Edward Teach as Captain Johnson called him—was no ordinary pirate but one who was careful to cultivate an incredibly fearsome image. He realized that for any violent criminal, intimidation was the key to success. If your opponent or victim is terrified of you before you have even raised a finger, then your task is made a lot easier. Blackbeard used his appearance as a weapon, both to intimidate his victims and to avoid unrest amongst his own crew.

Like many pirates, we know little about his early life. Like thousands of other seamen of his time, he remained anonymous and appeared in official records only after he started his piratical career. Captain Johnson claims that he was born in Bristol—probably around 1680—although a comprehensive search of the records there has failed to unearth any child called Teach. He then claims that Edward Teach "sailed some time out of Jamaica in privateers, in the late French war; yet though he had often distinguished himself for his uncommon boldness and personal courage, he was never raised to any command."[15]

This privateering background would have made him typical of many of the New Providence pirates, although his success as a privateer worked in his favor when, according to Johnson, Benjamin Hornigold "put him into a sloop that he had made prize of, and with whom he continued in consortship till a little while before Hornigold surrendered." In other words, Blackbeard started his piratical career as one of Hornigold's crew, sailing out of New Providence during 1716 and 1717. When he realized Blackbeard's potential, Hornigold became his pirate mentor and raised his protégé to the rank of an auxiliary captain.

The first mention of Teach in any official record came in March 1717, when a Captain Mathew (sic) Munthe ran his sloop aground on Cat Cay, on the western fringe of the Bahamas. While he was freeing his vessel he spoke to local fishermen, who told him a little about the piratical activities in New Providence. In a letter to the deputy governor of the South Carolina colony, Munthe reported that "five pirates made the harbor of Providence their place of rendevous vizt. Horngold, a sloop with 10 guns and about 80 men; Jennings, a sloop with 10 guns and 100 men; Burgiss, a sloop with 8 guns and about 80 men; White, in a small vessel with 30 men and small arms; Thatch, a sloop 6 guns and about 70 men."[16] That means that by the spring of 1717 at the latest, Blackbeard had his own command.

However, he was still cruising in concert with Hornigold. Captain Johnson wrote:

In the spring of the year 1717, Teach and Hornigold sailed from [New] Providence, for the Main of America, and took in their way a billop from the Havana, with 120 barrels of flour, as also a sloop from Bermuda, Thurbar, master, from whom they took only some gallons of wine, and then let him go; and a ship from Madeira to South Carolina, out of which they got plunder to a considerable value.[17]

This success hid a growing dissent amongst the pirates. Hornigold always claimed he was a privateer rather than a pirate, a fiction that he supported by limiting his attacks to French or Spanish targets. Blackbeard had fewer scruples, and although he was probably not directly involved in it, he would have supported the rebellion that took place that autumn, when Hornigold's crew deposed him from his captaincy. Hornigold returned to New Providence, where he teamed up with Henry Jennings to lead the pro-pardon group. Blackbeard then began operating on his own.

By late September 1717 Blackbeard was off Cape Charles in Virginia, where he captured the sloop *Betty*. After drinking her cargo of wine the pirates sank their prey, leaving her crew to row ashore in a longboat. In late October the *Boston News Letter* ran the story that a merchantman commanded by a Captain Codd was captured in the mouth of the Delaware River "by a Pirate Sloop called *Revenge*, of 12 Guns, 150 Men, Commanded by one Teach, who Formerly Sail'd Mate out of this Port."[18] The enigmatic reference to Blackbeard's earlier association with Philadelphia may suggest that he spent some time as a merchant sailor. The newspaper reported three other pirate attacks in the same area but did not mention Teach by name. He also captured three more prizes off the Virginia Capes and added another sloop to his force. Every time he captured a ship he also asked for volunteers to join his crew. This way he slowly built up his force.

The line in the *Boston News Letter* suggests another encounter. After mentioning the *Revenge,* it went on to claim that "on board the Pirate Sloop is Major Bennet, but has no Command." This is hardly surprising, as Major Bennet—actually Major Bonnet—was the owner of the *Revenge,* a pirate sloop that had the misfortune of encountering Blackbeard on the high seas. Blackbeard suggested to the inexperienced Bonnet that he should allow the professional pirates to run his ship for him, and so Bonnet became a de facto prisoner on board his own sloop. We will return to Major Stede Bonnet later, but for now his ship and his men were purloined by Blackbeard, who turned the *Revenge* into his flagship.

By late October Blackbeard was off New Jersey. This was the usual time when pirates headed south for the winter. The hurricane season was over for the year (it lasts from early June until November), and winter gales were starting to make the northern waters unpleasant. Consequently Teach set course for the Leeward Islands, and by November 17 the *Revenge* was 60 miles to the west of Martinique in company with a second pirate sloop. Lookouts spotted a large merchantman, and the pirates gave chase. She was overtaken and surrendered after only a token resistance. The prize turned out to be *La Concorde*, a well-built 200-ton French slave ship from Nantes, bound for Martinique. Teach led her into the secluded island anchorage of Bequia, where he set about converting her into his new flagship.

THE *QUEEN ANNE'S REVENGE*

La Concorde carried 16 guns, but Blackbeard had been collecting artillery, storing the guns and carriages in the holds of his two sloops. These guns were moved to the slaver, which was being transformed into the ultimate pirate ship. Teach would have cut down her stern structure and forecastle to make her more suitable as a fighting ship and removed the slave decks from her hold. By the time he had finished, the new ship—which he renamed the *Queen Anne's Revenge*—carried no fewer than 40 guns, making her one of the most powerful fighting ships in the Caribbean. He kept the *Revenge* but let his French prisoners sail off to Martinique in the smaller of his two sloops. As for *La Concorde's* miserable human cargo, they were left on Bequia, where they would soon be rounded up by the French captain and his men. Blackbeard then set off in search of another victim.

It was now late November 1717. His first prize was a small sloop, which he added to his fleet. Then off St. Lucia he captured the Boston merchantman *Great Allen*, en route from Barbados to Jamaica. The pirates kept her for a day, plundering her of anything they wanted, and then set fire to her. He went on to take three other smaller vessels—all sloops—before he encountered the sloop *Margaret*, off Crab Island near Anguilla. The importance of this encounter was that her captain—Henry Bostock—was the first of Blackbeard's victims to provide a detailed description of the pirate. He described "Capt. Tach" as "a tall spare man with a very black beard which he wore very long." This is probably the description that Captain Johnson used as the basis for his more exuberant one. It also gave rise to the pirate's nickname. From that point on he would be Blackbeard.

Johnson also describes a stand-up fight between Blackbeard and the warship HMS *Scarborough*. This never happened, although the *Queen Anne's Revenge* and the 30-gun frigate were both operating in the same part of the West Indies at the time. Powerful though his ship was, Blackbeard knew that his pirates were no match for the well-trained crew of a British man-of-war. News of the warship's presence was probably what made him leave the West Indies and head towards Hispaniola, where the Spanish were less likely to pose a threat. He probably spent Christmas in Semana Bay, on the eastern side of the island, before heading southwest towards the Gulf of Honduras with two ships—the *Revenge* and the *Queen Anne's Revenge*.

Blackbeard spent a month there—the same area of waters in which Charles Vane would cruise in a few months later, and where the unfortunate pirate was shipwrecked. Blackbeard was certainly more successful and spent his time attacking the logwood ships that frequented the Gulf. By late April the pirates had done all they could there, and so Blackbeard steered towards the north, passing through the Yucatan Channel on the western tip of Cuba, then sailing up the island's northern coast, through the waters of the Florida Straits. He captured a small Spanish sloop off Havana, then spent a few days lying off the wreck sites of the 1715 fleet off the eastern coast of Florida, where he captured another ship— either a brig or a sloop. That meant he now commanded a powerful squadron of four ships, including his 40-gun flagship, and a force of some 250 men. With all that power, it must have felt as if the whole of the Atlantic seaboard of the American colonies lay at his mercy. He would take full advantage of it.

On May 22, 1718, Blackbeard appeared off Charles Town (now Charleston), in the province of South Carolina. This was the beginning of one of the most unusual weeks in American colonial history. A string of sandbars separated Charles Town harbor from the ocean, and so, by guarding the only gap in the bar that could be used by large ships, Blackbeard managed to blockade the port. His first victim was the pilot boat that came out to help the newcomers over the bar. She was also escorting out the *Crowley*, a large merchantman bound for London, and Blackbeard captured her as well. The pirates captured a few more unsuspecting prizes over the next few days—mainly ships approaching the port whose crews had not heard of the pirate invasion. When the prizes dried up, Blackbeard decided to be even more audacious.

Captain Johnson describes his next move:

> Teach detained all the ships and prisoners, and, being in want of medicines, resolved to demand a chest from the government of the province; accordingly Richards, the Captain of the *Revenge*, sloop, with two or three more pirates, were sent up along with Mr. Marks, one of their prisoners, whom they had taken in Clark's ship, and very insolently made their demands, threatening that if they did not send immediately the chest of medicines and let the pirate ambassadors return without offering any violence to their persons, they would murder all their prisoners, send up their heads to the governor, and set the ships they had taken on fire.[19]

HOISTING THE BLACK FLAG

In the seventeenth century buccaneers fought under the national flag of their native country. Red was the color of choice, signifying that no quarter would be given. Some buccaneers embellished these flags with other symbols of death or threat. In French, such flags were known as *La JolieRouge*, "the pretty red." The English translated this as the Jolly Roger.

The first reported instance of a black flag being flown was in 1700, when the French pirate Emmanuelle Wynne flew a black flag decorated with a skull, crossed bones and an hourglass. By the time of the "Golden Age of Piracy" the color was closely associated with piracy. Like their red predecessors, these black flags stood for the threat of violence, for no quarter being given, and for danger. Any maritime victim would immediately understand the implication when an approaching vessel ran up the black flag.

Nowadays pirate flags are expected to have a skull and crossbones on them. Other variants—a skull and crossed swords, a skeleton, an hourglass (representing time running out), and drinking cups, representing a toast to death—were all commonplace. Everyone was aware of their associations. These symbols of death were grisly ways of reinforcing the flag's message, and all played their part in the process of intimidation.

The symbolism could make a specific threat. "Black Bart" Roberts designed a flag to show his hatred of two governors who challenged him from Barbados and Martinique. The flag showed a pirate figure standing on two skulls—one labelled ABH, the other AMH. These stood for "A Barbadian's Head" and "A Martiniquan's Head." Certain pirates came to be associated with certain flags, rather like the heraldic shields of medieval Europe.

Bartholomew Roberts's main flag showed a pirate holding an hourglass standing beside a skeleton holding a spear. Blackbeard flew a flag showing a skeleton holding an hourglass with a spear and a bleeding heart next to it, while "Calico Jack" Rackam flew a black flag with a skull surmounting a pair of crossed swords. Stede Bonnet flew one with a skull, flanked by a heart, a dagger, and surmounting a single bone. In fact the only pirate to fly anything akin to the skull and crossbones of pirate legend was Edward England.

Holding a town to ransom was something that had not been seen since the days of the buccaneers, and it was certainly a new experience for the colonial Americans. Moreover, threatening to cause all this mayhem just for a medicine chest was something unusual. While the South Carolina governor sent off for help, he knew that time was not on his side. The nearest Royal Navy warships were in Virginia's James River, and they would take a week to reach Charles Town. The port was reasonably well defended, but the abilities of the local militia were questionable, especially when they were faced with an attack by well-armed pirates. As a result:

> The [Carolina] government were not long in deliberating upon the message, though 'twas the greatest affront that could have been put upon them; yet for saving so many men's lives (among them Mr. Samuel Wragg, one of the council), they complied with the necessity and sent aboard a chest valued at between £300 and £400, and the pirates went back safe to their ships.[20]

Blackbeard had his medicine, but what he wanted it for has never been satisfactorily explained. A syringe used for treating venereal disease found on the wreck site of what was almost certainly the *Queen Anne's Revenge* may provide something of an explanation; his crew probably caught the disease during their winter sojourn around Hispaniola. Then again their recent visit to the Gulf of Honduras may have resulted in an outbreak of the flux—yellow fever. We can only speculate, but evidently the pirates considered the chest even more important than any other form of plunder. Of course, they did not go away from Charles Town empty-handed—the passengers on the *Crowley* alone are reported as having been stripped of around £1,500, the equivalent of as much as $400,000 today.

True to his word, Blackbeard raised the blockade and sailed off, heading north. He realized that if he delayed, the chances of being caught by Royal Navy warships would increase. What he needed now was a place where he could lie low for a bit, divide the plunder, and plan his next move. Although there was no real chance of being offered a pardon by Woodes Rogers, and he had just infuriated the South Carolina colony's governor, he had other options. A pardon was still being offered by the colony of North Carolina. This small colony lacked the powerful mercantile lobby that made neighboring Virginia a hotbed of antipirate feelings, while its rugged coast also provided the pirates with a place to hide out. However, Blackbeard had one small problem to overcome first. His flagship was too large to operate in North Carolina's sheltered waterways, and, prestigious though it was, it also acted as a direct challenge to the Royal Navy. Somehow he had to find a way to abandon her.

He hit on the perfect plan. On June 2 or thereabouts, Blackbeard appeared off Topsail Inlet, near the modern town of Beaufort, North Carolina. In those days the town consisted of a few fishermen's huts. The channel into the harbor was only 300 yards wide, and even at the time it was a tricky passage. Halfway through it, Blackbeard's helmsman turned the *Queen Anne's Revenge* hard to starboard, and she ran aground—hard. Teach called out to Israel Hands, who was following behind him in the sloop *Adventure*, asking him to tow the larger ship off. In the process Hands ran his sloop aground too. It is almost certain that Blackbeard and Hands had planned the whole thing. Although the *Adventure* might be repaired, the *Queen Anne's Revenge* was a complete loss—exactly what Blackbeard had wanted.

In June 1996 the wreck of what is thought to be the *Queen Anne's Revenge* was discovered in the waters off Beaufort, and since then the site has been surveyed and systematically excavated. A bronze bell dated 1705 was found, along with numerous cannons, weaponry, roundshot, and a small venereal syringe. Was it part of the medicine chest Blackbeard demanded from the citizens of Charles Town? Flakes of gold dust were also found—the kind of thing often carried by the crew of slave ships who visited the West African coast. It is hoped that one day the riddle will be solved and the wreck can be conclusively identified as Blackbeard's lost flagship. In the meantime, visitors to the North Carolina Maritime Museum in Beaufort can look at these objects, and imagine that they were once the property of Blackbeard and his men.[21]

LORD OF THE OUTER BANKS

The next part of the plan was to get rid of Major Bonnet. Using the excuse of the King's Pardon, Blackbeard sent Bonnet off to the colony's administrative seat in Bath Town, with instructions to obtain a provisional pardon for everybody. He left in a local vessel, while Blackbeard still held on to the sloop *Revenge* and the smaller Spanish sloop he captured off Havana. Blackbeard and his men busied themselves salvaging what they could from the wrecks, and he moved the plunder in the hold onto the smaller sloop. Meanwhile 17 of Bonnet's old crew prepared the *Revenge* for sea. Blackbeard then made his move. He collected all of Bonnet's men and marooned them on a deserted island across the inlet. Then he took the sails and cordage from the *Revenge* and sailed off in the Spanish prize, along with a small but carefully selected crew. A further 200 or so pirates were left on the beach in Beaufort. When Bonnet returned a few days later he was furious to discover that Blackbeard had pillaged his ship, stranded his crew, and absconded with the loot. That's what comes of trusting a pirate.

Bonnet took a week to set the *Revenge* to rights, and then he gave chase. He never caught up with Blackbeard, who by that time was safely hidden behind North Carolina's Outer Banks. Teach made his way to Bath Town, and in mid-June he accepted the King's Pardon from Governor Charles Eden and so officially turned his back on piracy. A reformed character, Blackbeard gave every impression of having turned over a new leaf. From that point on he would live off his piratical earnings, titillate polite Carolinian society with salty tales, and possibly indulge in a spot of coastal trading. He divided the plunder, which of course was more substantial when split among 30 men than among 250. The pirates must have enjoyed their sojourn in Bath Town, and the settlement's two makeshift taverns must have done a roaring trade.

This idyll would last for a few months, during which time Blackbeard established another, more secure base on Ocracoke Island, in the Outer Banks. He rented a house, and even—according to Johnson—married a young woman of 16, who, Johnson added, was his fourteenth wife. None of his marriages have ever been verified, so it is far more likely that the teenager became his mistress rather than his spouse. To keep his men occupied he took his sloop (which he renamed the *Adventure*) for little trips through the inland waters of the Outer Banks, and in September he even entertained Charles Vane and his men when they put in to the area after their escape from New Providence. News of this pirate gathering on the beach at Ocracoke reached Williamsburg, where the governor of Virginia was concerned that it heralded the creation of a new pirate base on his doorstep.

That was when Blackbeard returned to his own ways. He ventured further afield, and this time he encountered two French merchantmen off the Delaware Bay. He attacked and pillaged them, but according to the testimony he later gave to Governor Eden, Blackbeard found the ships floating and abandoned and came aboard them merely to establish salvage rights. The pirate was walking a legal tightrope, as he knew Governor Eden would have no option but to accept Blackbeard's word. However, if word got out that he had engaged in piracy, then he would immediately lose all legal protection. As a result he sank one of the ships, stripped most of the cargo from the other, then presented his case at a specially convened Admiralty Court in Bath Town held in late September. As Blackbeard thought, Eden had no choice but to accept the pirate's story.

For Governor Alexander Spotswood of Virginia, this was the final straw. He decided that he would deal with Blackbeard before he could become more of a threat, regardless of the pirate's legal standing. Consequently he organized a two-pronged assault. While Captain Brand of the Royal Navy led a force of sailors and Virginia militia overland to Bath Town, a smaller naval expedition would seek out Blackbeard at Ocracoke. The man he entrusted with this naval enterprise was Lieutenant Robert Maynard, an experienced officer and Brand's second-in-command on board the frigate HMS *Pearl*. As the *Pearl* and her consort HMS *Lyme* were too big to enter the shallow waters of the Outer Banks, Governor Spotswood hired two small sloops for the job—the *Ranger* and the *Jane*. Neither carried any guns, but they were crewed by 57 well-armed seamen—33 from the *Pearl* in the *Ranger*, and 24 from the *Lyme* in her consort. Maynard sailed in the *Ranger*, while the *Jane* was commanded by Mr. Hyde from the *Lyme*. To encourage these seamen, Spotswood offered a handsome reward for each pirate killed or captured and a bonus of £100 for Blackbeard himself—the equivalent of $23,000 today.

The two sloops sailed out of the James River late on November 17 and headed south, arriving off Ocracoke Island four days later. They arrived towards dusk, so Maynard decided to spend the night at anchor on the seaward side of the island before approaching the pirate lair first thing in the morning. As the light faded they glimpsed the topmasts of the *Adventure* behind the sand dunes on the island. They might even have heard the pirates, as that evening Blackbeard had company. A sloop from Bath Town had arrived late that afternoon, and the two crews—25 pirates and four locals—spent the evening drinking. The rest of Blackbeard's crew—another 24 men—was in Bath Town with Blackbeard's deputy Israel Hands.

The next day was a Friday, November 22, 1718. Maynard gave orders to get under way just before dawn, his sloops being towed into the inlet by their longboats due to a lack of favorable wind. The two sides were fairly evenly matched. Although Maynard had twice as many men as Blackbeard, the pirate sloop carried eight guns. A lookout on the *Adventure* spotted Maynard's force as it rounded the southern tip of the island. The pirate crew were roused, and a gun was fired at the nearest longboat, which immediately fled back to the relative safety of the *Ranger*. The battle had begun—a fight that would be remembered as one of the smallest yet bloodiest and most significant pirate engagements in history.

Maynard ordered the flags to be unfurled, and both of his sloops turned towards the enemy, the ships abreast of each other. Fortunately for Maynard, the pirates either didn't fire their guns effectively or didn't fire at all. When the two sides were within a hundred yards of each other the two captains hailed each other. Maynard recorded the conversation: "At our first salutation he [Blackbeard] drank Damnation to me and my Men, whom he stil'd Cowardly Puppies, saying, He would neither give nor take Quarter."[22] Other later accounts were more racy, but Maynard probably got it right. Both sides then exchanged small-arms fire, but the pirates may also have fired one of their guns, and the *Jane* was badly hit, Mr. Hyde killed, and five of her crew wounded. Effectively she was put out of action, as she fell astern and only rejoined the battle in its closing moments.

A broadside then ripped into the *Ranger*, killing six and wounding ten of Maynard's men. It seemed that Blackbeard was getting the better of the navy. The accounts vary, but one, two, or even all three sloops ran aground during this fight, and their crews tried to struggle free before the enemy could. Maynard probably stayed afloat, as—realizing the pirates planned to board him—he hid most of his crew belowdecks. Just before the two sloops crashed into each other, Blackbeard gave the order to throw *grenadoes* (grenades) onto the enemy's deck. In Johnson's words he then shouted that the enemy were "all knocked on the head, except three or four, and therefore let's jump on board and cut them to pieces."[23] At that moment Maynard's men surged up from below decks.

The hand-to-hand fighting that followed was brutal, with no quarter on either side. In the midst of the swirling melee, Blackbeard and Maynard singled each other out and fought their own form of duel. "Blackbeard and the lieutenant fired the first pistol at each other, by which the pirate received a wound." The pirate then drew a cutlass, which he swung at Maynard. The *Boston News Letter* picked up the story: "Maynard and Teach themselves begun the fight with their swords, Maynard making a thrust, the point of his sword went against Teach's cartridge box, and bended it to the hilt. Teach broke the guard of it, and wounded Maynard's fingers but did not disable him, whereupon he jumped back and threw away his sword and fired his pistol, which wounded Teach." The pirate had now been hit twice by pistol shot, but he still kept fighting.

With Maynard's sword broken, Blackbeard moved in to deliver a killing blow. At that moment one of Maynard's men slashed at Blackbeard, cutting his throat with his sword. Blackbeard remained on his feet, but he was mortally wounded.

As he was cocking another pistol he fell and was dead by the time he hit the deck. Of course the newspaper account was more lurid: "One of Maynard's men being a Highlander, engaged Teach with his broad sword, who gave Teach a cut in the neck, Teach saying well done lad; The Highlander replied, If it be not well done, I'll do it better. With that he gave him a second stroke, which cut off his head, laying it flat on his shoulder." However the end came, Blackbeard—the most notorious pirate of his age—was now dead.

The fight went out of the surviving pirates—or at least most of them. According to Captain Johnson, Blackbeard had "posted a resolute fellow, a Negro who he had brought up, with a lighted match in the powder room with commands to blow up when he should give him orders." This was Black Caesar, who tried to blow up the *Adventure* but was overcome by two prisoners held in the pirate ship's hold. By the time the fighting ended, eight pirates lay dead on the deck of the *Jane*, and the rest were either badly wounded or had jumped overboard and were swimming to the island. They were rounded up later, as were the five pirates still left alive on board the *Adventure*. Lieutenant Maynard had won his battle.

The cost had been high. Eleven British sailors had been killed in the short action and another 22 wounded —some of them badly. Maynard remained off Ocracoke for three more days, patching up the three sloops, burying the dead, treating the wounded, and rounding up the surviving pirates. He then sailed for Bath Town, which had just been captured by Captain Brand and his men. Of course Governor Eden of North Carolina was furious—Brand's action was tantamount to an invasion of one colony by another. While the lawsuits would fly around for years, Spotswood would be satisfied. Not only was Blackbeard killed and his sloop captured, but the pirates left behind in Bath Town had been captured without a fight. Maynard loaded up contraband seized by Brand then sailed home, with the severed head of Blackbeard hanging from his bowsprit.

On December 1 Maynard and his men rejoined their ships, and their pirate captives were turned over to the Virginia authorities. Their trial took place in Williamsburg's capitol building on March 12, 1719. There was no doubt about the verdict, despite some of the prisoners giving evidence against the others in the vain chance of escaping the gallows. Although the details of the trial have not survived, we can be sure that the case of the two French ships featured prominently as an example of an act of piracy committed after the King's Pardon had been granted. Only one man was given a reprieve—the remaining 15 were condemned to death by hanging. The exception was Samuel Odel, the Bath Town trader who, like the turtle-hunters of Jamaica who met "Calico Jack," was in the wrong place at the wrong time.

Just before the mass hanging, Israel Hands was also given a reprieve, having convinced the court that because of an argument with Blackbeard during which he was shot in the knee by his captain, he took no part in the attack on the French ships. He was still covered by the terms of the pirate pardon, and so was allowed to walk free. Within days the rest were dangling from makeshift gibbets that lined the roads from Williamsburg to Jamestown.

The strange thing about Blackbeard, or Edward Teach, is that for all his ferocious reputation, there is no evidence that he actually killed anybody, at least until his final battle with Lieutenant Maynard. Captain Johnson built up his fearsome image with tales like that of his filling the hold with burning tubs of brimstone and then challenging his crew to see who could stand the fumes the longest. Naturally he outlasted them all. The other was the wounding of Israel Hands, when Blackbeard and Hands were playing cards with guests. Blackbeard shot Hands with a pistol underneath the table, wounding his second-in-command and—according to Johnson—when asked why he did it, he was said to have replied: "that if he did not now and then kill one of them, they would forget who he was."

Today people remember Blackbeard for his appearance and his ferocity, not for his actions. More than most of the other pirates of his day he seemed to be a figure who developed a larger-than-life persona, whose image developed into something akin to a pirate caricature.

STEDE BONNET,
THE GENTLEMAN PIRATE

In most cases, we know very little about the lives of pirates before they broke the law. Stede Bonnet is an exception. Not only does Captain Johnson devote a whole chapter to him in his biography of pirates, but Bonnet also left behind a trail of evidence that supports Johnson's claims. In fact, the details of Bonnet's background were so sensational that at the time of his trial, the newspapers were filled with accounts of his background, his crimes, and his spectacular downfall. The novelty of Bonnet was that he never needed to turn to piracy at all. He was a gentleman, a prominent member of colonial polite society, and his flirtation with piracy was both ill conceived and dogged by disaster.

Johnson described him as "a gentleman of good reputation in the island of Barbados, [who] was master of a plentiful fortune, and had the advantage of a liberal education." At his trial in Charles Town the judge described him as "a gentleman that has had the advantage of a liberal education, and being generally esteemed as a Man of Letters."[24] That was essentially quite correct. Bonnet was born in England but moved to Barbados during the early 1700s. He bought and developed a sugar plantation outside Bridgetown, and by 1717 he was widely regarded as one of the more prosperous of the island's plantation owners. He was also considered highly respectable, having made a good marriage, involved himself in local politics, and become a major in the Barbados militia.

Then he threw everything away to become a pirate. Various reasons—a shrewish wife, a midlife crisis, or a major scandal—have all been suggested, but when questioned, his neighbors explained it by the onset of a "disorder of the mind." Whatever the reason behind his decision, Bonnet set about everything in a most unusual way. For a start he bought his own ship—something which any self-respecting pirate would simply not do. He opted for a large ten-gun sloop, an ideal pirate vessel, which he renamed the *Revenge*. Exactly what wrong he was seeking to avenge was never made clear. He then combed the taverns of Bridgetown for a sailing master and crew. While all other pirates called for volunteers, the inexperienced Bonnet had little option but to hire them and pay them wages. In fact the 70 crew members of the *Revenge* were probably the only pirates in history to earn a regular income from their work.

He sensibly avoided cruising the waters of the West Indies, where he might be recognized, and instead he headed for the Atlantic seaboard of the American colonies, which he reached at some time during the late spring or early summer of 1717. He spent a month cruising off the Virginia Capes, where he captured four merchantmen—the *Anne* from Glasgow, the *Endeavour* from Bristol, the *Young* from Leith, and the *Turbet* from his home island of Barbados. To cover his tracks a little he burned the *Turbet* after pilfering her cargo and setting her crew ashore. He then headed north towards New York, where he captured a sloop off the eastern tip of Long Island. Johnson claims that Bonnet further demonstrated his lack of understanding of pirate ways when he put in to a coastal settlement and bought rather than plundered the supplies he needed. The biographer then claims that Bonnet took the *Revenge* back down to the Carolinas, where he spent the winter, and that in the spring of 1718 he ran into Blackbeard somewhere between there and the Gulf of Honduras. This is another of those rare occasions when Captain Johnson got it badly wrong.

In November 1718 the *Boston News Letter* carried a story filed in Philadelphia on October 24. It reported that Blackbeard had seized a ship in the Delaware Bay, and that the pirate's ship was called the *Revenge*. It went on to say:

> On board the Pirate Sloop is Major Bennet, but has no Command, he walks about in his Morning Gown, and then to his Books, of which he has a good Library on Board, he was not well of his wounds that he received by attacking a Spanish Man of War, which kill'd and wounded thirty to forty men. After which putting into Providence, the place of Rendevouze for the Pirates, they put the afore said Capt. Teach on board for this Cruise.[25]

Major Bennet was obviously Major Stede Bonnet, and evidently Blackbeard and the gentlemen pirate crossed paths six months before Johnson suggests. Johnson's story about Bennet fighting a Spanish warship and putting into New Providence for repairs also fails to stand up to scrutiny.

However, the description of him in his "morning gown" fits in with Johnson's account of the relationship between the two pirates:

> The major was no sailor as was said before, and therefore had been obliged to yield to many things that were imposed on him during their undertaking, for want of a competent knowledge of maritime affairs ... To him [Blackbeard] Bonnet's crew joined in consortship, and Bonnet himself was laid aside, notwithstanding the sloop was his own; he went aboard Blackbeard's ship, not concerning himself with any of their affairs, where he continued till she was lost in Topsail Inlet, and one Richards was appointed captain in his room.

This is essentially correct, except that Blackbeard transferred his flag from his own smaller sloop to the *Revenge*, and Bonnet's sloop was not lost off Beaufort as Johnson suggests, although Blackbeard's next flagship was.

As Stede Bonnet became little more than Blackbeard's prisoner over the next eight months, and we have already covered Blackbeard's activities, we can jump ahead to June 1718, when Bonnet sailed from Topsail Inlet to Bath Town, in the North Carolina colony, where he hoped to secure the King's Pardon from Governor Eden. The original offer was open to pirates who "shall on or before the fifth of September, in the Year of our Lord 1718, surrender ... to any

Governor or Deputy Governor of any of our Plantations beyond the Seas." It then added that immunity applied only to crimes committed before January 1718. It did not cover the attacks made by Blackbeard (and therefore Bonnet) in the Gulf of Honduras or off Charles Town. However, provincial governors also had the right to waive this clause if they saw fit. And Blackbeard hoped that by sending the less threatening Bonnet to see Eden first, the North Carolina governor would be more amenable when it came to Blackbeard himself.

The plan worked, and Bonnet sailed back to Topsail Inlet clutching a provisional pardon. That was when he learned that Blackbeard had betrayed him, pillaging the *Revenge*, stranding the best of Bonnet's men on a deserted island, and absconding with all the plunder. The marooned men:

> remained there two nights and one day, without subsistence, or the least prospect of any, expecting nothing else but a lingering death; when to their inexpressible comfort they saw redemption at hand; for Major Bonnet happened to get intelligence of their being there, by two of the pirates who had escaped Teach's cruelty, and had got to a poor little village at the upper end of the harbor, sent his boat to make discovery of the truth of the matter, which the poor wretches seeing, made a signal to them, and they were all brought on board Bonnet's sloop.[26]

After rescuing his own men, Bonnet recrewed the *Revenge* from some of the other pirates whom Blackbeard had deserted at Beaufort, and, probably with the help of local fishermen, they worked hard to prepare the *Revenge* for sea. For once the name of Bonnet's sloop was completely appropriate.

If Bonnet had allowed logic to overcome anger, he would have realized he was on a fool's errand. He had a chance to walk away from piracy, but once the *Revenge* put to sea it was almost certain that his crew would call the shots, and they would revert to their old ways. He almost convinced himself and his men that becoming legitimate privateers was a better option. However, when news came that Teach was at Ocracoke, there was no turning back. The *Revenge* set off in pursuit, but, as Johnson put it, "it happened too late, for he missed of him there, and after four days' cruise, hearing no farther news of him, they steered their course towards Virginia." By the time the *Revenge* reached Ocracoke, Blackbeard was safely in Bath Town.

The first ship they encountered off the Virginia Capes was a small coaster, and Bonnet traded rather than pillaged. The *Revenge* then encountered a small sloop laden with rum, and this time Bonnet could not stop his men, who ransacked the vessel and drank her cargo. A string of prizes followed—two ships from Virginia bound for Glasgow carrying tobacco, a sloop carrying Virginia ham to Bermuda, and another carrying nothing but ballast. All chances of a pardon had now evaporated. The *Revenge* continued northwards towards the Delaware Bay, where Bonnet captured a sloop carrying furs to Boston. It was all slim pickings, and hardly worth giving up a pardon for. However, things picked up, probably when Bonnet decided he had no alternative. That July he captured five more vessels off the mouth of the Delaware River, and Bonnet decided to keep two of them—both small sloops. Sensibly the pirates then decided to head south, as their attacks would almost certainly attract the attention of the Royal Navy.

BATTLE IN THE CAPE FEAR RIVER

By this stage the sloop *Revenge* was badly in need of repair, so Bonnet put in to the Cape Fear River. Johnson suggests that "they stayed too long for their safety, for the pirate sloop which they now named the *Royal James*, proved very leaky, so that they were obliged to remain here almost two months, to refit and repair the vessel." The *Revenge*—now the *Royal James*—was ready for sea by mid-September. Unfortunately for the pirates, word of their presence had reached Charles Town, where the colony's governor had already sent two well-armed sloops out on an antipiracy patrol. The commander of the *Henry* and the *Sea Nymph* was Colonel William Rhett, whose orders were to "very much irritate the pirates who infest the coast in great numbers." Although his main target was Charles Vane, he was also on the lookout for Bonnet, or even Blackbeard. On September 26 the squadron lay off the mouth of the Cape Fear River, and, as Johnson recounts, "in the evening, the colonel with his small squadron, entered the river, and saw, over a point of land, three sloops at an anchor, which were Major Bonnet and his prizes." He decided to attack the next morning, on the incoming tide. Bonnet and his men saw the two arrivals, and at first they thought they were merchantmen. A closer inspection revealed the true identify of the mystery sloops, and so both sides prepared for battle at first light.

It was Bonnet who moved first, the *Royal James* creeping down the river in the predawn darkness, her guns primed and ready. Bonnet had 45 men on board, which meant he was outnumbered three to one. His best hope was to take Rhett by surprise, pass the enemy with guns blazing, then escape out into the open sea. Unfortunately, as the *Royal James* came within musket range of the two South

PIRATE JUSTICE

The way the authorities combated the spread of piracy during the golden age was by a combination of carrot, the granting of official pardons, and stick, hunting down wrongdoers then publicly trying and executing them. The best way to discourage more sailors from turning to piracy was to demonstrate that piracy led to a one-way ticket to the gallows.

If pirates were caught they faced a highly publicized trial, and when (rather than if) found guilty they would be condemned to death by hanging. In most countries, trials were conducted according to maritime or admiralty law. This meant there was no trial by jury, but instead the case was heard by a panel of appointed officials. The onus was on the accused to prove their lack of complicity. As most of the accused were barely literate, and no defense lawyers were appointed, it was inevitable that the prosecution would emerge triumphant. The whole process was less a matter of justice and more one of antipiratical propaganda, deterrence, and retribution.

Once a pirate was condemned to death, he was usually executed on the foreshore, deemed as being within the boundaries of the authority of admiralty law. This meant that gallows were often erected on the waterfront of ports—such as Execution Dock in London's Wapping. After a prayer from a chaplain or priest, the pirate was allowed a last speech, and then he would be hanged. The body would be left for a day and a half to be washed by the tides "as Admiralty law proscribes," after which the corpse would be cut down and buried in an unmarked grave.

Often, the dead pirate was not granted this last dignity. In keeping with the policy of deterrence, his body would be tarred to slow decomposition, then suspended in a cage overlooking a waterway. The bodies could take years to rot away, or be pecked to pieces by birds. These cages were positioned within sight of passing ships entering the port, so they would serve as a warning to others. The bodies of pirates such as William Kidd, Jack Rackam, and Charles Vane were used to reinforce the argument that piracy did not pay.

Carolina sloops, she ran hard aground. By that time the *Henry* and the *Sea Nymph* were under way and closed in on their victim. Then they too ran aground on hidden sandbanks. It was a ludicrous situation, with all three sloops stranded, and waiting for the incoming tide to lift them clear. They were all within musket range, so even if their guns could not bear, they could all fire small arms at each other. However, the ships were all heeling the same way—to starboard—but while the hull of the pirate ship protected her crew, the decks of the two pirate-hunters were exposed.

The two sides kept up the gun battle for five hours, by which time Rhett had lost 12 men dead and 18 more wounded, while Bonnet had only nine men wounded. However, it was the smaller *Henry* that freed herself first, and her skipper Captain Masters lay his sloop across the bows of the *Royal James* at point-blank range, where her four-gun broadside could sweep the pirate decks with grapeshot. Bonnet had no option but to surrender. Rhett spent the rest of the day rounding up his prisoners, freeing the pirate's own hostages, and tending to his wounded. He then set course for Charles Town, a port that was still furious at having been blockaded by Blackbeard.

The squadron reached Charles Town on October 3, and the pirates were locked up in the town's watch-house, guarded by a detachment of the South Carolina militia. Despite his crimes, Bonnet was still regarded as a gentleman and so was lodged in the private house of the local marshal. A few days later he was joined by his two officers—the master David Heriot and the boatswain Ignatius Pell, both of whom had promised to give evidence against their fellow pirates. The house was only lightly guarded, and so on the night of October 24 Bonnet and Heriot slipped past the guards and escaped. A reward of £700 was offered for their recapture, by which time the two men had stolen a canoe and tried to paddle their way to freedom. Then a storm blew in from the Atlantic, and the pair were driven back onto Sullivan's Island, near one end of the Charles Town Bar.

Unfortunately for them Colonel Rhett was out looking for them, and during the night of November 5 a patrol stumbled across the fugitives. In the exchange of fire that followed Heriot was killed, and Bonnet surrendered. The following morning Rhett marched his prisoner back to Charles Town. This time there was no gentleman's agreement to house him in comfort. He was taken straight to the watch-house and imprisoned with the rest of his crew. The trial had actually been under way for a week by the time Bonnet returned, so Bonnet was arraigned along with the rest of his men. Judge Nicholas Trot wasted little time in hearing the charges, and to speed things along he concentrated on the seizure of the sloops *Fortune* and *Francis* back in early August, when Bonnet was operating off the Delaware River.

All except two of the men—James Wilson of Dublin and John Levit of North Carolina—pleaded not guilty, the prisoners arguing that at the time of the attacks they intended to become privateers but were short of provisions and so borrowed what they needed from the two sloops. However, the court proved that they had plundered the ships, and benefited by sharing out booty of about £10 a head. That was enough to condemn all but four of the men, who joined the crew after the division of spoils. Consequently, on November 7, of the 33 men accused, 29 were sentenced to death for piracy. Bonnet was not one of them. His escape and late arrival at the trial, his position of command, and his standing as a gentleman all warranted a more detailed hearing.

The mass execution was set for the following day, November 8. At dawn 24 of the pirates were marched down to White Point, the southern tip of the city facing the Ashley River, and they were hanged in front of a large jeering crowd. That left five of Bonnet's crew still to face justice ... as well as Bonnet himself. The trial reconvened on November 10, and after two days Bonnet was found guilty. Therefore, on November 12, Judge Trot followed a long harangue about sin, repentance, and divine justice with the chilling words: "That you, the said Stede Bonnet, shall go from hence to the place from whence you came, and from thence to the place of execution, where you shall be hanged by the neck till you are dead ... and the God of Infinite Mercy be merciful to your soul." The following morning Stede Bonnet, former major and gentleman pirate, was hanged from the gallows on White Point, accompanied by the last few members of his crew.[27]

BLACK BELLAMY

If anyone could be described as Blackbeard's mentor, then it would be Benjamin Hornigold, who took him under his wing when he first arrived in New Providence. In fact Hornigold was very much the founding father of the Bahamian pirates, and several characters who would become pirate captains in their own right began their piratical careers sailing under his flag. Apart from Blackbeard, the most successful of these was Sam Bellamy.

Bellamy was an Englishman, born in Devon sometime around 1689. We know little about his early years, apart from the fact that he was already an experienced seaman and a candidate for a captaincy by the time he joined

Hornigold's crew. It has been suggested that like so many others, he served as a privateersman working out of Port Royal. Then again, according to Cape Cod legend, he was in love with Maria Hallett of Eastham, Massachusetts, but as he was an impoverished sailor her parents refused to let them marry. Consequently he headed south to seek his fortune. He certainly appears to have been caught by the outbreak of treasure fever following the shipwreck of the Spanish treasure *flota* of 1715. He formed part of Henry Jennings's expedition when he raided the Spanish salvage camp in Florida, and presumably arrived in the Bahamas as part of Jennings's crew. By 1716 Bellamy was in New Providence, where he served alongside Blackbeard as part of Hornigold's pirate crew.

Bellamy sailed on Hornigold's summer cruise of 1716, and in August or September he was given command of a captured sloop, the *Mary Anne*. Soon afterwards Hornigold and Bellamy decided to part company—the decision probably resulting from Hornigold's refusal to attack British merchantmen. The older pirate preferred to maintain the fiction that he was still operating according to his wartime "letter of marque," while Bellamy and many of the younger pirates had no qualms about attacking British shipping on the high seas. Certainly by the late summer of 1716, Bellamy was operating as his own captain, sailing in consort with the French pirate Olivier le Vasseur. The Frenchman was also known as La Buse (The Buzzard), although some records incorrectly label him as La Bouche.

The two pirates cruised the waters of the Virgin Islands, capturing several small prizes before returning to New Providence—possibly following a storm in early 1717. For La Buse this was probably his last independent cruise for some time, as by the summer of 1717 he was operating in consort with the pirate Christopher Moody. It was reported that Moody spent the summer cruising off the coast of the Carolinas in two ships. One of these was probably La Buse's own sloop. Incidentally, it was during this cruise that one of Moody's lieutenants— Thomas Cocklyn—was given his own command, and consequently sailed off in the captured galley *Rising Sun* to begin his own short career as a pirate captain. Moody would later accept the King's Pardon from Woodes Rogers but resumed his piratical career a few months later, when the crew of the sloop he was serving on mutinied off the coast of Hispaniola. In early 1719 Moody, La Buse, and Cocklyn would be temporarily reunited off the West African coast.

For his part Sam Bellamy was proving a successful pirate captain, having commandeered the merchant ship *Sultana* and converted her into a powerful square-rigged pirate ship of around 24 guns. He handed his sloop over to his friend and quartermaster Paul Williams (or Palgrave Williams), and the two vessels cruised in consort. Bellamy changed ships again in February 1717 when he captured the British slave ship *Whydah Galley* somewhere off the Bahamas—probably in the Bahamas Channel, between the islands and the Florida coast. She had been homeward bound from Jamaica, on the last leg of her triangular voyage between Britain, West Africa, and the West Indies. Named after the slave port on the West African coast, the *Whydah* was a fast, well-built vessel of 300 tons, and she was reportedly laden with a cargo of rum, gold dust, and money—reputedly as much as £20,000 ($39,000) in coin. As pirate hauls go, this was a pretty good one.

Bellamy made the *Whydah* his new flagship and fitted her out to carry 28 guns. Her former captain was given the *Sultana* in exchange. Bellamy and Williams resumed their cruise in the *Whydah* and the *Mary Anne*, heading northwards. During March they captured four more vessels off Virginia, one of which was added to Bellamy's small squadron. It was also one of these captures that resulted in the conversation between Bellamy and a merchant captain that was recorded in some detail by Captain Johnson. Although Bellamy's rail against the establishment may be more apocryphal than a genuine speech, it certainly demonstrates the views held by many pirates of the time.

When the merchant captain asked whether Bellamy planned to return his sloop after it had been pillaged, Bellamy replied:

> I am sorry they won't let you have your sloop again, for I scorn to do any one a mischief, when it is not to my advantage; damn the sloop, we must sink her, and she might be of use to you. Though you are a sneaking puppy, and so are all those who will submit to be governed by laws which rich men have made for their own security; for the cowardly whelps have not the courage otherwise to defend what they get by knavery; but damn ye altogether: damn them for a pack of crafty rascals, and you, who serve them, for a parcel of hen-hearted numbskulls.

He then launched into an even more bitter tirade:

> They vilify us, the scoundrels do, when there is only this difference, they rob the poor under the cover of law, forsooth, and we plunder the rich under the protection of our own courage. Had you not better make then one of us, than sneak after these villains for employment?

When the captain refused to consider joining the pirates, Bellamy supposedly retorted:

> You are a devilish conscience rascal, I am a free prince, and I have as much authority to make war on the whole world, as he who has a hundred sail of ships at sea, and an army of 100,000 men in the field; and this my conscience tells me: but there is no arguing with such snivelling puppies, who allow superiors to kick them about deck at pleasure.[28]

Shortly after this theatrical encounter the pirate squadron was caught in a storm—a southeasterly gale, which drove the *Whydah* and her two consorts northwards, past Delaware Bay and Long Island; by the time it abated they were in the waters of Massachusetts. Another version claims that Bellamy planned to establish a base on Roberts Island, off the coast of Maine—which, if true, shows that his association with New England might well have been a genuine one. Another version claims that the pirates captured a Nantucket merchantman laden with Madeira and were blind drunk by the time they reached Cape Cod.

Whatever the reason for being there, the pirate squadron was a few miles to seaward of Cape Cod on April 26, 1717, when another sudden storm came out of the southeast. Bellamy gave orders for his three ships to work their way further out to sea, but the *Whydah* was too slow, or her crew were too drunk, to escape the storm. Battered by 30 ft waves, the pirate ship was driven towards the shore by winds that reached 70 miles an hour—which is technically hurricane force. The *Whydah* struck a sandbar within sight of the beach, and she rolled over. The pounding waves then broke her back, and the *Whydah* disintegrated, scattering her 146-man pirate crew into the surf.

Only two men survived the disaster—Thomas Davis, a Welsh ship's carpenter who had been pressed into being a pirate a few months earlier, and John Julian, a half-blooded Native American from the Mosquito Coast of Nicaragua. While Julian was jailed and then disappeared—probably sold into slavery—Davis stood trial in Boston, where he was subsequently acquitted. One character witness described him as having had "a good Education in a Religious and Orderly Family, and that his Conversation, Carriage and Behaviour all that while was very decent and becoming."

As for their shipmates, locals from the nearby village of Wellfleet reported that over a hundred corpses littered the shoreline, lying amongst the detritus of their ship. The governor of Massachusetts, Samuel Shute, sent Captain Cyprian

Southack to the scene to search the wreckage and salvage what he could. By the time he arrived he found "at least 200 men from several places at 20 miles distance plundering the Pirate Wreck of what came ashore [when] she turned bottom up." Sam Bellamy's body was never found, so presumably he went down with his ship.

The prize sloop was driven ashore further up the coast, and the nine survivors were rounded up by the authorities. Of these, two were acquitted, and the remaining seven were hanged in Boston. That still left Paul Williams and the crew of the *Mary Anne*. He survived the storm, and may even have visited the wreck site a few days later, to see if he could recover any of the plunder. Another version claims that he had already parted company from Bellamy, and he sailed to Block Island off Rhode Island to visit his family, thereby escaping the fatal storm. This version is unlikely, as in May he was reported off Cape Cod, where he captured two merchantmen. He may even have entered Provincetown harbor. It seems that he was one of the sensible pirates who accepted the King's Pardon when it was offered, and so he retired from piracy during that winter.

In 1984 the wreck of the *Whydah* was discovered by wreck-hunter Barry Clifford. The wreck site has been excavated by Clifford and his team, and the artifacts are now housed in a purpose-built maritime museum in Provincetown, Massachusetts. There visitors can see the pirate ship's bronze bell, the slave shackles used by her former owners, the weaponry she carried, and even some of the plunder that for a few short months made the crew of the *Whydah* some of the richest pirates in the Americas.

THE SMALL-TIMERS

Not all the pirates mentioned in the various editions of Captain Johnson's *General History* began their careers in the Bahamas, nor did they all have such spectacular careers as Blackbeard, Charles Vane, or even Sam Bellamy. In fact at least one emulated the original buccaneer Pierre le Grand and began a piratical career in a rowing boat, while others were best described as violent, small-time pirates, whose short careers lacked the flair of their New Providence counterparts.

Richard Worley was certainly a man with big ideas. In late September 1718 he and eight companions stole a ship's longboat from New York harbor, and took it out to sea. After rounding Sandy Hook they headed south down the New Jersey shore, and 150 miles later they rounded Cape May and entered the Delaware Bay. That was the hunting ground of Blackbeard a year earlier, and his successes might well have encouraged Worley to embark on his venture. They continued on upstream, and off New Castle (just south of Wilmington, Delaware) they captured a shallop—a small sailing boat—transporting household goods into Philadelphia. There wasn't really anything worth stealing, so they continued on until they came across a small sloop, captained by a mulatto called Black Robbin. The pirates took his ship and a handful of men and left Robbin and the rest of his men their longboat.

Their next prize was a larger sloop, homeward bound from Philadelphia to Hull, and once again the pirates upgraded their ship. They then stood out to sea, heading for the Bahamas. They were lucky, as they narrowly missed HMS *Phoenix*, which came racing down from New York to intercept them as soon as word of their attacks got out. Captain Johnson claims that Worley captured a sloop and a brig among the islands, pressing more men from their crews. Worley now commanded a well-founded sloop armed with six guns and crewed by 25 men—although not all of them were willing volunteers.

The pirate biographer claims that Worley then put in to the North Carolina coast to "blacktop" (seal the lower hull with pitch) his ship, then sailed north towards the Virginia Capes. It was now late January 1719. The governor of the South Carolina colony was already on the offensive against the pirates, having just captured and hanged Stede Bonnet and his men. Johnson says that he fitted out two sloops, one of eight guns, the other of six, crewed by 70 men between them. From the description it is almost certain that this was Colonel William Rhett's force—the South Carolina sloops *Henry* and *Sea Nymph*. This means that they were already veteran pirate-hunters. On February 16 the two sides sighted each other in the mouth of the James River, and, thinking they were potential victims, Worley closed to intercept the two sloops.

Johnson takes up the story: "When the pirates saw how things went, they resolutely prepared themselves for a resolute defense; and though three to one odds, Worley and his crew determined to fight to the last gasp, and receive no quarters ... so that they must either die or conquer upon the spot."[29] This sounds like pure invention. Given the high number of pressed men in the crew, it is far more likely that most of the pirates hoped to surrender and claim they had been forced to join Worley's crew. The pirate-hunters both fired a broadside—probably one on each beam of the pirate sloop—then boarded in the smoke. Even Johnson agrees that the one-sided battle was over in a matter of minutes, and by the time the smoke cleared all but two of the pirates lay dead and the decks of the pirate sloop would have been awash with blood.

Worley and one other pirate survived the battle, although both men were badly wounded. While the biographer claims they were executed the following morning, "for fear they should die and evade the punishment as was thought due to their crimes," the records show they were both taken back to Charles Town to stand trial and were both executed on White Point, where Stede Bonnet had met his end four months earlier.

A similar career was followed by John Evans, a Welshman and former naval merchant officer, who in September 1721 (Johnson claims 1722) found himself in Port Royal without employment or prospects. Captain Johnson states that he had been the master of a sloop working out of Nevis, and on losing his job he made his way to Jamaica. He gathered together a group of three or four friends, and together they stole a large canoe—probably a piragua—and set off in search of victims. These small-time pirates began by landing on the north side of the island and robbing houses close to the shore. Off Dunns Hole in Saint Anne Parish they came across a small Bermudan sloop riding at anchor, and seized her.

They now had a four-gun sloop, which they renamed *Scowerer*. All Evans and his men needed now was a crew. They headed east, and off Puerto Rico they captured the merchantman *Dove* of New England. Almost as important as the provisions they stole from her were the four men they forced to join their pirate crew. Next came the British merchantman *Lucretia & Catherine*, which they captured off La Désirade near Guadeloupe on January 11, 1722, followed by two sloops in quick succession. Each yielded money and recruits. So far this had been a highly successful cruise, yielding plunder worth around £9,000.

Evans decided that the Lesser Antilles were getting dangerous, as his attacks were certain to invite the attention of the navy. Consequently he headed east again, bypassing Jamaica "where they took a sugar-drover," which probably means a small coastal vessel—one of many that transported raw cane along the coast to sugar refineries or distilleries. The pirates then headed towards the Cayman Islands, where they planned to careen their sloop. They put in to Grand Cayman, and Evans planned to go ashore—not to begin the business of cleaning his ship but to fight a duel. He and the boatswain had argued during the passage, and it had been decided to settle the affair "with pistols and sword, as is the custom among these outlaws."

When the time came the boatswain refused to fight, which prompted Evans to beat him with a stick, right there on the deck of the *Scowerer*. This was too much for the man, who pulled out a pistol and shot the captain stone dead. Before his crew could react the boatswain jumped overboard and swam for the safety of the shore. However, his shipmates rowed out and caught him, then shot him twice.

The death of Evans placed the remaining pirates in a quandary. The only man who could actually navigate the sloop was the mate from the *Lucretia & Catherine*, who had been pressed against his will. He refused to help them. We have only Johnson's account of what happened next, but it seems that for some reason the pirates went ashore, possibly to bury Evans, leaving the merchant ship's mate and a cabin boy back on board the *Scowerer*. Between them they cut the anchor cable and sailed her to the safety of Port Royal, leaving the pirates howling for revenge on the beach.

THE PSYCHOPATHIC EDWARD LOW

Another particularly unsavory pirate who started his career the same way was Edward Low, a man whom even Captain Johnson was hard-pressed to say anything good about. He was born in Westminster and took to crime as a pickpocket on the streets of London. However, he appeared to start life afresh when he took passage to the North American colonies, where he worked for a time as a seaman, then as a ship rigger in Boston. In late 1721 he joined the crew of a sloop that sailed to the Gulf of Honduras to take on a cargo of logwood.

While the cargo was being loaded Low led a mutiny, and tried to shoot the captain. He missed, and killed a crewman instead, which incensed the rest of the crew. Low and the dozen conspirators took to the ship's boat and fled. As Johnson then put it, "The next day they took a small vessel, and go in her, make a black flag, and declare war against the world." His first destination was the Cayman Islands—a popular pirate rendezvous—which he reached in December. There he ran into another pirate ship, commanded by George Lowther, and the two men decided to join forces, with Low initially serving as Lowther's quartermaster. Their partnership lasted for five months, until Low was able to establish himself as a captain in his own right. The reason for the split may also have been something to do with Low's violent temperament and strong antiauthoritarian views, which were probably not to Lowther's liking. On May 28, 1722, Lowther captured the brigantine *Rebecca* of Boston somewhere off the coast of Delaware or New Jersey and gave command of her to his quartermaster. The two pirate captains then went their own separate ways.

Lowther headed north towards New York in the *Ranger*, while Low took over the brigantine and converted her into a pirate ship. He had 44 men under his command. Low began his cruise by following Lowther north, capturing his first prize off Long Island six days later and two more in quick succession off the coast of Rhode Island. When he learned of the attacks the colony's governor sent out two pirate-hunters, but Low slipped away, rounding Cape Cod to reappear off Marblehead, Massachusetts. Johnson claims that he entered the harbor and plundered 13 vessels, taking one of them—a schooner—for himself, which he renamed *Fancy*. Although this is not supported by other records, he certainly acquired a New England schooner from somewhere. He handed his brig over to Charles Harris and kept the ten-gun *Fancy* for himself.

Realizing the New England coast was becoming dangerous for him, he headed back south towards the West Indies. The *Fancy* and the brig arrived there in mid-August, just in time to run into a hurricane—the same one which then went on to devastate Port Royal in Jamaica on August 22. Both vessels survived the onslaught, and, after putting in to a deserted Caribbean island for repairs, once again Low decided the navy was just too active, so he planned to head east across the Atlantic. Again, Captain Johnson gets the dates a little wrong here, and

The psychopathic pirate Edward Low.

it was probably late September when he arrived off São Miguel. In Ponta Delgada harbor the pirates captured several merchantmen and destroyed all but one of them, the sloop *Rose*, which was added to the pirate squadron.

Low then cruised the waters of the islands, capturing a French merchantman, which he ransacked, half-destroyed, and left to drift. Anyone who resisted was cut down or tortured. Johnson even claims that Low and his men "cut and mangled them in a barbarous manner, particularly some Portuguese passengers, two of whom being friars, they triced up at each arm of the foreyard, but let them down again before they were quite dead, and this they repeated several times out of sport." Worse was to come. After capturing another prize a few weeks later, Low became annoyed by the quality of the meals prepared by a pressed French ship's cook. He thought that the man, "a greasy fellow, would fry well in the fire, so the poor man was bound to the mainmast, and burnt with the ship, to the no small derision of Low and his Mirmidons." Their next stop was Madeira, then finding nothing to plunder they continued on past the Canaries to the Cape Verde Islands. There they were more successful, capturing at least eight prizes before quitting the islands and heading back towards the Americas.

Low and Harris reached the coast of Brazil before the end of the year, where Harris's vessel was lost, although he and his crew reached the safety of the *Fancy*. Low then worked his way northwards to Granada, where he encountered another Portuguese ship, an encounter that gave rise to another tale of cruelty. When he discovered that the captain had dropped his money bags into the sea, Low reputedly ordered his lips to be cut out, "which he broil'd before his face, and afterwards murdered him and his crew." Low gave one of his lieutenants, Anthony Spriggs, command of a newly captured sloop, and the two captains resumed the cruise, heading west towards the Gulf of Honduras.

By March 1723 Low and Spriggs were off the Honduran coast, where they captured a Spanish patrol ship, which had been harassing the British logwood cutters. Low massacred almost 60 of her crew. Harris was then given command of Spriggs's vessel, which suggests that Low had problems controlling his two subordinates. Harris renamed the ship *Ranger*. The pirates then sailed north, capturing several small vessels before they threaded their way through the Florida Straits and the Bahamas Channel to reach the Atlantic seaboard in mid-May. On May 27 they captured the New England ship *Amsterdam Merchant* off the South Carolina coast and a sloop, whose captain said something to offend Low. In response the pirate captain "cut off this gentleman's ears, slit up his nose, and cut him in several places on his body." Low was evidently not a man to be reasoned with.

Then on June 21 the pirates spotted a sail to leeward, off Long Island. They gave chase, only to find she was a 20-gun warship, HMS *Greyhound*, commanded by Captain Peter Solgard. The warship turned and gave battle. Low fled in the *Fancy*, leaving Harris to fight it out. After a running fight lasting two hours, the *Ranger* was captured and taken back as a prize to the *Greyhound's* home port of Newport, Rhode Island. There, on July 19, Harris and 24 of his men were hanged for piracy. Two more were found guilty but spared the gallows, while eight were acquitted.

Low fled north, capturing a small Nantucket sloop, "the master of which, one Nathan Skiff, a brisk young fellow, the pirates cruelly whipped naked about the deck, making his torture their sport, after which they cut off his ears, and last of all shot him through the head, and then sunk his vessel." These acts of extreme violence by Low against ship captains whom he captured seem to have become increasingly common, suggesting that he harbored a deep resentment against authority. Of course, he was also becoming increasingly psychopathic, and Johnson catalogs several similar acts during the next few months.

In late July he captured the large merchant ship *Merry Christmas*, which he converted into a 34-gun flagship. He also adopted the title of admiral. Next he headed across the Atlantic again, and in early September he captured a British sloop off the Azores. Half her crew were Portuguese, a nationality to which Low had clearly taken a dislike. According to Johnson he hanged all his Portuguese prisoners and let the rest go free. Another prize was captured off Ponta Delgada, after which Low resumed his earlier tour of the Canaries and the Cape Verde Islands. This time he put in to the West African coast, making landfall near Gallassee, then working his way down to Sierra Leone, where he captured a Royal African Company armed sloop called the *Squirrel*.

That is the last we hear of the psychopathic Edward Low. It was some time around the start of January 1724, and from that point on Low is not mentioned. One suggestion is that he was caught and hanged by the French. Johnson claims that Anthony Spriggs was given command of a prize called the *Delight* that had been captured off the Guinea Coast, and he promptly sailed off on his own account. It has also been suggested that around this time Low was deposed, marooned, then left to die. If so, then the likelihood is that this took place around the time of Spriggs's desertion. Johnson said of Low that:

In January last [1724], Low took a ship, called the *Squirrel,* Captain Stevenson; but what came of his afterwards I can't tell; we have had no news concerning him come to England … but I have heard that he talked of going to Brazil, and if so, it is likely we may soon hear of some exploit or other, though the best information we could receive, would be, that he and all his crew were at the bottom of the sea.

As for Spriggs, he renamed his ship the *Bachelor's Delight,* then sailed her to the West Indies, where he demonstrated both an ability to capture prizes and a cruel streak that matched that of the psychopathic Low. Johnson described the torturing of Portuguese captives, making them "sweat"—running around the mainmast until they dropped from exhaustion, encouraged by a ring of pirates armed with knives. He also traced their progress past St. Lucia and Martinique, then across the Caribbean to their old haunt—the Gulf of Honduras. There the pirates careened their ship. By April they were back in the West Indies, but off St. Christopher (now the island of St. Kitts) they fell in with a French man-of-war, which chased them out of the islands. Next Spriggs sailed north towards Bermuda, where he captured a New England schooner. He told her captain that he planned to sail in search of Captain Solgard of HMS *Greyhound,* but this act of bravado never took place.

Instead the pirates returned to the Leeward Islands, where on June 4 they captured a sloop off St. Kitts, whose crew were tortured by being hoisted into the yards on a rope, then dropped back to the deck. As if that wasn't enough, the survivors were whipped around the ship. Another prize carrying horses led to an impromptu shipboard horse race. Spriggs made his next appearance off Jamaica, but was chased westwards by two warships. Somewhere off the Yucatan coast Spriggs captured a sloop, which he gave to one of his officers called Shipton, after which the two sloops sailed around Cuba and into the Bahamas Channel. There they were pounced on by the two Jamaican warships again, and Shipton was driven ashore. The Spanish rounded up those of his crew who survived and took them to Havana, where they were executed.

As for Spriggs, he fled back the way he had come, and by January 1725 the *Bachelor's Delight* was back in the Gulf of Honduras. Johnson states that she was then cornered by a warship and driven ashore on Roatán. However, it has also been claimed that her crew deposed their captain, and, probably like Low before him, Spriggs was marooned and left to die. Certainly Philip Lyne, Spriggs's former quartermaster, began his brief independent career around that time and may have become the new captain of the Low and Spriggs band.

We know little about Lyne's career, save that in March 1726 he was captured by two Dutch pirate-hunters operating from Curaçao, where he was taken and tried. According to the *Boston News Letter*, in the courtroom he claimed to have been responsible for the deaths of 37 masters of vessels. It is hardly surprising that he was sentenced and hanged along with 19 of his men, in what became the last mass pirate hanging to take place in the Caribbean. The bloody trail left by Low, Spriggs, and Lyne had finally reached its end.

GEORGE LOWTHER

We know little about Edward Low's fellow pirate George Lowther, although his name suggests Scottish roots. In May 1721 he was serving as the second mate on board the *Gambia Castle*, a 16-gun ship belonging to the Royal African Company. The ship had just arrived off Gallassee (now Banjul), a town on a small island in the mouth of the Gambia River, where it was delivering a new 30-man garrison for the fort destroyed less than two years earlier by the pirate Howell Davis. The man in charge of the detachment was a Captain John Massey, who immediately fell out with the traders who ran Gallassee. He and Lowther conspired to take over the ship, and a few days later the two men led a successful mutiny, raised the black flag, and headed out to sea.

The pirates renamed their ship *Happy Deliverance* (although some accounts call her the *Happy Delivery)*, and Lowther was elected captain. He and Massey had a crew of around 50 men. Lowther decided to head towards the West Indies, making landfall near Barbados. There he captured his first prize, the brig *Charles* of Boston. Her capture was bound to alert the navy to his presence, so Lowther kept heading to the northwest until he arrived off Hispaniola. Massey was in favor of attacking the French settlements on Saint Dominique, but Lowther disagreed, preferring to remain at sea.

The result was that when they captured their next prize—a small sloop—Massey made off in her, taking ten men with him. Lowther continued on to the Cayman Islands and his meeting with Edward Low, the *Happy Deliverance* capturing several prizes along the way. Massey threw himself on the mercy of Sir Nicholas Laws, the governor of Jamaica, claiming that he only agreed to sail with Lowther in order to protect his men. As a gentleman he was believed and allowed to return to London. The authorities there were less forgiving, and in July 1723 Massey was duly tried, convicted, and executed for piracy.

When Lowther arrived in the Cayman Islands in December 1721 he came across the far smaller pirate force of Edward Low. The two bands decided to join forces, the smaller sloop was abandoned, and Low became Lowther's deputy, or quartermaster. Their alliance began with the pirate equivalent of an office Christmas party, which the rather puritanical Captain Johnson described as involving "unheard of debaucheries, with drinking, swearing and rioting ... resembling devils rather than men." When their hangovers cleared they sailed towards the Central American coast, where on January 10, they captured the 200-ton *Greyhound* of Boston. After capturing her, the pirates "not only rifled the ship, but whipped, beat and cut the men in a cruel manner, turned them aboard their own ship, then set fire to theirs." This violence had all the hallmarks of Low rather than Lowther.

In the western corner of the Gulf of Honduras they went on to capture two more Boston vessels, both brigs, which they destroyed, as well as four sloops—one from Connecticut, one from Jamaica, one from Rhode Island, and one from Virginia. One of these was returned, another was burned, and the last two were added to the pirate fleet. Low was given command of the Rhode Island sloop, although Lowther refused to let him operate on his own. An attempt to careen the *Happy Deliverance* ended in disaster when native tribesmen stormed the pirate camp, driving the seamen back to their ships. Although the pirates escaped, the *Happy Deliverance* and all of her stores were left on the beach, and the natives put her to the torch.

That left them with just two sloops—one commanded by Lowther (which he renamed the *Ranger*), and the other by Low. They made the joint decision to try their luck in the West Indies. They captured a brig off La Désirade near Guadeloupe, which they destroyed, but after learning that warships were patrolling the Leeward Islands, they headed north towards the Virginia coast. By this stage the two pirates were not getting on particularly well, largely because—as Johnson put it—Low was "proving always a very unruly member of the commonwealth." The decision made in late May 1722 that the two should go their separate ways was probably a mutual one, as it seemed that neither pirate quite liked or trusted the other.

After this separation Lowther sailed towards New York and Long Island, where he achieved nothing apart from the capture of a few fishing boats. Finally on June 3 he captured a New England ship, homeward bound from Barbados. She yielded a cargo of rum, sugar, pepper, and six slaves. The pirates looted her, then sent her on her way. Meanwhile Low was creating a furore off New England, so

Lowther deemed it sensible to head back south. Off the South Carolina coast they met the *Amy*, which was on her way from Charles Town to London. The pirate flag was hoisted on board the *Ranger*, but Captain Watkins refused to be intimidated and the *Amy* replied by firing a broadside.

Captain Johnson picks up the story:

> Lowther (not at all pleased by the compliment, though he put up with it for the present), was for taking leave; but the *Amy* getting the pirate between her and the shore, stood after him to clap him aboard. To prevent this, Lowther ran the sloop aground, and landed all the men, with their arms. Captain Watkins, the captain of the *Amy*, was obliged to stand off, for fear of running his own ship ashore.

Lowther might not have shown much bravery in the encounter, but he still had luck. Captain Watkins was unable to reach the *Ranger* for fear of running aground himself, so he lowered a boat and led a boarding party to set her on fire. A lucky shot from the pirates on the shore hit the longboat and killed Watkins; at this point his crew turned around and retreated back to their ship, which then sailed off, leaving the pirates in peace.

Lowther managed to refloat his sloop on the rising tide, although she had been badly damaged by both gunfire and the grounding. He also had dead and wounded men to deal with. Lowther took the *Ranger* northwards to a secluded inlet on the North Carolina coast, where he established a camp and set about repairing his sloop. Johnson claims that it took them several months, and that:

> He and his crew laid up all the winter, and shifting as well as they could among the woods, divided themselves into small parties, and hunted generally in the daytimes, killing of black cattle, hogs, etc., for their sustenance and in the night retired to their tents and huts, which they made for lodging; and sometimes when the weather grew very cold, they would stay aboard of their sloop.[30]

In the spring of 1723 they returned to sea, sailing north towards the Newfoundland Banks. There they captured the schooner *Swift* and stripped her of much-needed provisions, as well as pressing three seamen from her. They remained off the Banks throughout June and July, capturing several small vessels but not coming across any prize of real consequence. Finally Lowther decided to return to the West Indies, and in August he was rewarded by the capture of the brig *John and Elizabeth*. This proved a temporary break, as the waters of the Leeward Islands were empty, and the pirates only managed to capture two prizes in as many months. One of these was a French armed merchantman from Martinique, the other a British slave ship called the *Princess*.

By late September Lowther decided he needed to careen the *Ranger*, so he sailed south down the line of the Lesser Antilles to Blanco (the Isla la Blanquilla), lying off the Venezuelan coast. The ship was stripped of her guns and stores, and hauled into the shallows. At that critical stage another sloop appeared—the *Eagle* of Barbados, whose commander, Captain Moore, realized that the beached sloop was a pirate ship, He sailed into the bay and attacked. The bows of the *Ranger* were facing out to sea, so Moore anchored directly in front of her, with his broadside trained on the *Ranger's* bows. The *Eagle* raked the defenseless *Ranger* until she hauled down her black flag and surrendered. At that point Lowther and 12 of his men who were unwounded made a swift exit through their vessel's stern windows and ran up the beach to safety. The remaining 12 wounded pirates were all captured.

Moore landed with 25 men, but he could track down only five of the pirates. Instead he returned to his sloop, towed the *Ranger* off the beach, and set sail for the Spanish port of Cumaná, on the Venezuelan mainland. The Spanish governor sent a sloop to recover the pirates, but like Moore's men before them, they only rounded up a handful of them. These four prisoners were taken back to the mainland, where they were tried and sentenced to a lifetime of slavery. As a reward Moore was granted the *Ranger*. He then sailed to St. Christopher (St. Kitts), where his prisoners were handed over to the authorities.

Of these, three were acquitted, two were imprisoned then pardoned, and the remaining 11 were sentenced to death. On March 20, 1722 they were hanged on the beach outside Basseterre. George Lowther was never caught, nor were the three men and a boy who evaded the search parties on the Isla la Blanquilla. Johnson of course had the last word: "As for Captain Lowther, it is said that he afterwards shot himself upon that fatal island, where his piracies ended, being found, by some sloop's men, dead, and a burst pistol by his side."

THE PIRATE GOW

One of the romantic associations we have about pirates is that their activities are usually set against a backdrop of beautiful islands, fringed with palm trees, in a tropical azure sea. The career of Pirate Gow reached its climax against this same backdrop, except that there were no trees, and the azure waters were colder than normal. Instead of operating amongst the Leeward Islands of the West Indies, this pirate returned to his home waters of the Orkney Islands, off the north of Scotland.

In 1695 John Gow was born at Cairston, a farm just outside Stromness in Orkney. Like many Orcadians he took to the sea for a living, and by 1724 he was an experienced sailor, although out of a job. In Amsterdam he signed on as a crewman on the 24-gun galley *Caroline* of 200 tons, bound for the Canaries and Italy. It is fairly clear he was intent on piracy from the moment he signed on, as was his fellow recruit James Williams. During the voyage the two men worked on their shipmates, spreading dissent, and laying the seeds for a mutiny.

They struck on November 3, the first night at sea after leaving the Canaries, bound for Genoa. Gow and three accomplices set upon Captain Ferneau, shooting him with a pistol at close range, then throwing the badly wounded man overboard. Two officers—the mate and the supercargo (the owner's representative)—tried to hide in the hold, but Williams and another mutineer hunted them down and murdered them. The mutineers also killed the ship's surgeon, and then threatened their shipmates with a similar treatment if they did not do as they were told. Gow renamed his new ship the *Revenge* and set about converting her from a well-armed fast merchantman into a pirate ship. After hauling up the black flag he was ready to start hunting.

The pirates captured their first prize nine days later—the sloop *Delight* of Poole, bound for Spain with a cargo of cod. Off Gibraltar they captured the *Sarah* of Glasgow, carrying boiled salmon and smoked herring to Italy. It was hardly a great start to a piratical career. Both ships were ransacked and then sunk. Next, Gow ran down to Madeira to take on water and provisions, but the local governor realized he was dealing with pirates and refused to trade with them. Gow then sailed to the neighboring Ilha de Porto Santo, where he pretended to be a harmless British merchantman. When the governor came aboard to pay his respects, he was kidnapped and ransomed for the stores Gow needed. The pirates then headed back out to sea.

On December 18 they captured the *Bachelor* of Boston off the southern tip of Portugal. She was carrying a cargo of timber, so Gow's luck still had not changed. He let her go, after transferring most of his prisoners into her from his earlier prizes. For some reason he also decided to keep an American cabin boy, William Oliver, probably seeing him as a likely recruit. The *Revenge* was off Cape

Finisterre nine days later when she intercepted her first decent prize—the *Louis Joseph*, a French merchantman transporting Spanish wine from Cadiz. Gow's crew drank their way through her cargo, then sent the Frenchmen on their way, probably because they were too drunk to scuttle their victim. On board were Captain Cross of the *Bachelor* and Captain Somerville of the *Sarah*, whom Gow had prevented from sailing with the rest of his men.

Another larger French vessel was spotted on January 3, but Gow decided not to attack. This seeming act of cowardice infuriated James Williams, who tried to shoot Gow. Instead he was overpowered, wounded, and thrown into the hold. The *Revenge* headed south again, and three days later Gow captured his last prize—the *Triumvirate* of Bristol, which was carrying fish. After ransacking her Gow took her longboat and transferred his remaining prisoners aboard her, accompanied by Williams, who was still tied up. To add insult to injury, Gow told the Bristol captain to hand Williams over to the authorities, to be tried and hanged as a pirate. Captain Davis duly obliged, and in Lisbon the wounded pirate was handed over to the Royal Navy.

In two months John Gow had enjoyed a singular lack of success, and the revolt of his former friend Williams suggests that his 30-man crew were also disaffected. His solution was to quit the unprofitable waters of Iberia and to head north towards his native Orkney. There he hoped to be able to raid unprotected farms and houses near the coast and to hide out amongst the islands he knew from childhood. During the voyage north he changed the name of his ship to the less suspicious *George* and coached his crew in their alibi—they were a stormbound merchantman on her way to Stockholm.

He arrived in Stromness harbor around the middle of January 1725. While some might have wondered how he became so successful so quickly, most Orcadians kept their own counsel. To keep up appearances Gow even bartered with other ships in the harbor. Inevitably, though, things started to go wrong. Captain Watt of the *Margaret* recognized the former *Caroline* and knew that two of his old crew had joined her in Amsterdam. When he met one in the street he learned the whole story and realized that Gow and his men were pirates. He told the authorities. Then, ten of Gow's pressed men escaped in the ship's boat, rowing to the Scottish mainland, where they went their separate ways. Another deserter made it to Orkney's main town of Kirkwall, where he surrendered to the local magistrate, while the American cabin boy and another pirate hid themselves in Stromness until Gow set sail, then turned themselves in.

Now that everyone knew exactly what he was, Gow threw caution aside and press-ganged eight replacements, including his own teenage nephew. By this time the country was in an uproar, and so on February 10 he put to sea, where he would be relatively safe from the authorities. The only problem was that his ship was now undermanned, and the desperately needed task of careening was still only half completed. He needed another safer haven where he could finish the job and plan his next move.

Gow reverted to his old plan of raiding houses close to the shore. On the day he left Stromness, he led a landing party to the nearby small island of Gairsay, where he raided the house of the county sheriff. Fortunately for the household, news of the pirates had preceded them, and the raiders found nothing of value save £7 ($13.65) and a few silver spoons. He also kidnapped the sheriff's piper and two serving girls, who were presumably raped then set ashore on the neighboring island of Cava, in Scapa Flow. The *George* then sailed around the Orkney mainland, which separates the islands into two archipelagos. Once in the North Isles they continued on to Calfsound, an anchorage off the northern end of the island of Eday.

The island's main landowner was James Fea of Clestrain, whose home, Carrick House, overlooked the anchorage. As he approached the anchorage Gow handed the helm over to a local recruit, Robert Pottinger (Johnson incorrectly calls him Porringer), who came from the neighboring island of Westray. His local knowledge clearly did not extend to the anchorage, as the *George* ran hard aground on the Calf of Eday, a small island that formed the northern part of the sound. The situation was desperate but not disastrous, as the *George* could still be pulled off if Gow had a longboat. Unfortunately his longboat had already been stolen by his deserters, and the remaining little boat was too small to carry the anchor and men needed to pull her back into deeper water. Gow needed a boat.

Meanwhile Fea was watching the whole affair, and as word had already reached Eday, he guessed who the mariners were. He owned the only suitable boat on the island, and he ordered his men to stave in her lower planks, rendering her useless. He also sent a boat to Kirkwall asking for help. By the time a small boatload of pirates landed, Fea was ready for them. He encouraged them to eat and drink in the hamlet of Calfsound, while he invited the boatswain James Belbin back to Carrick House. On the path from the hamlet Fea's men jumped on the pirate, and the boatswain was tied up, then hidden in Carrick House. Fea then led his men back to Calfsound, where the remaining four pirates had been drinking heavily. They too were quickly overpowered and locked up.

PIRATE CODES

Once a pirate crew elected their officers, they often established a set of rules that governed life on board. A lot has been written about these pirate codes, or articles, and they have become enshrined in pirate fiction as an essential part of pirate life. However, it seems more likely they were guidelines, a code by which the shipmates lived together. Several pirates used these articles, which probably had their origins in the charters set out by the buccaneers in the seventeenth century. Those sailors who turned to piracy from privateering would also have been used to documents of this type, which set out how prize money or plunder would be divided or laid out compensation rates for injuries.

As pirate captains, quartermasters, and other officers were elected, and in most cases pirate ships were run along democratic lines, it made sense that they were unable to claim an unduly large share. However, as the one-time pirate and ship's cook Barnaby Slush pointed out, in order to justify their extra share, captains had to prove their courage to the men who elected them:

> Pyrates and Buccaneers, are Princes to [sailors], for there, as none are exempt from General Toil and Danger; so if the Chief have a Supream Share beyond his Comrades, 'tis because he's always the Leading Man in e'ry daring Enterprize; and yet as bold as he is in all other attempts, he dares not offer to infringe the common laws of Equity; but every Associate has his due Quota.

The most detailed set of pirate articles to have survived was drawn up in 1721 by Bartholomew Roberts and his crew, and these were quoted in full by Captain Johnson:

> I. Every man has a Vote in Affairs of Moment, has equal Title to the fresh Provisions, or strong Liquors, at any Time seized, & use them at pleasure, unless a Scarcity make it necessary, for the good of all, to Vote a Retrenchment.

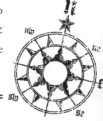

II. Every man to be called fairly in turn, by List, on Board of Prizes, because they there on these Occasions allow'd a Shift of Cloaths: But if they defrauded the Company to the Value of a Dollar, in Plate, Jewels, or Money, MAROONING was their punishment.

III. No Person to game at Cards or Dice for Money.

IV. The Lights & Candles to be put out at eight o'Clock at Night. If any of the Crew, after that Hour, still remained inclined for Drinking, they were to do it on the open Deck.

V. To Keep their Piece, Pistols, & Cutlash clean, & fit for Service.

VI. No Boy or Woman to be allow'd amongst them. If any Man were found seducing any of the latter Sex, and carried her to Sea, disguised, he was to suffer Death.

VII. To Desert the Ship, or their Quarters in Battle, was punished with Death, or Marooning.

VIII. No striking one another on Board, but every Man's Quarrels to be ended on shore, at Sword & Pistol Thus: The Quarter-Master of the Ship, when the Parties will not come to any Reconciliation, accompanies them on Shore with what Assistance he thinks proper, & turns the Disputants Back to Back, at so many Paces' Distance. At the Word of Command, they turn and fire immediately, (or else the Piece is knocked out of their Hands). If both miss, they come to their Cutlasses, and then he is declared Victor who draws the first Blood.

IX. No Man to talk of breaking up their Way of Living, till each has shared £1000. If in order to this, any Man shall lose a Limb, or become a Cripple in their Service, he was to have 800 Dollars, out of publick Stock, and for lesser Hurts, proportionably.

X. The Captain and Quarter-Master to receive two Share of a Prize; the Master, Boatswain, & gunner, one Share and a half and other Officers, one and a Quarter.

XI. The Musicians to have Rest on the Sabbath Day, but the other six Days and Nights, none without special Favor.[31]

Gow soon realized what had happened, but without a boat of any kind he was helpless. He resorted to trying to deal his way out of trouble. In response to a white flag waved from the Calf of Eday, Fea sent a boat across to investigate, and this soon became the go-between, carrying a string of messages from pirate captain to local laird, and back again. However, time was not on Gow's side. It was now February 17, and word of his presence off Eday had surely reached Kirkwall. To break the deadlock he seized William Scollay, Fea's go-between, which prompted the laird to land on the Calf of Eday at the head of a gang of seven armed men. In the negotiations that followed, Gow and two of his men were captured, and dragged onto Fea's boat. Without a leader the remaining pirates soon surrendered, but not before drinking the *George* dry.

By the time the sloop HMS *Weasel* arrived on February 26, it was all over. The 31 pirates were all in custody, and the *George* had been refloated. By the end of March Gow and his men were safely in London's Marshalsea Prison, where five of them agreed to turn informant in exchange for a pardon. While James Fea was rewarded for his efforts, he was also accused of stealing cargo from the *George*, although the accusations probably had more to do with his political affiliations than anything else. As for Gow and his men, they were tried on May 26, but Gow refused to make a plea or to give evidence. Threatened with torture, he decided to cooperate, and the trial soon reached its inevitable conclusion.

On June 11, 1725, Gow and six of his shipmates were hanged at Execution Dock in Wapping, while an eighth man—an Irish teenager—was transported to the Americas as an indentured servant for life. Another pirate was hanged on July 2, while the remaining pirates was released, having either turned informant or proved to the authorities that they had been pressed. Gow's nephew, William Clouston, was one of those who were acquitted. They were lucky, as the authorities were rarely so lenient. The execution of Gow and his men represented the last substantial pirate execution to take place in London. Two more small-time pirates were hanged over the next three years, but Londoners would no longer be able to flock to see the execution of a pirate captain and his crew. The days of the golden age of piracy were drawing to a close.

HOWELL DAVIS

In September 1718, two sloops—the *Samuel* and the *Buck*—dropped anchor off the northern coast of Hispaniola. It was less than two months since Woodes Rogers first arrived in the Bahamas, and the colony was in need of supplies. The sloops had come to trade, or rather to smuggle, as the Spanish authorities still forbade interlopers from trading with their colonies. Most of the crew had been pirates until they accepted the King's Pardon, and Captain Brisk of the *Buck*—the commander of the expedition—was probably still doubtful of their loyalty. He was quite right to be apprehensive, as that evening the crew mutinied and took over both of the vessels. The ringleaders of the mutiny were all former pirates—Walter Kennedy, Thomas Anstis, Christopher Moody, and Howell Davis—and Davis was elected captain.

Most of what we know about Howell Davis comes from Captain Johnson, although as his career developed his name started appearing in official letters and reports, as well as in the newspapers. Johnson claims that he was born in the South Wales port of Milford Haven in Pembrokeshire, "and was from a boy brought up to the sea."[32] In 1718 he was the first mate on the *Cadogan*, a Bristol slave ship, which was captured off the coast of Sierra Leone by the pirate Edward England, a man we shall hear more of later. Clearly England took a shine to the Welshman, as he handed the *Cadogan* over to him, with orders to take her to Brazil, where he was to sell the ship and its human cargo, then divide the proceeds amongst the crew. Instead the crew decided to remain on the right side of the law and sailed to Barbados. Davis was thrown into the Bridgetown prison and remained there for three months before the authorities decided he had no part in the piratical attack. On his release he took passage to New Providence, where he joined the crew of the *Buck*.

After the mutiny Captain Brisk and five of his crew were transferred to the *Samuel*, where Captain Porter and 17 others also refused to join the pirates. The two captains and their men were soon released, and allowed to return to New Providence in the *Samuel*, after—as Captain Johnson put it—"Davis having first taken out of her everything which he thought might be of use." Incidentally, in Johnson's account of the incident he got most of the story right but called the *Samuel* the *Mumvil Trader* and replaced Hispaniola with Martinique.

That left Davis with around 60 pirates and a six-gun sloop, although he now had the guns from the *Samuel* to add to his armament. He put in to Coxon's Hole, an unidentified hideaway that Johnson places on the eastern tip of Cuba, and if so was probably on the northern coast around Nicaro, directly north of Guantánamo. This anchorage was probably named after the English buccaneer John Coxon. After careening the *Buck* the pirates cruised the waters of the Windward Passage, where they captured several vessels—two French merchantmen, a ship from Philadelphia, and a few sloops. Howell Davis had got off to a good start, but he knew he dare not linger much longer in the area, as Woodes Rogers was bound to come looking for him. Rather than go elsewhere in the Caribbean, he decided to cross the Atlantic and try his luck off the West African coast.

This was not such a strange decision. The "bight" of West Africa was the area where most early eighteenth-century slave ships picked up their human cargo, either through established trading posts—many of them operated by the Royal African Company or by the Portuguese—or else by dealing directly with the African rulers in towns such as Whydah (or Ouidah) and Calabar. Davis considered the coast a rich hunting ground, although his reasoning might also have been that he knew those waters better than he knew the Caribbean. First the pirates visited the Cape Verde Islands, where Davis decided to put in to the small Portuguese island of São Nicolau. He spent a month there, having convinced the locals that he was an English privateer.

Then in February 1719 he broke his cover by raiding the roadstead of Porto Inglês, on the nearby island of Maio (Isle of May). The pirates helped themselves to whatever they could find from the small vessels in the harbor and then captured a much larger 26-gun vessel called the *Loyal Merchant*, which chose the wrong time to enter the port. Davis renamed her *Royal James* (Johnson calls her the *King James*) and abandoning the *Buck* took over this new prize instead. Although Johnson mentions a failed attack on the governor's residence on the principal island of Santiago—where Drake had led another unsuccessful attack 134 years before—there is no evidence that this incident actually took place. After all, by February 23 the pirates were off the West African coast, having made landfall at Gallassee in the mouth of the Gambia River, the place where George Lowther started his career.

The place was defended by a fort—Gambia Castle—owned by the Royal African Company, but when Davis arrived the defenses were only half finished. Its commander lived aboard the *Royal Ann*, a company ship moored in the harbor. Davis passed himself off as a merchant, but then under cover of darkness his crew manned their boats and attacked the *Royal Ann*, capturing her after a short fight. In Johnson's account Davis was invited to dinner, and captured the African Company commandant during the meal. However it happened, Davis then seized the fort and the town, and for the next few days Gallassee was a pirate town, and Davis's crew celebrated accordingly. Almost on cue a 14-gun pirate brig sallied into the harbor flying the *Jolly Roger*. The newcomer was none other than the French pirate Olivier le Vasseur—La Buse—and both pirate crews kept the party going for another week before heading south together. There they joined forces with yet another pirate, Thomas Cocklyn, who commanded the *Mourroon* of 24 guns. Davis was now part of a powerful pirate squadron.

In 1717 both Cocklyn and La Buse had been part of the pirate crew of Christopher Moody, who operated from New Providence. Moody regarded Cocklyn as something of a psychopath and so was happy to give him his own command—the galley *Rising Sun*, which Cocklyn renamed *Mourroon*. Then Moody's crew deposed him and elected La Buse as their new captain. As Moody had formed part of the original mutinous crew of the *Buck*, that meant that the three shipmates were reunited, and none probably trusted any of the others.

After the now customary two-day party to celebrate the meeting of the three ships, La Buse and Cocklyn declared Davis to be their pirate commodore, and together they decided to attack another Royal African Company fort, just down the coast at Sierra Leone. The real prize was not the fort but the six merchantmen sheltering beneath its guns. The pirates landed and assaulted the place, but, in Johnson's words, "Those who defended the fort ... had not the courage to stand it any longer, but abandoning the fort, left it to the mercy of the pirates." This was probably an exaggeration, as the African Company records report that the post held until the defenders had exhausted all their gunpowder. However, this was the one and only joint action taken by the three pirate crews, who fell out during the ensuing celebrations, "the strong liquor stirring up a spirit of discord among them."

The three groups went their separate ways, and according to Johnson, Howell Davis delivered the parting lines: "Hark ye, Cocklyn and La Bouse, I find by strengthening you, I have put a rod in your hands to whip myself, but I'm still able to deal with you both; but since we met in love, let us part in love, for I find that three of a trade can never agree." There was probably just too much bad blood between the three crews, and between Moody and his two former shipmates. Worse, a group who titled themselves lords set themselves up as Davis's lieutenants, and considered themselves superior to the rest of the pirate crew. Leaving the others to their own devices, Davis took the *Royal James* south towards Cape Three Points, on the coast of what is now Ghana. He captured and plundered two British ships on the way, then fought with a 30-gun Dutch ship that refused to surrender. She was captured after a long-running fight, and Davis kept her for his own use, renaming her *Royal Rover*. Walter Kennedy was given command of the *Royal James*.

His two ships then kept clear of the powerful Cape Coast Castle but put in to the slave trading anchorage of Anamabu (also written as Anamboe), some 13 miles further down the coast. Three British slave ships lay at anchor there—the *Royal Hind*, the sloop *Morris,* and the *Princess* of London. All were captured, along with a large number of slaves, money, bags of gold dust, and trade goods. Even more importantly, dozens of seamen volunteered or, more likely, were forced to join Davis's crew, including the second mate of the *Princess*. He was another Welshman, called Bartholomew Roberts, and he would go on to become the most successful pirate of the golden age.

From Anamabu the two pirate ships continued on to the east, but it soon became clear that the *Royal James* was leaking badly, and her pumps could barely keep her afloat. They beached her near Calabar and examined her hull, only to find her planking rotten and holed. They had no choice but to abandon her, and a crowded *Royal Rover* then set a course for the Portuguese island of Principe, 250 miles away to the south. When he arrived Davis had the audacity to pass his ship off as a British man-of-war. The deception worked—for a time. The Portuguese governor welcomed Davis and his men, and for two weeks all went well as the crew of the *Royal Rover* repaired their ship and replenished its stores. By now it was the first week in July. The only incident took place when a French ship tried to enter the harbor and Walter Kennedy led three longboats filled with men, who captured her. Davis had a ready excuse, and claimed that the Frenchman had been trading with pirates. The story was believed, and according to Johnson the governor even commended Davis on his men's zeal. Then it all went horribly wrong. A Portuguese-speaking slave escaped from the *Royal Rover*, swam ashore, and told the governor who his British guests really were. He also revealed Davis's plan to kidnap the governor and hold him to ransom. This time it was Davis who was outsmarted.

The following morning he went ashore as usual, accompanied by ten of his leading officers—the lords. The pirates accepted an invitation to visit the governor's house for drinks and never suspected the Portuguese until they walked into an ambush. The island's militia cut the pirates down with a concentrated volley, and Davis was badly wounded by a shot to the groin. He tried to drag himself away to safety but died in the attempt. As the story goes, "Just as he fell, he perceived he was followed, and drawing out his pistols, fired them at his pursuers; thus like a game cock, giving a dying blow that he might not fall unrevenged." Only Walter Kennedy and one other pirate escaped the ambush and were picked up by one of the *Royal Rover*'s boats.

Before the pirates could flee, they had to fight their way past the battery guarding the harbor entrance. Kennedy warped the ship round so her guns could bear, and opened fire. Within minutes the Portuguese had abandoned the battery and were running for the nearby woods. Kennedy landed with 30 men, overturned the guns, and returned to the *Royal Rover*. Meanwhile the pirates manning the captured French sloop began bombarding the town, although when she got too close she ran aground and had to be abandoned. Then the pirates sailed off, leaving a burning town, a wrecked fort, and the dead body of their captain behind them.

THE RISE OF BLACK BART

While everyone has heard of Blackbeard, Bartholomew Roberts (or "Black Barty") is virtually unknown to people who do not have an encyclopedic knowledge of pirates. However, he was far more successful than most and posed more of a threat to the authorities before he was finally cornered off the West African coast. One of the last of the pirates of the golden age, he was known as the "Great Pyrate" by his contemporaries, and his passing marked the end of the era.

Bartholomew Roberts, or "Black Bart," successfully terrorized the waters of the Americas and the West African coast before he was finally hunted down by Captain Ogle of the Royal Navy.

We have already described how he served as the second mate on board the slave ship *Princess* of London, which sailed from London in November 1718 and was forcibly recruited by Howell Davis when the *Princess* was captured off Anamabu at the end of May the following year. Roberts was born in the little Welsh hamlet of Newydd Bach sometime in the early 1680s. His original name was John Robert, but he changed his name after his encounter with Davis, if not before. After some two and a half decades at sea, he was an experienced seaman, with all the abilities needed to command his own ship. His nickname of "Black Bart" (or "Black Barty") stemmed from his dark complexion rather than any sinister streak. By all accounts he was regarded as good-looking—at least by the pockmarked standards of the day.

Following their escape from Principe the pirates headed southeast towards Cape Lopez—somewhere for them to recover. They also had to elect a new captain. Although the seven surviving lords—Thomas Anstis, Valentine Ashplant, Henry Dennis, Walter Kennedy, Christopher Moody, John Philips, and Thomas Sutton—were all experienced pirates, the election was open to the whole crew, not a small self-appointed elite. Realizing that the vote would go against any of the lords, and that Roberts would prove a popular choice, Dennis proposed him. As Johnson recounted:

> The speech was loudly applauded by all … [and] Roberts was accordingly elected, although he had not been above six weeks among them, the choice was confirmed by both the lords and the commoners, and he accepted of the honor, saying that since he had dipped his hands in muddy water, and must be a pirate, it was better being a commander than a common man.

Roberts began his captaincy by patrolling off Cape Lopez, and he was soon rewarded by his first prize—a Dutch slave ship—which he plundered on July 26, then sent on her way. The following day the *Royal Rover* ran across the English slave ship *Experiment*, which was captured and her crew pressed into service against their will. Her master, Thomas Grant, later recounted that the pirates took gold dust weighing 50 lbs, and that her crew remained involuntary pirates for another six months. After plundering the prize the pirates set her on fire. According to Johnson, Roberts then headed north towards Anamabu, but it seems more likely they remained off Cape Lopez, as records suggest that they then captured two more prizes there—a Portuguese and a British slaver. So far the cruise had been highly successful, but Roberts decided it was time to quit the West African coast. The crew were offered a choice between the Indian Ocean and Brazil and opted for the latter. Therefore, after pausing to take on water on São Tomé, an island south of Principe, the *Royal Rover* headed out into the Atlantic.

The transatlantic crossing took 28 days, and Roberts made his New World landfall at Fernando de Noronha, an uninhabited island some 175 miles off the Brazilian coast: "Here they watered, boot-topped their ship [scrubbed the hull], and made ready for the designed cruise." The cruise itself was something of a disaster. For the next nine weeks the pirates did not even see a sail, and the crew began to consider heading north into the Caribbean. Then, at the end of November, they approached Bahia and its anchorage, the Bay of All Saints. Bahia (now Salvador) was the Brazilian port fought over by the Dutch, Spanish, and Portuguese in the early seventeenth century. When Bartholomew Roberts approached its entrance he saw that the anchorage was filled with ships. It was the Lisbon fleet, the Brazilian version of the Spanish treasure *flota*. Despite the convoy being guarded by two ships-of-the-line and the harbor defended by shore batteries and forts, Roberts decided to attack.

Disguising the *Royal Rover* as a harmless merchantman, Roberts entered the anchorage under cover of darkness, guns loaded but housed, and his men ready for action. The guns on Fort San Antonio and San Pedro remained silent, and the pirates stealthily moved amid the lines of moored merchant ships without being challenged. Roberts came alongside one of the ships and captured her without the alarm being raised. He asked the captain which ship was the richest in the fleet, and he pointed out the *Sagrada Familia*, a 40-gun armed merchantman. Taking his prisoners on board the *Royal Rover*, Roberts cast off again and headed towards this new target. When the two ships came within hailing distance, in Johnson's words, "The master whom they had prisoner was ordered to ask how Seignior Captain did, and to invite him on board [the *Royal Rover*], for that he had a matter of consequence to impart to him."

The Portuguese captain was not fooled and ordered his men up from their berths. When Roberts saw them preparing their guns he knew the game was up, and "So without further delay, they poured in a broadside, boarded and grappled her; the dispute was short and warm, wherein many of the Portuguese fell, and only two of the pirates." By the time Roberts secured the *Sagrada Familia,* dawn was breaking and the anchorage was in turmoil. Worse, the two 70-gun

Portuguese ships-of-the-line were preparing for action. As he began towing the prize towards the open sea, the warships moved to intercept him. The closest one was gaining on the pirates, so Roberts altered course towards her. The Portuguese warship veered away, no doubt hoping to delay the fight until her consort reached her. Roberts was too wily for that and changed course again. Soon he was safely out of reach. The *Royal James* cast loose her prize, and the two ships sailed northwards, putting as much distance between them and the Portuguese as they could.

The raid on Bahia was a triumph, and from that point on it seemed as if Bartholomew Roberts could do no wrong. The *Sagrada Familia* was carrying 40,000 Portuguese gold moidores—the equivalent of 60,000 Spanish doubloons, or 240,000 pieces-of-eight (the equivalent of $23 million today). That did not take into account the jewelery the pirates found on board, including a spectacular diamond-studded cross that was being sent to the Portuguese king João V. Instead, Roberts presented it to the French governor of Guiana when the pirates put in to the Île du Diable (Devil's Island). Just over 130 years later the French would build their notorious prison on the same spot, but in 1719 the island was barely inhabited. They also captured a brig from Rhode Island, filled with provisions, which Roberts renamed the *Fortune* in celebration of his recent success.

That's when the fortune ran out. It was now late November—the end of the hurricane season—and Roberts was contemplating heading north into the heart of the Caribbean. However, one evening his lookouts spotted a brig, so Roberts took the *Fortune*—his fastest ship—and gave chase. William Kennedy stayed behind to guard the *Royal Rover* and the *Sagrada Familia*. Roberts had 40 men with him, including Moody and Anstis. He chased the brig into the night but lost her in the darkness. The following morning a storm appeared which pushed the *Fortune* further away from Devil's Island. It lasted for eight days, by which time the sloop was almost out of provisions.

As it would take a long time to work back to the island against the prevailing wind, Roberts sent a longboat ahead to bring Kennedy to his rescue. It came back a few days later, but it was alone. Kennedy had vanished, taking the *Royal Rover*, her Portuguese prize, and all the plunder with him. Roberts and his men were furious and swore revenge. However, for the moment he and his men were more concerned with finding the food and water they needed to survive than with tracking down the pirate who betrayed them.

THE ADMIRAL OF THE LEEWARD ISLES

Bartholomew Roberts started the second and greatest phase of his piratical career with a battered ten-gun sloop with the singularly inappropriate name of *Fortune* and 40 men. In an attempt to avoid another desertion he drew up a set of articles—a pirate code—which was signed by everyone on board apart from (according to Johnson) the Irish, whom he no longer trusted after the Kennedy betrayal. The idea was as much to bind everyone together by an incriminating document as an attempt to enforce discipline.

Roberts headed north to Tobago, where he ransacked the sloop *Philippa* from Barbados. Johnson mistakenly places this encounter off Deseada (now La Désirade), just to the west of Guadeloupe. He also claims that Roberts captured three prizes, two sloops and a Rhode Island brig, but in all probability these attacks were made off Barbados, as testimonies from the commanders of the sloops *Benjamin* and *Joseph* state that they were attacked by pirates near the island in early February 1720. Although these prizes were not large, they contained much-needed provisions. Johnson claimed that Roberts "then proceeded to Barbados, off which island they fell in with a Bristol ship of 10 guns, in her voyage out ... And after they had detained her three days, let her go." All these attacks were attracting attention, and three warships were ordered to track down the pirates off Barbados.

On February 19, 1720, Governor Robert Lowther gave permission for two ships to track down Roberts. One was Captain Graves's six-gun sloop *Philippa*, which had just limped into port from Tobago, and the other was Captain Rogers' 16-gun galley *Somerset* (actually spelled *Summersett*), which Johnson claims was from Bristol. They carried about 120 men between them—more than double the crew of the *Fortune*. However, Bartholomew Roberts may well have been reinforced, having come across another pirate, the Frenchman Montigny de Palisse, while he cruised off Barbados. Two days later the two pirate-hunters put to sea. The scene was set for another classic pirate sea battle.

However, it turned out to be something of an anticlimax. When the pirates sighted the two merchantmen, they gave chase and only realized they were pirate-hunters when the two sides were within pistol range. De Palisse immediately veered away and escaped to the south, but the *Fortune* and the *Somerset* traded broadsides. For all his desire for revenge, Captain Graves on the *Philippa* seemed to take very little part in the action that followed. Captain Rogers tried to board the pirate ship, but Roberts kept his distance, and, realizing he was outgunned, he too made his escape, cramming on sail and heading away towards the north. Rogers gave chase, but the pirates made good their escape by "throwing over their guns, and other heavy goods, and thereby lightening the vessel." Johnson states that following that little battle Bartholomew Roberts "could never endure a Barbados man afterwards, and when any ships belonging to that island fell in his way, he was more particularly severe to them than others."

After evading the pirate-hunters Roberts put in to Dominica to careen the *Fortune*, only to find 13 sailors who had been marooned there by the French. All of them volunteered to join his crew. The pirates spent the next few weeks dodging French naval patrols, sent out by the governor of Martinique when he learned that a pirate ship was in the area. This prompted Roberts to design a new flag, featuring an image of him, sword and hourglass in hand, standing astride two skulls. One was marked ABH ("A Barbadian's Head"), the other AMH ("A Martiniquan's Head").

It was now clear that the West Indies was a dangerous place for him, so Roberts decided to go where he was least expected and attack the fishing and whaling fleets that operated off Newfoundland. Both were lucrative businesses in 1720, and the pirates expected rich pickings. After sailing north, well away from coastal shipping on America's Atlantic seaboard, the *Fortune* arrived off the Newfoundland coast in late June 1720, and Roberts decided to attack the major fishing station of Trepassey, in the northeastern corner of Newfoundland. On June 21 the pirates sailed into the harbor "with their black colors flying, drums beating, and trumpets sounding." Rather than fight the invaders, the crew of the guardship *Bideford* abandoned ship and fled ashore, leaving the harbor completely defenseless. As Johnson recalled, "It is impossible particularly to recount the destruction and havoc they made here, burning and sinking all the shipping, except a Bristol galley, and destroying the fisheries, and [landing] stages of the poor planters, without remorse or compunction." Some 22 ships were captured that day, along with 250 small shallops. Roberts beat the seamen he caught for cowardice, particularly Admiral Babidge, whose job it had been to protect the fishing station.

Roberts abandoned his worn-out sloop in favor of the 16-gun Bristol galley, and the pirates then cruised off the Newfoundland Banks, capturing another ten ships—most of them French. One was a powerful 26-gun merchantman, which Roberts took for himself, giving her crew the Bristol ship instead. He renamed this new ship the *Good Fortune*, and for once it seemed the name was an appropriate choice. Almost immediately afterwards, Montigny de Palisse arrived in his sloop *Sea King*—apologizing for fleeing the fight off Barbados—and the two pirate ships continued the cruise in consort with each other. Several more prizes followed in quick succession during the middle two weeks of July—the *Richard* of Bideford, the *Willing Mind* of Poole, the *Expectation* of Topsham, the *Samuel* of London, the *Little York* of Virginia, the *Love* of Liverpool, the *Phoenix* of Bristol, and a sloop called the *Sadbury*.

Bartholomew Roberts's Newfoundland cruise was one of the most successful in the history of piracy, resulting in the pillaging or destruction of more than 40 ships—and hundreds of smaller craft. However, Roberts knew that the Royal Navy would retaliate by sending warships to the area, so he moved south again. By late August he was off South Carolina, where he captured a small vessel and stripped her of her water casks. After all, it avoided the risk of filling water barrels on shore. The same poor victim—Captain Fensilon—was later stopped by "Calico Jack" Rackam, who found nothing left to plunder. By September Roberts and de Palisse had returned to the West Indies and put in to La Désirade, where the pirates hoped to find smugglers to trade with.

Finding the anchorage empty, Roberts continued on down the line of the Western Antilles to Carriacou, one of the small Grenadines, between St. Vincent and Grenada. His voyage was speeded by a hurricane, which might explain why he chose such a small island to careen and repair his ship, well away from patrolling warships. He encountered the sloop *Relief* in the harbor, where Captain Dunn and his men were turtle hunting. Roberts persuaded the English captain to take some of the plunder the pirates had captured off Newfoundland, offering him an excellent deal if he traded it in St. Christopher (later called St. Kitts), the largest marketplace in the Leeward Islands.

After rejoining de Palisse the pirates followed Dunn north. They had agreed to rendezvous off St. Christopher on September 26, but their smuggler never showed. By the time Roberts arrived he was already in prison, facing charges of consorting with pirates. By way of revenge Roberts sailed the *Good Fortune* into the harbor of Basseterre, "where being denied all succour and assistance from the government, they fired in revenge on the town, and burnt two ships in the road." These ships—the *Greyhound* of Bristol and the *William & Martha*—also provided the pirates with a handful of new recruits. Giving up on his smuggler, Roberts sailed north to the tiny French island of St. Barthelemy, between St. Christopher and Anguilla.

The French governor lacked the power to resist, so he had little option but to cooperate with the pirates, "supplying them with refreshments ... and the women, from so good an example, endeavoured to outvie each other ... to attract the good graces of such generous lovers, that paid well for their favors." As well as indulging in rum and women, the pirates were also able to trade their goods with impunity. Roberts took the opportunity to rename his ship again, this time calling her the *Royal Fortune*. For his part de Palisse adopted Roberts's old name of *Good Fortune* for his sloop. Roberts also adopted an even fancier title, as a newspaper dated July 1721 reported, "They write from St. Christopher that Captain Roberts, who is the most desperate pirate of all who range these seas, now calls himself Admiral of the Leewards Isles." However, by the time the newspaper came out the Admiral was thousands of miles from the West Indies, terrorizing his way along the West African coast.

THE "GREAT PYRATE"

After quitting St. Barthelemy the pirates sailed west to the Virgin Islands, where Roberts captured a 22-gun brig off Tortola. As she was in much better condition than his own ship, Roberts transferred his men and cargo into her, and she became the new *Royal Fortune*. By the last week in October he was off St. Lucia, halfway down the chain of the Windward Islands, where he captured a brig and a sloop in Castries, the island's harbor. He kept the sloop as a store ship, then moved back north, past Martinique to Dominica. There, off the main harbor of Rouseau, the *Royal Fortune* overhauled a Dutch merchantman of 42 guns, which made her as powerful as a large warship. The two sides hammered it out, and this time de Palisse stayed to lend a hand. The pirates eventually captured the Dutch ship, and massacred her crew—the penalty for resisting so fiercely. She duly became the third *Royal Fortune*. After watching the massacre, the 15 small vessels in the harbor all meekly capitulated, while the ill-equipped guns of Fort Young remained silent.

From Rouseau the pirate flotilla (now a ship, a brig, and two sloops) sailed round to the Atlantic side of the island and spent an idyllic week holding a beach party. It was there that Roberts announced his decision to quit the West Indies and sail for West Africa. He sensibly pointed out that his force might be powerful but that it would also attract the attention of every warship in the Americas, and so Africa represented a safer option. Consequently in early November they sailed north towards Bermuda, where they picked up the trade winds that would carry them to Africa. True to form, Roberts even caught a prize—the *Thomas Emmanuel*—some 30 miles (48 km) off Bermuda. Then his luck changed.

In early December they came upon a Portuguese convoy off the Cape Verde Islands, and gave chase. Not only did the convoy elude them, but it also placed the pirates in a position in which the offshore winds made it near impossible to regain the African coast. Instead Roberts led his ships in a long sweep down towards Tobago, where they replenished their water supplies, then worked their way back up the line of islands to St. Lucia, where they spent a week taking on water and supplies and capturing passing vessels. He then followed a northwesterly course to reach Samana Bay on Hispaniola, where Roberts was forced to shoot a group of deserters led by Harry Glasby, the sailing master of the *Royal Fortune*.

Clearly morale was a problem. Roberts needed a few dramatic successes to bolster his men. On February 18, 1721, the *Royal Fortune* and the *Good Fortune* appeared off St. Lucia, where Roberts cut out a Dutch merchantman moored in Castries harbor. He then used her as a decoy, pretending to be a slaver. While his other ships remained over the horizon, Roberts took the Dutch ship in to Sainte Luce, on the southern tip of the island. There he was visited by several local sloops, all eager to exchange money for slaves. All of them were captured and plundered instead—their crews tortured, killed, or both. Roberts had his success.

Roberts lingered in the West Indies until late March, then sailed north towards Virginia. Morale was still poor, despite the capture of a large 26-gun French merchantman, which the pirates renamed *Sea King*. De Palisse chose that moment to go his own way. Left with only two ships, Roberts decided it was time to make another attempt to reach Africa. However, one more disaster lay in store. In late April, somewhere near Bermuda, the *Good Fortune* parted company with the pirate flagship, as her captain Thomas Anstis went his own way. This desertion left Roberts with only the *Royal Fortune*, his plunder, and some 228 men. In Johnson's words, "Accordingly they proceeded again for the coast of Guinea, where they thought to buy gold dust very cheap."

Roberts arrived off the Cape Verde Islands in late May, and after taking on stores he continued on to make his African landfall off the mouth of the Senegal River, where he captured two French sloops. Roberts kept them, and on the voyage down the coast towards Sierra Leone he renamed one the *Ranger*, turning her into a scouting vessel. By the time he reached Sierra Leone it was the end of June, and the anchorage was empty. His men spent six weeks there, until "the ships being cleaned and fitted, and the men weary of whoring and drinking, they bethought themselves of business."

The pirates moved on down the coast, and off the mouth of the River Cestos (on the coast of what is now Liberia) they came upon the Royal African Company Ship

Onslow, commanded by Captain Gee. When the pirates arrived most of the crew were ashore, and the ship was captured with relative ease. In fact, many of her crew volunteered to join Roberts's band. Roberts gave Captain Gee his own ship and commandeered the 40-gun *Onslow*, which duly became the fourth and last *Royal Fortune*. The cruise continued—the new *Royal Fortune* and the *Ranger* following the coast as far as Old Calabar (on what is now the eastern coast of Nigeria). The pirates arrived there in October, captured three slave ships from Bristol, and tried to careen their own vessels. However, the hostility of the locals prompted an early departure, so they continued down the coast to Cape Lopez, in modern-day Gabon. After watering, Roberts headed back towards the Gold Coast.

At Cape Appolonia (near the modern town of Abidjan on the Ivory Coast) the pirates captured the English slaver *King Solomon* and the Dutch *Flushing*, then sailed east to Whydah on the Slave Coast (now Ouidah in Benin). The open anchorage was crowded with 11 British, French, and Portuguese slave ships—all of which surrendered as soon as the pirates appeared on January 11, 1722. One of the slavers was added to the fleet, becoming the 32-gun *Great Ranger*, while the original sloop *Ranger* was renamed the *Little Ranger*. All the slave ship captains save one made a protection payment of eight pounds of gold dust. The exception—a slaver called the *Porcupine*—was burned to the waterline, with her human cargo still aboard her. This act of inhuman cruelty would not go unpunished.

The pirates were still at anchor off Whydah as dawn rose on February 5. Lookouts spotted a ship approaching. Roberts and his men had captured a slave ship the previous day and had spent the night drinking. Consequently the pirates were caught napping. The newcomer was HMS *Swallow* of 50 guns, commanded by Captain Challoner Ogle. Roberts sent the *Great Ranger* after her, the *Swallow* pretended to evade, and the chase continued over the horizon. Ogle then slowed down. When the *Great Ranger* was too close to escape Ogle sprang his trap and fired a broadside. A two-hour sea battle followed, by the end of which the *Ranger* was a bloody shambles. As Johnson reported, "They [the pirates] grew sick, struck their colors, and called out for quarter; having 10 men killed out right, and 20 wounded, without the loss or hurt of one of the King's men. She had 32 guns, manned by 16 French men, 20 Negroes, and 77 English."

Spectacular though this was, Captain Ogle realized he still had Bartholomew Roberts to deal with. On February 10 he reappeared off Whydah, and this time Roberts sailed out to give battle. The pirate captain now knew he was facing a British warship and that he stood no chance in a straight fight. His plan was therefore "to pass close by the *Swallow,* with all their sails, and to receive her broadside, before they returned a shot; if disabled by this, or if they could not depend on sailing, then to run on shore at the Point (which is steep to) and everyone to shift for himself." Bartholomew Roberts put on his finest clothes: "a rich crimson damask waistcoat and breeches, a red feather in his hat, a gold chain around his neck, with a diamond cross hanging to it, a sword in his hand, and two pairs of pistols hanging at the end of a silk sling slung over his shoulders." As he got under way Roberts also ordered the black flag to be hoisted.

Ogle recalled, "The pirate sailing better than us, shot ahead about half a gunshot." He fired a broadside, and then, "We continued firing (without intermission) such guns as we could bring to bear." Bartholomew Roberts was killed in the first salvo. Johnson wrote:

He [Roberts] had now perhaps finished the fight very desperately, if death, who took a swift passage in a grape-shot, had not interposed, and struck him directly in the throat. He settled himself on the tackles of a gun, which one Stephenson, from the helm observing, ran to his assistance, and not perceiving him wounded, swore at him, and bid him stand up, and fight like a man; but when he found his mistake, and that his captain was certainly dead, he gushed into tears, and wished the next shot to be his lot.

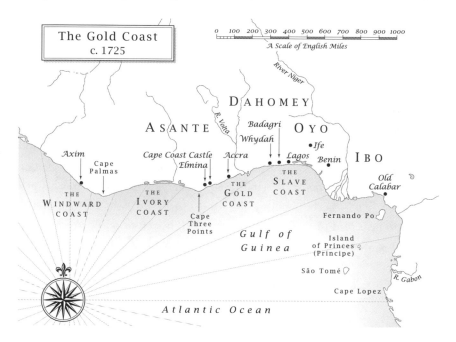

They presently threw him overboard, with his arms and ornaments on, according to the repeated request he made in his lifetime.

Johnson also recounted how the death of the pirate captain took the fight out of his crew: "Many deserted their quarters, and all stupidly neglected any means of defense, or escape." The *Swallow* continued firing, "till by favor of the wind we came alongside again, and after exchanging a few more shot, about half past one, his main-mast came down, being shot away ... At two she struck, and called for quarters ... the total of the men on board were 152, of which 52 were negroes."

The 'Great Pyrate' Bartholomew Roberts was dead, and those who survived of his crew were taken in chains to Cape Coast Castle, just along the coast from Whydah. The 72 African pirates were sold to the slave traders, while their remaining shipmates were imprisoned, then tried for their crimes. In what became one of the best-documented pirate trials ever, Roberts's crew were questioned in some detail about their activities. It began on March 28 and lasted just over three weeks. Finally, on April 20, 1722, 54 of the pirates were sentenced to death, while another 37 were spared the gallows but received lengthy sentences as indentured servants—which in the West Indies, where they were sent, amounted to a death sentence anyway. A further 74 pirates were acquitted, having proved they had been forced to join Roberts and his crew against their will. This mass hanging marked the official end of the golden age of piracy, although as always, there were still a few piratical loose ends to tidy up.

BLACK BART'S LORDS: KENNEDY AND ANSTIS

Two pirates who once sailed with Bartholomew Roberts went on to forge their own piratical careers. The first of these was Walter Kennedy, born to Irish parents in London in 1695. He reputedly began his criminal career as a pickpocket on the streets of London before gravitating to burglary. It seemed he put his past behind him when he became a sailor, and during the War of the Spanish Succession he served in the Royal Navy. In 1718 he served on board the sloop *Buck* during Woodes Rogers's expedition to the Bahamas, and later that year he was one of her crew members who mutinied off the coast of Hispaniola. He subsequently sailed with Howell Davis and then Bartholomew Roberts.

The last we heard of Kennedy was in late November 1719, when Roberts left him in charge of his flagship the *Royal Rover* when he went chasing after a prize.

His decision to desert Roberts was not taken lightly. Kennedy might have been left in charge, but his overbearing manner meant he was an unpopular commander. Most of his crew were pressed men, and he also had a prize ship to contend with and a group of Portuguese prisoners. He was also illiterate, and lacked the navigational skills normally expected of a pirate captain. All that held his crew together was his reputation for ferocity. To lighten his burden he emptied the prize *Sagrada Familia* of her cargo and handed her over to Captain Cane, whose sloop Roberts had recently captured. Cane sailed her to Antigua, thereby relieving Kennedy of his worries about prisoners. After waiting for 11 days for Roberts to return, he set course for the West Indies.

On December 15 he captured the small merchantman *Sea Nymph* near Barbados and kept the prize with him for a week before releasing the ship and her crew. He also took the opportunity to get rid of 16 of his most disaffected crew members. Next he headed to Virginia and spent a fruitless few weeks cruising off the mouth of the Chesapeake before heading south again towards warmer waters. His one encounter resulted in little plunder and the defection of eight more pirates, who chose to sail with the merchant captain rather than with Kennedy. Captain Knot deposited the men on the coast of Virginia, where they were all arrested and tried. Of the eight, two were eventually acquitted and the rest hanged for piracy, wishing "Damnation to the governor and confusion to the colony."

In February 1720 Kennedy in the *Royal Rover* captured the merchantman *Eagle* of New York, but following the drinking of her cargo, 48 men went aboard the prize and abandoned their old pirate ship, and Kennedy sailed away with them, taking the bulk of the Bahia plunder with him. That left just 25 men on the *Royal Rover*—too small a crew for a pirate ship of her size. These men sailed to the Danish colony of St. Thomas, where they hoped to surrender in exchange for a pardon. While most of her crew were ashore, the *Royal Rover* was spotted and captured by British pirate-hunters from Nevis, who towed the battered pirate ship as far as St. Croix. They left her there while they returned to Nevis to negotiate prize money, but in their absence the governor of Nevis sent the captain of HMS *Seaford* to recover the abandoned vessel. Unfortunately she foundered during the short voyage, and nobody earned a penny from her capture.

Meanwhile in the *Eagle*, Walter Kennedy made a landfall in Ireland, but his ship was damaged in a storm, and the pirates came ashore in Argyll, on the Scottish coast. The pirates split into two groups—Kennedy and one party elected to head south into England, while the remainder headed east towards Edinburgh.

This latter contingent was far from discreet, spending Portuguese gold coins on drink and women as they traveled. They were duly arrested and imprisoned in Edinburgh. Two of them turned informant, and in the subsequent trial the other nine were convicted. In late December 1720 the first batch of pirates was hanged outside Leith, and their shipmates followed them to the gallows two weeks later.

As for Walter Kennedy, he reached London and reputedly hid out in Deptford, across the river from his birthplace in Wapping. He was arrested—possibly for theft—and was subsequently identified by a seaman whose ship had been captured by Howell Davis off the West African coast. Despite his informing on his fellow runaways, only one of them was ever caught, and Kennedy was charged and convicted of his crimes. On July 21, 1721, he was hanged at Execution Dock in Wapping, after having made a short speech about the justice of Providence.

The next defector from Bartholomew Roberts was Thomas Anstis, who was another of the men who mutinied on the *Buck* off Hispaniola in 1718. Like Kennedy he was one of the lords, or inner cabal, of Howell Davis's crew, and he continued to serve as one of Roberts's most trusted lieutenants, eventually being given command of the powerful 18-gun pirate brig *Good Fortune*. In April 1721 he deserted Roberts during a passage from the Americas to Africa, and thereafter he forged his own piratical career.

In the West Indies he captured several small merchantmen, the first of which was the *Inwen* of Cork, whose carpenter, John Phillips, was forced to join the pirates. Worse, the pirates repeatedly raped one of the women passengers and then threw her overboard. They also almost killed a gentleman who tried to defend her. Anstis certainly doesn't come across as particularly pleasant, or intelligent, or even lucky. He spent the next six months careering wildly around the Caribbean, seemingly without any plan, and he was continually dogged by misfortune.

First he ran into two French warships off Martinique, who chased him out of the West Indies. Anstis fled to the Windward Passage and then moved on to the Gulf of Campeche, where he picked up a few small prizes and was joined for a time by Montigny de Palisse. His big success came on October 21, 1721, when he captured the large merchantman *Don Carlos* off the southern coast of Hispaniola. A week later the even larger *Morning Star* of Bristol fell into his hands. Anstis decided to keep her and gave her to John Finn, who was one of his lieutenants.

Their next attack took place off Tobago in December, and then, after a second unsuccessful cruise through the West Indies, the pirates were reported off Tortola—not the old buccaneer stronghold, but a smaller island off the

Venezuelan coast. That was in April 1722, by which time Anstis had been deposed as captain and Bridstock Weaver was now in charge of the *Good Fortune*. By that stage most of the 150-strong crew of the two pirate ships were having second thoughts about their chosen profession. They wrote a petition asking for clemency, which they handed over to the captain of the merchantman *Nightingale* that they encountered off Tortola. The plan was to rendezvous with their messenger in four months' time at an agreed location on the Cuban coast. This was a risky proposal, as it almost invited betrayal. The pirates were probably quite lucky that the authorities in Jamaica simply ignored their plea.

The pirates spent at least four months waiting in Cuba—possibly at Coxon's Hole, the hideaway once used by Howell Davis and therefore known to Anstis and some of the other veterans. However, Captain Johnson suggests they used a small island off the southwest coast of Cuba. He also mentions how they spent their time—living off the land and amusing themselves by dancing and holding mock pirate trials. In fact Johnson goes into some detail about this bizarre game, which involved the pirates appointing a judge and jury, and then trying one of their own. Finally the crews grew tired of waiting for a pardon that never came, and by the end of August they decided to return to piracy.

They resumed their hunting, traversed the Windward Passage and cruised off the southern coast of Cuba, but failed to capture any significant prizes. Then, in September, Finn ran the *Morning Star* aground off Little Cayman. Misfortune turned into disaster as two warships—HMS *Adventure* and HMS *Hector*—arrived on the scene just as Weaver and Anstis were trying to pull their consort off the reef. Although Finn and a few others managed to row over to the *Good Fortune*, which escaped capture, more than 40 of their shipmates were less fortunate and were rounded up by the navy.

Finn became the new captain of the *Good Fortune* and took her into the Windward Passage, then worked his way down the chain of the Leeward Islands until he reached Tobago in the spring of 1723. Some of the pirates deserted on a captured sloop, the *Antelope* of Dublin, so morale was at a low ebb. Those who remained had little to show for their efforts. They put in to a deserted beach to careen the ship, a task they had only just begun when the Royal Navy showed up again. On May 17 Captain Orm of HMS *Winchelsea* took his warship into the bay to capture the *Good Fortune*, but by the time he had negotiated the reef lying offshore, Anstis and a skeleton crew of 20 men had raised sail and escaped. However, Orm sent his men ashore and managed to capture John Finn.

As Johnson put it, "He was taken straggling with his gunner and three more, a day or two after their misfortune, by the men-of-war's men, and carried to Antigua, where they were all executed, and Fenn [Finn] hanged in chains." As for his former captain:

> Anstis, in the brigantine, escaped, by having a light pair of heels, but it put his company into such a disorder, that their government could never be set to rights again; for some of the newcomers, and those who had been tired of the trade, put an end to the reign, by shooting Tho. Anstis in his hammock, and afterwards the quartermaster, and two or three others, the rest submitting, they put in irons, and surrendered them up, and the vessel, at Curaçao, a Dutch settlement, where they were tried and hanged; and those concerned in delivering up the vessel, acquitted.[33]

That was the end of the chain of events that began that day off Hispaniola in 1718, when the crew of Woodes Rogers's trading sloop mutinied and took to piracy. Or rather, it was almost the end. John Phillips, the carpenter who was captured by Anstis in early 1721, was one of the lucky ones and deserted in the *Nightingale*. By 1723 he was working in the Newfoundland fisheries, where he decided that piracy was an easier life. On August 29 he stole a schooner (which he renamed the *Revenge*), and with a few accomplices he cruised the Atlantic seaboard, capturing as many as 30 vessels. His reign of terror lasted just over seven months.

Then, on April 15, 1724, he captured Captain Harradine's schooner *Squirrel* off the coast of Nova Scotia. Amongst his crew was John Fillmore, the great-grandfather of the thirteenth president. For once the pressed men and prisoners outnumbered the hardened pirates, and that night Harradine, Fillmore, and their shipmate Edward Cheeseman led a mutiny. In the brief fracas that followed Phillips was thrown overboard and the rest of his followers overpowered. Their trial and execution marked the last incident in the golden age, as by then it was clear to even the most desperate seaman that piracy did not pay. A string of high-profile trials and hangings had clearly demonstrated the point, and by the time Phillips's men were kicking on the end of a short rope, they had become the last of a breed. Ironically, later that same month, on May 24, 1724, Captain Johnson published his first edition of *A General History of the Robberies and Murders of the Most Notorious Pyrates*. The myth had already begun to supersede the reality.

7

THE PIRATE ROUND

THE LURE OF THE INDIAN OCEAN

Piracy was not just limited to the waters of the Caribbean and the west coast of Africa. While it is certainly true that most pirates were small-time criminals, whose sloops were too small to operate far from a friendly anchorage, other pirates were more adventurous. During the last decades of the seventeenth century, pirates began to sail down the African coast, round the Cape of Good Hope, and so entered the warm waters of the Indian Ocean. The big advantage of operating in these warm but distant waters lay in the wealth being shipped between India or the Far East and Europe. Ever since Vasco da Gama opened up a new sea route to the Indies in the late fifteenth century, European seafarers had made the long and dangerous journey, shipping the spices of the East to an appreciative market back home.

At first it was the Portuguese who held a monopoly of this trade, and their ships managed to break the Arab monopoly on the spice trade, transporting these exotic cargoes by sea rather than across the Arabian desert. Consequently vast fortunes could be made in trade with the Spice Islands of Indonesia or with the great coastal cities of the Indian subcontinent. By the start of the seventeenth century other European maritime nations had ventured into the Indian Ocean and begun challenging the Portuguese domination of the spice trade. The first of these was the Dutch East India Company, known as *Vereenigde Oostindische Compagnie* (or VOC), which was founded in 1602. The following year it opened up its first trading post in Indonesia, and by 1640 the Dutch rather than the Portuguese dominated trade between Europe and the East Indies.

During the second half of the seventeenth century the VOC maintained outposts at the Cape of Good Hope, in Persia, India, Siam, and China, in addition to its main trading colonies in the Indonesian archipelago, and it was generally considered to be the largest and richest private company in the world, maintaining a fleet of more than 150 merchantmen and almost 50 warships. However, it also had a rival. In 1600 Queen Elizabeth I of England signed a charter granting a monopoly of trading rights in India to a new organization—the Honorable East India Company (HEIC). In 1617 the Mughal emperor of India granted the English company trade rights, and over the next few decades the HEIC consolidated its hold on India. By 1690 it had established major fortified trading centers in Madras, Bombay, Surat, and Calcutta. At first it limited its main interests to cotton, silk, indigo, and tea, but it was only a matter of time before it began making inroads into the spice trade. It also had the right to print its own money, raise its own troops, and to protect itself from other interlopers. In effect it had become its own country.

This huge increase in trade in the region meant that by the end of the seventeenth century the Indian Ocean had become the perfect pirate hunting ground. Of course the European or colonial American pirates who ventured first into that part of the world certainly were not the first men to attack shipping in the Indian Ocean. Piratical attacks were recorded in the Indian Ocean centuries before the arrival of the Europeans, and small communities of pirates fringed the coast of India, Persia, and Arabia. The Turks maintained regular naval patrols in the region, as too did the Mughal emperors of India, but by the late seventeenth century these antipiracy operations had largely become a thing of the past. Consequently it was left to the Europeans to protect their own trading bases and ships and to launch punitive expeditions against local pirate bases.

In a later chapter we shall look at the way in which some of these local pirate enterprises operated and demonstrate that some pirate communities actually grew into what amounted to petty kingdoms. The Dutch and the English were already stretched by the need to protect their interests from rival European powers such as the Portuguese, the French, and to a lesser extent the Danes, and both England (Britain from 1707) and Holland were determined to secure their own share of the lucrative trade markets of India. The constantly shifting alliances and string of wars in Europe meant that nobody could really predict who the next enemy might be. The need to protect themselves against Indian and Arabian pirates placed even greater demands on the Dutch and the English. Consequently, by the time the European pirates first made an appearance, the resources of the two great trading companies were fully stretched. The pirates enjoyed a degree of freedom that they were unable to find in the relatively more crowded waters of West Africa, the Caribbean, or the Atlantic seaboard of North America.

The end of the seventeenth century also marked the heyday of the African slave trade. The Portuguese monopoly of slave trading on the west coast of Africa had been broken a century before, allowing English and French slave traders to establish their own trading links in the region. The English even organized the trade by means of another trading company, the Royal African Company, which, like its larger counterpart in India, maintained its own forts, trading stations and ships. During the last decades of the century, privateers had hunted the waters of West Africa in search of rich prizes, and so it was virtually inevitable that pirates would follow in their wake. It was also hardly surprising that some of the more adventurous of these pirates would continue their voyages further down the African coast to reach the Cape of Good Hope and the Indian Ocean, which lay beyond. What they found was a pirate's dream—rich and poorly protected prizes, a range of suitable hideaways to evade any pursuers, and a collection of European trading companies too busy fighting each other to worry about the threat of a pirate invasion. The result was that from around 1690 until the 1720s, the Indian Ocean became the most lucrative pirate destination in the world, and the men who sailed its waters were presented with opportunities that were simply not available anywhere else.

THE ROUNDSMEN: THOMAS TEW AND "LONG BEN" EVERY

The pirate threat which enveloped the Indian Ocean in the 1690s had its roots in Bermuda. That was where Thomas Tew from Newport, Rhode Island, found himself in 1692. Tew was wealthy enough to buy a share in a local sloop called the *Amity*. Nobody really knew where his money had come from, but one official later reported that "it was a thing notoriously known to everyone that he had before then been a pirate." In late 1691 a Captain Tew raided an island off Cape Cod, and while we can't prove it was the same man, the coincidences of name and place are suspicious. However, in 1692 the War of the Grand Alliance (1688–97) was at its height, and so Tew persuaded Governor Ritchier to grant him a privateering letter of marque that permitted him to attack the French. He decided to cruise off the West African coast, and so he headed out across the Atlantic in consort with another small Bermudan privateer commanded by a Captain George Dew (or Drew).

Captain Johnson suggests that Tew had little intention of limiting his attacks to the French:

> He thought it a very injudicious expedition which, did they succeed in, would be of no use to the public, and only advantage a private company of men, from whom they could expect no reward of their bravery … Wherefore, he was of opinion that they should turn their thoughts on what might better their circumstances.[1]

His crew seemed to be in full agreement, declaring "a gold chain or a wooden leg, we'll stand by you." When the two sloops were parted in a storm off the West African coast, the *Amity* sailed south, heading for the Cape of Good Hope. Once in the Indian Ocean they sailed north towards the Red Sea. The Bab el Mandeb ("Gate of Tears") was the Arab name for the 17-mile-wide passage between East Africa and the Arabian Peninsula which marked the boundary between the sea and the ocean. It was there that Tew and his men captured their first prize.

In July 1693 they sighted a "tall vessel" heading north into the Red Sea. According to Johnson the larger ship carried 300 soldiers, "yet Tew had the hardiness to board her, and soon carried her, and, 'tis said, by this prize, his men shared near three thousand pounds a piece." It was a stupendous achievement. The prize turned out to be a warship belonging to the great Indian Mughal emperor Alamgir I (also known as Aurangzeb), and she yielded up a fortune in specie, gems, ivory, spices, and silks. The pirates learned that the ship was the flagship of a convoy, and five more vessels were somewhere in the area. Tew wanted to give chase, but he was overruled by his quartermaster and the majority of his crew, who wanted to safeguard the treasure they had just won. As Johnson put it, "This differing of opinion created some ill blood amongst them, so that they resolved to break up pyrating, and no place was so fit to receive them as Madagascar; hither they steered, resolving to live on shore and enjoy what they got."[2]

According to Captain Johnson, Tew met up with another pirate off Madagascar who had made the same voyage into the Indian Ocean. Captain James Misson and his ship *Victoire* had recently arrived in Madagascar, where the French pirate had apparently established a fortified piratical settlement he called Libertaria. Tew and his men certainly spent a few months in Madagascar, probably on St. Marie's Island, and it has even been claimed that Tew used the island as a base from which he attacked and captured a Dutch East Indiaman somewhere off the Cape of Good Hope. However, the probability is that this mysterious Captain Misson was little more than a literary fiction dreamed up by Johnson.

When Tew decided to return to America his quartermaster and about half his crew remained behind in Madagascar. In April 1694 he sailed into the harbor of Newport, Rhode Island. As his prize had been captured from a non-European power, Governor John Easton of the Rhode Island colony treated Tew and his men more as successful privateers than as the pirates they really were.

Tew found himself feted as a hero, and after selling his share of the plunder he was even invited to pay his respects to Governor Benjamin Fletcher of New York, a meeting that many alleged was because Fletcher wished to back Tew in further ventures. When he was criticized for consorting with a known pirate, Fletcher wrote to his masters in London, reporting that he found Tew an interesting character, and that "at some times when the labors of my day were over it was some divertissement as well as information to me, to hear him talk."

The celebrity of the pirates was caused by the sensational scale of their success. As a contemporary New Yorker wrote, "We have a parcel of pyrates called the Red Sea Men in these parts who got a great booty of Arabian gold." Fletcher was not alone, as other New York and New England businessmen, most notably the New York ship owner Frederick Phillips, were eager to finance further ventures into the Red Sea—a lucrative privateering voyage that was soon dubbed the Red Sea Round.

After paying off his Bermudan backers, Tew returned to sea in November 1694, armed with a fresh privateering letter of marque provided by Fletcher. Johnson claims that Tew returned to Madagascar, where once again he joined forces with Captain Misson. It seems more likely that he operated in consort with four other New Englanders—Thomas Wake, William Want, Thomas Jones, and Captain Glover. All were eager for their share in the riches of the East. Tew may well have become the commodore of a pirate squadron, and Johnson even dubbed him "Admiral of the Fleet." Another of these pirate ships was the *Fancy*, commanded by Henry Every (Captain Johnson spelled his surname "Avery," but this is at odds with most contemporary accounts).

By June 1695 the pirates were back in Tew's old hunting ground of the Bab el Mandeb. What happened next is a little unclear, but it appears Tew decided to attack a large southbound Indian merchantman, part of a convoy bound for the Indonesian island of Surat. His target was possibly the Mughal treasure ship *Ganj-i-Sawai*, which was escorted by the well-armed Indian warship *Fateh Mohammed*. He launched the *Amity* into the attack against the escort, only to be met by a broadside. Johnson claimed that "in the engagement, a shot carried away the rim of Tew's belly, who held his bowels with his hands some small space; where he dropped." The original Red Sea Roundsman was killed, and apparently his death 'struck such a terror in his men that they suffered themselves to be taken, without making resistance."[3] At that point the story of the "Red Sea Roundsmen" is taken up by Henry Every.

For a man who has been touted as the most successful pirate of them all, we know very little about Every before he joined Tew's pirates. Johnson claimed he was born at Plymouth in Devon and was "bred to the sea." Other accounts describe him as the son of a Plymouth innkeeper or the son of a wealthy ship owner, born in the early 1650s. Another intriguing fact is that apparently he was known as John Every, but the name Henry appears in all surviving letters and papers, including those written by the man himself. The name Benjamin Bridgeman has also been associated with him, although this may well have been little more than a temporary alias, used after his return home.

He may (or may not) have spent some time in the Royal Navy, and during the late 1680s he showed up in the Caribbean, the captain of a sloop that collected cargoes of logwood in the Gulf of Campeche. It has also been claimed that shortly after 1690 he sailed with a privateer-turned-pirate called "Red Hand" Nicholls, who operated from the Bahamas. Much of this was probably the invention of his admirers—after all, he was one of the few pirates (apart from Blackbeard) whose life was dramatized on the London stage.

In 1693 "Long Ben, alias Every" is mentioned in the papers of the Royal African Company, where he was described as a rather unscrupulous and unlicensed slave trader. Until the end of the century the Royal African Company held a monopoly of slave trading on the West African coast, but the trade suffered from the activities of interlopers such as Long Ben. Finally in 1698 it bowed to the inevitable and granted noncompany ships permission to operate from its ports, as long as they gave the company a 10 percent share of the profits. In 1694 Every reappeared in the historic record, this time as the first mate of a fast 46-gun privateer called the *Charles II*. (Johnson calls her the *Duke*, no doubt confusing her with the Bristol privateer operated by Woodes Rogers, and he names her commander as a Captain Gibson. In fact Johnson's account of the life of Henry "Avery" is one of the few areas in which the pirate biographer got things badly wrong.) In June she set sail from Bristol, bound for Martinique in the West Indies, and her captain held a letter of marque authorizing him to prey on French shipping.

The *Charles II* put in to La Coruña in northeast Spain, but the crew were discontented enough for Every to stage a mutiny, probably when the captain was ashore. Historian Jenifer Marx claims that the unrest was caused by the crew not having been paid for eight months—an unlikely situation in a ship that had recently left her homeport. Whatever the reason, the mutinous crew elected Every as their captain, renamed the privateer the *Fancy*, and set a course for the Indian Ocean in search of plunder. On the way south they committed their first piratical acts—plundering three English and two Danish ships in the Cape Verde Islands—but the rest of the long voyage appears to have been uneventful, at least until they reached their chosen hunting ground.

The *Fancy* made her landfall in the Comoro Islands and put in to Johanna Island (now Nzwani) for water and a much-needed careening. It was there that Every captured another ship—a French pirate vessel, of which nothing is known. Every then penned a bizarre letter, the contents of which he hoped would be passed to the captains of all English ships operating in the Indian Ocean. In it he claimed, "I had not wronged any English or Dutch, nor ever intend whilst I am commander." He signed it, "As yet an Englishman's friend, Henry Every." It seems that he was still trying to pretend he was a law-abiding privateering captain rather than the pirate captain of a mutinous crew. Nobody was fooled.

By June Every had reached the Bab el Mandeb, by which time he was already cruising in consort with Thomas Tew. He took part in the same attack on the Mughal convoy in which Tew was killed, and he probably shadowed the convoy after the survivors of Tew's crew were taken aboard the *Fateh Mohammed* as prisoners. He then made his move, isolating the Mughal warship, then attacking her. His target may well have been damaged in her short engagement with Tew's *Amity*, as this time she did not seem to put up much of a fight. Every rescued the pirate captives, massacred the Indian crew, and helped himself to plunder, which was later valued at around £50,000 (the equivalent of $12 million). This was a substantial achievement, but it was still only a third of the treasure captured by Tew two years before. This meant that for Every it was only the start.

He continued to chase the convoy, and this time his goal was the treasure ship *Ganj-i-Sawai*. She was a tough opponent, mounting 62 guns and carrying some

Henry Every (also written as Avery) was one of the few pirates who knew when to quit. After capturing a fortune from a treasure ship in the Indian Ocean, he managed to evade justice and almost certainly retired with his ill-gotten gains.

500 Mughal soldiers. However, the *Fancy* was more maneuverable, she had a respectable 46 guns, and her 150-man crew had recently been augmented by the 40 or so prisoners recaptured from the *Fateh Mohammed*. Things started to go badly wrong for the Indian ship almost as soon as the battle started. First, one of her guns exploded, killing some of her crew, injuring others, and causing confusion. Then a lucky shot from the *Fancy* brought down the treasure ship's mainmast, which made her almost impossible to control. Every was able to rake his opponent, causing devastation aboard the Indian ship.

He then brought the *Fancy* alongside and boarded her. It was an extremely rash move, as the Indians still outnumbered the pirates by at least four to one. A bitterly contested hand-to-hand battle began—or at least it was bitterly contested by most of the participants. The aristocratic Mughal captain Ibrahim Khan fled belowdecks and sought refuge in his cabin, leaving his men to fight the pirates on their own. Still the fight could have gone either way, but gradually Every and his men gained the upper hand, and after some two hours the Indians finally surrendered. The decks would have been strewn with the dead and wounded, the pirates alone losing 20 men in the hard-fought action.

Still, the *Ganj-i-Sawai* now belonged to Every, and even the most rapacious members of his crew would have been stunned by the plunder that was now theirs. The booty—specie, precious stones, silks, and more—was valued at somewhere between £325,000 and £600,000, and included no fewer than half a million gold and silver coins. Even this seems not to have been enough for the pirates, who tortured the passengers and crew in an effort to find more. Women passengers either killed themselves to avoid a worse fate or were passed over to the *Fancy*, where the crew used them without mercy. After several days of rape, plunder, torture, and killing, the pirates continued on their way, leaving the survivors on board the plundered Indian ship to pick up the pieces.

What happened next was something of an anticlimax. Every sailed to the French island of La Réunion, where he shared out most of the loot, giving each man £1,000 (about the same as $250,000), plus a handful of gems as a bonus. He then quit the Indian Ocean, heading north to the Bight of Biafra, where he put in to the Portuguese island of São Tomé for supplies. They then set sail for the West Indies, putting in to St. Thomas in the Virgin Islands, where they sold some of their plunder. Every discovered that news of his attacks had already reached the Americas and that he was a wanted man. He was too notorious for the regional governors to grant him a pardon, despite the bribes Every and his men could offer them. Instead the pirate captain made the decision to break up the crew, and everyone went his own way.

For his part Henry Every and some of his men probably took passage to Ireland on a sloop called the *Isaac*, landing there in the summer of 1696. Although several of his crew were arrested in Ireland or England, the trail of Henry Every went completely cold. It was said that he took on the alias of Benjamin Bridgeman and was last seen in Ireland. Others claim that he retired from the sea, and ended his days as a country gentleman. Captain Johnson was less generous, claiming that Every ended up back in his native Devon, where he was swindled out of his money and died in poverty. The truth is that nobody really knows what happened to him. History has labeled Henry Every "the Arch Pirate"—the one that got away with it. He probably did. Unlike many of those who followed in his footsteps, Henry Every knew to quit while he was ahead. That probably made him the most successful pirate of them all.

CAPTAIN KIDD THE PRIVATEER

An altogether less fortunate character was William Kidd, who is probably the best-known pirate after Blackbeard. His notoriety actually stems more from the dramatic circumstances of his trial and execution than from anything he actually achieved. He was also one of the last of the "Red Sea Roundsmen" who sailed into the Indian Ocean in search of a fortune. In fact, it has been argued that he was really not a pirate at all—only a privateer who made a few errors of judgment that ended up costing him his life.

For years it was assumed he was born in Greenock in Scotland, although recent evidence suggests he came from Dundee, on the other side of the country. Born in January 1654, he had a tough childhood, his father dying when he was five and his mother reduced to receiving handouts from a seafarers' benevolent society. He went to sea and spent the next few decades learning his trade and gaining responsibility. Then in February 1689 the 35-year-old Scotsman appeared on the Isle à Vache off Hispaniola, where he joined the crew of the French privateer *Sainte Rose*, a filibuster based in Petit Goâve. While this might have been a smart enough move at the time, news of the outbreak of the War of the League of Augsburg meant that he was in a difficult position, operating in the middle of an enemy fleet. However, Kidd had a plan.

He bided his time, and when Jean du Casse led the French filibusters in an attack on St. Kitts, Kidd made his move. When most of the French crews were ashore assaulting Fort Charles, Kidd, his accomplice Robert Culliford, and six other Britons doubled back and returned to the fleet. They managed to overpower the sailors guarding a 16-gun brig and then fled to the neighboring island of Nevis, where they received a hero's welcome. The governor let him keep the ship (which was renamed the *Blessed William*), and over the next year Kidd turned himself from being a down-and-out seaman into a successful privateering captain. Then it all went wrong. On the night of February 2, 1690, Robert Culliford stole the *Blessed William* while Kidd was ashore on Antigua, leaving her captain stranded on the beach. It took him the better part of the year to find another ship—a 16-gun French prize which with a sense of irony he called the *Antigua*. Kidd sailed to New York as soon as he heard that Culliford had been seen there, but he missed the pirates, who had been welcomed by the unpopular acting governor. Kidd therefore played his part in ousting him and helped install a more suitable candidate in the governor's residency. He was now a hero again, rewarded for his efforts and the toast of the town.

It was there that he met Sarah Bradley Cox Oort, the youngest and most eligible widow in the city, and in May 1691 they married. Kidd's fortunes had been transformed in the few years since his arrival on the Isle à Vache, and he was now regarded as a privateer captain of repute and a worthy member of polite New York society. Over the next few years he played the part of the dutiful husband, his wife giving birth to two daughters—Elizabeth and Sarah. He became a merchant captain, voyaging to the West Indies and back, and he even made a few privateering ventures on behalf of the colonies of New York and Massachusetts. In 1695 he sailed to England in the *Antigua*, hoping to win more lucrative privateering contracts. That was when it all started to unravel.

Kidd secretly harbored a desire to become a captain in the Royal Navy. Despite his modest success he lacked the political clout or aristocratic pedigree even to consider such a possibility. However, he ran into an old New York acquaintance, Richard Livingston, who in turn introduced him to Richard Coote, the Earl of Bellomont. Livingston convinced the earl that his fellow Scot would make an ideal commander of a 34-gun privateering vessel he was building called the *Adventure Galley*. Bellomont agreed and offered to fund the venture, along with a group of his political friends, Lord Romney, the Earl of Salisbury, Lord John Somers, and Admiral Edward Russell—all members of the ruling Whig government. Consequently Kidd was drawn into a web from which he would be unable to escape. He sold the *Antigua* to raise money for his stake in the venture.

However, the terms of the agreement left little scope for Kidd and his crew to reap a decent profit from the venture—at least if they abided by the terms of the agreement.

In December 1695 Kidd was presented with a letter of marque authorizing him to attack the French and another one six weeks later that allowed him to hunt down pirates. By that time the *Adventure Galley* was almost ready for sea, and so in early April 1696 Kidd headed down the River Thames and into the open sea. His first stop was New York, where he recruited more crewmen—sailors whom the governor described as "men of desperate fortunes." He added that "'twill not be in Kidd's power to govern such a horde of men under no pay."[4] After all, privateers operated on a strict "no prey, no pay" policy, and without a string of prizes the crew could easily become disaffected. Despite this Kidd lingered in port for three months, spending time with his family and putting his affairs to rights. He finally set sail in September, bound for the Indian Ocean. This in itself was a curious decision—he had clearly set his heart on the tracking down of the "Red Sea Roundsmen" rather than French merchant ships, which could more readily be found in the West Indies.

On January 28, 1697, the *Adventure Galley* made landfall in Madagascar. Before Kidd arrived he may well have considered launching a direct attack against the main pirate base on the northeast side of the island. However, he probably thought that his crew were too few to take on the pirates in a direct assault. Instead he lingered on the coast, figuring out what to do next, hoping that a pirate ship would happen to pass by. Eventually he and his men grew tired of waiting and headed north to Johanna Island, where they came across the *Scarborough*, an English merchantman. Kidd sailed to intercept her but found his way blocked by a new arrival—the 40-gun East India Company warship *Shirley*. He backed off, and the trio eventually anchored off the island, where Kidd was eager to stress his good intentions. The East India Company captain would later report to his superiors that he was certain Kidd was a pirate, or at least planned to become one.

A bout of sickness amongst his crew kept Kidd in the Comoro Islands for a few more months, and he lost the best part of a third of his crew from "the bloody flux." He managed to scrounge a few replacements from other ships, but these all seem to have been hardened pirates, men the other captains were glad to get rid of. It was July before he was able to set sail again, and this time he headed towards the Red Sea, where he hoped to intercept the pirates as they lay in wait for another

Mughal convoy. In fact, Kidd may already have been entertaining ideas of carrying out such an attack himself. After all, he hadn't captured anything, he was running out of money, and his crew were becoming increasingly restless. In that situation the idea of attacking a non-European ship must have seemed appealing.

On August 15 the *Adventure Galley* was in the Bab el Mandeb. Kidd did not find any pirates, but he did run into a Mughal convoy. Without hesitation Kidd ran up a French flag, and attacked—an act of piracy he hoped he could explain away when the time came. Unfortunately the Indian ships were being escorted by the East India Company warship *Sceptre*, of 30 guns. Unknown to Kidd the emperor had hired the Company to protect his shipping, and so the *Adventure Galley* began her pirate-hunting career by encountering another pirate-hunter. As soon as he realized his mistake, Kidd turned about and disappeared—but the damage had already been done. Kidd had been branded a pirate in the eyes of the East India Company.

CAPTAIN KIDD THE PIRATE

Kidd was now desperate. He decided to head to the Malabar coast and loitered off the Indian port of Goa in the hope of encountering an unescorted Indian merchantman. His crew were now on the verge of mutiny, so when he encountered a small Arab merchantman he attacked and captured her. He eventually let her go but kept her English captain with him as a local pilot. He also had a running fight with two Portuguese warships, but there was still no sign of any lucrative Indian merchantman. Kidd was well aware that his crew planned to revolt, and when he overheard his gunner William Moore discuss mutiny, Kidd decided to crush the dissent by brute force. There was a brief exchange of curses—Kidd called the gunner a lousy dog, and Moore retorted, "If I am a lousy dog, you have made me so; you have brought me to ruin and many more."[5] Incensed, Kidd picked up a wooden bucket and smashed Moore over the head with it. The gunner was knocked unconscious and died the next day. This—and the subsequent capture of a Dutch prize, the merchant vessel *Rupparell*—helped stave off the mutiny. However, it was now November, and Kidd had little to show for 18 months of effort.

His big chance came on January 30, 1698, while the *Adventure Galley* cruised off Cape Cormorin, the southern tip of India. A lookout sighted a large ship— the *Quedah Merchant*—an Indian vessel homeward bound from the Far East. Kidd ran up the French flag and ordered her to heave to. Her English captain

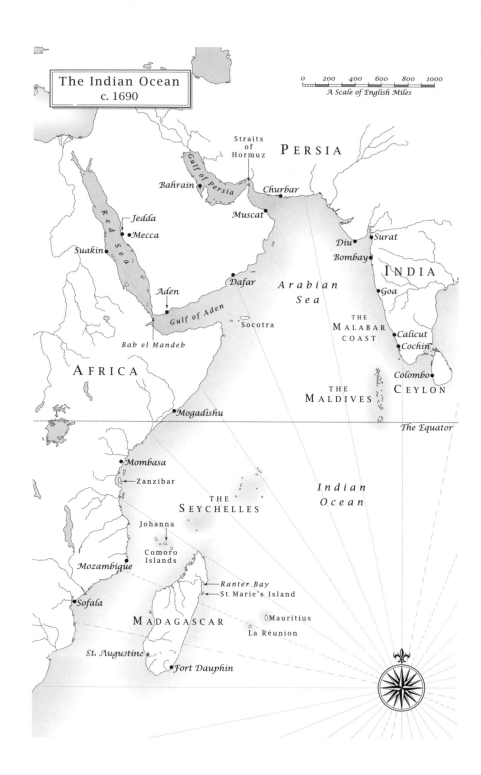

The Indian Ocean
c. 1690

A Scale of English Miles
0   200   400   600   800   1000

PERSIA

Straits
of
Hormuz

Gulf of Persia

Bahrain

Churbar

Muscat

Jedda

Mecca

Red Sea

Suakin

Diu

Surat

Bombay

INDIA

Dafar

Arabian
Sea

Goa

Aden

Gulf of Aden

THE
MALABAR
COAST

Calicut

Cochin

Bab el Mandeb

Socotra

AFRICA

Colombo

CEYLON

THE
MALDIVES

Mogadishu

The Equator

Mombasa

Zanzibar

THE
SEYCHELLES

Indian
Ocean

Johanna

Comoro
Islands

Mozambique

Sofala

MADAGASCAR

Ranter Bay

St. Marie's Island

Mauritius

La Réunion

St. Augustine

Fort Dauphin

complied, and Kidd and his men ransacked the ship, then took her into the nearby Portuguese-run port of Quillon (now Kollam). Kidd sold most of the cargo of silk, satin, and muslin for a bargain price (probably around £7,000), and used the money to pay his crew the equivalent of £25 apiece, the equivalent of about $6,000. It wasn't much, but it was sufficient to buy their loyalty until Kidd made it home. He kept the rest of the plunder, mainly specie, to pay off his backers, although he also promised his men a share of this hoard when the ship returned to New York.

He now had three ships—the *Adventure Galley*, the *Rupparell*, and the *Quedah Merchant*. It was just as well, as his privateer flagship was beginning to fall apart, rotted by her year in the Indian Ocean. One suspects that the owners of the Castle Shipyard in Deptford had cut a few corners in order to build the *Adventure Galley* in just five weeks. On April 1, Kidd put in to St. Marie's Island (now Nosy Boraha) on the northeast corner of Madagascar. This was the pirate den he had balked at attacking a year before, and it says a lot about Kidd's circumstances that he now sailed into the harbor without any fear of attack. It meant he was now one of them. However, one of the pirate ships in the port was the *Revenge* (formerly the *Mocha Frigate*), commanded by none other than Robert Culliford, the man who stole Kidd's first ship, the *Blessed William*.

To add insult to injury the bulk of Kidd's crew now defected to Culliford, leaving him with barely enough to make the voyage home. Feelings must have been running high in the port, but Kidd had little choice but to make a brave face of it and prepare for the return voyage. The *Adventure Galley* was beyond repair, so he abandoned her and his Dutch prize, and in November he sailed for home in the *Quedah Merchant*. Kidd must have known that he would face a hostile reception back in New York or London, and he must have spent the voyage wondering just how he would get away with it. His big hope was that his influential backers would support him and understand that his mutinous crew had forced his hand.

Kidd's first port of call in the Americas was Hispaniola, where he discovered that he was a wanted pirate, and that his backer Lord Bellomont was now the governor of New York. He decided to leave the *Quedah Merchant* and some cargo in Antigua, then took passage north with the bulk of her cargo. He put in to Gardiner's Island off the southern tip of Long Island, where he buried the bulk of his plunder—an insurance policy in case Bellomont did not support him. He then wrote both to the governor and to Robert Livingston, asking for help.

Bellomont was in Boston at the time, so after visiting his family Kidd made his way there, arriving on July 1, 1699. If he expected a friendly reception he was disappointed. The earl refused to see him, and five days later Kidd was arrested and thrown into jail.

He confessed where he had hidden the stolen goods, and within weeks Bellomont had recovered specie, jewels, and cloth valued at around £14,000 (about $3.3 million today). Although Kidd claimed that far more still remained on board the *Quedah Merchant*, the governor ignored this blatant attempt to strike a bargain. The bottom line was that while Kidd had been away the political climate had changed. England and France were no longer at war, and the privateers had been recalled. This inevitably led to an increase in piracy, so the government had adopted a tougher stance against it. Consequently any association with a known pirate would seriously harm Bellomont's career—and those of his fellow Whigs. Besides, as the governor of New York his legal share of the pirate plunder would probably be greater than his share of the profits from the "privateering" venture. In other words, Kidd was being thrown to the wolves.

The story of Captain Kidd's trial is probably better known than his piratical exploits. In March 1700 he arrived in England and immediately became the epicenter of a political storm. During the two months he was held in Newgate Prison, the Tory opposition (supported by the East India Company) demanded that Kidd name his Whig backers, while Bellomont's colleagues avoided a political scandal by destroying all the evidence they could that linked them to the unfortunate prisoner. Kidd still believed he would be exonerated through the intervention of these influential men, so he kept silent during two hearings held before a House of Commons committee.

The trial began on May 8, and Kidd was charged with five acts of piracy and one of murder (the killing of William Moore). As the proceedings were governed by admiralty law, his counsel was denied the chance to speak on his behalf, so Kidd was forced to maintain his own defense. This was made even more difficult because the murder trial was conducted in front of a jury in a different court, while the piracy charges were heard before a panel of admiralty appointees. Denied access to the evidence he needed to support his story, and condemned in advance by agents of the East India Company and by both sides of the political divide, the outcome was never in doubt. Kidd was duly found guilty of piracy and murder.

The whole business had taken just three days, and without doubt the main aim was to avoid further political scandal rather than achieve any sort of justice.

All Kidd could manage to say after his death sentence had been read out was "My Lord, it is a very hard sentence. For my part, I am the innocentest person of them all, only I have been sworn by perjured persons."[6] The judge was having none of it, and set the date of the execution for two weeks' time. Kidd probably still hoped for a reprieve from the gallows, but Bellomont and his friends kept well away.

On Friday May 23, 1701, a cart brought Captain William Kidd and nine other pirates to Execution Dock in Wapping, the procession headed by an official carrying a ceremonial oar—the symbol of the authority of the Admiralty. By all accounts he was drunk, having been granted a last request to be able to drown his sorrows in rum the night before. A gallows had been set up on the foreshore of the river, as under Admiralty law the execution had to take place below the high water mark. Then a last minute reprieve arrived—but not for Kidd. Instead, six of the other pirates were granted amnesty and were led away to safety. Kidd must have realized that this was it. A crowd of jeering onlookers watched as Kidd was led to the scaffold, and a minister prayed for his soul. His last slurred words were uttered—protesting his innocence—and then, as a psalm was sung, the block he stood on was kicked away and he danced his final dance.

Of course that was not the end of the affair. His body was then hung in a cage on the banks of the River Thames, as a warning to would-be pirates. Then came the claims, demands, and recriminations over the plunder—a long-running legal tussle that involved Bellomont, the government, and the Admiralty. It was never satisfactorily resolved, and the bulk of the Gardiner's Island plunder was eventually shipped to London, where it was used to fund the building of the Greenwich Hospital by Sir Christopher Wren. Then there was the business of Robert Culliford. In September 1698 he captured the Mughal treasure ship the *Great Mohammed*. He was back in St. Marie's Island when a squadron of Royal Navy warships appeared, bearing news of a newly offered royal pardon—part of William III's carrot-and-stick approach to piracy. He was still arrested though, as the attack on the Indian ship came after the terms stated in the amnesty.

Culliford stood trial on the same day as Kidd, but for some not wholly explained reason he was reprieved and set free—an opportunity never offered to the more famous captain. It has been argued that the man who robbed Kidd of his first command then gave evidence in return for his freedom—and so robbed him of his life as well. William Kidd and his nemesis Robert Culliford were probably the last of the "Red Sea Roundsmen." After their passing, the East India Company managed to patrol the waters of the Indian Ocean, so preventing any fresh wave of attacks, although the rump of the pirate colony supposedly first established by Captain James Misson would survive until the next great pirate outbreak a decade and a half later. While Madagascar would remain a pirate haven, none of those who remained had the skill or ability to follow in the footsteps of the great roundsmen.

THE MADAGASCAR PIRATES

The story Captain Johnson tells of the founding of an idyllic pirate community called Libertaria was probably little more than the retelling of a myth. He claimed that around 1695 the colony of Libertaria was founded by the French pirate Captain Misson and suggests it was located on the island of St. Marie, lying off the northeastern coast of Madagascar. The island's main anchorage of the Baie de Forbans provided good protection from storms, while the island itself was well provided with food and water, and the local population was tolerant of visiting mariners. Above all, Madagascar itself was ideally located astride the main sea route between Europe and the Orient. All shipping plying between the ports of India, China, and the Spice Islands of Indonesia had to pass close to Madagascar before it reached the Cape of Good Hope. In other words St. Marie was piratical paradise. It is little wonder it came to be associated with a pirate utopia.[7]

The legend of Captain Misson is really a tale of idealism. A supposed native of Provence, James Misson is said to have served in the French Navy Royal, where he met Father Caraccioli. This rather unorthodox priest called for the establishment of an egalitarian commune, in which everyone was equal, without distinctions of race, class, or creed. Whether these admirable virtues really did find a voice in a mysterious priest and an even more mysterious pirate captain is open to question. It is far more likely that both men were concocted as a means of explaining the foundation of a community that was little more than a literary invention.

Madagascar—exotic, unexplored, and largely free from tribal conflict—seemed the ideal place to found this kind of colony. After all, the social structures adopted by pirates were already extremely liberal for their day, and what might be construed as a social experiment was merely a pirate settlement run on democratic lines, following a generally held code of piratical conduct. Johnson's account simply pandered to widespread tales of pirate kingdoms, fueled by the wealth and abundance that many Europeans imagined was there for the taking in the Indian Ocean. On St. Marie's Island, as in other known pirate haunts in the area such as Ranter Bay (now the Baie d'Antongil) and Saint Augustine's Bay, both on

Madagascar's east coast, the remoter islands of La Réunion and Mauritius to the east, and Johanna Island to the northwest, visiting pirate crews seem to have been welcomed by those who were already there. In effect this pirate utopia was little more than interaction governed by the principles laid down in pirate codes, such as the articles drawn up by the buccaneers of the Caribbean.

Far from being an example of a social utopia, this was merely a pragmatic way of controlling life beyond the reach of the law. Johnson also claimed that the pirates eventually settled down to become farmers, holding the land in common: "No Hedge bounded any particular Man's Property." Plunder was "carry'd into the common Treasury, Money being of no Use where every Thing was in common." The British historian Christopher Hill argues that Johnson's chapter was merely a political essay, disguised as pirate history. He proposes that this vision was based on the ideas espoused by the English Levellers during the late 1640s: "all land in common, all people one." It hardly sounds as if this creed was designed to govern life amongst a disparate collection of maritime renegades and criminals. In fact, there are clear indications that, just as in any criminal society, some men rose to the top. In the late 1690s the pirate Abraham Samuel styled himself King of Port Dolphin (Fort Dauphin, now Taolanaro in southern Madagascar), while another pirate, James Plantain, called himself the King of Ranter's Bay. So much for an egalitarian pirate utopia.

What is clear is that for a decade or so, St. Marie and these other anchorages provided a fairly safe refuge for pirates. A recent exploration of the Baie de Forbans on St. Marie's Island has not only produced what is probably the wreck of the *Adventure Galley* but also the remains of several other suspected pirate ships, which were probably abandoned for the same reason as William Kidd's flagship. The visit to the Baie de Forbans by a Royal Navy squadron in 1699 may well have marked the end of Madagascar's heyday as a pirate sanctuary. Many of the pirates there—including Robert Culliford—accepted the offer of a pardon, while others, such as John Bowen and Thomas Howard, gave up piracy to live as settlers. When Woodes Rogers visited the Cape of Good Hope in 1711 he spoke to two former pirates from St. Marie's Island, who told him that fewer than 60 or 70 pirates now remained in Madagascar, "most of them very poor and despicable, even to the natives."

It seemed that by the start of the eighteenth century the Indian Ocean had seen the last of the pirates. However, they would return for one last hurrah. St. Marie's Island also provided a backdrop for one of the most unusual pirates of the golden age. It probably all began with John Halsey, an American privateer-turned-pirate. He arrived in St. Marie's Island in 1706, then for more than two years he used the decaying pirate haven as a base. His greatest success came in August 1707, when he captured two British ships off Mocha (now in Yemen), but soon after his return his ship and her two prizes were destroyed in a typhoon. Halsey died on St. Marie's Island soon afterwards, and his crew joined the other "poor and despicable" inhabitants of the island.

The next to appear was the Englishman Christopher Condent (sometimes called Congdon), who was one of the pirates who fled New Providence with Charles Vane in 1718. He soon went his own way, and off the Cape Verde Islands he captured a small Dutch sloop-of-war, which he renamed the *Flying Dragon*. He sailed for the Cape of Good Hope via the coast of Brazil, and by the summer of 1719 he had reached Madagascar. In St. Marie's Island he came across the survivors of Halsey's crew, and he used their local knowledge to good effect, spending the next year cruising the waters of the Red Sea and the northern Indian Ocean in search of prey. In October 1720 he captured an Arabian merchantman off Bombay, which yielded a substantial fortune in plunder—possibly as much as £150,000.

Condent was another pirate who knew when to quit. He sailed to St. Marie's Island and dispersed the crew of the *Flying Dragon*. In fact, archaeologists think they have now identified her remains lying at the bottom of the Baie de Forbans, not far from the wreck of the *Adventure Galley*. Condent and 40 of his men then headed east to the French island of La Réunion, where he negotiated a pardon from the French governor. The story goes that some 20 of these men went on to settle on the island, while Condent married the governor's sister-in-law, then retired to St. Malo in Brittany, where he set himself up as a merchant.

The next one to try his luck was Edward England, who despite his name was actually an Irishman, whose original name was probably the less dramatic Edward Seegar. During the War of the Spanish Succession (1702–14) he served as a privateer, working out of Jamaica, and like so many others he then gravitated towards New Providence, where his name was linked with William Winter, another small-time pirate. England accepted Woodes Rogers's pardon, then returned to his old ways. He was operating off the West African coast in early 1719, and he may well have encountered Howell Davis during his cruise, as the names of the two pirates were both identified as operating off the Guinea coast at the same time. By this time he had replaced his sloop with a larger vessel called the *Pearl*.

He kept another of his prizes, and after renaming her the *Victory*, he gave command of her to his quartermaster, John Taylor, another New Providence renegade. They decided to head south to the Cape of Good Hope and then try their luck in the Indian Ocean. It was somewhere along the East African coast, or more likely in Madagascar, that Captain Johnson claims that they spent a few months, where they "Liv'd there very wantonly for several weeks, making free with the Negroe women." From the description it sounds like St. Marie's Island. Eventually England and Taylor grew tired of these diversions and returned to sea, cruising in consort off the northwest coast of India. Again, England moved into one of his prizes, a 34-gun three-masted ship he called the *Fancy*.

Edward England operated off the coast of West Africa and the Indian Ocean, where his pirate ship the Fancy *fought a duel with the East Indiaman* Cassandra. *However, England lacked the ruthlessness needed to be a successful pirate captain, and he was eventually deposed, then left to end his days in poverty on the beach in Madagascar.*

A little after noon on August 27, 1720, the pirates made a landfall at Johanna Island, where they put in for water and supplies. However, they were not alone. The pirates found three ships already at anchor—a small Dutch Indiaman and two larger vessels, both British East Indiamen. The *Greenwich*—the smaller of the two British ships—and the Dutch vessel both cut their anchor cables and fled, but Captain James Macrae of the Indiaman *Cassandra* elected to stay and fight. While Taylor chased the two fleeing ships in the *Victory*, England steered the *Fancy* towards the waiting Indiaman. As the Scottish captain wrote in his report, the two other ships "left us engaged with barbarous and inhuman Enemies, with their black and bloody Flags hanging over us."[8]

What followed was a real slog of a sea battle. The lack of wind made it difficult to maneuver, so the two simply blazed away at each other. The fight lasted for three hours, and both sides fired broadsides into the other at close range until both vessels were holed and damaged. At one point England tried to use long oars ("sweeps") to bring the *Fancy* alongside the *Cassandra*, but, as Macrae put it, "by good Fortune we shot all her Oars to Pieces, which prevented them, & by consequence saved our lives." However, it was clear that the better armed pirate ship was winning the fight, and so Captain Macrae decided to run his battered ship onto the beach. His crew scrambled ashore and hid out on the island for several days before surrendering to the pirates.

This involved throwing themselves on the mercy of the pirates—men who had just seen dozens of their shipmates killed or wounded. To Macrae's surprise England turned out to be an extremely generous victor, and he granted the British sailors their freedom. Taylor was furious and accused England of being far too lenient. The pirate ignored him and allowed Macrae and his men to limp away in the shattered and leaking *Fancy*, which somehow made it to the safety of Bombay. The doughty Scotsman was feted as a hero and went on to become the governor of Madras.

Meanwhile England had Taylor in the *Victory* pull the *Cassandra* off the beach, and then set about turning her into his new flagship. However, the rift between the soft-hearted England and the callous Taylor reached a head six months later, in early 1721. As Johnson put it, "He [England] was soon abdicated and pulled from his government, and marooned with three more on the island of Mauritius." Marooned and abandoned by his own men, England and his companions managed to sail across the Indian Ocean in "a little boat of staves, and odd pieces of deal," and he reached the safety of St. Marie's Island. There he "subsists at present (1724) on the charity of some of their brethren." England reportedly died shortly afterwards.[9]

As for John Taylor, he continued his cruise in the *Victory* and the *Cassandra* after marooning his former captain, capturing a string of Arabian and European prizes off the Indian coast. He returned to St. Marie's Island, where he met Olivier le Vasseur, who had once sailed with Christopher Moody, Howell Davis, and Sam Bellamy. Taylor gave the veteran French pirate command of the *Victory*. The two pirates sailed to La Réunion, where they came across the *Nossa Senhora de Cabo*, a homeward-bound Portuguese merchantman which was transporting the Count of Ericeira. The Portuguese ship had been dismasted in a storm and proved to be easy pickings, being captured after a brief boarding action. The ship was laden with plunder, most notably a hoard of diamonds that the count planned to present to King João V of Portugal. Instead the jewels were divided between the pirate crew.

Le Vasseur replaced the rotten *Victory* with the *Cabo* (which was renamed *Victory*), and the pirates sailed to the East African coast, where they lay low for a time while a squadron of British warships scoured the Indian Ocean for them. The two men then split up. Le Vasseur destroyed the new *Victory* and disappeared, possibly retiring somewhere on Madagascar but more likely taking passage home to France. Taylor decided it was clearly no longer possible to return to St. Marie's Island, so instead he headed east across the Pacific, reaching Panama in May 1723. Although Spain and Britain were at peace—at least for the moment—the governor accepted Taylor's present of the *Cassandra* in return for a pardon and a safe passage to the Caribbean coast. What happened to him after that is something of a mystery, although one report claims he became an officer in the Armada de Barlovento.

England, Taylor, and le Vasseur were the last of the Madagascar pirates. In 1721 the same squadron from which Taylor and le Vasseur had hidden destroyed any remnants of pirate havens in Madagascar, while the French did the same in Mauritius and La Réunion. For the first time in decades the British, French, and Portuguese were at peace with each other, and their governments cooperated in an effort to end all piracy in the Indian Ocean. It was the end of the Pirate Round, and just as in the waters of the Caribbean or on the coast of West Africa, organized piracy became a thing of the past.

8

LAST OF THE PIRATES

THE LATIN AMERICAN PROBLEM

The end of the golden age of piracy did not necessarily mean the end of pirate attacks. However, these became isolated incidents, and any such outbreaks were soon dealt with by the navies of the leading maritime powers, which for the most part meant Britain. The government campaign against the pirates had clearly been successful, and in theory European and colonial ship owners could now sit back and watch the profits roll in. However, life was rarely that simple. The eighteenth century was dubbed the Age of Reason, but rationality didn't always apply to merchant seamen. Instead the period was marked by a near-constant string of wars, which were principally fought between Britain and France, and which frequently involved one or more of the other maritime powers.

First there was the War of the Quadruple Alliance (1718–20) in which amazingly the French and the British joined forces against the Spanish. A rare two decades of peace were followed by the War of the Austrian Succession— also known as the War of Jenkins' Ear (1740–48)—which saw wide-ranging naval action in the Mediterranean, the Caribbean, and the English Channel. Then came the major contest of the Seven Years' War (1756–63), when British naval supremacy was established on both sides of the Atlantic. The French were out for revenge, and therefore the American War of Independence (1775–83) was seen as the perfect vehicle to inflict a humiliating defeat on the British. The great Anglo-French struggle resumed following the overthrow of Louis XVI in the French Revolutionary Wars (1792–1802) and came to a head in the Napoleonic Wars (1805–15). In between came a host of other smaller conflicts, the most important of which was a series of wars of independence in Latin America and the War of 1812 (1812–15). What all these wars meant for sailors was that privateering became extremely lucrative, and by the end of the string of conflicts this form of state-sponsored piracy had become big business.[1]

This meant that when the wars ended in 1815, thousands of privateers found themselves out of work. While most found regular employment, a few turned to piracy or operated under dubious letters of marque, issued by rebel governments whose authority was not recognized by the rest of the world. The biggest sources of these privateering licences were the emerging countries of Latin America. When the French launched their devastating invasion of Spain in 1808, many Spanish colonies in the Americas seized the opportunity to rebel against their colonial overlords. The Latin American Wars of Liberation that followed soon engulfed most of South America, and the rebel juntas in Venezuela, Colombia, and Ecuador all embraced privateering as a means of striking out against their Spanish masters.

By 1826, Peru and Chile had become independent states, while Ecuador, Colombia, and Venezuela had effectively freed themselves of the Spanish. While Mexico had gained its independence in 1821, the rest of Central America was still in turmoil. Only Cuba remained under Spanish control, although it too was ravaged by guerrilla fighting and by the lack of effective Spanish government in some of its remoter provinces. The problem caused by these privateers did not go away after independence, as many kept on attacking Spanish shipping, claiming that they held their letters of marque from juntas who were still fighting for their independence. Others simply crossed the line from privateering into piracy and attacked anyone they wanted. Not all of these pirates were capable of operating on the high seas—some were little more than collections of local fishermen and bandits, who attacked passing shipping as a means of supplementing their income. In effect the Caribbean had become a dangerous and semi-anarchic place, where a once powerful central authority had been replaced by a patchwork of warlords, revolutionary juntas, and petty rulers.

This coincided with a postwar boom in shipping. As the war economies of Europe and the United States turned to manufacture, the growing demand for materials created by the Industrial Revolution meant that the volume of shipping on the world's sea lanes increased dramatically. For the most part these ships operated without hindrance. However, those who sailed through pirate hot spots such as the Caribbean placed themselves in danger. An example of one such attack was the plunder of the American brig *Washington*, which was seized by pirates off the coast of Cuba in 1822. Captain Lander reported that the Hispanic pirates who swarmed aboard his vessel stole food, cooking equipment, clothing and a compass, as well as $16 in cash. This was hardly piracy on a grand scale, but it was certainly typical of the opportunist attacks carried out on Caribbean shipping during this period. The American captain was fortunate to have escaped with his life—in several instances the pirates massacred the crew, following the old pirate adage that dead men tell no tales.

In a few cases the pirates ranged further afield, attacking ships on the high seas and roaming across the Atlantic as far as the European coast. However, unlike the great upsurge of piracy a century earlier, these oceangoing pirates were exceptions to the rule, and this time the maritime powers were better prepared and willing to cooperate to bring the pirates to justice. For the most part the main antipiracy force at this time was the Royal Navy, whose ships were used to patrol known pirate hot spots. However, since attaining its independence in 1783 the United States of America had become a major mercantile power. The size of the American merchant fleet increased dramatically during the years immediately following the end of the Anglo-American war in 1815, and by 1820 American ships had come to dominate the maritime trade of the Caribbean. This meant that American shipping was particularly badly hit by the increase in piratical attacks.

As the number of attacks increased, maritime insurance premiums soared, and consequently American ship owners demanded that their government do something. From 1820 on, major efforts were made by both the U.S. Navy and the Royal Navy to stamp out piracy in the Caribbean. This response involved three main stages. The first was the patrolling of major shipping lanes such as the Florida Straits and the Bahamas Channel. That was followed by a series of aggressive naval patrols in pirate waters, in which pirate ships of all sizes were hunted down and destroyed. Finally, attacks were launched against known pirate bases, particularly those on the coast of the Gulf of Mexico and along the northern coast of Cuba. This was supported by a diplomatic mission, in which the Spanish authorities in Cuba and the fledgling nations of Central and South America were encouraged to deal with the pirate problem within their own territorial boundaries. The result of all this was that by the late 1820s the pirate problem had been almost completely eradicated, and the waters of the Caribbean were once again deemed safe for maritime trade. This success was reflected by the great maritime insurers Lloyds of London, when in 1829 they removed their special insurance tariff for voyages to or from the Caribbean.

THE LAST PIRATES OF THE CARIBBEAN

We have already mentioned the rise of piracy in the years following 1815, but it is worth looking at the scale of the problem. In 1823 the American national newspaper the *Niles Weekly Register* reported that between 1815 and 1823 over 3,000 acts of piracy had taken place in the Gulf of Mexico and the Caribbean. In 1820 there were 52 piratical attacks in the Florida Straits alone, of which 27 were against ships flying the American flag. That year, insurance premiums were raised to a higher level than during the recent War of 1812, when British and American ships were regularly attacked by each other's privateers.

The newspapers of the period were filled with horror stories. For instance, in February 1819 the *Boston Daily Advertiser* carried a report from the supercargo of the American brig *Emma Sophia*. He claimed:

> On Saturday nineteenth [December 1818] between the Bahama Bank and Key Sal we were boarded and taken possession of by a small schooner of about 30 tons, having one gun mounted on a pivot and 30 men. She manned us with twelve men, Spaniards, French, Germans and Americans, and carried us towards the Florida coast ... every man had a knife about a foot long, which they brandished, swearing they would have money or something more valuable, or they would kill every soul of us.[2]

One of these small-time pirates was the Frenchman Louis-Michel Aury, who was a privateer based in Cartagena during the Latin American Wars of Liberation. When the Spanish reconquered the city in 1815 he turned to piracy, cruising the waters of the Gulf of Mexico and attacking shipping of any nationality he could find. Then in 1817 he arrived off Amelia Island in northeastern Florida, where a revolt was taking place against Spanish rule. He landed, claimed to represent the Mexican Republic, and duly annexed the island in the name of the Mexican government. In effect he turned the place into a pirate haven, where slaves were illegally sold to buyers on the Florida mainland. Two months later a force of U.S. Marines landed, rounded up the pirates, and put an end to Aury's island state. This move was followed a year later by the American annexation of Florida.

Another area troubled by pirates was the Gulf of Mexico. By far the most notorious of these was Jean Lafitte, a smuggler who turned to piracy, and whose close association with New Orleans has become part of the city's folklore. Today he is viewed as something of a romantic hero—a man who helped save the city from the British and who epitomized the carefree spirit of the Louisiana Cajuns. Of course the truth is somewhat different. His birthplace is usually given as Bayonne in southern France, sometime around 1780. He probably left the country at the time of the French Revolution, and by 1809 at the latest he and his brother Pierre were living and working in New Orleans, where they reputedly ran a blacksmith's shop. It appears that if this ever existed it was just a front, as their real business was smuggling.

In 1810 Jean Lafitte was named as the leader of a group of smugglers, pirates, and illicit traders who operated from "the Kingdom of Barataria," a bay on the western side of the Mississippi Delta, just south of New Orleans. Then in 1812 the brothers were arrested and charged with smuggling and illegal trading—charges of piracy were dropped through lack of evidence. The pair were released on bail, then promptly escaped to Barataria where they resumed their activities. According to a well-known New Orleans legend, when the newly elected Louisiana governor, William Claiborne, put a price of $500 on the head of Jean Lafitte the following year, the showman smuggler responded by offering ten times that for the head of the governor. Unfortunately there is no evidence that this dramatic exchange ever took place.

Barataria Bay was linked to the Mississippi River by a network of small rivers and bayous, and Lafitte and his colleagues used these waterways to transport goods between the Gulf of Mexico and the city, and stood ready to use them as a means of escape if the authorities came looking for them. Lafitte's main base was a barrier island called Grand Terre, to which slave owners and merchants came from the city to trade directly with Lafitte and his men. The authorities raided the island in September 1814, and although Jean escaped, his brother was captured and the base destroyed. Then three months later the British arrived and landed a small army, which attempted to assault New Orleans. This time Lafitte and his men sided with the American authorities and played a part in repulsing the British assault in an engagement known as the battle of New Orleans (1815).

In retrospect Lafitte probably backed the wrong side. In the aftermath of the American victory, General Andrew Jackson and Governor Claiborne refused to deal with the Baratarians, and within two years Jean Lafitte was forced to flee from Louisiana. He moved to Galveston (then still known as Campeche) in what is now Texas, a port that existed on the fringes of the authority of the Spanish government in Mexico and that served as a marketplace for frontiersmen, slave traders, pirates, and Mexican traders. One of these slave traders was Jim Bowie, who later achieved fame because of his knife and his participation in the defense of the Alamo. By 1818 it was claimed that 20 pirate schooners operated out of the port—including those operated by Lafitte—and that Galveston had become a leading center for the sale of slaves and plunder looted by Lafitte and his men in the Gulf of Mexico. However, a hurricane flattened the port later that year, and Lafitte's operation suffered a major setback.

At this stage there was no antipiracy squadron, but attacks on American ships operating out of New Orleans resulted in the U.S. Navy sending a Lieutenant Kearney, captain of the USS *Enterprise,* to deal with the problem. The *Enterprise* was a 14-gun brig, and Kearney threatened to bombard the port unless the pirates dispersed. Lafitte prevaricated, but ultimately he had no choice. Then in May 1821, according to an eyewitness, "Lafitte set fire to Campeche. Men aboard the USS *Enterprise* saw it burst into flames … When they went to shore at dawn they found only ashes and rubble. The ships of Lafitte were gone …" What happened to Jean Lafitte afterwards remains a mystery.[3]

As for Lieutenant Kearney, he went on to enjoy another success, when in October 1821 the USS *Enterprise* caught the fleet of the Rhode Island native Charles Gibbs, a former privateer and now one of the most notorious pirates on the Cuban coast. Although Gibbs and his men escaped ashore, Kearney succeeded in capturing or destroying all of his pirate squadron. However important this success was, it was still an isolated success. What was needed was a more organized response to the pirate threat in American waters.

Then in November 1822 the captain of the U.S. naval schooner *Alligator* was killed in a brush with the Cuban pirate Domingo—an event that inflamed public opinion. This was the final straw for the American government. Consequently four weeks later President Monroe ordered the formation of an antipirate squadron, charged with clearing the pirates from the waters around Cuba and the Gulf of Mexico. The commander of this new force—the largest peacetime assembly of American naval power—was Commodore David Porter, a veteran of the War of 1812 and America's earlier campaign against the Barbary pirates.

The fleet that congregated in Key West in Florida was perfect for the job. Dubbed the Mosquito Fleet it consisted mainly of small, shallow and fast schooners and brigs, supported by a paddle steamer and even a decoy ship—a merchantman armed with hidden guns. By early 1823 Porter was ready, and he began operations that April—his first success coming within days, when two of his schooners captured a pirate ship off Matanzas in Cuba. Within a month Porter was able to write to the Secretary of the Navy, reporting that "I can now say with safety that there is not a pirate afloat in this part of Cuba in anything larger than an open boat." What he failed to add was that it was the British who actually captured the flagship of Diabolito ("Little Devil"), the most notorious of all these small-time Cuban pirates.

Cuba was a particularly difficult place to operate, as the Spanish resented the American presence, and some regional administrators even seemed to condone piracy. American consuls reported that the Spanish mayors in the ports of Matanzas and Caibarien were in league with the pirates, as was the governor of the western province of Pinar del Rio. Both areas lay close to the busy shipping lane of the Florida Straits. Certainly pirates such as Charles Gibbs appear to have bought political protection in return for sharing their plunder with the local authorities. Another problem was that it was often difficult to tell the difference between pirates and local fishermen, which increased the risks of some kind of diplomatic incident. However, as Porter's fleet began to gain the upper hand, Cuban merchants began lobbying the Spanish authorities to support his actions using their own military forces. By December 1823, when President Monroe announced his Monroe Doctrine, he noted "the co-operation of the invigorated administration of Cuba."

In fact the Spanish soon began complaining that Porter was too successful—many former pirates simply turned their backs to the sea and began new careers as Cuban brigands, attacking targets on land rather than on the high seas. One of these was Charles Gibbs, one of the last of the Cuban pirates to remain at large. After being driven ashore by Porter he reinvented himself as a brigand and proved highly successful for several years. In 1830 he returned to sea but was captured after leading a failed attempt to take over a ship. He was taken to New

York to stand trial, where he confessed to the murder of over 400 people. He was hanged in Ellis Island early the following year. By then piracy had become a thing of the past. In fact by early 1825 piratical attacks were virtually unknown in Cuban waters, and international shipping could once again pass through the Florida Straits without the risk of attack.

THE *BLACK JOKE*

Although the pirate crisis had passed, a few isolated incidents of piracy still took place in the Caribbean or the Atlantic. These were made all the more shocking because of their rarity, and consequently the small-time pirates who still remained at large were given far more notoriety than they probably deserved. One of the worst of these early nineteenth-century pirates was Benito de Soto, a Portuguese (or Spanish) seaman who convinced his shipmates to turn pirate. In late 1827 he was serving on board an Argentinian slave ship *Defense de Pedro*, which had sailed from Brazil to the west coast of Africa and was anchored off Luanda, in Angola. Supported by the first mate, de Soto staged a mutiny and took over the brig. The captain and his supporters were either cast adrift in an open boat or simply thrown overboard, and for good measure de Soto disposed of the mate as well, leaving him in unquestioned control of the ship. Appropriately enough he renamed her the *Black Joke*.[4]

De Soto sailed to the Caribbean, where the brig's cargo of slaves was sold in the slave markets of Santo Domingo. The pirates then headed south, working their way down the chain of the Lesser Antilles, chasing and capturing every ship they encountered. In every case the crew of the vessel were murdered and the ship burned or scuttled. This meant that there was nobody left to report the crime or describe who had attacked them. The only trail left by the *Black Joke* was a string of missing ships.

After reaching Trinidad they continued on southwards, working their way down the South American coast towards Brazil and Argentina—the crew's home waters. By this time the authorities had worked out what was happening, and word was sent to the Latin American ports, warning merchantmen not to sail alone. In fact the Brazilian government began organizing convoys as a means of protection—all because of one small pirate ship.

As de Soto found the seas empty of shipping, he decided to follow the transatlantic shipping route that led from Brazil towards the Cape of Good Hope. In the age of sail, ships traveling from Africa to the Indian Ocean would

The head of the latter-day pirate Benito de Soto, after his execution in Gibraltar in 1832. One of his victims identified the Portuguese pirate on the streets of the port, and de Soto was arrested. Before his death he reputedly mounted the scaffold unaided and slipped the noose around his own neck.

sail far out into the South Atlantic to take advantage of trade winds, which would then sweep them close to the Brazilian coast. From there westerlies would lead them southeast towards the southern tip of Africa. Similarly, ships heading toward Europe would follow another route closer to the African shore, but still keeping well out into the Atlantic. By operating where these two trade routes crossed, the *Black Joke* would be in a perfect position to intercept shipping while keeping well away from land. As more ships started to disappear in the mid-Atlantic, the maritime governments began to become concerned that a pirate was operating in the area. Consequently homeward-bound British East India Company ships were ordered to wait at St. Helena for a naval escort, which would then convoy them into safer waters.

On February 21, 1832, de Soto came across the *Morning Star*, a British barque returning home from Ceylon. The *Black Joke* fired into the merchantman at point-blank range, killing several of her crew and forcing the *Morning Star* to heave to. De Soto ordered her captain to row over in his launch, and when he did the man was cut down by de Soto's cutlass—apparently because the pirate thought he took too long to comply. Reputedly, he cried, "Thus does Benito de Soto reward those who disobey him," as he struck the British captain. The pirates then used the launch to board the *Morning Star*, where they embarked upon an orgy of destruction, killing several of the men, raping the women passengers, and locking the survivors in the hold. After looting the ship the pirates scuttled her, then rowed away to safety. De Soto sailed off, leaving the *Morning Star* sinking steadily. It was the same trick he had pulled several times in the past.

Unfortunately for de Soto, this time it went wrong. The crew managed to free themselves and manned the pumps. Consequently they were able to keep their ship afloat while they repaired her hull. The following day another ship appeared—a British merchantman—and the passengers and all but a skeleton crew were taken to safety. That meant that for once there were witnesses. News of the attack eventually reached Britain, where accounts of his rape of the female passengers and the murder of wounded soldiers on board inflamed the passions of the public. Overnight he and his men became the most wanted criminals in the Western world. Of course de Soto was oblivious to all this. He presumed that the crew and passengers had gone down with their ship and that there was nobody left who could identify him.

Then came one of those strange coincidences. The surviving wounded soldiers had been dropped off in Gibraltar, where there was a large military hospital.

By now it was early April, and the *Black Joke* was cruising off the Spanish port of Cadiz, where the pirates hoped to sell their plundered cargo of silks and spices. Then a storm arose, and the *Black Joke* was flung onto the lee shore. De Soto and most of his crew survived the disaster and decided to make their way to the nearby port of Gibraltar, where they hoped to find another ship that they could take over once it put out to sea. The paths of one of the soldiers and the pirates crossed, and de Soto was identified and arrested. The governor agreed to extradite the prisoners to Cadiz, where they were duly tried, sentenced, and hanged. The Spanish form of execution was unusual, involving the condemned man riding to the gallows in a cart, seated on his own coffin. After the noose was tightened the cart was pulled away, and the rope did the rest.

Another early-nineteenth-century pirate who made the headlines was Pedro Gibert, although he was singularly less successful than de Soto. Strangely enough, both pirates made the same mistake—they both left survivors behind who could identify them. Although it has been claimed that Pedro Gibert was the son of a Spanish nobleman, it is far more likely that he was born somewhere in South America in around 1800. The confusion often arises from his title of "Don," which was something he adopted for himself, rather than a rank that was his by birth. For a time he had sailed as a privateer, working for the junta that governed Colombia and preying on Spanish shipping in the Caribbean. However, by the late 1820s that was all in the past, and he had reinvented himself as a smuggler and illegal slave trader. He certainly had the perfect vessel for the job—a fast 150-ton Baltimore clipper (schooner) called the *Panda*, crewed by a dozen men who didn't have too many scruples.

Then in the early 1830s Pedro Gibert decided to try his hand at piracy. He already had a base—a secluded inlet somewhere on Florida's east coast, probably in the Saint Lucie River, which allowed easy access to the Bahamas Channel. On September 20, 1832, the American brig *Mexican* was passing through the Florida Straits on its way from Salem, Massachusetts, to Buenos Aires in Argentina. When Captain Isaac Butman spotted a schooner heading out from the Florida Keys to intercept him, he decided to alter course and keep his distance. The mystery vessel gave chase, and eventually the American brig was overhauled. Captain Butman tried to fire his guns, but the roundshot turned out to be the wrong caliber for the barrels. Realizing he was helpless, he went below and hid the ship's money chest—$20,000 in coin, with which he planned to buy his next cargo.

The mystery ship turned out to be the *Panda*. When Gibert and his men boarded the *Mexican,* they locked up the crew in the forecastle and then ransacked the ship. When they could not find any money the American captain was dragged out of the forecastle, then beaten and tortured until he told them where he had hidden it. Gibert now had what he wanted and prepared to return to the *Panda*. According to the American captain, when one of his crew asked what he wanted done with the prisoners, he replied, "Dead cats don't mew. You know what to do." However, rather than kill them outright, the pirates kept their prisoners locked up, then set fire to the ship. They then sailed away, leaving the American sailors to die.

However, one of the sailors managed to escape by squeezing out through a skylight. He freed his companions, and together they fought to bring the blaze under control. Somehow they managed it, but Butman made sure to keep a small fire going, so that the pall of smoke would still suggest that the *Mexican* was burning to the waterline. Once the pirate ship had sailed over the horizon

The pirate schooner Panda *was commanded by "Don" Pedro Gibert, a ruthless cutthroat, smuggler, and slave trader who preyed on shipping in the Florida Straits during the early 1830s. The schooner was captured by the Royal Navy off the West African coast, and Gibert was extradited to the United States, where he was executed.*

the American sailors put the fire out completely, put their ship to rights, then sailed northwards again, away from the *Panda*. The *Mexican* eventually limped home, where news of the attack outraged the American public. Soon a worldwide hunt was under way for Don Gibert and his pirate crew.

Unable to return to Florida, Gibert decided to try his luck on the far side of the Atlantic. Eight months later, in early June 1833, Gibert was off Cape Lopez on the West African coast, where he planned to collect a cargo of Gabonese slaves—a trade that was now officially banned, although illegal trading still continued. This meant that amongst other nations, Britain maintained an antislavery patrol in the area, in which warships looked out for illegal traders just like Gibert. Of course they were also well aware of Gibert and his activities, as the British Admiralty had already notified its captains to watch out for the pirates. The ten-gun brig HMS *Curlew*, commanded by Captain Henry Trotter, had been on slave patrol for three years, and so when its sailors sighted the *Panda* anchored off the Nazareth River (now the Olibatta, the northern mouth of the Ogowe River in Gabon) they realized she was a slaver. Although most of the pirates escaped ashore, Gibert and a dozen others were captured.

Trotter soon realized who his prisoners were. The *Panda* was destroyed by an accidental explosion, but the pirates were duly brought to Britain, where their capture was reported to the American ambassador. The brig HMS *Savage* then transported the prisoners to Massachusetts, where they stood trial in November 1834. In a Boston courtroom the pirates were faced by the crew of the *Mexican* they had left to die. The outcome was inevitable. While two of the pirates were acquitted and six more were given long prison sentences, Gibert and three others were sentenced to death. On June 11, 1835, Gibert and his companions were hanged—the last pirates to be executed on American soil. The pirate attack perpetrated by these men was really an isolated case, as by that time piracy on the high seas had become a thing of the past—at least in American waters. However, the great expansion of maritime trade in the nineteenth century meant that merchant ships began regularly to sail through other waters that were far from safe.

BROOKE AND THE MALAY PIRATES

While piracy was a worldwide phenomenon, it rarely had a global impact. Instead, incidents of piracy tended to flare up in different regions and then die away when maritime powers in the region found a way of dealing with the problem. However, the growth of maritime trade in the eighteenth century meant that European and American merchants began to establish trade routes across the globe, and this in turn brought them into contact with regional pirates whose influence had rarely been felt beyond their own shores. Similarly these foreign ships were seen as lucrative prizes for many who would otherwise have been content to eke out a peaceable living from the sea.

For example, the Angrian dynasty that operated off the west coast of India in the early eighteenth century would hardly have been noticed by non-Indian historians had they not begun to prey on European East Indiamen. As a result the British undertook a major campaign against the Angrian pirates during the 1750s, and their fleets and bases were destroyed. Similarly the pirates who operated in the Red Sea and the Persian Gulf had little impact on the world until European traders became the victims of piratical attacks. The result was a string of punitive expeditions, which culminated in the British launching a large-scale assault on the Arabian pirates in the years following the end of the Napoleonic Wars.

The growth of trade with China in the nineteenth century meant that a new series of trade routes were opened up beyond the Spice Islands of the East Indies. This brought European and American ships and their crews into contact with a new set of pirates—those who operated in the waters of the South China Sea, the Philippines, and the Malay Archipelago (now Indonesia). For the most part these were coastal pirates, operating within tightly confined geographical areas. However, some of these regions, such as the Malacca Straits between the Malay Peninsula and Sumatra, or the Makassar Straits between Borneo and the Celebes, became maritime bottlenecks where these European traders sailed close to the shore. This made them tempting prey for the Malay pirates.

During his travels through the Malay Archipelago in the late 1850s, the British naturalist Alfred Russell Wallace described his encounter with local pirates:

Opposite us and along the coast of Batchian, stretches a row of fine islands completely uninhabited. Whenever I asked the reason why no one goes there to live, the answer was always, 'for fear of the Maguindanao pirates.' The scourges of the archipelago wander every year in one direction or the other, making their rendezvous on some uninhabited island, and carrying desolation to all of the settlements around ... their long well-manned praos escape from the pursuit of a sailing vessel by pulling away right into the wind's eye, and the warning smoke of a steamer generally enables them to hide in some shallow bay or narrow river or forest covered inlet until the danger is past.[5]

In another passage he wrote:

> A small prao arrived which had been attacked by pirates and had a man wounded ...
> The natives were of course dreadfully alarmed as these marauders attack their villages,
> burn and murder and carry away their women and children as slaves ... The next day
> the praos returned and we had definite information that these scourges of the Eastern
> seas were really among us. One of the praos had been attacked as it was returning ...
> They had four large war boats and fired a volley of musketry as they came up and sent
> off their small boats to attack. Two other praos were also plundered and the crews
> murdered to a man.

The coast of Borneo, the Celebes (now Sulawesi), Sumatra, Java, and the
Philippines were all perfect pirate havens, where a lack of central authority
and easy access to these maritime bottlenecks meant that piracy thrived. The
exceptions were a few small enclaves controlled by Europeans, such as the trading
posts established by the Dutch, or else areas where strong tribal leaders managed
to keep the pirates at bay using their own forces. The head-hunting Dyaks of
Borneo were generally acknowledged to be the worst pirates in the region, and
these were the fierce raiders described by Wallace. They ranged throughout the
region and developed a name for attacking European shipping sailing between
Borneo and the Malay Peninsula.

Then there were the Ilanun people from the Philippines, who harassed
Spanish shipping operating in Philippine waters. They also launched slaving
raids throughout the region, selling their captives in the slave markets of the
East Indies. Another formidable group were the Balanini or Sulu pirates
from the north of Borneo (now Sabah). Their main stronghold was on the
island of Jolo, in the Sulu Archipelago off the north of Borneo, although
they operated throughout the region. Other pirate communities included the
Bugis of Sulawesi, who divided their time between trading and piracy and
were described as "the most mercenary, bloodthirsty, inhuman race," while
the Atjeh (Achin) and Riau pirates operated in the strategic Malacca and
Sunda Straits—on either side of their home island of Sumatra. For the most
part these pirates used *proas* (also known as *praos*, *praus* or *prahus*)—shallow
drafted canoes—although some variants were also employed, such as the
corocoro, a fast sailing vessel fitted with outriggers, which could be powered by
sail or oar.[6]

While the Dutch generally tolerated these pirates as long as their own ships were not attacked, the British proved more proactive. The most celebrated European pirate-hunter of the time was Sir James Brooke (1803–68), the "White Rajah of Sarawak." As the effective ruler of a small state in the middle of the Malay Archipelago, Brooke waged a private war against the Dyaks during the 1840s and 1850s, supported on occasion by the Royal Navy and by the Dutch. However, it was not until 1861 that a joint Anglo-Dutch force was sent into the region to stamp out piracy in the archipelago, and this, combined with similar Spanish expeditions, finally managed to subdue the pirates. While the threat of pirate attacks remained, these were no longer considered a serious threat to European shipping. That, after all, was the main reason why most outsiders cared about the Malay pirates in the first place.

9

CHINESE PIRATES

PIRACY IN THE SOUTH CHINA SEA

Over the centuries piracy ebbed and flowed around the world, appearing and disappearing again according to the whims of circumstance—and naval power. However, in Chinese waters the threat of piracy remained constant for seafarers for more than a thousand years, probably longer. The first recorded incidence of piracy in the South China Sea took place in AD 589, around the time the emperor Wen unified China under the banner of his Sui Dynasty. However, it is almost a certainty that piracy flourished long before, as the fragmented petty states provided piracy with the perfect political climate it needed in order to prosper. Minor warlords dominated long stretches of the Chinese coast, their ships trading, raiding or conducting piratical attacks with equal ease. It was only when the emperor Wen and his dynasty managed to impose some degree of central authority that the power of these local warlords was temporarily checked.

This proved short-lived, and it was not until the Ming Dynasty in the thirteenth and fourteenth centuries that Imperial authority extended into the coastal provinces, mainly by threatening local rulers with invasion and execution if they did not stop misbehaving. While this meant that these rulers acknowledged the emperor as their feudal master, it still did not mean they didn't involve themselves in piracy when it suited them. This might have been a golden period for China, as her merchants ranged as far as the Indian Ocean, but it was also a boom time for the pirates. It was only in the fifteenth century that the Chinese came up with a solution. They paid the local rulers to suppress piracy in their own waters. As many of them were the same people responsible for the attacks, the policy was bound to fail. The Chinese government continued to adopt this pragmatic approach for the next five centuries.

In fact the whole business of piracy was different in China from anywhere else in the world. For a start, piracy was highly organized. Rather than operating in individual ships or even small groups, pirates congregated into fleets. Instead of occupying small pirate havens, Chinese pirates tended to control large sections of the coast, and ruled them much as if they were local warlords. Indeed a few of them were the very people the Chinese authorities paid to suppress piracy in their own waters. While this policy certainly reduced regional involvement in piracy, it also meant that some of these dubious local rulers became little more than bandits who enjoyed the protection of the emperor. However, for the most part these Chinese pirate confederations or empires kept well away from politics, and simply ruled their pirate fiefdoms as independent states. Their strength lay in their numbers—both the regional rulers and the emperor lacked the naval strength to do more than patrol their own local sea lanes. As a result, for five centuries the pirates were allowed to operate unchecked. Piracy in the Far East was eventually suppressed by the European powers, whose steamships and modern armaments were able to decimate the older fleets of pirate junks. It was not until the Europeans arrived with their steam-powered warships that the problem was finally dealt with.

Of course China was not the only country in the Far East to suffer from piracy. The coastal waters of Japan were plagued by pirates well into the sixteenth century, while we have already examined the tribal piracy that went on in the islands of the Philippines and the Malay Archipelago. Another pirate hot spot was the coast of what is now Vietnam. Before the 10th century the region was just another Chinese province, but from AD 939 onwards it ran its own affairs—at least until the French arrived in the nineteenth century. However, the Vietnamese still had to pay an annual tribute to the Chinese emperor, and the country remained divided into small semiautonomous provinces, similar to those found along the Chinese coastline. Local rulers used piracy as a means of protecting their own fiefdom at the expense of their neighbors. Piratical activity reached a peak during the Tay Song Dynasty (1778–1802)—a period of widespread rebellion and decentralization. Even the reunification of Vietnam by the Nguyen Dynasty did little to check the influence of these petty pirate kingdoms, and it was only through the intervention of the European powers (primarily the French) that the power of the Vietnamese pirates was finally broken.

The arrival of the first Europeans in the late sixteenth century brought traders into contact with these pirates, and, just like the Chinese and Vietnamese rulers themselves, the Europeans had to reach some form of accommodation with the pirates in order to trade. Their arrival coincided with the rise of the first large-scale pirate empire—that of the Chinese warlord Cheng Chi-Lung (or Zheng Zhi-Long, 1604–61), who operated in Fujian province. His power showed that, in China, piracy and politics were intertwined—Cheng combined his role as a pirate leader with those of a province administrator, a leading merchant trader, and even an admiral in the Imperial Navy. His son Cheng Ching-Gong (or Zheng Cheng-Gong, nicknamed "Koxinga") would expand this pirate empire into what was effectively the most powerful maritime power in the South China Sea.

It was only with the growth of European colonialism in the nineteenth century that the European maritime powers brought their naval might to bear on the problem of piracy in Chinese waters. Their successful defense of their trading enclaves during the Opium Wars of the mid-nineteenth century involved the employment of a naval force in the region, and this presence remained for the best part of a century, protecting the interests of European merchants against local warlords and pirates alike. Their technological advantage over the Chinese (and Vietnamese) pirates meant that relatively small naval forces were able to conduct punitive expeditions that succeeded in destroying the naval power of these pirate kingdoms, allowing European commerce to prosper without the constant threat of attack. In effect a combination of colonial police work, maritime steam power, and shell-firing naval ordnance brought an end to a thousand years of pirate domination in the South China Sea.

KOXINGA

The first of the three great Chinese pirate empires was based in Fukien province, opposite the island of Taiwan. Cheng Chi-Lung was a surprising pirate chief.[1] After all, he was more of a merchant than a sea robber, although he also dabbled in politics as well as piracy. He served his business apprenticeship with a Chinese merchant, working both in Japan (where he found a wife—Tagawa Matsu) and with Dutch traders, who had recently established an outpost on the Penghu (Pescadores) Islands in the Formosa (now Taiwan) Straits. He may well have dabbled in piracy during the early 1620s, using the Dutch port as a base and acting more as a Dutch privateer than as a pirate.

When his trading mentor died in 1623 his merchant fleet and escorting war junks were passed to Cheng. He established himself in Taiwan, but a growing rivalry with the Dutch encouraged him to move his operation to Hsiamen (Xiamen), the main port in the Amoy Islands, and other ports in Fukien, on

THE JUNK

For centuries the junk was the mainstay of Chinese and Southeast Asian maritime shipping, equally suitable as a merchant trader or as a pirate ship. It was the Portuguese who first coined the name *junco*, a derivative of the Indonesian *djong*. The junks used by the pirates of the South China Sea were little different from the junks encountered by Marco Polo centuries before, and their motor-powered descendants can still be seen today.

Most pirate junks were converted from trading junks, armed with several guns (including numerous small swivel pieces called *lantakas*), and crewed by as many as 200 men. Some of the largest pirate junks were over 100 ft long, with a beam of 20 ft, and carried three masts. The largest seagoing pirate junks had a substantial cargo space in the hold, part of which was used to store powder and shot. Junks were also divided into numerous small compartments belowdecks, which offered some form of protection against flooding if they were hit by enemy shot. This made them a lot less fragile than they looked.

Although the Europeans sometimes described junks as being primitive craft, mariners recognized that they were ideally suited to the waters of the South China Sea, being fast, reliable, and commodious.

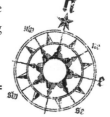

291

the other side of the Formosa Straits. While the mercantile arm of his maritime empire suffered from Dutch competition, the Europeans were traders, not pirates, and as long as Cheng avoided attacking Dutch ships, his pirate fleet was able to operate without any restriction. One of his most daring ventures was a large-scale raid on shipping in the mouth of the Yangtse River, an attack that secured his reputation as the unrivaled master of the Chinese seas. Within a decade his pirate war junks cruised as far afield as the Vietnamese coast and the Yellow Sea, and merchant ship owners were forced to pay him protection money in order to remain in business.

They were not the only ones who paid Cheng off. In 1641 the Ming emperor Chu You-Jian (Chongzhen) needed help in countering the revolt that would eventually cost him his throne. Consequently he appointed Cheng as his admiral of coastal waters, and charged him—of all things—with the suppression of piracy. The pirate chief was even paid an Imperial salary for three years, until the Manchu rebels captured Beijing and Chu You-Jian was forced to commit suicide.

Cheng Chi-Lung played a large part in these events, having aligned himself with the Ming successor Prince Tang in 1645. He ruled Fukien in the name of the Ming Dynasty, but in 1649 he was persuaded to change sides, so allowing the Manchus to capture the province. His actions helped secure the end of Ming resistance, and therefore the new Manchu (Qing) Dynasty rewarded Cheng for his efforts. He remained in charge of Fukien for another two decades, until the activities of his son led to his being called to Beijing in 1661. There the great pirate chief was held accountable for his son's actions, and he was executed. However, his son, nicknamed Kuo Hsing Yeh, or Koxinga, meaning "Lord with the Imperial Surname," would wreak a terrible revenge.

Koxinga was born in 1624, most probably during his father's stay in the Japanese port of Nagasaki. He was raised in Fukien, and during the late 1640s he took part in his father's military campaign on behalf of the Ming Dynasty. From around 1650 onwards, he also ran the twin family businesses of trade and piracy, leaving his father to concentrate on his political responsibilities. Much has been written about Koxinga the pirate chief, the Taiwanese hero, and the Ming loyalist. Although many of the legends that surrounded him fail to stand the test of historical scrutiny, the pirate chief certainly became a figurehead for anti-Manchu resistance—the defender of the older Ming civilization. One of these legends describes how he captured the city of Changchow (Zhangzou) from

A Scale of English Miles

0   100   200   300   400   500

The China Seas
c. 1800

Mouth of
Yellow River
to 1853

KIANGSU

Yellow River

CHINA

Nanking

Shanghai

Hankow

Changchow

Ningpo

Yangtze River

CHEKIANG

Wenchow

East
China
Sea

Foochow

FUKIEN

Tamsui

KWANGSI

GUANGDONG

Amoy

Canton

FORMOSA

Chiang-p'ing

Pearl River

Kowloon

Haiphong

Tien-pai

Hong Kong

Red River

Macao

Hanoi

Lei-Chou
Peninsula

South
China
Sea

Gulf
of
Tonkin

Ch'iung-choo

HAINAN

THE
PHILIPPINES

Hue

INDOCHINA

the Manchus, only to find that his mother had died during the siege. As the story goes, he went to the temple, then burned his old clothes as a symbol, and declared his intent: "In the past I was a good Confucian subject and a good son. Now I'm an orphan without an Emperor—I have no country and no home. I have sworn to fight the Manchu army to the end, but my father has surrendered and my only choice is to be a disloyal son. Please forgive me."[2]

At first he operated in Fukien, enjoying the protection of his father. However, as the new commander of the pirate fleet he concentrated his attacks on Manchu shipping. He then followed this up with a more aggressive policy, leading rebel forces in a series of raids and amphibious attacks against Manchu territory. Inevitably the military might of the Manchus meant that he was forced back and eventually had to abandon the mainland of Fukien. He took refuge just off the coast in Chinmen, a port in the Amoy Islands, where the Manchus were unable to reach him. A military stalemate followed that lasted for a decade, although Koxinga still served as a focal point for anti-Manchu resistance.

The high point of his military endeavors came in 1659, when he led a pirate fleet up the Yangtse River as part of a combined rebel assault on the Manchu capital of Nanking (Nanjing). The enterprise was a disaster, as the Manchus were able to trap the pirate fleet in the river, and then destroyed it using massed batteries of artillery. Koxinga managed to escape, but the rebel cause was lost. While Koxinga's anti-Manchu resistance is verified by historical sources, the suspicion is that his exploits have been exaggerated by later historians. He is often portrayed as a sort of Chinese Robin Hood figure, whereas the truth was probably quite different.

The Dutch traders who operated in the region certainly painted a somewhat different picture. While they describe Koxinga as a rebel, they suggest that politics were only a secondary concern for him. First and foremost, Koxinga was a pirate. The Amoy Islands (then called the Zsu-ming prefecture) just off the coast of Fukien provided him with an ideal base for operations. While the Manchus dominated the mainland, including his father's province of Fukien, Koxinga ruled the seas—and ran his pirate empire. He continued his father's policy of offering protection money to merchants from Korea to Vietnam, while his pirate junks attacked anyone who refused to pay. Unlike his father, Koxinga was prepared to take on the Dutch, who reported to Amsterdam that Koxinga's pirate junks regularly attacked Dutch shipping off both the Penghu Islands and also the new Dutch colony of Taiwan. For a decade he maintained complete control over the coastal waters from the Mekong Delta to the mouth of the Yangtze.

The disaster at Nanking in 1659 meant that for the first time, Koxinga was on the strategic defensive. His naval power had been weakened, and there was now no guarantee that the Manchus would not commit their overwhelming resources to an assault on the Amoy Islands, whose proximity to the Chinese mainland made them an obvious target. He also lost his one ally in Fukien when, in 1661, the Manchus executed his father in retaliation for his son's resistance. This meant that Koxinga needed a more secure base.

In 1661 he launched an amphibious attack on Formosa, landing on the southern tip of the island near the modern city of Kao-hsiung. The Dutch had built a powerful fortress—Fort Zeelandia—on a sandy spit which defended their main settlement of Oranjestad (Orange City, now Tai-nan). On April 30 Koxinga blockaded the settlement with a fleet of 400 pirate junks, while his army of 25,000 men laid siege to the fort. The siege that followed lasted for nine months, but with no prospect of relief, and most of his 2,000-man garrison stricken by thirst, hunger and disease, Governor Coylett had no option but to surrender. On February 1, 1662, the Dutch surrendered Formosa to Koxinga, who accepted control of the island in the name of the Ming Dynasty.

The capture of Formosa was a triumph for the pirate chief, but he did not live long enough to enjoy the spoils of war. Later that year he died of malaria, although there were rumors that his death was the result of a seizure, following a disagreement with his son. Today, Kuo Hsing Yeh (Koxinga) is seen as a hero, both in Taiwan and in mainland China, where his reputation as a defender of Ming culture and civilization seems to have outweighed his crimes as a pirate warlord. Taiwan even boasts a shrine to Koxinga, which makes him the only pirate ever to be considered a religious deity. After his death Koxinga's pirate empire was taken over by his son Cheng Ching, or Zheng Jing (1642–81), who held Formosa against the Manchus for two more decades. However, he was unable to hold together the great pirate fleet, and it fragmented soon after Koxinga's death. This left Formosa open to invasion, and in 1681 the Manchus overran the Amoy and Penghu Islands and then attacked Formosa. Cheng Ching died fighting the invaders, and although his followers continued fighting for another two years after his death, the island eventually fell to the Manchus.

THE GREAT PIRATE CONFEDERATION

After the collapse of the great pirate empire of Koxinga, piracy in Chinese waters became a fragmented business, in which no one pirate chief or warlord was able to unite the various groups under a single banner. This lasted for a century, a period when individual provincial rulers acted as both pirates and traders, and when their influence extended no further than the boundaries of their own territorial waters. Then Cheng Yih appeared, and within a decade he had created a pirate empire that rivalled that of Koxinga.[3]

As the son of a Chinese pirate operating in Vietnamese waters, Cheng Yih (or Zheng Shi) was literally born into the business. In fact it has been suggested that his family had been pirates for generations, although this was probably little more than an attempt to link his empire with that of Koxinga. This was a time when Vietnam was in turmoil, as the Tay Son rebels were busy wresting control of the country from the Nguyen lords, who had ruled it for centuries. Cheng's rise was set against the backdrop of this conflict, and by the time it ended the pirate had become the leading maritime power in Vietnamese waters. However, the reestablishment of order meant that his presence would soon be considered a threat to the new Vietnamese rulers. Consequently in 1801 he moved his operation along the coast to the Chinese province of Guangdong (Kwangtung), a center for the opium trade. In the process he took control of the smaller pirate fleets he encountered along the coast, and so his power grew as he headed east.

In April 1804 he took on the Portuguese and blockaded their trading port of Macao for at least two months, defeating a small Portuguese squadron sent to break the pirate blockade. This prompted the British to intervene, and the following year the Royal Navy began escorting British shipping and that of their political allies in the waters off Hong Kong, Macao, and other European enclaves on the Chinese coast. However, the threat posed by Cheng Yih was still growing. In 1805 he formed a pirate confederation, uniting the Chinese pirates who operated along the coast of the South China Sea into one mighty pirate empire. He divided this force into six fleets, each known by a color—black, white, red, blue, yellow and green. Each fleet was also given a particular area to operate in, which helped ensure that the fleets would not fight each other or interfere in each other's operation.

Cheng Yih retained a nominal control over the other pirate fleets, but he kept control of his original fleet for himself. This force of some 200 pirate junks became the Red Flag Fleet and was based in the provincial capital of Canton (now Guangzou). By the time of his death in 1807, Cheng Yih's Red Flag Fleet had trebled in size—some 600 pirate junks crewed by some 30,000 men, making it the largest pirate fleet in the South China Sea. Of course this was only part of his power base—in time of need he could also count on the rest of his pirate confederation, whose commanders had agreed to help each other in time of difficulty. That meant that Cheng Yih could call upon as many as 1,200 junks and 150,000 men—the largest pirate confederation in history. Protection money was demanded from Chinese merchants and coastal communities, and Cheng Yih's junks seemed able to roam at will, attacking ships or demanding payment with impunity.

The reason Cheng Yih could get away with this was that the Chinese government had failed miserably in its attempts to deal with piracy. In fact it

Chinese pirates depicted running amok in a coastal village during the early nineteenth century.

seemed more intent on limiting the impact of European traders than it did on protecting its own national trade routes. Any Imperial response to the pirate threat required the support of provincial governors, many of whom were either in league with the pirates or were pirate leaders themselves. In the event that sufficient force could be gathered for a punitive expedition, Cheng Yih simply gathered his forces. If one pirate fleet was threatened, the other colored fleets would be summoned, and the threat would be repelled. In effect the pirate confederation was invulnerable to attack. However, after his attack on the Portuguese, Cheng Yih was at pains to discourage attacks on European traders. After all, while he might be able to deal with the forces of the Chinese emperor, the combined naval might of these foreigners might be a different matter entirely.

Cheng Yih was at the height of his power when he died in late 1807, probably by being washed overboard during a storm. His wife Cheng Shi (or Zheng Yih Sao, which means wife of Cheng Yih) took over control of the Red Flag Fleet and somehow managed to hold together the rest of the pirate confederation. She is also sometimes referred to as the Widow Cheng, or as Madam Cheng. She was aided in this takeover by Cheung Po Tsai (or Chang Po), the young male lover (and adopted son) of her husband Cheng Yih, who duly transferred his allegiance and affections to the pirate leader's wife.[4] According to tradition Madam Cheng first came to the attention of the pirate leader when she worked as a prostitute in Canton. She went on to rule a pirate empire.

Madam Cheng proved to be a natural pirate leader, and over the next few years she developed a reputation for ferocity and skill, building the Red Flag Fleet up into a force of some 800 pirate junks and completely dominating the coastal waters from Hainan as far as Formosa. Unlike her husband, Madam Cheng refused to be intimidated by the Europeans. In September 1809 she kidnapped a group of seven British seamen from an East Indiaman anchored off Canton. They were eventually released after a ransom was paid, and one of them—Richard Glasspole—left an account of his experiences. He described the code of laws under which Madam Cheng governed, in which theft, disobedience, or rape was punishable by death, and lesser crimes such as desertion involved the cutting off of an ear, a thumb, or even a limb. The result of this severity, according to Glasspole, was to create a force that was disciplined, resolute, and united.

However, the whole empire started to break down. Unable to defeat the pirates on the high seas, the Chinese authorities adopted a carrot-and-stick approach. First came the stick—supervised by Pai Ling, the new provincial governor of

Guangdong. He declared war against the pirates operating around Canton and solicited European help to defeat them. First he resettled thousands of inhabitants of coastal settlements further inland, thereby denying the pirates a source of revenue and provisions. Supported by European warships and a flotilla of fireships, the Cantonese fleet cleared the local waters of pirates by the end of the year. Then came the carrot. The emperor offered a pardon to all Chinese pirates, and the terms were generous enough to be tempting. One of the first to accept the offer was Cheung Po Tsai, who defected to Pai Ling in early 1810, taking most of the Red Flag Fleet with him. This was a severe blow to Cheng Shi, who had just been elected as the new head of the great pirate confederation. In theory that made her one of the most powerful women in China. In reality her world was falling apart.

The pirate leader Madam Cheng (Cheng Shi, or Zheng Yih Sao) took over control of a large pirate fleet in the early nineteenth century and went on to rule the largest pirate confederation in China.

The confederation was in disarray, as many saw the benefits of accepting the pardon, which opened up lucrative Imperial markets that had hitherto been denied to the pirates. Worse, the five remaining colored banner fleets began fighting one another, as some accepted the pardon—and Imperial rewards—while others held out. Some, like Cheung Po Tsai, became pirate-hunters and actively campaigned against their former comrades. By the end of the year Cheng Shi was forced to admit defeat, and she accepted the pardon herself. However, she was allowed to retain her own small force of ships and men, and she remained an influential figure in Guangdong; for the next three decades she ran the biggest opium smuggling operation on the Chinese coast. For his part, Cheung Po Tsai went on to become a highly respected Imperial admiral, although it was still suggested that he never quite turned his back on his old piratical ways.

SHAP'-NG-TSAI

The threat of piracy receded slightly during the early nineteenth century, but it never went away completely. The Chinese policy of bribing regional officials and their carrot-and-stick policy clearly reaped dividends. However, three decades after the collapse of Cheng Shi's great pirate confederation, the Europeans and the Chinese had come to blows, the friction caused by the import of Indian opium into China on board British ships. When the Chinese seized ships carrying the drug, the British reacted with military force, initiating a conflict known as the First Opium War (1839–42). It ended with the Chinese being forced to sign a humiliating trade agreement that further opened up the country to European trade. Hong Kong Island was occupied by the British in 1841 and was formally ceded to Britain a year later. Canton also became an open port, and by 1843 it became the center of a thriving opium trade. From there the drug was smuggled along the coast to other ports, and by encouraging smugglers the trade also encouraged piracy—an occupation adopted by many smugglers in their spare time.[5]

While the Chinese navy should have been powerful enough to deal with this problem, its recent encounter with the Royal Navy had left it defeated and demoralized, in no condition to fight a major antipiracy campaign beyond the waters surrounding the major ports. Shap'-ng-Tsai was one such smuggler-turned-pirate, who was based in Tien-pai (sometimes called Tin Pak—now Dianbai), in the western corner of Guangdong province and 175 miles west of Hong Kong. He offered protection to smugglers in exchange for money, and during the 1840s this business expanded until he was able to extort payment from coastal shipping operating between Hainan Island and Canton, and from many coastal communities in between.

By 1849 his fleet had grown to 70 pirate junks, and his protection racket had been extended as far as Vietnam. Then he made the mistake of attacking treaty vessels—the European and American carriers who shipped opium into the treaty ports. He captured one American and three British opium-carrying clipper ships, which led to a panic in the treaty ports that disrupted trade. If Shap'-ng-Tsai had limited his piratical attacks and the extortion of protection money to Chinese victims, then the foreigners would probably have left him alone. However, an attack against Western ships was a completely different matter.

In September 1849 the Royal Navy commander of the Hong Kong Squadron was given orders to attack the pirate lair—a punitive expedition that had been demanded by the East India Company, whose shipping had been disrupted. Consequently the Scottish-born Commander John Hay led a squadron of steam warships into Tien-pai, only to find the pirates had already fled. Tipped off by his spies in Hong Kong, Shap'-ng-Tsai had led his pirate fleet westwards towards the safety of Haiphong in Vietnam, leaving Commander Hay with nothing to show for his efforts except the destruction of the pirate base and the recapture of around 100 trading junks, which had been held in the port while the pirates waited for their owners to pay a ransom for them. He also destroyed a secondary pirate base at Bias Bay, between Macao and Tien-pai.

According to Admiralty law these captured junks were now prizes of the Royal Navy, and once the expedition returned to Hong Kong they were sold in auction to the highest bidder. In this case the bidder turned out to be none other than an agent of Shap'-ng-Tsai, who simply recouped the cost of the sale from the ship owners—and added a substantial handling fee in lieu of his lost ransom. It was clear that a second naval expedition would be needed to deal with the pirate fleet, so once again Commander Hay was ordered into action.

In late October his squadron tracked the pirates down in the Red River (Hong Ha) Delta, just north of the Vietnamese port of Haiphong. First Commander Hay blockaded the mouth of the river to prevent any escape, and then he led part of his fleet into action against the pirates—three steam warships (including the East India Company armed paddle-steamer *Phlegethon*)—supported by a squadron of Imperial Chinese junks. The pirates were taken by surprise, and their junks were still at anchor when Hay arrived. The battle was therefore extremely one-sided—steam against sail, shell against roundshot—and by the end of the engagement 58 pirate junks had been captured or sunk. Some 1,800 pirates were killed in the battle, either by British or Chinese gunfire or else by the local Cochin villagers.

As for Shap'-ng-Tsai, he escaped up the Red River in a small junk, one of six to survive the battle. The British were unable to pursue. The Chinese then solved the problem of the pirate being still at large by offering him a pardon. Not only did Shap'-ng-Tsai accept it, but according to some sources he went on to hold a commission in the Imperial Navy, helping to scour Chinese waters for pirates. The incident also led to a permanent Royal Navy presence on the Chinese coast, and over the next few years it continued its antipiracy operations, working in conjunction with the Chinese government and the East India Company. Consequently, by the mid-nineteenth century the waters of the South China Sea were deemed clear of pirates, a victory achieved through a combination of Chinese pragmatism and Western firepower.

10

MODERN PIRACY

DANGEROUS WATERS

Piracy is not a thing of the past, a romanticized form of crime from the pages of history. It still happens every day, and the victims don't always live to tell the tale. In recent years piracy has hit the headlines as even the largest supertankers have fallen victim to attack by gun-wielding cutthroats.[1] As an example, in April 2007 the International Chamber of Commerce (ICC) issued a warning: "There has been a marked increase in attacks and hijackings off the southern part of Somalia, particularly off Mogadishu. The attacks are mainly targeted towards vessels with cargo for Somali ports. Vessels are advised to steer well clear of Somalian waters at all times." Over the past two decades organizations like the ICC have been monitoring pirate attacks and have identified clear pirate hot spots where attacks are commonplace events. The waters of Indonesia, Somalia, India, Sri Lanka, Bangladesh, Burma, West Africa (especially Nigeria), the Philippines, Brazil, Colombia, and Venezuela have all been identified as high-risk areas.

Piracy in these dangerous waters is not a new phenomenon. In the early nineteenth century the waters of the Persian Gulf were plagued by pirates, and it took a major initiative by the British East India Company to stamp out these

303

nests of pirates. The same was true in China during the early 20th century, when a collapse of central authority led to rule by local warlords—a situation reminiscent of the one described in the previous chapter. The maritime powers—mainly represented by the Royal Navy and the U.S. Navy—took an active part in stamping out piracy on the Chinese rivers, as it did in other pirate hot spots of the prewar world such as the Malay Archipelago, Central America, and the Philippines. For the most part these pirate attacks were isolated incidents, or at worst they represented a temporary resurgence in maritime crime. Other piratical acts were also reported around the globe—the attack on a British merchant freighter in a small North African port, the plunder of an Australian fishing boat in the South Pacific, or the murder of a lone American yachtsman off the coast of Cuba. None of these incidents warranted the dispatch of a punitive expedition, but, when required, the maritime powers considered antipiracy operations to be part of their job.

Whereas previously the most vulnerable category of mariner was considered to be the yachtsman, nowadays even the crews of the largest vessels in the world are placing themselves at risk when they sail into these dangerous waters. Before the Second World War, 20th-century piracy was virtually unknown, and only sporadic incidents were reported around the world. Since then it has been on the increase, and within the past two decades the number of reported incidents has climbed dramatically. There are various reasons for this. First, the postwar trend is for navies to become smaller and more specialized. While in the past the maritime powers had the ships to patrol likely trouble spots, and could always send a gunboat, now merchant ships are largely left to their own devices on the high seas. Many smaller governments lack the resources to patrol their own waters, let alone to hunt for pirates on the high seas. Often these governments control the very waters in which the pirates like to operate.

Modern-day pirates now enjoy all the advantages of technology—radios, radar, satellite navigation, automatic weapons, and high-performance boats. This gives them an advantage over their historical predecessors. Above all there is a lack of regulation on the high seas due to a shortage of interest, of international goodwill, and of resources. The erosion of national maritime fleets has been partly to blame. These days the majority of the world's merchant shipping sails under a flag of convenience—that of Liberia, Panama, or Honduras—rather than under the merchant marine flags of the major maritime powers. In fact it is only comparatively recently that piracy has been regarded as a serious form of international crime, worthy of combating on the international level. Meanwhile the pirates have prospered.

In 1985, the first year the ICC began recording pirate attacks, there were some 50 recorded incidents of piracy around the world. This total increased steadily every year—just over 200 in 1998, 300 in 1999, and on to a peak of 445 in 2003. These are only incidents involving register ships—they ignore the hundreds, if not thousands, of attacks against yachts, small fishing boats, or other vessels not big enough to make the grade. A third of all these pirate attacks took place in the Malacca Straits. However, the news is not wholly bad. In the last few years the number of incidents has been on the decrease. According to the Piracy Reporting Center of the International Maritime Bureau (IMB), a wing of the ICC, there were 329 attacks in 2004, 277 in 2005, and 239 in 2006. The agency credited the improving situation to better levels of international cooperation, particularly the presence of international antipiracy patrols in the Malacca Straits, and in other pirate hot spots around the world.

Disregarding the risks inherent in sailing through the waters of a modern war zone, the most dangerous stretch of water in the world is generally regarded to be the Malacca Straits, the 550-mile- (885 km) long waterway separating the Malay Peninsula and the island of Sumatra. More than 50,000 ships a year pass through these waters, making it one of the busiest maritime bottlenecks in the world, as well as the most dangerous. Many of these ships are the largest vessels afloat, the supertankers and bulk carriers that dwarf even the largest ocean liner. A quarter of the world's annual oil supply passes through these waters, the equivalent of 11 million barrels of oil each day. Ships have to slow down while they thread their way through such a busy waterway—which makes them vulnerable to attack by well-armed pirates operating in fast speedboats or inflatables.

The only bright spot was that the 2006 report by the IMB showed that the number of attacks in the Malacca Straits had dropped dramatically during the last few years, and in 2007 there were only 11 pirate incidents in this strategic narrow waterway. While much of the credit for this lies with the large-scale naval and intelligence-gathering campaign waged by the international maritime community, the authorities were unable to stamp out piracy altogether. It almost looks as if the local pirates are biding their time, waiting for the warships to go away. In this respect they are little different from the pirates of the golden age, avoiding areas where the navy is known to patrol, and either moving elsewhere to continue their trade or else adopting more legitimate pursuits until the situation improves.

The obvious effect of this is that piratical incidents have been on the increase in the neighboring waters of Indonesia, with 79 attacks recorded in 2006 alone. However, a campaign by the Indonesian navy has meant that attacks decreased to 50 incidents the following year. Another pirate hot spot is Chittagong in Bangladesh, where 46 attacks were recorded in 2006. The port is now listed as the most dangerous anchorage in the world. Although almost all of these attacks were conducted by opportunistic small-time pirates armed with knives and metal pipes, the trend is certainly a worrying one. Other hot spots highlighted in the IMB's latest report are the waters of Nigeria (12 attacks), the Gulf of Aden (10), Malaysia (10), Tanzania (9), and Peru (9).

Another danger spot that is rapidly climbing the piratical league table is the coast of east Somalia. The threat of piracy in this region was first highlighted in 1989 when the German-built cruise ship *Seabourn Spirit* was attacked on the high seas, some 70 miles off the Somalian coast. Just before 6:00 a.m. on November 5 two speedboats approached the liner, having been launched from a mother ship. The boats raked the liner with machine-gun fire and rocket-propelled grenades (RPGs), and one crewman was injured. Fortunately the well-trained crew of the liner were able to prevent the attackers from boarding. Somalia is now regarded as a particularly dangerous region, in which 19 major attacks were reported in 2005 alone. The country exists in a political vacuum, and the lack of a functioning government makes it easier for pirates to use the country as a base.

One of these attacks took place on June 27, 2005, launched against the Kenyan-owned MV *Semlow*, which was transporting a cargo of rice to Somalia as part of a UN food program designed to relieve tsunami victims. Somalian pirates attacked and captured the ship under cover of darkness as she approached the port of Harardhere, and her ten-man crew were held hostage for over three months. As one of the captured crewmen reported: "These pirates are worse than the pirates we read about in history books ... These Somali pirates are better armed, and they want ransom, not just our goods." The lack of authority in the country means that it is difficult for the international maritime community to offer any firm response, apart from patrolling the international waters off the coast, warning passing shipping, and hoping that the Somalians will one day be able to police their own waters. Unfortunately, many so-called government organizations are either pirates themselves or represent a local warlord. In November 2006 the crew of the cargo vessel MV *Veesham* were bemused when the ship was boarded and captured by a group of ten Somalian pirates, who sailed their prize into the Somalian port of Obbia. There a group of militia loyal to the Union of Islamic Courts recaptured the ship after a protracted gun battle, and returned it to their former owners. In places like Somalia, it is often very difficult to work out who the "good guys" really are.

TACTICS AND TERRORISM

In his book *Dangerous Waters*, author John Burnett highlighted the problem:

> There has been traditionally an ill-defined distinction between piracy and terrorism. Following the attacks on the World Trade Center and the Pentagon, governments worldwide finally began to take notice that there had been a war at sea long before September 11. The inevitable conclusion was reached—there is very little difference between the two crimes. The International Maritime Bureau and others in the maritime industry have called the bombing of the USS *Cole* in Aden harbor an act of piracy. The attack hammered home that we can no longer afford to ignore piracy, or deny its close relationship with terrorism. The stakes are too high.[2]

In other words, many pirate attacks were probably the work of terrorists—men who attacked for political or religious reasons instead of just for plunder. It was only after the event that the Western world woke up to the fact that piracy had become as much a tool of the terrorist as hijacking or bombing.

In the charged political atmosphere following September 11, 2001, and the Coalition invasion of Iraq, it is sometimes difficult to tell where piracy stops and terrorism begins. In the Western press the term "terrorist" has been increasingly applied to pirates, regardless of their political or religious motives. In many cases, once these highly publicized attacks were investigated by the IMB it was clear that profit rather than political gain was the only motive. One of the big problems is the official definition of piracy as an attack that takes place on the high seas. Many incidents that occur within a harbor, or even within a country's 12-mile limits, are deemed local crimes rather than piratical acts or can even be labeled as terrorist attacks in an effort to whip up world opinion. In other places the waters in which attacks take place are disputed by neighboring countries, so it is often unclear exactly who should control them. This can sometimes lead to situations in which the supposed good guys are just as likely to attack passing shipping for political or monetary gain as any local pirate crew.

For instance, the lack of a functioning government in Somalia means that even semilegitimate organizations such as the local coast guard have reportedly taken part in attacks. Groups such as the National Volunteer Guard, the Somali Marines, and the Somali Coastal Defense Force have all been identified as pirates, operating under the smokescreen of legitimacy. For instance, in 2000 the MV *Bonella* was attacked off the Somalian coast by 26 pirates in two speedboats. The merchant captain later said, "I told them that we didn't have any money, but the general of the Somali Coast Guard cocked his pistol and pointed it by my head saying: 'Captain, no ship travels without money. Do you really want to lose your life just as I am about to set your ship free?'" The pirates kept the captain and crew prisoner for five days while they tried to use her to capture other passing ships. When they found she was too slow, the pirates plundered her and left. Clearly this Trojan Horse approach—using an innocuous-looking vessel as a lure—is a tactic that has proved popular. In January 2006 the USS *Winston S. Churchill* intercepted an Indian freighter that had been captured off the Somalian coast several days earlier. The pirates were reportedly using her as a base for other attacks.[3]

The deckhouse of the German yacht Jan Wellem III, *photographed after the vessel was attacked by pirates off the Venezuelan coast in March 2001. Fortunately the owners were armed and managed to drive off the pirates after a short exchange of gunfire.*

This semilegitimate approach is not just a ploy used by Somalian pirates. In recent years the Chinese Coast Guard has been involved in a number of incidents, which are either the result of official Chinese policy (which is unlikely), or the actions of Chinese officials who adopt a cavalier approach to their work. It is also possible that these represent the actions of real pirates, who use the Chinese as a cover for their illegal activities. For example, in June 1995 a Chinese customs cutter stopped the Panamanian-registered freighter MV *Hye Mieko* in international waters. The freighter had sailed from Singapore two days before, bound for Cambodia with a cargo of cigarettes and cameras. A dozen men in Chinese uniforms seized the vessel and sailed it over 900 miles through international waters until it reached the Chinese port of Shanwei. There the vessel was impounded on suspicion of smuggling. The Chinese subsequently denied any knowledge of the customs cutter and charged the vessel's owner with trying to smuggle cigarettes into China. Clearly the Chinese government does not engage in piracy, but evidently some official either sanctioned the operation or else covered it up. The truth will probably never come out.

One equally worrying trend is the changing nature of modern piracy. While in the past most attacks involved the temporary seizure of a ship while it was plundered, more recently the trend has been to augment this with kidnapping or hostage-taking—which only serves to blur the boundaries between piracy and terrorism even more. In 2006, 188 pirate attacks involved the taking of crew members or passengers as hostages, while 77 involved outright kidnapping. Of these, almost half of the hostages were taken in Somalian waters, although Indonesia came a close second. In most cases the hostages were simply held until the ship owners paid for their release or until the hostage-takers released them, often with their ship. In this respect the pirates are simply acting in a manner reminiscent of the Cilician pirates who plagued the Ancient Mediterranean—the people who took Julius Caesar hostage and held him to ransom. Hostage-taking is generally seen as a criminal act, not a terrorist one.

Kidnapping is a different matter. Of the 77 reported incidents in 2006, 25 maritime kidnappings took place off Sri Lanka (all in one incident), while 49 people—mainly oil workers—were kidnapped off the coast of Nigeria. The big difference between hostage-taking and kidnapping is that while the former is usually resolved after the payment of money, kidnapping is often accompanied by political as well as monetary demands. An example was the capture of the Jordanian-registered MV *Farah-3* off Sri Lanka in December 2006, when pirates armed with automatic weapons and explosives captured 25 crewmen but later released them into the hands of the International Red Cross. The pirates were reportedly members of the Tamil Tigers, a group that the international community has labeled a terrorist organization. The situation in Nigeria is a little different, as although a regional tribal independence movement (the Movement for the Emancipation of the Niger Delta) has been linked to piratical attacks and the kidnapping of foreign oil workers, the local political situation is so muddled that the real identity of the culprits is unclear. In some cases the victims have even included members of the Nigerian armed forces, charged with protecting foreign oil workers from attack. It seems that the disruption of oil production was the primary objective behind the attacks and kidnappings, which suggests that either the pirates have a political agenda or they are simply being destructive—just like the pirates of the golden age who destroyed ships' cargoes for the sheer hell of it.

An altogether more worrying example of maritime kidnapping took place in April 2007, when the paramilitary Iranian Revolutionary Guards seized 15 British servicemen while they were carrying out a routine stop-and-search mission in the Shat al Arab waterway. There is little doubt that this attack constituted an act of piracy, but the motives were purely political rather than financial. While the Iranian government may not have directly sanctioned the piratical attack, they were quick to reap whatever diplomatic benefit they could from the incident. The danger is that other rogue states or even terrorist organizations may well resort to piracy as a means of furthering their political agendas. In international law maritime terrorism is defined as a piratical act intended to influence a government or group of individuals. This means that the rebels in the Niger Delta or the Iranian Revolutionary Guards in the Persian Gulf are both tarred with the same legal brush, regardless of the more complex economic or diplomatic issues involved. The problem for sailors and oil workers alike is that while regular piratical attacks are dangerous enough, in this new form of piracy the stakes are much higher.

11

PIRATES IN FICTION

Fifteen men on a dead man's chest
Yo ho ho and a bottle of rum
Drink and the devil had done for the rest
Yo ho ho and a bottle of rum.

Long John Silver has a lot to answer for. In *Treasure Island*, published in 1883, the Scottish author Robert Louis Stevenson created the ultimate pirate, the figure everyone thought of when a mental image of a pirate was required. Of course fictional pirates existed long before *Treasure Island*. At the same time as Captain Johnson's pirate biography was proving a runaway success in early eighteenth-century London, a play called *The Successful Pirate* was drawing crowds to the Drury Lane Theatre—a production based on the exploits of the Red Sea Roundsman Henry Every. This meant that even while the last of the pirates of the golden age was still at large, the business of romanticizing them had already begun. In the early nineteenth century, romantic fiction writers and poets rediscovered piracy as a source for dramatic plots and exotic locations. For example, Lord Byron's poem *The Corsair* (1814), Sir Walter Scott's novel *The Pirate* (1821), and Giuseppi Verdi's opera *Il Corsaro* (1848) all provided the same thing—a sanitized, rose-tinted view of the pirate world, in which pirates were romantic heroes and rebels against authority rather than simply a bunch of unwashed cutthroats.[1]

Treasure Island was probably the most influential children's book ever published, and it first appeared as a serial called *The Sea Cook, or Treasure Island* in a children's magazine called *Young Folks* (1881–82). This original title showed that, at least in Stevenson's mind, Long John Silver rather than Jim Hawkins, the boy hero, was the central character. For Stevenson, his hero was not a romantic figure but a frightening symbol of pirate reality—a man who would make you walk the plank rather than wax lyrically about the freedom of the open sea. In *Treasure Island*, Stevenson introduced all those other elements of piracy that have now become the bedrocks of pirate mythology. He was responsible for putting parrots on pirate shoulders, for wooden legs, black eye patches, the Black Spot, and of course "fifteen men on a dead man's chest." Above all, it was Stevenson who came up with the idea of buried treasure and maps where "X" marks the spot.

Actually, the real inventor was probably Lloyd Osbourne, Stevenson's American stepson. Stevenson and his family were spending a late summer holiday in Braemar, in the Scottish Highlands, and the Scottish weather was proving as fickle as ever. One day Stevenson came across the 13-year-old Lloyd coloring in a map he'd drawn—the map of an island. As Osbourne later recalled:

> Stevenson came in as I was finishing it, and with his affectionate interest in everything I was doing, leaned over my shoulder, and was soon elaborating the map and naming it. I shall never forget the thrill of Skeleton Island, Spyglass Hill, nor the heart-stirring climax of the three red crosses! And the greater climax still when he wrote down the words 'Treasure Island' at the top right-hand corner! And he seemed to know so much about it too—the pirates, the buried treasure, the man who had been marooned on the island. 'Oh, for a story about it', I exclaimed, in a heaven of enchantment, and somehow conscious of his own enthusiasm in the idea.

Within three days Stevenson had penned the first three chapters, and the rest of the family helped him steer the plot to its climax. Within weeks the first chapters were offered to the editor of *Young Folks*, and within two years *Treasure Island* appeared in print. The rest is history.

Treasure Island has never been out of print and remains one of the best-loved books of all time. There have been over 50 film and television versions of the story, from the first silent *Treasure Island* (1920) to the latest French adaptation—*L'Île aux Trésors* (2007). Of these, probably the most notable is the Walt Disney version, filmed in 1950—the first live action film ever attempted by the studio. Child actor Bobby Driscoll played Jim Hawkins, while the British-born Robert Newton came up with the definitive portrayal of Long John Silver, complete with his strong West Country accent and all those guttural utterances of "Arrrr, Jim lad." These were immediately added to Stevenson's caucus of pirate myth, and every self-respecting pirate impersonator for the past six decades has aped Newton's manner of speech. Newton made his name playing these rough, wizened characters, and six years later he revisited the role (and the accent) when he played the lead in *Blackbeard the Pirate*.

The next great work of pirate fiction was *Peter Pan*, written by another Scotsman, J. M. Barrie (1860–1937) and first performed in London in 1904. Barrie first wrote the play as a novel, *The Little White Bird*, and then adapted the work for the stage. The story of the boy who refused to grow up proved an instant success, and Captain Hook became an instantly recognizable pirate villain, although he and his crew were portrayed more as figures of fun than as real pirates—a far cry from the dangerous villains who populated *Treasure Island*. As well as pirates with hooks instead of hands, the stage version of *Peter Pan* also gave us pirate hats emblazoned with the skull and crossbones, and walking the plank. While no self-respecting pirate of the golden age would have bothered with such nonsense, they have become just as much part of the whole pirate image as Stevenson's piratical affectations.

Within a decade the popular perception of the pirate would change yet again. Instead of villainous cutthroats or comic buffoons, the new breed of fictional pirates would be true heroes—youthful, quick-witted, honorable, clean-cut Englishmen who fought for a higher cause, who righted wrongs, and who saved aristocratic ladies in distress. The man responsible for this was Rafael Sabatini, an Anglo-Italian author who single-handedly invented the genre known as the swashbuckler. While his books have been derided as being a "*Boy's Own*" style of adventure fiction, Sabatini anchored his piratical world in the writings of Exquemelin and Johnson, although his heroes were entirely of his own invention. His first successful novel was *Scaramouche* (1921), set in the French Revolution, but the following year he produced *Captain Blood*, which set the standard for the swashbucklers that followed. His other pirate novels included *The Sea Hawk*, *The Black Swan*, and two more Captain Blood books.

His success came just at the right time. *Captain Blood* was published just two years after the release of the first film version of *Treasure Island*, and Hollywood immediately realized the potential of Sabatini's novel. *Captain Blood* appeared on the silver screen in 1924, with Warren Kerrigan playing the title role. While the film itself was uninspiring, it led to two more—*The Sea Hawk* (1924) and more memorably *The Black Pirate* (1926), in which Douglas Fairbanks played the swashbuckling hero. He was the first screen hero to stick a knife in a sail and slide down to the deck, and he also walked the plank, killed a pirate captain in a sword duel, and rescued the princess. The floodgates had been opened, and the pirates of the silver screen would remain a staple of Hollywood for another three generations.[2]

The 1930s and 1940s saw a profusion of talking-picture "swashbucklers," many of which were based on Sabatini's novels. The best of these was probably the talking-picture remake of *Captain Blood* (1935), which launched the career of the unknown Errol Flynn as the swashbuckling hero. He returned to piracy in *The Sea Hawk* (1940), a wartime patriotic romp that owed little to Sabatini's original book. Another piratical classic of the time was *The Black Swan* (1942), in which Tyrone Power played a fictional pirate serving alongside a bombastic Sir Henry Morgan, while other mainstays of the genre—Maureen O'Hara and Anthony Quinn—both made their first appearance under the black flag.

While the pirate genre continued into the early 1950s, tastes were changing, and the tendency was for these later pirate films to parody what had come before. For example, in the *Crimson Pirate* (1952) Burt Lancaster reprised Fairbanks's earlier role in *The Black Pirate*, but as a former circus acrobat he placed an even greater emphasis on swinging on ropes and sliding down sails. However, there was one last piratical hurrah, with Robert Newton appearing in both *Blackbeard the Pirate* and *Long John Silver* and the aging Errol Flynn and Maureen O'Hara enjoying one last pirate romp in *Under All Flags*. These were the last of their kind—for two decades at least one or two swashbucklers had come out every year, but from the late 1950s they became a rarity.

While most swashbuckling heroes were fictional, sometimes they crossed paths with real pirates—Blackbeard, Morgan, Kidd, and others. In most cases these historical pirates were simply there to be outsmarted by our piratical heroes, two-dimensional villains who come across as even more bumblingly incompetent than Captain Hook or more fundamentally evil than Long John Silver. A prime example is the film *Captain Kidd* (1945), in which Charles Laughton portrayed the unfortunate privateer as an evil schemer. By contrast, one of the few swashbucklers in which the actual hero was based on a real pirate is *The Buccaneer*, in which the part of Jean Lafitte was played by Frederic March in the 1938 version and by Yul Brynner in the 1958 remake. Even then the screen pirate was shown as a suave gentleman—two terms that were probably never applied to the real pirate.

For almost half a century piracy was never really considered a box office draw. Of course there were pirate films—*Swashbuckler* (1976) with Robert Shaw, *Yellowbeard* (1983) with Peter Cooke, *Pirates* (1986) with Walter Matthau, *Hook*

The severed head of Blackbeard, hanging from the bowsprit of the naval sloop Jane *after his death off Ocracoke Island in 1718. Today the romantic view of piracy portrayed by Hollywood belies the brutal reality.*

(1991) with Dustin Hoffman, and *Cutthroat Island* (1995) with Geena Davis were probably the most notable of these. There were a few others, including at least three versions of the Robert Louis Stevenson classic, one of which was *Muppet Treasure Island* (1996), in which even Tim Curry was unable to break completely from the Robert Newton version of Long John Silver. While some of these were competent enough films in their own right, none of them took the box office by storm.

Then along came Johnny Depp. The idea of basing a film on a rather dated Disney attraction may have been strange enough, but Depp's portrayal of a pirate captain—foppish swagger, slurred speech, and rather camp demeanor—sent alarm bells ringing in the Walt Disney Studios. They need not have worried. *Pirates of the Caribbean: The Curse of the Black Pearl* (2003) proved a smash hit and earned Disney a small fortune. The sequels *Pirates of the Caribbean: Dead Man's Chest* (2006), *Pirates of the Caribbean: At World's End* (2007), and *Pirates of the Caribbean: On Stranger Tides* (2011) were equally successful, which suggests that for all the zombies, sea creatures, and giant whirlpools, the business of cinematic piracy is still alive and well.

For his part, Johnny Depp was hailed as having reinvented the screen pirate—a new combination of Errol Flynn, Robert Newton, and everybody else. When reporters asked him whom he used for inspiration, Depp named Keith Richards as his role model, mixed with a touch of Iggy Pop and Errol Flynn. He added that pirates were "like the rock stars of their time," which goes a long way towards explaining why he chose that particular persona. In fact just about the only person he didn't cite was Captain Charles Johnson. Despite this, both Robert Newton's Long John Silver and Johnny Depp's Captain Jack Sparrow owe more than a passing nod to Johnson's descriptions of pirates such as Blackbeard and Bartholomew Roberts. In fact, it could be argued that compared to Blackbeard, with his wild beard, burning pieces of slowmatch stuck in his tricorne hat, and ferocious eyes, Jack Sparrow looks positively mundane. That remains one of the charms of these characters—pirate reality will always be every bit as colorful as pirate fiction.

CONCLUSION

THE REAL PIRATES OF THE CARIBBEAN

For a pirate historian, one frequently asked question is whether you feel any affinity for the pirates of the golden age, for men like Blackbeard, or "Calico Jack" Rackam, or "Black Bart" Roberts. If you think about it, it's a strange question. It assumes that just because you try to learn what you can about a person, you somehow approve of what they did. Robert Graysmith, who wrote about the Zodiac Killer in northern California, was frequently presented with the same question. Even Truman Capote was asked the same thing when *In Cold Blood* was published in 1966. The difference is, unlike the other criminals, our pirates did not commit their crimes within living memory. This somehow makes the question less personal, less of an accusatory suggestion of complicity. The simple answer is no, I don't feel any affinity for them, and if I were given the chance I probably wouldn't like to meet them either, especially on the high seas. However, I do admit to being fascinated by them, by their crimes and by their lives. I want to know what drove them to follow the life they chose, and how they expected things to turn out.

What is interesting is that when Alexander Exquemelin first published *Buccaneers of America* in 1676 and Captain Charles Johnson *A General History of the Robberies and Murders of the Most Notorious Pyrates* in 1724, both men were almost certainly asked the same question. Both books were written at the very end of the two great pirate eras—the age of the buccaneers and the golden age of piracy. Seamen who had been the victims of pirate attacks were still walking the streets, and might well have been the first to accuse Johnson of romanticizing the criminals he wrote about. In fact, buccaneer attacks and pirate incidents were still taking place. This immediacy might well have been part of the reason why both books were such an instant success. However, this does not explain why the books were quite so popular, and why they have remained in print ever since. The likelihood is that people in late seventeenth-century Amsterdam or early eighteenth-century London were just as fascinated with pirates as we are today.

Many of the reasons for their appeal have already been mentioned—men who rejected the constraints of a law-abiding society, who lived life to the full, sailed away to exotic destinations, who took whatever they wanted … everything that the average book reader might have dreamed about but was never going to do. By reading about pirates they were living pirate lives by proxy, and mentally escaping to a bold new world of adventure. It is much the same today. It is fairly easy to see why children have always had a strong fascination with piracy, or why the subject has long been a staple of junior fiction. Pirates were anti-authoritarian figures who were allowed to stay up late and weren't made to have a bath. The attraction for adults runs along similar lines—the autonomy of the individual, the freedom from social obligations, and the ability to escape the banality of modern life are all important. Adult and child alike see pirates as exotic, romantic, and free-spirited.

Unfortunately, most of this image is the work of pirate fiction rather than fact. Most people don't want to consider that pirates were simply sailors who rebelled against a brutal and oppressive system of labor. The romanticism of piracy ignores the fact that conditions were still harsh, that fever and disease were commonplace, or that life expectancy was measured more in months than in years. Pirate historians such as David Cordingly, Robert Ritchie, Richard Zacks, Peter Earle, Jan Rogozinski, and I have all done our best to strip the fact from the fiction, but we are all swimming against the tide. Although we keep telling people that pirates didn't walk the plank, bury treasure, draw maps showing where the plunder was buried, or capture galleons filled with pieces-of-eight, most people simply don't want to know. The pirates of popular myth are too entrenched to challenge, and the best we can hope for is to make a few people aware that there was another, less romantic, side of the pirate coin.

Another important factor is that when most people think about historic rather than fictional pirates, they think of the people described by Captain Johnson. These all date from one brief historical period, the so-called golden age of piracy, which at most lasted for 40 years, between 1690 and 1730. In fact, this period was probably a lot shorter—and the real pirate heyday only lasted for one brief decade, from 1714 to 1724. This was the period of Blackbeard, "Black Bart" Roberts, Charles Vane, "Calico Jack" Rackam, Anne Bonny, Mary Read, "Gentleman" Stede Bonnet, Howell Davis and several others. Piracy had existed since man first launched a dugout canoe, so why are we so obsessed with a few characters who lived in the early eighteenth century? I suppose the real answer is publicity. These people were written about by Captain Johnson, and their activities have been the inspiration for most of the pirate fiction out there, including the *Pirates of the Caribbean* film series.

While this book certainly concentrates on this important period, it also covers other crucial pirate eras, such as the age of the Elizabethan "sea dogs," the buccaneers, or the nineteenth-century pirates of the South China Sea. In a way these are easier periods to deal with, as the reader is less encumbered by the baggage of pirate mythology. While this book will never seriously erode the popular image of the pirates of the golden age, it may allow readers to question some of these myths and give them a glimpse of the real pirates of the Caribbean. If this has allowed you to understand these people a little more clearly, or even to develop some affinity with them, then so much the better.

NOTES

Full publication details are provided the first time a work appears in a chapter's endnotes; thereafter only the author's name is given, unless more than one work by the same author is quoted in the chapter.

CHAPTER 1—PIRATES OF THE ANCIENT WORLD

1. George Bass, *A History of Seafaring* (London, 1972), p. 20; Angus Konstam, Leo Marriot & George Grant, *Warships* (London, 2001), pp. 10–12.
2. Bass, pp.20–21.
3. H. A. Ormerod, *Piracy in the Ancient World: An Essay on Mediterranean History* (Chicago, 1967), pp.22–25, 90–98.
4. Plutarch, *Lives of Alexander the Great and Julius Caesar* (reprinted London, 1886), pp. 103–05.
5. Ormerod, pp. 190–204.

CHAPTER 2—MEDIEVAL PIRATES

1. Angus Konstam, *The Historical Atlas of the Viking World* (New York, 2002), pp. 60–63.
2. Quoted in Konstam, p. 64.
3. Quoted in Konstam, p. 65. An online translation of the *Annals of St. Bertin* can be found at www.medievalsources.co.uk/stbertin.htm.
4. Walter Göttke, *Die Hölle von Helgoland* (1924). He also adapted the poem as a song, using a traditional church melody.

5. This account of Eustace's activities is extracted from the writings of Matthew Paris, available online through the Stanford University website (www./standish.stanford.edu/). For a more detailed account of the activities of Eustace the Monk, see Glyn Burgess, *Medieval Outlaws: Eustace the Monk and Fouke Fitz Waryn* (London, 1997), pp. 32–78. The work is a translation of the thirteenth-century French romance *Li Romans de Witasse le Moine*.

6. For a full account of the life of Gráinne Ní Mháille, see Anne Chambers, *Granuaile: Ireland's Pirate Queen c.1530–1603* (Dublin, 2003).

CHAPTER 3—SEA DOGS OF THE RENAISSANCE

1. J. H. Parry, *The Spanish Seaborne Empire* (London, 1966), pp. 137–51; Timothy R. Walton, *The Spanish Treasure Fleets* (Sarasota, FL, 1994), pp. 30–35.

2. Walton (1994), pp. 44–64; Angus Konstam, *Spanish Galleon, 1530–1690* (Oxford, 2004), pp. 17–19.

3. David Cordingly (ed.), *Pirates: Terror on the High Seas* (Atlanta, GA, 1996), p. 18; Hugh Thomas, *The Conquest of Mexico* (London, 1993), pp. 568–69.

4. Juliet Barclay, *Havana, Portrait of a City* (London, 1993), pp. 33–52.

5. For a fascinating account of Hawkins's third voyage, see R. Unwin, *The Defeat of Sir John Hawkins: A Biography of his Third Slaving Voyage* (London, 1960).

6. Unwin, pp. 152–60.

7. Lloyd Hanes Williams, *Pirates of Colonial Virginia* (Richmond, VA, 1937), pp. 80–117; Angus Konstam, *Elizabethan Sea Dogs, 1560–1605* (Oxford, 2000), pp. 29–30.

8. Williams, p. 141; David Cordingly, *Under the Black Flag: The Romance and the Reality of Life Among the Pirates* (London, 1995), pp. 31–32; Konstam, *Elizabethan Sea Dogs*, pp. 43–44.

9. Konstam, *Elizabethan Sea Dogs*, pp. 44, 62–63.

10. Angus Konstam, *The Armada Campaign, 1588* (Oxford, 2001), pp. 37, 41.

11. Ibid., p. 41.

12. Kenneth R. Andrews, *Elizabethan Privateering during the Spanish War, 1585–1603* (Cambridge, 1964), pp. 134–36, 199–204.

13. For a detailed account of the Cadiz Expedition, see Williams, pp. 158–60; Arthur Nelson, *The Tudor Navy: The Ships, Men and Organisation, 1485–1603* (London, 2001), pp. 124–30.

14. Nelson, pp. 193–202.

15. Ibid., pp. 202–03.

CHAPTER 4—MEDITERRANEAN CORSAIRS

1. John F. Guilmartin, *Gunpowder and Galleys* (London, 1974), pp. 61–41; John F. Guilmartin, *Galleons and Galleys* (London, 2002), pp. 126–36.

2. Jan Rogozinski, *Pirates! An A–Z Encyclopedia* (New York, 1995), pp. 16, 178–79; David Cordingly (ed.), *Pirates: Terror on the High Seas* (Atlanta, GA, 1996), pp. 80–81; Angus Konstam, *The History of Shipwrecks* (New York, 1999), pp. 46–47.

3. Rogozinski, p. 179; Konstam, p. 47.

4. Rogozinski, pp. 349–50.

5. Guilmartin, *Galleons and Galleys,* pp. 137–51. For a full account of the battle, see Angus Konstam, *The Battle of Lepanto, 1571* (Oxford, 2003).

6. Quoted in Ernle Bradford, *The Great Siege, Malta, 1565* (London, 1961), p. 35.

7. Quoted in Christopher Lloyd, *English Corsairs of the Barbary Coast* (London, 1981), pp. 72–82.

8. Ibid., p. 97; J. R. Powell, *Robert Blake, General-at-Sea* (London, 1972), pp. 252–72.

9. For an account of the American attacks against the Barbary pirates during the nineteenth century see Joshua London, *Victory in Tripoli* (Hoboken, NJ, 2005).

CHAPTER 5—BUCCANEERS

1. David Cordingly, *Under the Black Flag: The Romance and the Reality of Life Among the Pirates* (London, 1995), pp. 12–13. For an overview of Dutch maritime policy and the effect of the Dunkirk privateers on Dutch shipping see C. R. Boxer, *Dutch Seaborne Empire, 1600–1800* (London, 1965).

2. Pablo E. Pérez-Mallaína, *Spain's Men of the Sea: Daily Life on the Indies Fleet in the Sixteenth Century* (Baltimore, MD, 1998), pp. 50–52, 95–98; J. H. Parry, *The Spanish Seaborne Empire* (London, 1966), pp. 262–64. For an examination of Spanish defensive policies in the Caribbean, see Timothy R. Walton, *The Spanish Treasure Fleets* (Sarasota, FL, 1994).

3. Quoted in Hilary Beckles, *A History of Barbados* (Cambridge, 1990), p. 7. Also see Cruz Apestegui, *Pirates of the Caribbean: Buccaneers, Privateers, Freebooters and Filibusters, 1493–1720* (Barcelona, 2002), pp. 140–46.

4. Alexander O. Exquemelin, *Buccaneers of America* (Amsterdam, 1678, reprinted New York, 1969), pp. 67–69.

5. For a detailed overview of the military campaigns of this period, see John A. Lynn, *The Wars of Louis XIV, 1667–1714* (London, 1999).

6. For a detailed discussion of the identity of Captain Johnson, see Angus Konstam, *Blackbeard: America's Most Notorious Pirate* (Hoboken, NJ, 2006), pp. 1–4.

7. Apestegui, pp. 151–56. In addition Paul Sutton, *Cromwell's Jamaica Campaign* (Leigh-on-Sea, 1990) provides a highly detailed account of the conquest of Jamaica.

8. Dudley Pope, *Harry Morgan's Way* (London, 1977), pp. 96–98.

9. David Cordingly and John Falconer, *Pirates: Fact & Fiction* (London, 1992), pp. 38–39; Cordingly, pp. 49–50.

10. Pope, pp. 349–56; Apestegui, pp. 174–80.

11. Cordingly, pp. 50–51. Another account of Braziliano's debauchery is found in Exquemelin, pp. 81–82. Also see Angus Konstam, *The History of Shipwrecks* (New York, 1999), pp. 86–87.

12. Exquemelin, pp. 79–80. Also see Konstam, *The History of Shipwrecks*, pp. 86–87.

13. Exquemelin, pp. 106–107, p. 193; Konstam, pp. 82–83; Apestegui, pp. 160–61.

14. Pope, pp. 151–52.

15. Ibid., pp. 149–50. Also see David F. Marley, *Pirates: Adventurers on the High Seas* (London, 1995), pp. 48–50.

16. Quoted in Marley, 50. Also Exquemelin, pp. 138–39; Pope, pp. 168–69.

17. Exquemelin, p. 154.

18. Quoted in Marley, p. 54.

19. For a full account of the political situation surrounding Morgan's commission as admiral, see Pope, pp. 217–19.

20. Exquemelin, p. 193.

21. A detailed account of Dampier's voyage is provided in Diana and Michael Preston, *A Pirate of Exquisite Mind: The Life of William Dampier* (London, 2004).

22. Ibid., pp. 329–30.

23. Although Exquemelin deliberately omits mentioning much about French buccaneering activities in the Caribbean, Louis le Golip, *The Memoirs of a Buccaneer* (London, 1954) provides a useful account, while the subject is also discussed in depth by Marley and Apestegui.

24. Exquemelin, p. 223, also p. 69.

CHAPTER 6—THE GOLDEN AGE

1. For a broader account of these military and naval conflicts, see John A. Lynn, *The Wars of Louis XIV, 1667–1714* (London, 1999).

2. Angus Konstam, *Blackbeard: America's Most Notorious Pirate* (Hoboken, NJ, 2006), pp. 41–43.

3. Ibid., pp. 36–40.

4. Captain Johnson, *A General History of the Robberies & Murders of the Most Notorious Pyrates* (London, 1724, reprinted by Lyons Press, New York, 1998), pp. 13–14. Also see Konstam, p. 107.

5. Johnson, pp. 103–10. Also see Konstam, pp. 158–59.

6. Johnson, p. 107.

7. Quoted in Konstam, p. 117.

8. Quoted in Konstam, p. 120.

9. Johnson, p. 121.

10. Ibid., p. 131.

11. Ibid., p. 131.

12. Ibid., p. 131.

13. Quoted in David Cordingly, *Under the Black Flag: The Romance and the Reality of Life Among the Pirates* (London, 1995), p. 64. This and all other information concerning the trial is drawn from the transcript of the proceedings, published in 1721.

14. Johnson, p. 60.

15. Ibid., p. 46. For a discussion of Blackbeard's early career see Konstam.

16. Quoted in Konstam, p. 64.

17. Johnson, p. 46.

18. Quoted in Konstam, pp. 69–70.

19. Johnson, p. 49.

20. Ibid., p. 49.

21. The excavation of the wreck and the conservation of finds were undertaken through the cooperation of the state of North Carolina, academic archaeological teams, and the salvors who originally located the wreck. The conserved collection is now displayed in the state-run museum.

22. Quoted in Konstam, p. 251.

23. Johnson, pp. 56–57. The quotes describing the fight which follow are also gleaned from the same source.

24. Ibid., pp. 63, 77.

25. Quoted in Konstam, p. 70. Also see Johnson, p. 64.

26. Johnson, p. 65.

27. Ibid., p. 79.

28. This speech was included in the original 1724 version of Johnson (Chapter 28). Quoted in David Cordingly (ed.), *Pirates: Terror on the High Seas* (Atlanta, GA, 1996), p. 111.

29. Johnson, p. 273.

30. Ibid., pp. 286.

31. Ibid., p. 180–81.

32. Ibid., p. 132.

33. Ibid., p. 268.

CHAPTER 7—THE PIRATE ROUND

1. This speech was included in the original 1724 version of Johnson (Chapter 22). Quoted in David Cordingly (ed.), *Pirates: Terror on the High Seas* (Atlanta, GA, 1996); Jan Rogozinski, *Pirates! An A–Z Encyclopedia* (New York, 1995), pp. 337–38.

2. Captain Johnson, *A General History of the Robberies & Murders of the Most Notorious Pyrates* (London, 1724, reprinted by Lyons Press, New York, 1998), p. 34.

3. Ibid., p. 35. For a further interpretation of the relationship between Tew and Every, see Cordingly, pp. 147–51.

4. Quoted in Richard Zacks, *The Pirate Hunter: The True Story of Captain Kidd* (New York, 2002), p. 20.

5. Johnson, p. 352.

6. Ibid., p. 358.

7. Ibid., pp. 35–40. The theme of Madagascar as a pirate utopia is explored in Cordingly, pp. 124–39; Jan Rogozinski, *Honor Among Thieves* (London, 2000), pp. 165–84.

8. Johnson, pp. 85–87.

9. Ibid., 89.

CHAPTER 8—LAST OF THE PIRATES

1. An account of the privateering elements of these wars is provided by David Cordingly (ed.), *Pirates: Terror on the High Seas* (Atlanta, GA, 1996), pp. 164–87; David J. Starkey, E. S. van Eyck and J. A. de Moor (eds.), *Pirates and Privateers: New Perspectives on the War on Trade in the Eighteenth and Nineteenth Centuries* (Exeter, 1997), pp. 10–28; Angus Konstam, *The History of Shipwrecks* (New York, 1999), pp. 142–55.

2. Quoted from the *Boston Daily Advertiser*, February 1819. A detailed account of the operations of pirates operating in the Florida Straits is provided by Colin Jameson, 'Porter and the Pirates', in *Florida Keys Sea Heritage Journal* 4:4 (1994).

3. Ibid., 14. Also see Cordingly, pp. 82–84; Konstam, pp. 156–57.

4. Konstam, pp. 160–61.

5. Alfred Russell Wallace, *The Malay Archipelago* (London, 1869) Vol. I, pp. 264–65.

6. Cordingly, pp. 189–92.

CHAPTER 9—CHINESE PIRATES

1. Tonio Andrade, "The Company's Chinese Pirates: How the Dutch East India Company Tried to Lead a Coalition of Pirates to War Against China, 1621–1662" in the *Journal of World History*, December 2004, pp. 415–44 provides a useful account of Koxinga's early career.

2. Ibid., p. 421.

3. David Cordingly (ed.), *Pirates: Terror on the High Seas* (Atlanta, GA, 1996), pp. 220–25.

4. Ibid., pp. 229–31.

5. Ibid., pp. 233–35.

CHAPTER 10—MODERN PIRACY

1. By far the most striking account of modern piracy is provided by John S. Burnett in *Dangerous Waters* (New York, 2002). His findings are corroborated by reports published by the International Marine Bureau, a department of the International Chamber of Commerce. Their information has been used in the compilation of this chapter. Their reports are available online at www.iccwbo.org and www.icc-ccs.org/imb/overview.php

2. Burnett, p. 284.

3. U.S. Navy Report, published on their official website (www.navy.mil), Story Number NNS060121-01.

CHAPTER 11—PIRATES IN FICTION

1. For a more detailed look at the role of literature in our perception of piracy see David Cordingly and John Falconer, *Pirates: Fact & Fiction* (London, 1992), pp. 10–12, 37, 49, 54.

2. A brief account of "Pirates of the Silver Screen" is provided by Cordingly & Falconer, pp. 68–69, and David Cordingly, *Under the Black Flag: The Romance and the Reality of Life Among the Pirates* (London, 1995), pp. 174–76. Jan Rogozinski, *Pirates! An A–Z Encyclopedia* (New York, 1995) provides an almost complete catalog of pirate films, listed by title.

SELECT BIBLIOGRAPHY

Albury, Paul, *A History of the Bahamas* (London, 1975)

Andrews, Kenneth R., *Elizabethan Privateering during the Spanish War, 1585–1603* (Cambridge, 1964)

Apestegui, Cruz, *Pirates of the Caribbean: Buccaneers, Privateers, Freebooters and Filibusters, 1493–1720* (Barcelona, 2002)

Baer, Joel, *Pirates of the British Isles* (Stroud, 2005)

Barclay, Juliet, *Havana, Portrait of a City* (London, 1993)

Bass, George, *A History of Seafaring* (London, 1972)

Beckles, Hilary, *A History of Barbados* (Cambridge, 1990)

Blackmore, Howard L., *Armouries of the Tower of London: Catalogue: Volume 1: Ordnance* (London, 1977)

Blake, John, *The Sea Chart: The Illustrated History of Nautical Maps and Navigational Charts* (London, 2004)

Boxer, C. R., *Dutch Seaborne Empire, 1600–1800* (London, 1965)

Bradford, Ernle, *The Great Siege, Malta, 1565* (London, 1961)

Burg, B. R., *Sodomy and the Pirate Tradition* (New York, 1983)

Burgess, Glyn, *Medieval Outlaws: Eustace the Monk and Fouke Fitz Waryn* (London, 1997)

Burgess, Robert F. & Clausen, Carl J., *Florida's Golden Galleons: The Search for the 1715 Spanish Treasure Fleet* (Port Salerno, FL, 1982)

Burnett, John S., *Dangerous Waters* (New York, 2002)

Chambers, Anne, *Granuaile: Ireland's Pirate Queen c. 1530–1603* (Dublin, 2003)

Clifford, Barry, *The Pirate Prince: Discovering the Priceless Treasures of the Sunken Ship Whydah* (New York, 1993)

Clifford, Barry, *The Black Ship: The Quest to Recover an English Pirate Ship and its Lost Treasure* (London, 1999)

Cordingly, David, *Under the Black Flag: The Romance and the Reality of Life Among the Pirates* (London, 1995)

Cordingly, David (ed.), *Pirates: Terror on the High Seas* (Atlanta, GA, 1996)

Cordingly, David & Falconer, John, *Pirates: Fact & Fiction* (London, 1992)

Dodson, Leonidas, *Alexander Spotswood: Governor of Colonial Virginia* (Philadelphia, PA, 1932)

Earle, Peter, *The Sack of Panama* (London, 1981)

Earle, Peter, *Sailors: English Merchant Seamen 1650–1775* (London, 1988)

Earle, Peter, *The Pirate Wars* (London, 2003)

Exquemelin, Alexander O., *Buccaneers of America* (Amsterdam, 1678, reprinted New York, 1969)

Forbes, Rosita, *Sir Henry Morgan: Pirate and Pioneer* (Norwich, 1948)

Gerhard, Peter, *Pirates of New Spain, 1575–1742* (New York, 2003)

le Golip, Louis, *The Memoirs of a Buccaneer* (London, 1954)

Gosse, Philip, *The Pirate's Who's Who: Giving Particulars of the Lives & Deaths of the Pirates & Buccaneers* (New York, 1925, reprinted by Rio Grande Press, Glorieta, NM, 1988)

Gosse, Philip (ed.), *The History of Piracy* (New York, 1925, reprinted by Rio Grande Press, Glorieta, NM, 1988)

Guilmartin, John F., *Gunpowder and Galleys* (London, 1974)

Guilmartin, John F., *Galleons and Galleys* (London, 2002)

Hayward, Arthur L. (ed.), *Lives of the Most Remarkable Criminals* (London, 1735, reprinted by Dodd, Mead & Co., New York, 1927)

Hewitson, Jim, *Skull & Saltire: Stories of Scottish Piracy* (Edinburgh, 2005)

Hympendahl, Klaus, *Pirates Aboard!* (New York, 2003)

Johnson, Captain Charles, *A General History of the Robberies & Murders of the Most Notorious Pyrates* (London, 1724, reprinted by Lyons Press, New York, 1998)

Johnson, Paul, *A History of the American People* (New York, 1997)

Jones, Hugh, *The Present State of Virginia* (Richmond, VA, 1912)

Konstam, Angus, *The History of Pirates* (New York, 1999)

Konstam, Angus, *The History of Shipwrecks* (New York, 1999)

Konstam, Angus, *Elizabethan Sea Dogs, 1560–1605* (Oxford, 2000)

Konstam, Angus, *Pirates: Terror on the High Seas* (Oxford, 2001)

Konstam, Angus, *The Armada Campaign, 1588* (Oxford, 2001)

Konstam, Angus: *The Historical Atlas of the Viking World* (New York, 2002)

Konstam, Angus, *The Pirate Ship, 1660–1730* (Oxford, 2003)

Konstam, Angus, *Lepanto: 1571* (Oxford, 2003)

Konstam, Angus, *Spanish Galleon, 1530–1690* (Oxford, 2004)

Konstam, Angus, *Blackbeard: America's Most Notorious Pirate* (Hoboken, NJ, 2006)

Konstam, Angus, Marriot, Leo & Grant, George, *Warships* (London, 2001)

Lee, Robert E., *Blackbeard the Pirate: A Re-appraisal of his Life and Times* (Winston-Salem, NC, 1974, reprinted John F. Blair, Winston-Salem, NC, 2002)

Little, Benerson, *The Sea Rover's Practice: Pirate Tactics and Techniques, 1630–1730* (Dulles, VA, 2005)

Little, Bryan & Sansom, John (eds.), *The Story of Bristol: From the Middle Ages to Today* (Tiverton, 2003)

Lloyd, Christopher, *English Corsairs of the Barbary Coast* (London, 1981)

London, Joshua, *Victory in Tripoli* (Hoboken, NJ, 2005)

Lynn, John A., *The Wars of Louis XIV, 1667–1714* (London, 1999)

Lyon, David, *The Sailing Navy List: All the Ships of the Royal Navy, Built, Purchased and Captured, 1688–1860* (London, 2001)

Marley, David F., *Pirates: Adventurers on the High Seas* (London, 1995)

Mather, Cotton, *The Tryals of Sixteen Persons for Piracy* (Boston, MA, 1726)

Mather, Cotton, *The Vial Poured upon the Sea: A Remarkable Relation of Certain Pirates* (Boston, MA, 1726)

May, W. E., *A History of Marine Navigation* (Henley-on-Thames, 1973)

Moore, John R., *Daniel Defoe, Citizen of the Modern World* (Chicago, 1958)

Nelson, Arthur, *The Tudor Navy: The Ships, Men and Organisation, 1485–1603* (London, 2001)

Ormerod, H. A., *Piracy in the Ancient World: An Essay on Mediterranean History* (Chicago, 1967)

Parry, J. H., *The Spanish Seaborne Empire* (London, 1966)

Pawson, Michael & Buisseret, David, *Port Royal, Jamaica* (Oxford, 1975)

Pérez-Mallaína, Pablo E., *Spain's Men of the Sea: Daily Life on the Indies Fleet in the Sixteenth Century* (Baltimore, MD, 1998)

Plutarch, *Lives of Alexander the Great and Julius Caesar* (reprinted London, 1886)

Pope, Dudley, *Harry Morgan's Way* (London, 1977)

Powell, J. R., *Robert Blake, General-at-Sea* (London, 1972)

Preston, Diana & Michael, *A Pirate of Exquisite Mind: The Life of William Dampier* (London, 2004)

Rediker, Marcus, *Between the Devil and the Deep Blue Sea: Merchant Seamen, Pirates and the Anglo-American Maritime World, 1700–1750* (Cambridge, 1987)

Rediker, Marcus, *Villains of all Nations: Atlantic Pirates in the Golden Age* (Boston, MA, 2004)

Reinhardt, David, *Pirates and Piracy* (New York, 1997)

Riley, Sandra, *Homeward Bound: A History of the Bahama Islands to 1850* (Nassau, 2000)

Ritchie, Robert C., *Captain Kidd and the War against the* Pirates (Cambridge, MA, 1986)

Roberts, Nancy, *Blackbeard and other Pirates of the Atlantic Coast* (Winston-Salem, NC, 1993)

Rogozinski, Jan, *Pirates! An A–Z Encyclopedia* (New York, 1995)

Rogozinski, Jan, *Honor Among Thieves* (London, 2000)

Sanders, Richard, *If a Pirate I Must Be* (London, 2007)

Stanley, Jo, *Bold in her Breeches: Woman Pirates across the Ages* (London, 1995)

Starkey, David J., van Eyck, E. S & de Moor, J.A. (eds.), *Pirates and Privateers: New Perspectives on the War on Trade in the Eighteenth and Nineteenth Centuries* (Exeter, 1997)

Stevenson, Robert Louis, *Treasure Island* (London, 1883)

Sutton, Paul, *Cromwell's Jamaica Campaign* (Leigh-on-Sea, 1990)

Thomas, Hugh, *The Conquest of Mexico* (London, 1993)

Unwin, R., *The Defeat of Sir John Hawkins: A Biography of his Third Slaving Voyage* (London, 1960)

Wallace, Alfred Russell, *The Malay Archipelago* (London, 1862)

Walton, Timothy R., *The Spanish Treasure Fleets* (Sarasota, FL, 1994)

Williams, Lloyd Hanes, *Pirates of Colonial Virginia* (Richmond, VA, 1937)

Winston, Alexander, *No Purchase, No Pay: Sir Henry Morgan, Captain William Kidd and Captain Woodes Rogers in the Great Age of Privateers and Pirates, 1665–1715* (London, 1970)

Woodbury, George, *The Great Days of Piracy in the West Indies* (New York, 1951)

Zacks, Richard, *The Pirate Hunter: The True Story of Captain Kidd* (New York, 2002)

INDEX

INDEX